THE ABIY PROJECT

TOM GARDNER

The Abiy Project

God, Power and War in the New Ethiopia

HURST & COMPANY, LONDON

First published in the United Kingdom in 2024 by
C. Hurst & Co. (Publishers) Ltd.,
New Wing, Somerset House, Strand, London WC2R 1LA
Copyright © Tom Gardner, 2024
All rights reserved.

The right Tom Gardner to be identified as the author of
this publication is asserted by him in accordance with
the Copyright, Designs and Patents Act, 1988.

Distributed in the United States, Canada and Latin America by Oxford University
Press, 198 Madison Avenue, New York, NY 10016, United States of America.

A Cataloguing-in-Publication data record for this book
is available from the British Library.

ISBN: 9781911723103

Printed and Bound in Great Britain by Bell & Bain Ltd, Glasgow

www.hurstpublishers.com

*To all those whose lives have been upturned or cut short
by the wreckage of these years*

CONTENTS

CONTENTS

PART THREE
CRISIS

PART FOUR
WAR

ACKNOWLEDGEMENTS

Whatever understanding of Ethiopia I have accrued over the years is owed to a list of friends and sources as long as the Blue Nile River. All know who they are. But to my sadness and regret, none of those living in the country today can—for reasons of safety—be acknowledged publicly in these pages. Suffice to say, without the knowledge, insight and wisdom they shared with me, combined with their often boundless hospitality, this book never would have been possible. One day, I hope, we will meet again for a *buna*, this time on me.

Many others also contributed in myriad ways: reading drafts, answering phone calls, giving tips, lending books and sharing contacts. Among the older generation of *feranjis*, Patrick Gilkes, Christopher Clapham, Guenter Schroeder and Dan Connell were especially generous with their rich compendia of knowledge accumulated over many decades. Among the country's diaspora, over the years Aaron Maasho, Mekonnen Firew Ayano, Adem K. Abebe, Haileselassie Amha, Mohammed Ademo, Ezana Tefera, Michael Woldemariam, Tsedale Lemma, Juweria Ali, Zecharias Zelalem and many others routinely enriched my reporting and sharpened my analyses. Among my *feranji* contemporaries, Benedikt Kamski, Andrew DeCort, Jonah Wedekind, Terje Østebø and Mehdi Labzaé all supplied troves of data as well as invaluable feedback. Samuel Gebre deserves special mention for his patient advice and clear-eyed contributions, from inception to completion.

The Society of Authors helped with a travel grant which enabled a research trip to America in 2022. My editors at *The Economist* backed the years of reporting across Ethiopia and the Horn which facilitated the rest. None of it, though, would have been possible without the untiring support of my mother, Amanda, who encouraged me to begin, or the love and inspiration of Claire, who gave me the confidence to finish. I could not have done it without you.

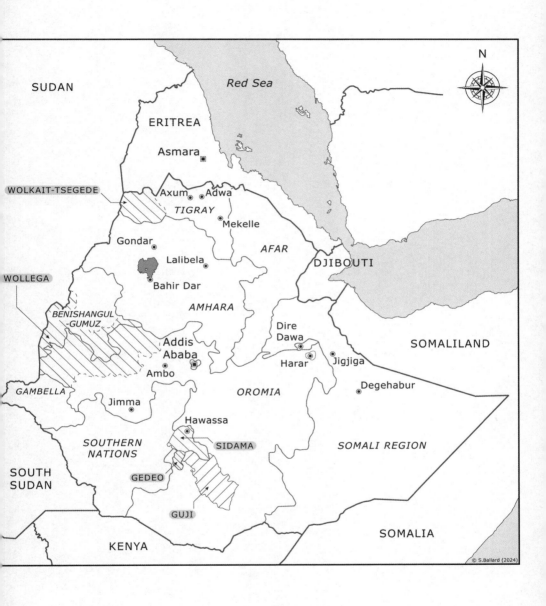

LIST OF ABBREVIATIONS

ADP   Amhara Democratic Party

ANDM   Amhara National Democratic Movement

CUD   Coalition for Unity and Democracy

EFFORT   Endowment Fund for the Rehabilitation of Tigray

EHRC   Ethiopian Human Rights Commission

ENDF   Ethiopian National Defence Force

EPLF   Eritrean People's Liberation Front

EPRDF   Ethiopian People's Revolutionary Democratic Front

ESAT   Ethiopian Satellite Television and Radio

GERD   Grand Ethiopian Renaissance Dam

INSA   Information Network Security Agency

METEC   Metals and Engineering Corporation

NaMA   National Movement of Amhara

NISS   National Intelligence Security Service

ODP   Oromo Democratic Party

OFC   Oromo Federalist Congress

OLA   Oromo Liberation Army

OLF   Oromo Liberation Front

OMN   Oromia Media Network

ONLF   Ogaden National Liberation Front

OPDO   Oromo People's Democratic Organisation

LIST OF ABBREVIATIONS

PP	Prosperity Party
SEPDM	Southern Ethiopian People's Democratic Movement
SNNPR	Southern Nations, Nationalities and Peoples Region
TDF	Tigray Defence Forces
TPLF	Tigrayan People's Liberation Front

LIST OF ILLUSTRATIONS

1. Abiy and Isaias Afewerki at the reopening of the Embassy of Eritrea in Addis Ababa (Minasse Wondimu Hailu/Getty Images)

2. Abiy takes Ursula von der Leyen for a drive around the capital (Eduardo Soteras)

3. The new Addis Ababa skyline (Charlie Rosser)

4. The Ethio-Djibouti Railway (Charlie Rosser)

5. *Qeerroos* arriving in Addis Ababa (Tom Gardner)

6. Supporters of the prime minister gather in Meskel Square (Charlie Rosser)

7. Supporters of Ginbot 7 welcome the rebel movement's returning leaders (Charlie Rosser)

8. Joyful OLF supporters gather for a rally in Meskel Square (Tom Gardner)

9. Jawar Mohammed (Charlie Rosser)

10. Meret Sisay, 18, was forced to flee her home in West Guji twice in 2018 (Tom Gardner)

11. Getachew Reda (Charlie Rosser)

12. People stand next to an exploded tank near the village of Mezezo, Amhara (Eduardo Soteras)

13. Amhara militiamen pose at their base (Eduardo Soteras)

14. An Amhara militiaman bows in front of a church (Eduardo Soteras)

15. A man welds the window of a shop next to graffiti depicting Abiy (Eduardo Soteras)

16. The Epiphany of Saint George celebrations in Lalibela (Tom Gardner)

17. The battlefields of Adwa in Tigray (Claire Wilmot)

INTRODUCTION

"I am sorry, I don't know anything about Abiy Ahmed."

The message flashed up on Signal, a secure messaging app, from someone I had been told to call Napoleon. It was the middle of 2023, six years after I had first arrived in Ethiopia, and one year after I had left in the midst of a war which was tearing it apart. Though that war had recently cooled, another one was heating up. Ethiopia was lurching from crisis to crisis and behind each of them loomed one figure larger than any other: Abiy Ahmed.

Napoleon was in America. He had known Ethiopia's prime minister when the two of them had worked together as cyber-intelligence officers in the 2000s. Our mutual contact had prepped him for my call, and assured me that he was ready and willing. Just one day earlier, Napoleon had told me himself, over text message, that he would share with me what he knew of the character of the man who, five years earlier, had won control of the Ethiopian state. Now, though, Napoleon was having second thoughts. When I tried to ring, he blocked my number.

It was an iron law: the closer someone had been to Abiy, the less likely they were to talk about him. From childhood neighbours, to friends from church, to allies-turned-enemies in politics—even those living far away in safe countries in the West were often too afraid to speak with me. Some would read my messages and then block my number. A few would reply, promising to schedule an interview, only to disappear. Many would not answer my calls at all.

In 2018, a few months after Abiy became Ethiopia's prime minister at 42 (though even his press team weren't exactly sure of his age), one of his most trusted confidants had picked up the phone to me. Once I had introduced myself, he promised to call back. He never did.

Around the same time, I sat through an hour in the company of a psychotherapist thought to have more influence over the prime

1

minister than almost anyone else. We talked about different schools of psychoanalysis and their relevance for understanding Ethiopia's political crisis. But when I asked him to tell me about his friend, the country's most powerful man, the conversation ended. Friends and foes alike: when it came to Abiy, speaking in public always carried risk.

Over the following years living and working in Ethiopia, I spoke with as many people as possible who had known and worked with Abiy. Despite the appearance of openness which characterised his early days in power, almost everyone agreed he was an enigma. Nobody could claim to fully understand him. Later, as their lives, and those of all Ethiopians, were profoundly altered by the political decisions he made, many sought further explanations: who is Abiy, really, and what does he want?

I've never met him in person. Over the years, requests for interviews went unanswered. An offer extended in 2019 to the editors of *The Economist*, which was later retracted, was made on the condition that I wouldn't accompany them. Three years later, amid a campaign waged against me online by his supporters, the government accused me of siding with his enemies. My press accreditation was revoked, and I was given forty-eight hours to leave the country. By then, it felt as though for the best part of a decade I had been chasing a shadow.

* * *

This book is a chronicle of the years I spent in Ethiopia before and during Abiy's time in office, the most tumultuous period in the country's recent history. It is also an attempt to peel back the layers of myth which have built up around the man himself. At first sight, he is neither especially captivating nor menacing. Handsome and clean-cut, with a neat goatee, he has a cherubic smile that can knock people off balance. One journalist who met him likened him to a prosperous estate agent. He often comes across as impishly youthful.

But there are many Abiy Ahmeds. One is an aspiring emperor longing for a glorious past. When I left Ethiopia in 2022, he was building a palace for himself in the hills above the capital so grandiose that it was said to cost at least $10 billion—paid for at least in part by the United Arab Emirates—and cover a greater area than Windsor, the White House, the Kremlin, and China's Forbidden City combined. All over the country, meanwhile, older palaces from a previous era were being rehabilitated, while several new high-end lodges, each in itself a miniature palace, were under construction. When

INTRODUCTION

Abiy was a young boy, he would tell people, his mother had prophesied that he would be Ethiopia's "seventh king": the seventh ruler since Menelik II, the emperor who created the modern Ethiopian state in the late nineteenth century. "Don't forget: he's a king," a colleague of his would one day joke. "And the seventh king needs seven palaces."

Another Abiy is a forward-looking moderniser. Just as I left the country, he was also finalising Ethiopia's first-ever science museum: a temple to a hyper-modern vision of national progress built on scientific discovery and artificial intelligence. Here was the new Ethiopia Abiy sought to build: a country of 'smart cities', robo-cops, biometric identification cards, virtual reality simulation and cutting-edge surveillance. Some have likened him to a Silicon Valley 'tech bro'.

Abiy confounds and contradicts. Like a Pentecostal Putin, he is part-preacher, part-spy. He is fervently messianic but, at the same time, capable of pragmatism. At times, he seems like a Machiavellian mastermind, ruthlessly eliminating his enemies and outfoxing his rivals. "Everything is a conspiracy," one of his colleagues later admitted. "I don't think anybody in Ethiopia is as good a chess-player as him," said another. But he is also a gambler, for whom chaos is an opportunity that can be turned into a blessing. How much Abiy planned his path to power versus how much he simply reacted to events has never been fully explained—and may well never be. Ethiopia's road to civil war in 2020 was littered with unsolved murders, whose perpetrators will never be brought to justice, and other unresolved mysteries. Its shaky aftermath has proven no less inscrutable.

But he may also be remembered as the iconic African leader of our age: a distinctly contemporary bricolage of styles and influences—both old and new; national and cosmopolitan; African, Western and Middle Eastern. In the pantheon of Ethiopian history, he is a figure at once profoundly familiar and utterly novel: both a Christian nationalist, in the prophetic mould of the nineteenth-century emperor Tewodros II, and a corporate CEO who uses 'positive-thinking' and 'self-help' jargon to boost the productivity of his staff. Coming to power at a time of international upheaval—the world of Donald Trump, Xi Jinping and Vladimir Putin—Abiy applies twenty-first-century techniques of online propaganda and disinformation just as he resurrects the courtly politics of imperial Ethiopia. As the global order splinters and traditional alliances fray, Abiy wants to be friends with everyone yet loyal to none.

* * *

The world got Abiy wrong. When he came to power in 2018, he was feted in the West as a liberal reformer, one who would shepherd an Ethiopia bedevilled by factional politics and competing identities into a democratic and 'post-ethnic' future. As the first national leader in Ethiopia's modern history to identify as Oromo, the largest but historically among the more politically under-represented of the country's many ethnic groups, Abiy was thought to be a unifier after years of fracture. In 2019, a year after he made a historic peace deal with Eritrea, Ethiopia's smaller neighbour which seceded in 1993, he was awarded the Nobel Peace Prize. The Nobel committee's chair said the prize recognised Abiy's "efforts to achieve peace and international cooperation, and in particular his decisive initiative to resolve the border conflict with neighbouring Eritrea." She also praised Abiy's domestic reform efforts, including the release of tens of thousands of prisoners and the return of once-banned opposition groups. Accepting the prize at a ceremony in Oslo, Abiy declared war "the epitome of hell for all involved. I know because I was there." But little more than a year later, one of the worst wars of the twenty-first century had erupted in Ethiopia's northern region of Tigray. Abiy was not alone responsible for it. But he was arguably more so than anybody else. He may well go down as the most controversial recipient of the 123-year-old prize since at least Henry Kissinger in 1973.

And I misjudged him, too. In 2018, I argued in an article in *Foreign Policy* that Abiy was not really a populist—and that if he had to be described in terms imported from abroad, then what he most closely resembled was a liberal democrat. This was wrong, even at the time: Abiy was never a liberal, and nor was he ever a democrat. But it remains true that he is not a conventional populist. Unlike some of the authoritarian demagogues of our age—Jair Bolsonaro, for instance, or Binyamin Netanyahu—Abiy came to power with a certain vision of the Ethiopia he wanted to see. That isn't to say he had a clear policy programme, or a rigid ideological agenda, for achieving it. Like any populist, he could be deceptive and dishonest, allowing different constituencies to believe whatever they wanted about him, however contradictory. He also conflated his own fate with that of the nation, believing himself to be indispensable, and deployed rhetoric that was often hateful, xenophobic and—on occasion—arguably even fascistic. But his mission in government wasn't only amassing power and enriching himself. It was also about remaking the whole of Ethiopia in his own image.

* * *

INTRODUCTION

This isn't a conventional biography of Abiy. It is a book about the society which made him, and which he, in turn, has sought to reshape. Abiy, more than any of his recent predecessors, has become, in the words of a top US official, the Ethiopian government's "pre-eminent decider". More than anyone else, for better or worse, it is Abiy who has made history. But he hasn't, to paraphrase Marx, made it just as he pleased.

The country Abiy came to lead is tormented by a bloody past. It remains, in important ways, the world's last empire: a fragile, fissiparous federation of peoples held together by force. Until the second half of the last century, it also remained one of the very final bastions of both feudalism and slavery. Alone in Africa, Ethiopia largely escaped European colonial rule. This made it a moral beacon to the world, and also bequeathed it the strongest indigenous state apparatus anywhere on the continent. At the same time, though, the absence of a foreign colonial overlord meant its population had lacked—the brief wartime interlude of Italian occupation notwithstanding—a single enemy to unite against. The story of modern Ethiopian history is therefore, to a striking degree, one of fractious internal rivalries over perennially scarce resources, particularly between elites from the country's three most powerful ethnic groups, the Amharas—considered by many Ethiopians to have been indigenous African colonisers—the Oromos, and the Tigrayans, the smallest of the three, who comprise just six percent of the population but had, in recent decades, held preeminent power.

Abiy sought to transcend this difficult history: to wipe away the complexities of identity, ideology and nation-building in a single stroke and build afresh. But, instead, he was consumed by it. A central aim of this book is to show how Abiy's highly idiosyncratic and personalised rule heightened what sociologists might call the Ethiopian state's 'structural contradictions' to the point of near total collapse. As the country's disrupter-in-chief, who took a sledgehammer to an already delicate set of political arrangements, Abiy was the prime catalyst for the country's spectacular unravelling after 2018.

This isn't a definitive account of the Abiy years. By definition, it's an outsider's view. As a foreign journalist, I was privileged to have access to people and places that many Ethiopians did not: to senior politicians and foreign embassies, to active frontlines and distant borderlands. I could speak to those with political power and those excluded from it. With the help of interpreters, I could interview people from almost any region, in almost any of the country's eighty-plus languages. But my position as a foreign journalist from the West, and the advantages that afforded me, also limited my perspective and narrowed my focus. In the following pages, not every twist and turn of the past decade has been explored in full, nor each and every corner of the country addressed in equal measure. Some may disagree with my conclusions; others may wish I had gone further. Mine will be far from the final word: if there is ever to be one, it would come from Ethiopians themselves. With time, many more books will be written, and many more stories will be uncovered. While my account is primarily interested in the role of ideas, ideologies and identities as the motors of recent Ethiopian history, others may choose to place greater emphasis on the part played by economic and material factors. The world's understanding of what happened in Ethiopia under Abiy will—I hope—continue to grow.

That makes this, in essence, a first draft of history. And so, it is to history, first, that we must turn.

* * *

Note on the text

This book is the product of hundreds of formal interviews, and countless informal conversations, in-person and online exchanges, with Ethiopians of all persuasions, as well as many well-informed foreigners. These took place over the course of nearly eight years, mostly between 2017 and 2023, and took me to countries well beyond Ethiopia, including Eritrea, Sudan, Kenya, Somalia, Britain, Germany, France and America. Where possible, I've endeavoured to identify my sources by name, though many agreed to speak with me only under conditions of strict anonymity. Even some of those living outside Ethiopia feared greatly for the safety of their relatives back home if they criticised the government openly. Diplomats were often able to speak freely with me off-the-record only. However, in the interests of both transparency and scholarly rigour, where relevant I've sought to provide useful additional information—a source's political or ideological leanings, for instance—which might help readers in assessing why, when and where they chose to speak with me. So far as possible, those foreign diplomats who are no longer serving in an official capacity are identified by their name or, at least, the country they represent.

In Ethiopia, traditional naming conventions mean people have a single given name, followed often by their father's (and then grandfather's) name. There is no concept of the division into Christian name and surname as usual in the West. The book's central protagonist is thus, on second mention, "Abiy", not "Ahmed". Non-Ethiopians, once introduced, are thereafter referred to by their surname.

Political and ethnic labels are sensitive in Ethiopia. Some Ethiopians do not identify with a particular ethnic group; indeed, there is no such thing as ethnic purity in a diverse country whose populations have long lived, loved, fought and worked together. Given the undeniable salience of ethnicity in Ethiopian political and social life today, however, identifying people by their primary ethnic affiliation is often unavoidable. Where relevant, though, I try to refer to Ethiopians who explicitly describe themselves as being of 'mixed' heritage by more appropriate or important markers of identity, such as political or ideological preference.

Conversely, many others reject the idea of 'ethnicity' and prefer to talk of 'nationality': many Oromos, for instance, describe the Oromo as a 'nation', not merely an 'ethnic group', regarding the latter as dismissive or even pejorative. For simplicity's sake, however, I refer to 'Ethiopian' as a 'nationality'—as it appears so on passports—and sub-national groups as 'ethnicities'. This is neither a political nor a value judgement. Ideological labels such as 'Ethiopianist' and 'ethno-nationalist' are likewise used for the sake of simplicity, despite their shortcomings. These are terms with general currency in contemporary Ethiopian political discourse, albeit disputed.

PART ONE

REVOLUTION

1

"OUR FOREFATHERS"

THE LONG STRUGGLE OVER HISTORY

The stairs rose elegantly, twisting towards the heavens. At the top was the small, octagonal room where Emperor Menelik II had prayed for God's blessing as he dramatically enlarged Ethiopia's territory in the last decades of the nineteenth century. The watchtower, as this wing of the palace was known, was also a perfect vantage point for the monarch to survey the open plain beneath its windows: the manor houses of his provincial lords; the peasants in their *tukul* huts along the banks of the rivers which gurgled from nearby Mount Entoto. It was here that Menelik founded Addis Ababa, the Ethiopian capital, in 1886. And it was on the same spot, a decade later, that he installed the country's very first telephone line—a thread to gather the disparate and disconnected lands Menelik called his kingdom into a modern nation-state. The grand palace built on a hilltop became the heart of each regime that succeeded his, through empire, war and revolution.

In time it would become the ideal place to view not just the capital's growth, but the whole sweep of Ethiopia's history in the decades that followed. To the north, beneath the hills which Menelik had shrouded in eucalyptus trees imported from Australia in order to alleviate a shortage of firewood, were districts built by Italian colonists in the 1930s that had once been racially segregated. To the south-west stood a grand circular building, in the distinctive style of an Ethiopian monastery, made for the national bank in the 1960s during the modernising phase of the reign of Ethiopia's last emperor, Haile Selassie—the most feted, and later most hated, of Menelik's successors. A soaring bronze monument nearby commemorated the socialist revolution of 1974. Further in the distance were rows of hulking tower blocks, built during the era of the Ethiopian

People's Revolutionary Democratic Front (EPRDF), the rebel movement which seized power in 1991.

One hundred and thirty-three years after Menelik had founded the city, his successor, Abiy Ahmed, refurbished the palace and opened it as a public museum.[1] In the symbolic heart of what he re-christened "Unity Park", an ornate banquet hall designed by architects shipped in from India, stands the museum's centrepiece: a waxwork replica of the late emperor himself. Seated proudly on his original mahogany throne, and with his trademark wide-brimmed hat, no other exhibit inspires such emotion in the museum's visitors. So revered was the model Menelik that some of those who made pilgrimages after it was unveiled in 2019 were seen prostrating themselves in deference.

In the eyes of his devotees, Menelik was the man who had made Ethiopia great. Ten years after establishing the capital, he had fought off the Italians in the would-be colonists' first ill-fated invasion. Victory at the Battle of Adwa by his army of perhaps over 100,000 men, drawn from all corners of the empire, secured Ethiopia's international reputation as a bastion of African independence and pride. Over the following century, and only briefly interrupted by an Italian fascist occupation between 1936 and 1941, it remained the continent's sole indigenous state to resist the 'Scramble for Africa' embarked on by Europe's industrial powers in the late nineteenth century. After his triumph at Adwa, and equipped with modern arms supplied from overseas, Menelik then turned his attention southwards. In a series of bloody but stunningly successful campaigns, from the far western border with Sudan, where his armies enslaved those they captured, to the Somali deserts in the east, the emperor conquered— or rather, in his eyes, restored—territories which many Ethiopians believed to be divinely ordained as theirs but lost in the tumult of earlier centuries. By the time of his death in 1913, the empire's borders extended beyond even their legendary fourteenth-century peak. If God was on their side, as many Ethiopians had long believed, then Menelik was his most exalted earthly representative: Ethiopia's "*emaye*", or mother, a term of endearment said to evoke the maternal benevolence of his long reign.

Haile Selassie, for his part, was a determined centraliser, who clipped the power of the empire's provincial magnates and expanded the state's administrative and coercive powers to a degree without precedent in its history. Over the course of a reign which spanned four decades, from his coronation in 1930 to his overthrow in a military coup in 1974, Ethiopia's last emperor transformed the feudal regime he inherited from Menelik's daughter, Empress Zewditu, into something which resembled the absolutism of early modern Europe.[2] For the first time, the country had a national army, a modern bureaucracy, a bi-cameral parliament as well as schools and a university based on the Western model. After his return from exile in Britain, where he had spent the years of Italian wartime occupation, he inaugurated factories, built dams and, by launching a national airline, opened Ethiopia up to the world.

Even more than Menelik, it was Ethiopia's last emperor who furnished the ruling dynasty with myths of its own divine provenance. Menelik and his royal descendants from the Amharic-speaking highland province of Shewa, Haile Selassie claimed, could trace an unbroken bloodline back some 3,000 years. It was a lineage which, according to legend, had begun in a union between the Old Testament King Solomon of Jerusalem and the Queen of Ethiopia, known as the Queen of Sheba: it was their illegitimate son, the first Menelik, who was said to have brought with him to Ethiopia the fabled Ark of the Covenant of Christian lore.[3] In 1931, the freshly crowned emperor introduced Ethiopia's first-ever constitution. But rather than separate the state from the church, it explicitly declared the person of the monarch to be sacred, God's anointed. Such was the religious devotion Haile Selassie inspired (and encouraged), both at home and—in the Rastafarians who proclaimed him the Messiah—abroad, that desperate pilgrims would travel the length of the country just to receive his touch.

Though he ended his days in opprobrium, his star dimmed by a devastating famine in the north which his government had failed to address, Haile Selassie remained an icon for millions of Ethiopians throughout the subsequent decades, and a figure of global stature who counted Mao, Queen Elizabeth II, John F. Kennedy and Charles de Gaulle among his personal acquaintances.[4] When he was finally laid to rest in 2000, his remains having been disinterred from beneath the palace latrine where the soldiers who had deposed him reputedly threw them a quarter of a century earlier, tens of thousands of people gathered in the streets outside Addis Ababa's St George's Cathedral for his state funeral.

Among the late emperor's most enthusiastic latter-day admirers was Abiy Ahmed. As prime minister, he would revel in regaling visitors with stories of the monarch's contribution to Ethiopia's unity, progress and independence; one foreign journalist given a personal tour of the palace noted the prime minister's particular fascination with Haile Selassie's royal emblem, a crowned lion holding a flag.[5] In the classical-style Throne Hall where Haile Selassie had once conducted state business, Abiy installed a waxwork replica of the 'King of Kings', as the late monarch was known, similar to the one of Menelik next door. Meanwhile, Haile Selassie's own Jubilee Palace, built in the 1950s and situated a stone's throw down the hill from Menelik's, was lovingly restored as well.[6] "We are proud of the bravery of our forefathers," Abiy told foreign dignitaries and local businessmen at the inauguration of Unity Park in October 2019. "We aren't ashamed of their mistakes."[7]

But historical commemoration is never—anywhere—a neutral act. In Ethiopia, there is scarcely anything more explosive. On the same day Abiy unveiled Unity Park, prominent politicians from his own ethnic group, the Oromo, snubbed the event and instead made a televised visit to a memorial for Oromo victims of Menelik's military campaigns in the south. The armies of the former emperor committed mass atrocities, they argued, so he shouldn't be celebrated. "It's like a Democrat promoting the Confederacy," one opposition politician complained. When anti-government demonstrations broke out in Oromia, Abiy's home region, just days after the museum's inauguration, 'Menelik' was the word on every protester's lips.

They were following a well-established script. When the Marxist junta, later known as the "*Derg*", seized power from Haile Selassie in 1974, imperial statues were torn down. Some were dumped in the overgrown garden of the National Museum, where they would remain decades later; others were destroyed. So great was the anti-monarchical, revolutionary fervour that when books were thrown on bonfires, Haile Selassie's autobiography was among them. Conversely, when the incoming EPRDF, fresh from having, in turn, ousted the Derg in 1991, tried to remove a nearby statue of Menelik II, large protests erupted in its defence. Three decades after that, in 2018, 2020 and again in 2023, violent protests broke out in the same vicinity—sparked, in large part, by popular anxieties about the statue's fate.

There are few countries where the past weighs quite as heavily on the present as it does in Ethiopia—a country whose history, as one of its scholars observed in 1972, has "a particular tendency to repeat itself."[8] Emperors like Menelik consciously modelled themselves on their predecessors, waging wars against neighbours or rebellious provinces which often seemed like re-enactments of earlier ones.[9] When they died, or were overthrown, the bloody struggles to succeed them followed patterns set centuries before; eras of centralised rule were typically followed by periods of chaotic disintegration.[10] To slow the gyre, or to subdue unruly subjects, successive imperial regimes resorted to spectacular displays of force. Over the centuries, imperial armies inflicted cycles of forced conscription, atrocity and famine on Ethiopia's rural populations. Wars were recurrent, and so were revolts.[11] "My people are bad," the pioneering centraliser and mid-nineteenth century Christian firebrand, Emperor Tewodros II, once lamented. "They love rebellion and hate peace." And so he crushed them: burning churches, devastating villages and pillaging fields.[12] It was a recipe for violent repression that would be repeated by almost all his successors in turn.

Rarely were the miseries forgotten. Even—or perhaps especially— today, the echoes of old traumas continue to reverberate. In Ethiopian politics, present-day debates and controversies continue to follow tramlines set by battles decades, even centuries, in the past. Arguments about the nature and the legacy of the empire continue to rumble; even today's wars continue to be fought, at least in part, in its name. Reflecting on his own country's struggle to reconcile its modern identity with its bloody origins, the African American writer James Baldwin once observed that "history is not the past; it is the present."[13] In Ethiopia, likewise, it is history that lies at the very heart of the questions that continue to roil it: what the country is now, what it has been—and what it could be in the future.

* * *

Controversies about Ethiopia's imperial past revolve around two fundamental questions. First, is Ethiopia an ancient nation, perhaps several thousand years old, or is it rather the product of a rapacious modern empire, with roots going back little more than 130 years to the eve of Menelik II's reign?[14] Secondly, and very much relatedly: is Ethiopia one single nation, or is it, in fact, an assemblage of many different ones?

For most of its history, the power to tell Ethiopia's national story was the preserve of foreign observers—European missionaries, diplomats and explorers—and local chroniclers, who were often members of the Ethiopian Orthodox Christian clergy. Both tended to stress the country's ancient provenance and its Christian character. According to what later became known as the 'Great Tradition' in historical writing about Ethiopia, the country's roots could be traced back, uninterrupted, as far as the ancient Axumite Empire.[15] Centred on the northern highlands in what is today the region of Tigray, and flourishing between the fourth and seventh centuries AD, this scarcely remembered polity is believed to have extended, at its peak, as far as modern-day Yemen, and to have enjoyed access to vast international trade routes linking the Roman Empire to the Middle East and India. Crucially, though, in terms of the enduring narratives of nationhood which it spawned, it was through the Axumites, and the conversion of Emperor Ezana in the fourth century AD, that Christianity was said to have first arrived on Ethiopian soil. Out of this, so the 'Great Tradition' had it, came an indigenous script (*Ge'ez*), a patriotic peasant army, settled agriculture and a feudal aristocracy. The result was a well-organised Christian state, able to withstand foreign threats and preserve a recognisably homogenous culture over more than a millennium.[16]

For most of this history the idea of Ethiopia was inextricably entwined with the Ethiopian Orthodox faith.[17] Sealed off from the outside world by the impenetrable terrain of the highland plateau at its heart, Ethiopia's reputation in Europe and the Middle East in the Middle Ages was that of an unchanging Christian island in a sea of Islam. For most Christian Ethiopians, this was underscored by the foundational text of their nationhood, a mediaeval church epic known as the "*Kebre Negast*", which asserted that the people of Ethiopia were God's chosen.[18] Waves of conquest by Muslim armies, in particular those in the sixteenth century led by a certain Ahmed ibn Ibrahim al-Ghazi (who Christians would nickname "*Gragn*", "the left-handed"), served only to harden such convictions. The 'trauma of Gragn', as the destruction visited upon their ancient monasteries and churches became known, echoed through the centuries, hardening the popular image of a Christian fortress under siege.

Equally important to this traditional view of Ethiopian history was the special place it granted to the highland cultures which dominated the region and claimed direct descent from the Axumites. These were the ethno-linguistic groups who today call themselves Tigrayans and Amharas (plus modern-day Eritreans), who, for much of their history, were described collectively as "*Habeshas*", and by outsiders as Abyssinians.[19] To be Ethiopian meant, to the traditionalist mind, being *Habesha*, which in turn meant practising Orthodox Christianity and speaking the most widely-used 'Semitic' languages—Amharic and Tigrinya—believed to derive from the ancient church tongue of *Ge'ez*. According to this school of history, the mass migrations of southern peoples, who spoke neither language, into parts of the northern highlands in the sixteenth and seventeenth centuries were, in essence, alien invasions. The most numerous among these latter peoples were those who spoke Afan Oromo, a 'Cushitic' tongue, and are today known as Oromos, Ethiopia's largest ethnic group. They were explicitly cast as outsiders: "*Galla*", meaning strangers or infidels.[20] Well into the twenty-first century it was common for *Habesha* highlanders to disparage Oromos as 'savage' and, in essence, foreign—restless nomads who had originated across the ocean from as far away as Madagascar. Popular highland beliefs and scholarly erasure were often mirrored in the real-world of coercive nation-building, and the story of the incorporation of the Oromo into the Ethiopian state one of successive bouts of warfare and frequent atrocities.[21]

Subsequent generations of Ethiopian and Western scholars pushed back, arguing—sometimes convincingly, at times more tenuously—that Oromos and other southern peoples had long been part of a 'Greater Ethiopian' cultural sphere. Despite the enormous linguistic diversity which characterised Ethiopia, so such scholars argued, there existed nonetheless an underlying pan-Ethiopian identity—a shared universe of tradition, syncretic practices and history, even in those parts of the empire in which Islam historically predominated.[22] Especially important to this account was the central role played by Oromo notables in the eighteenth-century imperial court of Gondar, where Afan Oromo was briefly the official tongue, and, a century later, their presence as warriors and even commanders in Menelik's armies. So thoroughly integrated were they in the life of the empire, it has been argued, that many Oromos came to see themselves as no less *Habesha* than Amharas and Tigrayans themselves.[23] Though modern 'Ethiopianist' scholars like these rejected the jaundiced notion that Oromos and other southerners outside the *Habesha* highland marrow couldn't be real Ethiopians, they shared the traditional assumption of an essential unity and continuity in Ethiopian nationhood. There was only 'one Ethiopia', in other words, and it was immemorial.

By the mid-1960s, however, a new generation of dissident intellectuals was coming of age. Centred, ironically, at the very seat of learning which Haile Selassie had established so as to furnish the empire with the loyal bureaucrats required to maintain it—Haile Selassie I (later, Addis Ababa) University—this rising cohort were the product of a far-reaching social transformation in the decades after World War Two. Between the university's founding in the 1950s, and the eve of revolution in 1974, Ethiopia's student population had ballooned. A total of less than 1,000 students expanded eight times over, of which a large proportion spent time studying abroad in America and Europe.[24] Education and experience overseas had sharpened the students' criticisms of their emperor's autocratic methods, as well as their economy's woeful under-development. Encounters with members of other ethnic groups, moreover, either on college campuses or in the countryside where students were sent by the emperor as a part of a programme of national service, dramatically increased popular appreciation of the empire's inequalities. Had the late imperial state and economy been advancing rapidly enough to absorb them all, many students might, in the end, have chosen to look the other way. But they weren't, and despite their education, the students' prospects for employment in Ethiopia upon graduation were decidedly grim.

Taking inspiration from the decolonisation movements then sweeping across Africa, as well as the revolutionary spirit which flourished on college campuses across much of the West, the Ethiopian university students who came of age at this time grew ever more radical. Many of them were free-thinking iconoclasts. All of them, almost without exception, identified as socialist or were otherwise left-leaning. For the first time, the whole gamut of inherited assumptions—that the country's civilisation was ancient and august; that there existed something ineluctably 'Ethiopian' about its many diverse subjects—was put under the microscope. From the pages of the student press, and in the slogans of the demonstrations they organised against the ageing emperor, the future revolutionaries proceeded to mount an unprecedented assault on the foundational precepts of Ethiopian nationhood.[25]

Their conclusions were empire-shaking. Ethiopia, said Wallelign Mekonnen, the most prominent of their cohort, was quite simply an invidious fiction. According to this new mode of thought, there was no such thing as an 'Ethiopian' at all. What there was, instead, was merely a tapestry of disparate and distinct peoples—Tigrayans, Oromos, Somalis and the like—among whom the most powerful by far were the Amhara. To be Ethiopian, the student radicals alleged, paraphrasing the Algerian de-colonial theorist, Frantz Fanon, was to wear an "Amhara mask": to speak Amharic, practise Orthodox Christianity, adopt an Amharic name and don traditional Amhara garb.[26] Out of these student interventions, which gradually became more revolutionary as the late 1960s turned into the 1970s, came the idea of an overarching, and existentially pressing, 'national question'. Leftist Ethiopian students took it upon themselves to resolve it. In doing so, often by drawing explicitly on Marxist models from overseas such as the Soviet Union and Yugoslavia, they would irrevocably alter the terms of discussion about Ethiopia's past—and blast open radically new avenues for the empire's future.

That the student movement, the name by which they would be remembered, was able to mount such a challenge stemmed from a set of conditions particular to the empire in the second half of the twentieth century. Ever since Haile Selassie's hurried flight from Ethiopia at the moment of the second Italian invasion in 1936, the final emperor's sheen, once so powerful as to place him far beyond the reach of public criticism, had been wearing thin. While his fellow countrymen had waged a campaign of patriotic resistance against the Italian occupation, whose horrors included dropping mustard gas on civilians as well as a ghoulish massacre of up to 20,000 residents of Addis Ababa in 1937, Haile Selassie spent the intervening years in Bath, England.[27] Though he had returned to reclaim the throne in the company of the British army, the emperor was, by the latter days of his reign, seen by many younger Ethiopians as a doddery autocrat, whose anti-democratic instincts extended as far as an outright ban on political parties of any kind. His government's signal failure to transform the empire's still feudal economy was an increasing source of embarrassment; the episodic recurrence of famine in the countryside a national travesty. Repeated attempts at land reform, what the idealistic students would later call returning 'land to the tiller' from the hands of the nobility, had been persistently blocked. In 1960, army officers staged a coup—the first in its history. It failed, but the spell which had long held back criticism of the emperor had finally been broken.[28]

The reign of Haile Selassie had also seen a sharpening of the empire's ethnic inequities. Consciously modelling his nation-building on the lines pursued by eighteenth- and nineteenth-century European states like France, the emperor significantly ramped up the assimilationist policies of his predecessors. In the name of "*andinet*", or unity, Amharic was to be vigorously promoted as the nation's lingua franca. Land in the southern territories conquered by Menelik was increasingly liable for expropriation by predominantly Amhara landlords.[29] Power in the imperial court, meanwhile, was concentrated in the hands of a few Amhara nobles drawn disproportionately from the province of Shewa from which Menelik and Haile Selassie both hailed.[30]

Rebellious populations were dealt with harshly. Between 1941 and 1974, not a decade passed without a major revolt somewhere in the provinces: in Tigray in the 1940s (crushed with the help of the British air force); among the Oromos of Bale in the 1960s; by the Yejju Oromo in

Wollo in 1948 and again in 1970. Many Amharas also revolted against Haile Selassie's regime, but the favourable correspondence of language, religion and, quite often, class, meant that in the eyes of many other Ethiopians they were undoubtedly the ones on top. 'Amhara', in the popular imagination, in effect meant power;[31] Amharic, so some southerners said, meant "the tongue that punishes you".[32] Much like the hazy line between, for instance, Englishness and Britishness, the distinction between an Amhara identity and an Ethiopian one—what in Amharic was called "*Ethiopiawinet*"—had under Haile Selassie become almost non-existent. Such was the energy with which the emperor had pursued his policy of national unification that by 1961 it was illegal even to ask someone their ethnic identity.[33]

Resentment of what was generally understood, throughout much of the empire, to be 'Amhara rule' had been growing steadily over the preceding decades.[34] That a handful of Tigrayans and Oromos, in particular, were represented in the upper ranks of the imperial regime was considered largely incidental. So too was the fact that many Amharas, not least Haile Selassie himself, might be considered of mixed ethnic stock.[35] By the 1960s, even the province of Tigray, long an intrinsic part of the empire whose people had never really seen themselves as colonial subjects before, was well on the way to becoming a cauldron of anti-imperial ferment.

Part of the grievance in Ethiopia's northern-most province was dynastic. In truth, Haile Selassie had allowed Tigray greater autonomy than anywhere else in his domain.[36] Nevertheless, Tigrayan nobles decried the loss of imperial primacy to Amhara, and specifically Shewan, monarchs: the last Tigrayan emperor, Yohannes IV, had died in battle fighting Sudanese invaders in 1889. Many Tigrayans also blamed Yohannes's successor, Menelik II, for agreeing to hand the largely Tigrinya-speaking territories known as Eritrea over to the Italians in the aftermath of the Battle of Adwa, severing their 'natural' homeland in two.

Perhaps more fundamentally, though, the discontent reflected Tigray's relative economic weakness. Under Haile Selassie, it had been effectively bypassed by economic development, such that on the eve of the revolution in 1974 there wasn't a single factory in the entire province.[37] Food shortages continued to ravage the remote Tigrayan highlands like almost nowhere else in the empire. Destitute young Tigrayans began to emigrate, mostly to Eritrea or Addis Ababa, in such numbers that their compatriots were recorded likening them to Land Rover jeeps, crossing the hills from every direction.[38] A distinctively Tigrayan identity, formed out of a sense of relative marginalisation, and defined in opposition to Amhara and the remote imperial elite in Addis Ababa, began to crystallise.

Among Oromos, too, a new national self-consciousness was beginning to emerge. In 1963, a group of educated and assimilated senior army officers established the Macha-Tulama Self-Association, the very first pan-Oromo organisation of its kind. Their stated aim, to promote Oromo culture and language, was remarkably modest. Their complaints, which included that the few educational institutions which existed in Ethiopia back then were mostly in the north, were also well-founded. By 1970, only 10 percent of the student population was Oromo, and almost none of them Muslim.[39] But the emperor nonetheless viewed the organisation as a threat to Ethiopia's unity, and banned it in 1967. Its leader, a former Ethiopian general called Tadesse Birru, was thrown in prison—transforming him into a martyr for the movement which would soon become known as Oromo nationalism.

Even more up in arms by this time were the Tigrinya-speakers across the northern border with Tigray in Eritrea, among whom opposition to Haile Selassie was distinct, both in its cause and its scale. Unlike the rest of Ethiopia, Eritrea between 1889 and 1941 had been an Italian colony, and its population had over the decades acquired an identity quite separate from the rest of those in the *Habesha* heartlands. On Haile Selassie's return from exile, the Italians had been driven out and Eritrea placed under British administration until 1950, when the UN General Assembly had voted for a federation between Eritrea and Ethiopia, "under the sovereignty of the Ethiopian crown." This arrangement had ensured that Eritreans enjoyed an unusual degree of autonomy, which included their own elected regional government, as well as certain freedoms, such as a vibrant press, unthinkable in the rest of the empire. But Haile Selassie, receptive to those voices in Eritrea that demanded full union with the 'motherland', and deaf to those who wanted nothing to do with it—a sentiment especially common among Muslims from the coastal lowlands—proceeded with a policy of creeping annexation. In 1962, his government succeeded in pressuring the Eritrean parliament to disband itself, turning Eritrea into just another province of the Ethiopian empire.

For Ethiopia, a direct benefit of the new arrangement was access to the sea. The emperor quickly set about developing ports on the Red Sea coastline, namely at Massawa and, further to the south, Assab. Ethiopia built up a navy. But the emperor also moved quickly to crush Eritrea's fledgling democracy. Political parties were banned, and schools forced to switch from Tigrinya to Amharic. Armed Eritrean resistance, beginning with the establishment of the Eritrean Liberation Front (later swallowed up by the Eritrean People's Liberation Front, or EPLF), was the almost immediate result.[40] The Eritrean war of liberation lasted the next three decades, becoming Africa's longest-running insurgency and claiming perhaps a quarter of a million lives.[41]

* * *

When the imperial regime finally collapsed in 1974, following months of strikes and protests in Addis Ababa amid a terrible famine in the north, the coup de grâce would be delivered not by rebels in the provinces but by the very institution supposed to represent the emperor's modern, unified nation: the army. The officers responsible, which included the junta's future leader, Mengistu Hailemariam, proceeded to sweep away the old order with no less fervour than the sans-culottes of Revolutionary France or the Russian Bolsheviks of 1917. With a single swoop, the entire edifice of feudalism was no more, as private property was nationalised, land collectivised and the nobility liquidated. It was, by some estimates, the most comprehensive revolution to have ever occurred anywhere on the continent. America, for decades the empire's most reliable foreign ally, promptly cut diplomatic ties. The Soviet Union swiftly took its place.

But the revolution would bring no resolution to the 'national question', nor decisive answers to the arguments about history and identity which burned beneath it. The Derg was no less authoritarian, and in the end no less nationalistic, than the regime it had ousted. Though it drew on the revolutionary ideals and slogans of the student movement—of which some officers had themselves been members—it had no interest in handing power to it. Just like the imperial armies of centuries past, which spilt blood in God's name, or the power of emperors to inflict divine punishment, the atheistic Derg pursued its enemies with a fury as righteous as it was unrelenting. In the 'Red Terror' which followed the coup, tens of thousands of Ethiopians, including many of the students and former students who at first supported the Derg, were murdered, mutilated and tortured in the name of class revolution.[42] When Somalia seized the moment to prey on its weakened neighbour, the Derg responded by calling upon the Ethiopian masses to defend the motherland—in doing so drastically inflaming the same militaristic nationalism which the students had been first to question. After the invading Somalis had been defeated in

1978, thanks in large part to Soviet and Cuban assistance, the Derg turned its attention to the north, and to the intensifying insurgency in Eritrea. This too, at first, was vanquished. The Derg's rallying cry became "*Ethiopia Tikdem*": Ethiopia First.

In the chaos of the revolutionary years, the student movement, and the political parties it spawned, splintered. Some of their disagreements could appear arcane: the wisdom of Leninist urban struggle versus Maoist rural insurgency, the place of the 'proletariat' in the revolution.[43] Their readiness to settle disputes by executing rivals was also troubling. But beneath the sometimes obscure Marxist jargon and, some would later argue, a prevailing cult of violence, were deep questions about the nature of Ethiopia and the sort of country they wanted to build.[44] For some students, in particular those who went on to join the multiethnic—though notably Amhara—Ethiopian People's Revolutionary Party, the problem of unequal relations between Ethiopia's constituent peoples was ultimately economic, and could be solved only through cross-ethnic class struggle. But among others, who came mostly from the empire's peripheries, the primary axis of oppression in Ethiopia was not class but rather ethnicity. For this latter camp, the key influences were, variously, Lenin, whose writings on colonialism and the 'national question' were in vogue across much of what was then called the 'Third World', and Stalin, whose 1913 treatise, "Marxism and the National Question", had formed the basis for the confederal arrangements of the similarly multiethnic Soviet Union. From the late 1970s, their ideas about nationalism by then complemented by Chairman Mao's theories of peasant insurgency, these students would take to the countryside to mobilise the rural masses in the name of national liberation. Chief among this camp were the Tigrayan and Oromo students soon to re-emerge as the Tigrayan People's Liberation Front (TPLF) and the Oromo Liberation Front (OLF). Their stated goal was "national self-determination" up to and, most controversially, *including* secession. They took up arms and joined the EPLF in its fight to bring down the Derg.

Abstract demands like 'national liberation' concealed quite a range of opinion. For many Oromo nationalists, following Lenin, it meant nothing short of an independent Oromia free from Ethiopia's colonial yoke. Likewise, Eritrean nationalists also deemed their condition to be a colonial one. Having coalesced, by the late 1970s, under the banner of the EPLF (the ELF having been crushed in a bout of internecine warfare), they were soon to fall under the sway of a gangly but charismatic college dropout with a penchant for Maoist military literature called Isaias Afewerki.[45] Like the OLF, their goal was complete secession.

Among the Tigrayans, however, slightly less radical, albeit more distinctively Stalinist, positions typically predominated.[46] Under the leadership of a ferociously intelligent former medical student from Addis Ababa University called Meles Zenawi, it would be the Tigrayans who proposed what would eventually become the country's new constitutional order: a radical, bracingly non-liberal blueprint for national renewal. Ethiopia was to be restructured as a voluntary federation made up of what were called, again in language derived from Lenin and Stalin, "nations, nationalities and peoples". The constituent units of the new federal state were to be the country's diverse ethnic groups. Each would be granted the right to self-determination including secession. 'Amhara rule', and a singular Ethiopian national identity, were to be forever consigned to history.

The Derg, fatally weakened by the end of communism and Soviet military support, fell in 1991. With it came down the whole model of coercive nation-building pioneered by Menelik II—or, arguably, Tewodros II—and codified by Haile Selassie. It had long reached its sell-by-date. Through his forced conscription and endless wars in the peripheries, Mengistu had, for his part, turbocharged it to the point of near total collapse. Ruinous economic policy, and more than a decade of civil war, had destroyed whatever faith many Ethiopians might still have had in the national project. In the north, popular alienation had been compounded by another devastating famine in 1984, made worse by the Derg's practice of denying food to rebel-held areas in Tigray and Eritrea.[47] Hundreds of thousands had died, serving only to fuel the very ethno-nationalist tendencies which Mengistu had aimed to trample. The TPLF, now rebranded as a Leninist-style vanguard party at the helm of the multiethnic coalition known as the EPRDF, marched on the capital with the support of fighters from the EPLF and OLF. Few in Addis Ababa stood to defend the dying regime. Mengistu simply fled.

Having seized control of the central state, the TPLF set about putting into practice its own answer to the 'national question'. Under the new federal constitution, enshrined in 1995, Ethiopia was divided into nine ethnically based, semi-autonomous states and, in Addis Ababa and Dire Dawa, two chartered cities. The largest ethnic groups were granted powers to teach and administer in their own tongues, promote their own cultures, and recruit and train their own security forces. Eritrea, following a referendum in 1993, was allowed to peacefully secede, taking the former empire's Red Sea coastline with it. The new government in Addis Ababa argued that with the country's meagre resources no longer consumed by a bloated military, national development could finally take priority. On the eve of the EPRDF's ascension to power, Ethiopia was among the poorest and least industrialised countries on earth. Over time, the Marxist-inspired EPRDF optimistically reasoned, ethnic loyalties would gradually wither as people grew richer.

But the 'national question' wouldn't disappear, and the underlying ethnic tensions which had always animated it would anything but diminish. From the outset, the EPRDF and its then-allies, the OLF and the EPLF, faced opposition from multiple quarters: from former Derg officials who had fled abroad; from Amharas, who felt demonised by a new federal dispensation which cast them as historical oppressors; and from erstwhile rivals in the student movement with scores to settle. Coalescing in the diaspora, above all in Washington DC, these opponents of the EPRDF immediately mounted a campaign of virulent agitation against both the new federal system and its Tigrayan architects. They styled themselves as 'pan-Ethiopians', or more simply, 'Ethiopianists', in contrast to the 'ethno-nationalists' in the TPLF and OLF. They were often, though not always, Amhara.

At rally after rally, in the opinion pages of newly established opposition magazines, as well as on the airwaves, Ethiopianist activists in the diaspora declared the motherland to be in peril. The new constitution represented, said a former Derg official, nothing less than a "dagger blow aimed at the very heart of the integrity of the Ethiopian state."[48] What had soon become known as 'ethnic federalism' would, they argued, inevitably lead to disintegration along the lines of the Soviet Union and Yugoslavia, two comparable multinational federations which both broke apart in the early 1990s. Some pointed to how the new identity cards issued by the EPRDF forced people to choose an ethnicity, though many Ethiopians, especially those in Addis Ababa, were of mixed heritage. Others also noted that by redrawing the national map along ethno-linguistic lines, boundaries between groups which had once been porous had now been fixed. As in Yugoslavia, they warned, the result would be bloody disputes over territory and resources. More extreme voices, however, simply alleged the whole arrangement to be a sinister Tigrayan plot to dismember Ethiopia, beginning with the TPLF's acquiescence in Eritrean independence.[49]

Oromo and other ethno-nationalists, by contrast, had other grievances. The EPRDF was always at pains to present itself as a coalition of equals, in which Oromos and other marginalised groups could finally have their say. But for much of the following decades, the TPLF, though it represented only a small minority of the overall population, remained on top. From 1995, the then forty-year-old Meles, whose intellectual firepower wowed Western interlocutors no less than his coalition colleagues ("he just *ate* books", one US official gushed), took up the reins in the Prime Minister's Office. Having previously been the transitional government's interim president, he would remain in place until his untimely death in 2012. Tigrayan officers, meanwhile, were firmly ensconced at the helm of the newly-constituted federal army and national intelligence. According to what, over time, became an exaggerated but widely-held popular view, 'Amhara hegemony' had been replaced by a Tigrayan one. What was more, such critics argued, the new leadership had succeeded only in perpetuating the very same pathologies of the empire. Though the 1995 constitution granted the new regional states significant powers, for most of the 1990s and 2000s these would remain only theoretical. Like each twentieth-century Ethiopian regime which preceded it, the TPLF-led EPRDF monopolised power and governed firmly from the centre.[50] In this sense it was, despite its name, neither revolutionary nor democratic.

But what it did achieve was the second-longest period of stable government in modern Ethiopian history. Only the reign of Haile Selassie surpassed it.[51] One reason for this, in its founders' eyes, though certainly not its critics', was that the EPRDF was an essentially pragmatic project, one which aimed at finding a middle ground between competing poles of history, ideology and identity. Holding Ethiopia together, the EPRDF believed, meant containing multiple contending forces at any one time, by force if necessary: revanchist Ethiopian nationalism in the Christian Amhara mould in one moment; rising ethno-nationalism in the old empire's peripheries, above all among the Oromo, in another. It also required, though this was less often noted, keeping religious fundamentalism and extremism in check. Not one opposition party, the EPRDF insisted, was fit to do all this.

Certain of the wisdom of the path they had chosen, the ruling coalition's leaders were also clear-headed about what they wanted to achieve: rapid development and a country at peace with itself. Though it was the gun which had brought them to power, it was to be rapid economic growth, they reasoned, that would keep them there. For a while the strategy worked. But over time success bred blindness, and a complacency in the face of their project's flaws. Not many of the EPRDF's leaders in the early 1990s, for instance, would ever have imagined that the questions raised by the students three decades before would eventually return with a force quite unlike anything seen previously. Nor would they have predicted just how fatal the blow to their project would one day be. Indeed, in 2018, it would finally unravel. But perhaps the greatest shock of all was that the person to deliver the last rites was one of the EPRDF's most direct beneficiaries—who would emerge from deep within their own ranks.

2

ABIYOT

THE EARLY LIFE OF ABIY AHMED

Abiy Ahmed was a child of revolution. Born two years after the fall of Emperor Haile Selassie in 1974, his mother—like many others in those years—named him "*Abiyot*", an Amharic word meaning "revolution". In Beshasha, a small countryside town in the distant southwest of Ethiopia dominated by Muslim Oromos, it was a name which would soon mark him out for all the wrong reasons.

Haile Selassie's overthrow had initially been met with great enthusiasm in the empire's distant rural provinces.[1] The imperial district of Jimma, whose eponymous capital was a day's walk from Beshasha through undulating hills and pristine jungle, was no different. The ousting of an emperor who had crushed what remained of the erstwhile Kingdom of Jimma's cherished autonomy and, in 1932, abolished its revered Islamic monarchy, had given the revolution special significance there.[2] For Jimma's landless Oromos, moreover, the revolutionary promise of 'land to the tiller'—the wresting of land out of the hands of feudal landlords into those of the indigenous rural peasantry—held as much appeal at the time as it did for any of imperial Ethiopia's downtrodden subjects. Over the decades since Jimma's incorporation into Menelik II's empire, the Christian Ethiopian state had imposed itself with gradually increasing severity. Under Haile Selassie, more and more land had been confiscated by absentee landlords, and, for the first time, Orthodox churches had begun to appear in the district.[3] With the revolution, though, its days finally seemed numbered. For the first time in modern Ethiopian history, the Oromo of Jimma, or the "*Galla*" as they were then still disparagingly known by highland Ethiopians, stood on the brink of emancipation.

But by the time that Tezeta Wolde, the fourth wife of Ahmed Ali, a Muslim Oromo better known by the honorary Abba Fita, had given birth to their fourth and youngest child, Abiyot Ahmed Ali, two years later, the revolution's promise was already beginning to sour.[4] In 1975, college students sent to Jimma to organise the peasantry and socialise the land clashed violently with local police and landowners.[5] By the close of that same year, Ethiopia's centuries-old monarchy had been abolished and the state's ancient marriage to the Orthodox church had been dissolved. Ministers and relatives of the late emperor, who was allegedly strangled in his bed that August, had been lined up and executed. The cabal of army officers known as the Derg had emerged from the shadows.

Its rule, which stemmed paradoxically from both a reactionary military coup and a genuine social revolution, was harsh to a degree almost without precedent in Ethiopian history. First in Addis Ababa, then spreading to smaller towns like Jimma, the regime and its radical affiliates began hunting down young dissidents deemed 'enemies of the state'. Each morning bodies littered the streets, following nightly executions and running battles between the government and the newly formed rebel groups. By the following year, Mengistu Hailemariam, with his chilling disregard for human life, had assumed absolute power. Though he was said to have Oromo or otherwise southern origins, he and the Derg officers around him had thoroughly absorbed the chauvinistic Ethiopian nationalism of the old imperial state. The most senior Oromo officer among them, Teferi Benti, was executed in 1977. Though the Derg in its early days acknowledged the existence of a still unresolved 'national question', officially recognising Ethiopia's linguistic diversity and even producing school manuals in some fifteen local languages, the problem of enduring Amhara and Orthodox Christian power would be left basically untouched until the close of the following decade.[6] Amharic remained the language of government, and in much of the country local power continued to reside largely in the hands of Christian, Amharic-speaking functionaries.[7]

Ahmed Ali, on the eve of the Derg's landmark nationalisation of land, was a relatively well-to-do coffee farmer with several of his own plots and shops in the town centre.[8] He was not, therefore, altogether typical of the Oromo peasantry, and certainly not those elsewhere in rural Ethiopia who lacked both land of their own and the prestige associated with the former Kingdom of Jimma. Nationalisation, however, had left Ahmed Ali with just his home, his shops, and the mouths of many children to feed. Over the next decade, as the Derg's repression became more ferocious, and rural resistance to it mounted, Ahmed Ali threw in his lot with the

Oromo Liberation Front (OLF)—sheltering its fighters then roaming the nearby forests, and helping to raise food and money for their campaigns. Beshasha would become a stronghold of Oromo resistance. Ahmed Ali ordered his youngest son to stop calling himself Abiyot, and go by the less politically fraught "Abiy" instead.[9]

The early lives of Ethiopia's leaders have often been shrouded in veils of rumour and myth. Just as their enemies had sometimes sought to puncture their legitimacy by casting doubt on their origins, so had leaders and their courtiers purposefully obscured them in order to enhance their mystique. Meles was frequently accused by his critics of hiding his Eritrean roots. Mengistu, whose true past was never fully established, was said to have kinship ties to an Amhara lord.[10] But, crucially, even the lowliest of origins could be an asset for an Ethiopian leader. Both Mengistu and Menelik II, for example, were also rumoured to be the sons of southern slaves.[11] By mirroring the master-narrative of Ethiopian nationalism—that anyone could rise to the pinnacle of the state, provided they cloak themselves in the culture, symbols and, at least until 1974, the national religion— such rags-to-riches stories could be powerful tools of legitimisation.[12] The iconic Emperor Tewodros II, after all, had first started out as a "*shifta*", or rural bandit.

This was a lesson seemingly not lost on Abiy, of whose early life little is known for sure. On coming to power in 2018, he rarely spoke of his childhood, either mystifying it through reference to his mother's prophecy—that he was born to rule Ethiopia—or muddying it, by curating certain details differently depending on the audience. "He told so many stories," recalled a colleague of his. "He'll tell you one thing in the evening and the opposite the next morning." As an adult, Abiy was known to assure friends and followers that his upbringing had been more comfortable than might be assumed for someone from Beshasha; that he had always slept on clean sheets, for instance, and travelled everywhere by car.[13] But at other times he painted a picture of backbreaking poverty, describing his hometown as no more than a simple village, bereft of electricity, television and paved roads, in which he and his siblings had studied into the night under kerosene lamps and fetched water from nearby springs.[14] Family and friends who knew him then have been reluctant—or too afraid— to speak publicly about what they know of his past, seeding the ground for endless rumours and conspiracy theories about it. He later explained that because he was certain he would rise through the political ranks, he had actively avoided being photographed.[15] Until the publication of an authorised biography, *Sewyew* ("The Man"), written by a former public relations officer from his time as a state minister, there were no known images of him before the start of his political career.[16]

There is little doubt, however, that the young Abiy didn't get along particularly well with his father. Friends recalled that he rarely spoke warmly of him; on occasion, one said, the prime minister hinted that Ahmed Ali had mistreated his mother. When Ahmed died in 2019, reportedly at the age of 105, Abiy made no public mention of it and paid only a hasty visit home for the funeral. In any case, the feeling may well have been mutual. Abiy appears to have spent little time in his father's care. "His siblings say Abiy was cruel growing up," said one former resident of the district, now living overseas, who had known Ahmed Ali and his family well. "Even his father used to speak of him this way." Abiy's Oromo opponents would later make much hay out of a local rumour that Abiy was not, in fact, Ahmed Ali's biological son at all—a claim which the prime minister himself didn't trouble much to dispel. One former colleague recalled him telling them in the early 2000s, when still a young army officer, that his real father was an ethnic Gurage from the south. Many others have insisted he was Eritrean.

What is more certain is that Abiy's mother was Orthodox Christian, a marked rarity in the area at the time. Though she had formally converted to Islam, raising her children Muslim and being buried as one upon her death in 2017, Tezeta continued to dress as a Christian and would for the rest of her days be seen crossing herself as she passed by Beshasha's sole Orthodox church on saints' days. Officially hailing from Burayu, a multiethnic town near Addis Ababa, her son would describe her in public as an Oromo.[17] Those who knew her in Beshasha, however, recalled that she spoke the language with an accent so thick that many assumed she was Amhara—speculation consistent with claims later made privately by several Oromo officials that she was the daughter of an Amhara Orthodox priest in Burayu. What originally brought her to the area around Jimma is unclear, though Abiy later said that she had followed her older brother, also a priest, who had arrived in the town a year earlier.[18]

In any case, poor migrants from distant parts of the country were not unusual in Jimma at the time. The once-royal city, known to the Italian occupiers in the 1930s as "Little Rome" for its prosperous colonial-style downtown district, was home to the largest market in all south-western Ethiopia, thanks to its thriving trade in coffee, *khat* and, for much of the period, slaves. Later, during the Derg years, it had been a popular leisure destination for party cadres from Addis Ababa—in part, it was said, due to its reputation for prostitutes. Tezeta, who had two children already before she married Abiy's father, was by all accounts a strong-willed and independent woman, who raised Abiy and his siblings more or less alone in a dilapidated house from which she sold traditional *tej* honey wine for a living. "She was hard on the kids, often yelling at them," recalled a neighbour. "But she was a strong woman for that time. Back then it was unusual for women to come to the city to buy or sell goods—that was a job for the men or older children—but she had lived alone before, doing all those things, so she just carried on like that."

Tezeta appears to have had a profound influence on her youngest son, instilling in him a sense of personal destiny quite at odds with his reputation at the time as a troublemaker with a patchy record in school. "My mother was a hero," Abiy later said. "She was sturdy, like the women who can cook two or three pots at a time."[19] No doubt conscious from an early age of his relatively lowly social rank, as a younger and less-favoured son, it was from her that Abiy seems to have drawn much of his titanic self-belief. When they were alone together, Abiy later wrote, Tezeta would call him "Moti"—the Afan Oromo term for "King". It was from her, he added, that he had learnt that to be a leader one must match words with deeds, and that with enough determination and grit anything could be possible.[20] Even at primary school, he claimed, his peers had marked him out as one destined for greatness.[21] "All the students knew me as a king," he later recalled. "And so, I read and strove with the assumption that kingship would come."[22] If there was a single thread running through all Abiy's public utterances it would be the expression of the simple but firm belief that, thanks to his mother, he knew he was sent by God to rule.

* * *

Abiy would have been fourteen years old by the time the Derg fell in 1991. After seventeen years of brutality and incompetence, Mengistu's regime had finally collapsed, leaving behind it a population exhausted and broken by war, famine and upheaval. "This revolution made us all old," remarked a woman in Jimma to a visiting anthropologist that year.[23] More than that though, it had bequeathed to Ethiopia's once untouchable sense of national identity a profound, perhaps terminal, crisis. Mengistu's militant 'Ethiopia First' nationalism, briefly triumphant in the late 1970s as the great mass of the Ethiopian public was roused to defend the country against invasion by neighbouring Somalia, had by the end of the following decade almost rent the country apart. By the time the EPRDF took over, almost every corner of the map, and each major ethnic group, boasted an armed liberation movement of one sort or another—the best known being the TPLF and EPLF in the north, and the OLF in the south. With the formal secession of Eritrea in 1993, and the ultimately doomed bid by ethnic Somalis in the east to follow suit the following year, the country in which Abiy came of age in the early 1990s seemed to be battling for its very survival.

When fighters from the OLF stationed themselves in a military camp near Beshasha, Abiy's hometown, in the early months of the transition, the start of a process by which they were supposed to one day lay down their arms, the Oromo nationalism which they espoused was still an inchoate force. 'Oromia', as it would soon become known, was then little more than a patchwork of provinces divided by clan, religion and, to a certain extent, ideology. Some such as the Christian Oromos of the central highlands, to which group Abiy's mother officially belonged, were known for their often staunch commitment to Ethiopian nationalism. Many others, not least Abiy's Muslim father, spoke little Amharic and possessed no great love for either Christian Ethiopia or its national myths. Beyond their common language, Afan Oromo, there was little on the surface that would unite Abiy, the son of a Muslim farmer in the southwest, with an educated Orthodox Oromo living in Addis Ababa.[24] Both might, in theory, have pointed to a shared ancestral myth, and many, including Abiy, might have possessed a gut awareness of a collective Oromo identity.[25] But until the redrawing of the national map in the 1990s, Oromia, as a simple matter of administrative and legal fact, didn't exist. It would have to be built.

The OLF, briefly the EPRDF's junior partner in the transitional government of these years, would be instrumental for the project of Oromo nation-building. Two OLF members sat on the Boundary Commission, established in 1991, and it was thanks to them that 'Oromoland' acquired its current territorial shape, stretching from the Kenyan border all the way to the southern rim of Amharic-speaking Wollo in the northern highlands.[26] The OLF also set about injecting the Oromo public with a strong dose of national self-consciousness and cultural pride.[27] As its fighters flooded the countryside in Oromia's far-west in 1991, aiming to fill the vacuum left by the disintegration of the Derg, they came armed not just with guns but also with the books and pamphlets with which they sought to acquaint the Oromo public with their own national story. "We opened offices in every building in every village and in every small town," Chala Lata, one of the OLF's founders, later recalled. "And then we taught the cadres."

Abiy, growing up in the 1980s, was educated in Amharic, and though he could speak Afan Oromo fluently, never learnt to write it. By contrast, Oromos growing up in the 1990s were, for the first time in the history of the modern Ethiopian state, not only to be administered in their own language but taught in it too. "We told them to speak fluent, clear Afan Oromo only—not to mix it with other languages," Chala recalled. Over the coming years Oromia would go on to acquire many of the trappings of a modern state of its own: an Oromo state president; educated, Afan Oromo-speaking civil servants; Oromo police; Oromo courtrooms; Oromo state-owned corporations and banks; an Oromo flag. It was out of this, arguably for the first time, that an Oromo 'nation' in a real and tangible sense emerged. "I was Ethiopian, by default, until 1991 when the OLF came in," recalled Ahmed Nuru, who was a teenager in western Oromia at the time. Like thousands of other Oromos, Ahmed left Ethiopia in the early 1990s and moved to Minneapolis, Minnesota, where he became an indefatigable anti-EPRDF activist. "The OLF came with a spotlight and we saw what was underneath. I've hated Ethiopia ever since." Like many of his generation, Ahmed was now an Oromo first, and an Ethiopian second.

Relations between the OLF and their EPRDF allies, however, had come under strain almost from the first day of the transition. Within just months of taking over Addis Ababa, the OLF had cried foul, accusing Meles Zenawi and the EPRDF leadership of replicating the Derg's monopolisation of power by blurring party and state once more, by arresting and killing opposition members, and by seizing control of local government offices across Oromia. As the first free elections approached in 1992, violent clashes broke out. Shortly before the vote, the OLF pulled out entirely and announced its return to armed struggle. Much of western and southern Oromia returned briefly to civil war.

The overwhelming preponderance of Tigrayan fighters at the helm of the EPRDF's troops in this period would also cast a long and contentious shadow. Of an army numbering about 100,000 soldiers in 1991, some 90 percent were estimated to be Tigrayan. "Almost all the soldiers I remember from then were Tigrayan," recalled Jawar Mohammed, another Muslim Oromo with a mixed religious upbringing—in his case in the eastern district of Arsi—who would go on to play a hugely prominent role in Ethiopian politics. "And it's kind of weird, because I really did admire them. They were so egalitarian when they first came to our area. They understood us, and we understood them. But I also couldn't reconcile that with the killing they were doing." As war between the EPRDF and the OLF simmered in the 1990s, the young Jawar would side with the rebels. Abiy, almost a decade his senior, did the opposite.

Exactly why Abiy, still in his mid-teens, joined the EPRDF's Oromo wing, the Oromo People's Democratic Organisation (OPDO) has never been fully explained. Abiy himself has rarely spoken candidly about it in public, and over the years conflicting accounts have accumulated. Based on what can be pieced together reliably, though, it seems that the formative moment took place in the wake of the OLF's departure from the transitional government in June 1992. It was in these weeks that OLF fighters broke out of their camps in western Oromia, including one just five or so kilometres from Beshasha, with many of them subsequently fleeing into the surrounding forests to organise a new insurgency. Pursuing them over the coming weeks, so as to round them up for re-education camps, were troops from the TPLF and OPDO, as well as a few sympathetic local residents. Among the latter, so the OLF believed at the time, was Abiy's older brother, Kedir. According to former OLF sources from the area, the rebels believed Kedir to be a government agent who had given the whereabouts of a prominent OLF-supporting elder to a local Eritrean merchant known to have links to the TPLF. The elder was then killed. Whether Kedir had actually passed on the information which led to the elder's death is not known. But the OLF soon captured him, and then, in an apparent act of revenge, murdered him.

According to some of Abiy's childhood friends, the OLF fighter who pulled the trigger was a local man called Mulugeta. Several years later, on returning to his hometown, Abiy was said to have made a public show of forgiving him. As prime minister, he would never mention his family's tragedy in public. But in the immediate aftermath of the killing, while still a young teenager, Abiy appears to have been deeply shaken by it. "I think losing his brother at that age was a turning point in Abiy's life," Miftah Hudin Aba Jebel, a childhood friend, later told a local reporter. "We were young, and I remember one night Abiy asking me to join the struggle. To be honest, it was difficult for me to understand what he was saying."[28] According to his father, Abiy, who was then still a schoolboy in Agaro, fled briefly for Addis Ababa—cutting short his formal education.[29] It was around this time, according to most accounts, that he attached himself to the OPDO. In an interview many years later Abiy said he had been just fourteen years old.[30] He never completed high school.

To join the OPDO in the early 1990s was controversial. Formed by the TPLF as a sort of surrogate party in the late 1980s, its earliest members were Oromo captives from the Derg's army. It therefore lacked entirely both the OLF's revolutionary credentials and the TPLF's military discipline. Indeed, right from the outset it was profoundly unpopular in most of Oromia and would remain so throughout the next decades. As its fighters had spread across western Oromia in the early 1990s, those most likely to enlist were either army captives or the most desperate of the many young men and women whose schooling or salaries had been interrupted by the war and change of regime. "People were suffering," recalled a senior OPDO official who also entered the party at this time. "Some didn't have enough to eat. So hungry teachers, hungry students, hungry labourers all joined the OPDO." Among those recruited from around Jimma at the same time as Abiy were Muktar Kedir, a future president of Oromia who was then working in a flour mill, as well as a friend who would grow up to be Abiy's chief personal bodyguard. Whereas a generation earlier the OLF and the TPLF had been founded by a cohort of unusually educated and ideologically committed student radicals, the early OPDO attracted much less dedicated members. "In those days, those who were educated, fit and relatively intelligent were attracted to the OLF," the OPDO official admitted. "There was a clear demarcation." Merera Gudina, the most influential Oromo civil opposition leader until the rise of Jawar in the 2010s, would later dismiss them as "non-unionised factory workers who just show up for the day job ... no ideology, no commitment to anything."

But Abiy's decision to join them was an early sign of political acumen. Though the creation of Oromia had heralded unprecedented opportunities for advancement for young Oromo men of his generation, it soon became clear that these wouldn't be made available to everyone. Whatever the OLF's popular credentials, it was to be out of power for the next three decades: anyone associated with it would be cut out, too. By 1993, the OPDO was the only game in town. As a distinctly and self-consciously Oromo elite emerged for the first time over the coming decades, Abiy was to make sure he was part it.

* * *

Details of Abiy's life over the next few years are no less murky than those of his early childhood. For about one year, Abiy later said, he served as a non-military OPDO cadre in a district of Jimma called Limmu.[31] Due to his young age, he would have started out as little more than an errand boy, or what was called a "*manjus*", delivering tea and carrying out odd jobs for the cadres. But like all new recruits to the EPRDF at this time, most of whom came from Oromia and southern Ethiopia, he would at some point have been sent for several months of 'political training'. There, among other things, he would have been taught the EPRDF's distinct version of Ethiopian history—much of which, by stressing the modern and essentially Amhara character of the former empire, overlapped considerably with the nationalist revisionism of the OLF. He would also have been schooled in Leninist theory, 'Revolutionary Democracy', the plight of Ethiopia's many subjugated 'nations and nationalities', as well as in the paramount importance of keeping religion and politics separate. These were the fundamental precepts which had guided the radical wing of the student movement a generation earlier, and which underpinned the federal constitution of 1995. The more rigorous the indoctrination, so the logic went, the less likely new recruits like Abiy would ever repudiate them.

In 1993, having failed to finish high school and being therefore unable to attend one of only two public universities in Ethiopia then, Abiy transitioned from the OPDO to the national army and became a regular soldier.[32] For several years in the early 1990s he was stationed at a military camp near the far-western town of Begi in the territory of Wollega, a centre of OLF activity going back to the Derg era. There he fell under the command of Colonel Gudeta Olana, an Oromo officer who taught him to be an army radio operator. During these years he would take part in missions against OLF guerrillas, while also picking up the basic Tigrinya language skills which would help him ingratiate himself with the army's still overwhelmingly Tigrayan hierarchy.

He also became known as something of a hellraiser. Those who knew him back then recalled him roaring around the camp on a motorbike, for instance, or chewing *khat*, a local stimulant, and getting drunk on local "*tej*" honey wine in nearby bars. Some have also suggested that it was in Begi that he first came to be known, controversially, as a womaniser—allegations which would dog him, if only in quiet whispers, for much of his professional life. By some accounts he was very nearly discharged from the army on account of his behaviour, only to be rescued at the last minute by his already well-evident personal charm.

In 1995, having avoided being thrown out of the army, he was briefly deployed to Kigali as a member of the United Nations peacekeeping force in the wake of the Rwandan genocide. (In an intriguing footnote, Rwanda's president Paul Kagame would later tell American diplomats during the Tigray War that he remembered the future Ethiopian prime minister from this time.) In Rwanda, Abiy later said, he had met a French woman who had fallen in love with him, and begged him to elope with her. "How little she could have thought of me," he later mused, "of the man who would be a king."[33] He would remain in the army for the next fifteen years, at one point in the mid-2000s being sent home to Beshasha, where he was to play a role in defusing tensions between Christians and Muslims there. By then, in keeping with the constitutional separation of the military from politics, he had ceased to be an active member of the OPDO.

His personal ties to the Oromo ruling party, however, had remained strong—thanks largely to a connection which would prove more consequential for his career, and the course of Ethiopian politics, than almost any other. The contact in question was Abadula Gemeda, a disarmingly gregarious, high-living OPDO commander who, under Meles, would go on to become Ethiopia's defence minister and later a landmark president of Oromia. Born an Orthodox Christian with the name Minase Woldegiorgis, he had started out as an ordinary soldier in the Derg's army before being captured by the TPLF in the early 1980s. Later acquiring his nom de guerre—Aba Dula, a traditional Oromo martial rank—in the early 1990s, he had been one of the founding members of the OPDO. Over the next three decades nobody until Abiy would wield as much power and influence over Oromo politics. Much of the party's subsequent transformation would later be credited to him. "All this was Abadula's creation," said Mohammed Ademo, a prominent Oromo activist who briefly joined Abiy's administration. "You cannot write the history of the OPDO without him."

There are differing accounts of exactly how they first met. One of his friends later said Abiy come into contact with Abadula through the latter's driver—another young OPDO recruit from Jimma—as early as 1994.[34] Another claimed the two men didn't really cross paths until almost a decade later. What is clear, though, is that the two were, for a while, like father and son. "Wherever Abadula went, Abiy went with him," recalled a close mutual friend. According to insiders who have known him longest, Abiy for a while camped out at the older man's home and, in the early 2000s, even fathered a child with one of Abadula's relatives. When

Abiy became prime minister, Abadula would take up position as his formal and, later, informal advisor. "Abiy owes his rise to Abadula," said Jawar, who also befriended the older politician as a precocious secondary school pupil in the early 2000s. "He was his godfather." Were it not for Abadula's blessing, Abiy may well have found it impossible to overcome his lack of both academic and formal military qualifications in his quest for power. Thanks to Abadula, Abiy would also rise unusually quickly through the military to the rank of lieutenant-colonel. For a thrusting young man of his ilk this might have been proof enough that charm, confidence, and a dash of good luck were all that were needed to get ahead in life. Yet with war breaking out in the north again in 1998, there would soon be another element to add to the mix: God's favour.

3

KINGDOM OF GOD

ETHIOPIA'S PENTECOSTAL TURN

"Like Sarajevo, 1914," Meles observed. "An accident waiting to happen." Few outsiders imagined a light skirmish on 6 May 1998 at Badme, a border village of which few had heard, could spiral into full-scale war. One observer at the time likened it to "two bald men fighting over a comb." Yet, for two full years, two of the world's poorest countries bled themselves to exhaustion. Young men charged across the no-man's-land between their trenches in battles reminiscent of the First World War. By the time a ceasefire was signed in June 2000, as many as 100,000 soldiers may have died, and half a million civilians had been forced from their homes.[1]

Neither side was blameless. Following Eritrea's peaceful secession in 1993 the two countries had enjoyed a brief honeymoon. Citizens were allowed to move seamlessly between them. Isaias Afewerki, by then independent Eritrea's first and only president, publicly mulled eventual political union as well as economic integration; some even imagined a "United States of the Horn of Africa". But frictions between the ruling parties on either side of the border—the TPLF and the EPLF—and between their respective leaders had never really disappeared. In Tigray, resentment still lingered of what was perceived to be a superiority complex harboured by their relatively wealthier Eritrean cousins, an attitude said to stem in part from the latter's relatively advanced industrial growth during the era of Italian colonisation. Also festering were memories of the EPLF's hand in the 1984–5 famine in Tigray, when Isaias and colleagues blocked the road used by aid workers to deliver food to TPLF-held areas following a particularly bitter disagreement between the two organisations over their divergent interpretations of the 'national question'.[2] In Eritrea, meanwhile, suspicions of Tigrayan designs on their hard-won territory persisted. Favourable trade and currency agreements struck in the early 1990s had given Eritrea the whip hand over the Ethiopian—and in particular the Tigrayan—economy. Irredentist sentiments within the TPLF and also the wider Ethiopian public, which had never truly come to terms with Eritrean independence, had gradually mounted.

In 1996, as Isaias departed for Asmara following a heated meeting with Meles in Addis Ababa, his aircraft caught fire.[3] With the Eritrean president now convinced the Ethiopian prime minister had tried to assassinate him, relations between the two governments collapsed. Over the next year unresolved tensions over their shared border and interdependent economies would worsen dramatically. Both sides prepared for war. By early 1998, munitions production in Ethiopia had gone into overdrive; in a final escalation the Eritreans dispatched troops to seize the land which they claimed the Tigrayans had unlawfully occupied.[4]

Just like the Tigray War twenty-two years later, it was a conflict which many observers struggled to comprehend. From the outside, each misstep had seemed avoidable, a mutual slide into war which appeared entirely illogical and benefitted no one. But at the same time, as in 2020, once war became thinkable it took on an air of inevitability. Ethiopia's northern borderlands, after all, had endured centuries of conflict.[5] Peace along the frontiers had historically been the exception, never the rule. Not even a decade had passed since the Derg's guns fell silent before the new conflict erupted.

The TPLF and the EPLF, moreover, were children of the student movement: born of revolution and forged in war. Both were Leninist vanguard parties, guided by closed circles of elites among whom a culture of secrecy had almost always prevailed. Violence, and the settling of difference through arms, were hard-wired into them. Traditions of negotiation and compromise were absent in both. Over the course of the next two years both societies would be dramatically militarised once again.[6] Ethiopia, just seven years on from the reactionary nationalism of the Derg which had nearly broken it, was gripped once more by jingoistic fervour.[7] Eritrea, ultimately unable to prevail against a neighbour thirty times its size, would harden over the coming years of frozen conflict into a garrison state kept alive by forced conscription.

Two decades later a video clip from the war circulated online. It shows an army band led by Getish Mamo, a friend of Abiy's from Jimma, performing to a gaggle of soldiers near the front line in northern Tigray.

Just briefly, the future prime minister flashes on screen. Slim, and wearing a denim jacket, he jumps onstage to kiss his friend on the forehead, patting down his collar and fondly straightening his shirt. It is the only known video of Abiy from his youth, and it is striking how much of the future politician is visible in it: the cheery optimism; the warm, tactile affection; the ease under the spotlight. Later he can be glimpsed dancing in the crowd, his head thrown back in laughter.[8]

Yet for Abiy, the defining experience of the war was not the youthful excitement evoked by these few seconds of video. Indeed, if his later testimony can be trusted, there was perhaps nothing in his early years which shaped him more than the gruelling slog of the trenches between 1998 and 2000. "I have seen brothers slaughtering brothers on the battlefield," he recalled in his Nobel Prize acceptance speech in Oslo in 2019. "I have seen older men, women, and children trembling in terror under the deadly shower of bullets and artillery shells." What was more, the tragedy of the war had been particularly personal for him. As he recounted in his Nobel speech, his whole army unit had been wiped out by an Eritrean artillery attack. He was the sole survivor.

This was not entirely true: one other comrade had also escaped unharmed.[9] But it was precisely when Abiy, then a junior radio operator in a signal interception unit stationed not far from Badme, had briefly stepped outside the foxhole to position his antenna—or, as he would sometimes tell people, to take a call from the future army chief General Samora Yunis—that the fateful shell landed. Indeed, it was Abiy who had been left to radio their superior in Addis Ababa, a certain General Teklebrhan Woldearegay, to relay the news.

Occurring at the apocalyptic height of the final Ethiopian offensive in Eritrea, shortly before the fighting stopped, Abiy had managed to narrowly escape death at perhaps the most dangerous period of the whole war. Many Tigrayans, including the then head of the Ethiopian army, General Tsadkan Gebretensae, would later rue these weeks as a missed opportunity to press home their advantage and remove Isaias altogether. So bitter were the ensuing internal ructions over Meles's ultimate decision not to advance that the TPLF would splinter the following year. But Abiy, looking back, would remember June 2000 for other reasons. This was the moment, he later told his fellow churchmen, that God's purpose was revealed to him and he resolved to become a Pentecostal Protestant.

* * *

Converting to Pentecostalism was, on the surface, unusual for someone of Abiy's background. His father, after all, was not only a Muslim but a respected local elder who was said to have donated some of his land during the reign of Haile Selassie for the construction of a mosque.[10] As a child, Abiy had attended classes at a Koranic school in the nearby town of Agaro, and would later make much of his close relationship there with a renowned Islamic scholar who went on to be the chief imam of Addis Ababa's Grand Anwar Mosque.[11] Converts to Pentecostalism were, moreover, always far more likely to come from Ethiopia's traditional Orthodox communities than from its much more separate Muslim ones.

Even so, by joining one of the country's biggest Pentecostal denominations, the Ethiopian Full Gospel Believers' Church, in his early twenties, Abiy was emblematic of the most significant demographic transformation in Ethiopia of the entire EPRDF years.[12] In the 1960s, 'Pentes', as both Pentecostals and more staid Protestants are known in Ethiopia, had made up less than one percent of the national population. Mostly confined to the non-Orthodox southern and western fringes of the empire, where Haile Selassie had allowed Protestant missionaries to operate as agents of modernisation, they were maligned for much of this period, stigmatised for their association with the West and condemned as traitors to Ethiopia's national destiny as the last home of true Christian faith. When Full Gospel Believers tried to register with the authorities in 1967, the emperor rejected its application. Under the atheistic Derg, the nadir for Ethiopia's embattled Pente minority, Full Gospel members were publicly flogged as punishment for refusing to chant socialist slogans.[13]

Yet by the time Abiy took power just four decades later, Protestantism, and in particular its more 'charismatic' Pentecostal variants, had exploded—so much so that Pentes accounted for perhaps as much as a quarter of the population. For many of those living through a period of such rapid social and economic change, the new faith, with its hopeful stress on individual empowerment and salvation, coupled with its modern, even capitalist aesthetic, seemed to offer a far more empowering message than the fatalist conservatism of traditional Orthodoxy. In many parts of the country, especially in Oromia and the wider south, big and brash new churches had begun to sprout on almost every street corner. Most of this growth had come at the expense of the Orthodox church.[14]

For a country defined, even after the iconoclasm of the student movement and the Derg, by the entwining of national identity with the ritual and hierarchy of the continent's oldest church, it was a profound shift. Not because, as Orthodox critics often contended, the loyalty of Pentes to the Ethiopian state was innately compromised. Many Oromo nationalists, to be sure, were Pentes, including several of the founders of the OLF, in part because sermons were conducted in Afan Oromo, rather than Ge'ez, the ancient language of Orthodox liturgy, and in part because of the presence of American, German and Swedish missions in the nationalist movement's western heartlands. But really that was to confuse cause with effect: for much of its twentieth century history, Protestantism had tended to spread fastest in those places where the penetration of the Ethiopian state and its Orthodox institutions had always been shallow. Much more striking, in fact, were the efforts the new churches went to distance themselves from foreign missions—whose leaders had often looked down on their Ethiopian congregants—and instead burnish their patriotic credentials. As Abiy and his allies would one day go on to demonstrate so vividly, to be a Pente certainly didn't require jettisoning the fundamental Christian mythos at the heart of Ethiopian nationalism. Indeed, perhaps partly for fear of being accused of wayward loyalties, it would often mean doubling down on it. Belina Sarka, for instance, a renowned Pente preacher with whom Abiy was personally close and whom he would often describe as a father figure, was famous for his exceptionally extravagant depictions of Ethiopia as a chosen nation. His prophetic vision, of an Ethiopia rich and prosperous within just three decades, was one which Abiy later echoed in much of his own rhetoric as a prime minister.

But the rise of Pentecostalism would impact Ethiopian political culture in other, more novel ways, and in particular through its strong association with the growing individualism of the era. In part, this stemmed simply from the fact that Pentecostalism tended to free people from familial control and from traditional obligations to share their wealth, liberating them to fashion themselves as they wished and make new kinds of economic choices. From the early 2000s it had become evident that parts of the country which had seen a boom in private businesses were often also those where Pentecostalism was particularly thriving.[15]

But the change was distinctly ideological, too. Pentes, not least Abiy himself, could be deeply hostile to socialism. As early as the 1960s it had been apparent that many of the early Pente students had deliberately eschewed the Marxism-Leninism of their peers—choosing conversion and personal salvation as their own act of youthful rebellion—and quite self-consciously defined themselves in opposition to the left-wing student radicals of the same generation. Over the years, connections with

American Evangelical groups made by Ethiopians in the diaspora had the effect of further hardening the anti-socialist leanings of many Ethiopian Pentes. Among these was Abiy: despite his schooling in EPRDF doctrine, he would later spend considerable time moving in such circles in America. Among his closest friends in the diaspora, for example, was a wealthy Oromo pastor and businessman called Gemechis Desta Buba, whose core pastoral message—as seemingly reflected in his flourishing business empire in Ethiopia—was the importance of individual effort and personal uplift. (Once Abiy became prime minister Gemechis would be heard telling congregants that his friend was a prophet.) "Abiy hates Marx. He really hates Marx. And he hates Marx because Marx was an atheist," noted an Ethiopian scholar who met with Abiy on several occasions before he became prime minister. "He believes Ethiopia went wrong because, in the 1960s and 1970s, it imported foreign, i.e. atheist, ideas. So what he really wants to do is bring God back into politics."

Often more important for most Pentes, though, was simply the act of conversion itself. In part because Pentecostalism stressed the personal relationship between the individual and Christ, which meant throwing off the shackles of the Orthodox church's conservative traditions, joining the Pente fold often inspired a novel sense of possibility: the power to transcend one's personal circumstances, however desperate they might be. Because conversion to Pentecostalism often corresponded with moving to the city, bringing rural migrants into contact with new cultures, religious influences and people, it also helped shape new identities and communities.[16] Abiy was, in this regard, again quite typical of his generation.[17] After the war with Eritrea ended in 2000, he moved to Addis Ababa, where he was appointed by Abadula, Ethiopia's defence minister between 2001 and 2005, to lead a new ICT agency for Oromia. There he would also meet his future wife, Zinash Tayachew, an Amhara from the seventeenth-century city of Gondar and a member of Getish Mamo's army band, who was then working as Abadula's secretary. Like Abiy, she was a soldier, with an aristocratic grandfather who had played a prominent part in the resistance movement against the Italians in the 1930s. Together they would join the same church in Addis Ababa around the same time, with Zinash, who otherwise shied away from the limelight, later reinventing herself as a popular gospel singer. "Before they converted, they were both vagabonds," recalled a mutual friend. "Abiy smoked and chewed *khat*. But all that stopped after they converted." Soon they would have three daughters and, later, an adopted son.

For most Pentes, at first, social and cultural change didn't translate into significant political ambition. Ethiopia's earliest Protestants, wary of the legacy of intolerance and repression which had blighted their short history, had typically avoided formal party politics. Abiy's own church had long forbidden party members from obtaining leadership positions. But from the 2000s, as new churches mushroomed and their leaders grew in confidence, so a rising Pente generation, often inspired by tendencies originating in America, sought to emancipate themselves from the quietist constraints of Ethiopia's mainline Protestant churches. Now, for the first time, they looked to enter politics.

One of those influences was explicit about this. 'Dominionist' or 'seven mountain' theology, as it was variously called, encouraged Pentes to take over the state, one convert at a time, by expanding their influence over business, politics and culture. This was, in effect, a Christian version of the Marxist idea of a 'long march through the institutions', and over the course of the 2000s such thinking had been gradually infiltrating some of Ethiopia's younger Pentecostal churches.[18] Though Full Gospel Believers' Church officially rejected this kind of thinking, Abiy would almost certainly have encountered it. "Definitely he believes in Dominion Theology," said one of his fellow Full Gospel churchmen. Among its most prominent advocates in the 2010s was Mehret Debebe, a psychiatrist, self-help coach and Pente preacher whom Abiy would later invite to give talks to officials in the ministry of science and technology. Mehret would go on to become one of the most influential of all Abiy's informal advisors in the Prime Minister's Office.

The impact which Prosperity Gospel theology, another powerful trend in this period, had on the political outlook of Ethiopia's Pentes was less direct. Long abhorred by both Orthodox and Protestant traditionalists for its supposedly unseemly—even heretical—celebration of earthly success as a sign of God's blessing, Prosperity theology had never been formally embraced by the country's Pentecostal establishment. Abiy's own, relatively traditionalist church was, again, one of the stauncher opponents. Nonetheless, spearheaded by a new generation of charismatic pastors universally known, by the mid-2010s, as the 'Prophets', Prosperity Gospel was rapidly becoming ubiquitous in much of the country.[19] The consequences of this would be just as much political as they were cultural.

Flashily dressed and renowned for exorcising demons from the bodies of the faithful, nothing quite rivalled the Prophets in embodying the transformations underway in Ethiopian society in these years. With their business empires and sometimes global followings, the Prophets were individualistic, cosmopolitan and often ruthlessly entrepreneurial. They were, needless to say, nothing like traditional Ethiopian religious figures. Yet in Abiy they had a kindred spirit. Like him, they had rags-to-riches stories with which to enchant their followers: Prophet Suraphel Demissie, to pick just one example, grew up an orphan in the southern city of Hawassa, but by the middle of the 2010s had hundreds of thousands of YouTube followers and a swanky office in Addis Ababa. Like Abiy, they also assured their followers that glittering success was attainable not just for them but for anyone who strived for it. And most importantly, they straddled the line between politics and religion, with many of them pronouncing Abiy in 2018 to be a fellow prophet sent by God to heal Ethiopia's ethnic divisions. The following year, several publicly endorsed his newly formed, and tellingly named, Prosperity Party. Between 2020 and 2022 many would also lend their moral support to his military campaign in Tigray.

Pentes entering politics alongside Abiy thus brought with them an overtly religious conception of statecraft, with the potential to influence government and society in profound and consequential ways. What this wasn't, though, was something entirely novel or fundamentally alien to Ethiopia's political culture. Indeed, for most of the country's history, under an imperial monarchy ordained by God, there had never been a meaningful distinction between politics and religion, or church and state. Even decades after the 1974 Revolution, Ethiopia had remained one of the most devout nations on earth: in the late 2010s, some 98 percent of Ethiopians still described themselves as "very religious".[20] Moreover, Abiy's predecessor as prime minister, Hailemariam Desalegn, had also been a devoted Pentecostal, albeit from a small and dissident church.[21] Like Abiy, Hailemariam believed his mission in politics was heaven-sent, and expressed his opposition to Marxism in explicitly religious terms: when Meles recruited him into the EPRDF in the 1990s, he recalled, the first question he asked the then prime minister was whether the ruling coalition were "communists". After leaving office in 2018, Hailemariam would go on to be ordained as a church minister.

But as a loyal disciple of Meles and a reliable product of the EPRDF, Hailemariam had been studiously careful to observe the secular state's limits. His official speeches made no mention of God. As prime minister, he refrained from commenting publicly on religious matters. Though he was, like Abiy, a critic of the student movement's secular, socialist legacy,

Hailemariam was politically too weak ever to openly challenge it. It would, therefore, take the rise of Abiy's younger generation of Pentes—bolder and better connected—to restore God to its place at the heart of Ethiopian politics.

* * *

As prime minister, Abiy would never be an entirely conventional Pente politician. There was, for instance, no mention of religion at all in his 2019 political tract, *Medemer*. He was close to several Orthodox leaders, including some virulently reactionary ones, and he enjoyed warm relations with many Muslims clerics, too. To the horror of fundamentalist Pentes he even spoke warmly of *Irreecha*—a traditional Oromo thanksgiving festival which many Christians regarded as 'pagan', and which he would allow to be celebrated annually in Addis Ababa's iconic Meskel Square. Later, many committed Christians also questioned why a man so ostentatiously God-fearing could appear so unmoved by the mass bloodshed committed in his name.

But there was also little reason to doubt the centrality of religion to his political project. Pastor Bekele Woldekidan, one of Abiy's earliest spiritual patrons in the Full Gospel's church, later recalled how Abiy would turn up at his office to tell him of his conviction that he was destined to be prime minister from his very early twenties.[22] Over the years, many others—from party colleagues to foreign officials—would also encounter the same unblinking, righteous self-belief. "I don't see any contradiction between Abiy's words, his rhetoric and his actions," an advisor in the Prime Minister's Office told me many years later. "It's the biggest driving force in his life. He genuinely believes he is God-anointed." In office, when asked to explain the thinking behind one of his flagship religious projects—bringing Ethiopia's Pente churches together under a single Ethiopian Evangelical Council—the prime minister explained that, though the constitution formally kept state and religion separate, "that doesn't mean they shouldn't work together". Addressing a large private gathering of his fellow churchmen he then went further. "You want a strong institution," he told a sceptical attendee who probed him on his plans for the council. "But I want to expand the kingdom of God."[23]

4

UNDERSTANDING INSA

INSIDE THE SURVEILLANCE STATE

To catch the eye of his new boss, Abiy had an idea. One day in the early 2000s the young radio operator walked into the office of General Teklebrhan Woldearegay, then the head of Military Intelligence's Technological Information Department, and presented him with a proposal. He had recently written his own Amharic-to-English dictionary, he told the older Tigrayan officer. Now he needed money to publish it. Could the Ministry of Defence help?

It was a canny move. Although the defence ministry didn't have funds for such a proposal, which was quickly shelved, the young Oromo officer now had his foot in the office door of one of the military's leading lights. Teklebrhan, with whom he had hitherto had little contact, reasoned that if Abiy could write a dictionary then he must speak good English. And so, he invited him to join his team working on a joint intelligence project with America's National Security Agency (NSA).

For nearly two decades under the Soviet-backed Derg, ties between America and Ethiopia had been all but severed. With the more pragmatic EPRDF in power in the 1990s, however, they had swiftly recovered. Soon, relations between the countries had returned to a strength familiar to Ethiopians of an older generation, who remembered how, in the latter part of Haile Selassie's reign, Ethiopian troops had even fought alongside American ones in Korea. Yet it was the years following the September 11th terror attacks in 2001 which would really come to count as golden ones for what, to many Ethiopians, was their country's most valuable diplomatic alliance. Under Meles's tutelage, the EPRDF succeeded in positioning itself as America's closest and most reliable regional partner for its 'war on terror' across Africa and the Middle East in the 2000s. "Ethiopia was the point of reference for security for the whole region," recalled Alex Rondos, a former EU special envoy to the Horn of Africa. "Meles had managed to wind the United States around his little finger." So great was Ethiopia's clout in Washington by the middle of the decade that when it invaded Somalia in 2006 to topple an Islamist government in the capital Mogadishu, America would even come to its aid. By the late 2000s, Ethiopian airstrips were being used by American bombers; intelligence from American satellites was being shared with the Ethiopian military; and Ethiopian commandos were being trained by American special forces for counterterrorism operations.[1] Ethiopia had become what foreign policy wonks called an American 'anchor state', pivotal for regional order and for guaranteeing Western interests in the Horn and the geo-strategically vital Red Sea trade route. Under the EPRDF it would send more troops to UN peacekeeping missions than any other on earth. In return, Ethiopia became the top recipient of American aid in all of Africa.[2]

It was thus with American help that in 2006 Ethiopia established what was to become its own version of the NSA, the Information Network Security Agency (INSA). Originally the brainchild of General Tsadkan Gebretensae, Ethiopia's army chief until he fell out with Meles in the Ethio-Eritrea war, INSA's original purpose was to intercept and analyse intelligence gathered primarily from Somalia. Given the simmering hostilities which continued through the 2000s, it was also to target Eritrea. Envisioned as a high-tech, civilian-military hybrid, INSA was to complement—and soon rival—the civilian intelligence agency, the National Intelligence and Security Service (NISS). Charged with keeping Ethiopia's growing digital infrastructure safe from foreign threats, it would later play a role in monitoring and censoring the internet. But although it had the power to intercept radio and cyber transmissions from abroad, and to interpret geospatial satellite imagery, it was not, at first, intended to be a domestic spy agency.[3] Teklebrhan would become its first director, and Abiy, who had been sent along with five colleagues to study cryptography in South Africa for six months between 2002 and 2003 in preparation, was to head its department of Information Security Assurance. For his first four years at INSA, Abiy's primary job was to help protect government and military agencies from cyber-hacking. He was among a small Oromo cohort in a leadership which, like that of the military, was still visibly dominated by Tigrayans. "Abiy was a fast communicator, young and Oromo—that's why he was chosen," explained one of his Tigrayan superiors. "His main talent was communicating with people."

Abiy would later describe his years at INSA as among the best of his life. It was during his time in the cyber-intelligence agency, he later claimed, that he came of age politically, becoming aware of both the strengths and weaknesses of the EPRDF and the need for reform.[4] The work also brought him into closer contact with American officials, allowing him to spend some time on US training programmes and cultivating some valuable foreign links in the years before he became prime minister. "I was the one who would send intelligence from this part of the world to the NSA, about Sudan and Yemen and Somalia," he later boasted to the *New Yorker*. "The NSA knows me. I would fight and die for America."[5]

But, more importantly, it was during this period that Abiy would build the social networks to facilitate his political career and acquire the friends who would go on to become his most trusted allies. Much like Putin, who was moulded by his years inside Russia's KGB intelligence services, so Abiy was unmistakeably the product of INSA and Ethiopia's opaque, and largely unaccountable, military intelligence establishment. Perhaps more than anything else, it was by quickly rising through the ranks of INSA that Abiy was able to master the darker art of palace politics for which he would one day be so well-known. "You cannot understand Ethiopian politics today without understanding INSA," recalled a former employee of the agency who was close to Abiy at the time, and remained friendly with him afterwards. "All the politics now was first tried there."

One by one Abiy had begun collecting powerful friends. Some of them were politicians. In South Africa, for instance, he had established contact—through Abadula—with Bereket Simon, then Ethiopia's information minister and Meles's right hand man in the EPRDF. (Bereket had happened to be in Pretoria for medical treatment at the same time.) On his return to Ethiopia, Abiy would use his new relationship with the senior government minister to help him establish links to other senior Amhara figures in the EPRDF, and to help Teklebrhan in lobbying Meles on INSA matters. Meanwhile, he also courted wealthy businessmen and senior army officers. By the early 2000s, he was already friendly with Samora Yunis, the chief of staff who would later be one of the very few senior Tigrayan officers not to join the TPLF's side in the Tigray War.

Most importantly, though, by the time INSA had been established in the mid-2000s, Abiy was on familiar terms with Meles himself. Though still in his very early thirties, and without any academic qualification beyond his diploma from South Africa, Abiy and Teklebrhan would regularly meet with the prime minister to brief him on developments at INSA, sometimes just the two of them. By some accounts—though these are heavily disputed—it was Abiy who played the decisive part in convincing Meles to establish INSA as a fully independent agency, rather than as just a wing of military intelligence.[6] Later, as prime minister himself, Abiy would describe how he would use such opportunities to win Meles's favour, for instance by passing him notes with eye-catching proposals or ideas. "Abiy was one of the very young, very sharp guys on the Oromo side," recalled a senior American official who was close to the former prime minister at the time. "And he was trusted."

Close colleagues from this time, however, painted a more ambiguous picture of the rising star. On the one hand, it was clear Abiy could be extremely personable. "He's friendly; he hugs people, he smiles; he texts you his best wishes, invites you to things," recalled Berhane Kidanemariam, a Tigrayan then in charge of Walta TV, a state-affiliated media outlet. Berhane noted how often the young cyber-intelligence officer would seek him out in his Walta office to take him for lunch at expensive hotels. "He was generous, and his life was extravagant. He'd give money to a beggar if he saw one; if you complimented his shoes, he'd go and buy a pair for you." Even so, the amount of time Abiy spent networking like this often rankled. "He was restless. He couldn't sit still for more than three minutes," complained an INSA colleague who sat near him in the office. "You'd just see him in the compound, roaming and talking. I never saw him deliver anything."

Others alleged that Abiy used his position in INSA to build a political following. To win the loyalty of his colleagues, some recalled, he was known to make lavish promises, including—among other things—of jobs and perks in the future. "He was neat, really neat," one former INSA employee recalled. "With everyone else you could tell when they'd spent all the night in the office: they'd have red eyes from sitting too long in front of the computer; they'd look dishevelled. Abiy wasn't like that. His hairline was always clean; he wore lotions; he had new shirts every morning. But then he'd stand up in a meeting and make all these promises, like, 'in two years you'll all have a house and we'll make sure you're set for life.' But it was just never going to happen. I remember thinking, 'I didn't even get my salary on time this month!'"

There were also some darker allegations. "He was focused on gaining power by any means," claimed one of his superiors. "He was using his position to advance his own interests." Technically, monitoring the phone calls of ordinary Ethiopian citizens was not part of INSA's mandate. From the outset, though, its leaders had been keen to acquire both the capability and legal authority for it—sparking a fierce turf war with NISS, Ethiopia's official spy agency. In the end, the latter prevailed and NISS retained its formal monopoly over domestic surveillance. But, according to some former colleagues, this didn't deter senior INSA figures from eavesdropping on private phone calls. Among the more serious allegations from this period was that they had managed to bug the communications of a prominent Oromo businessman, who was accused of working with the OLF. Though the agency lacked the legal power to monitor phone calls, it had the authority and capability to gather and store private email communications in Ethiopia.[7] "We were monitoring everyone's emails," said a close colleague. "We had access."

Some of these claims haven't been definitively proven, and given the closed character of Ethiopia's security agencies, likely never will be. Despite the allegations, a striking number of those who worked at INSA around this time have since remained loyal to him. "INSA had nothing to do with domestic abuses," said another colleague. "That was NISS's realm. INSA was prohibited by law from spying on anything domestic." But it's worth noting that as prime minister a decade later, Abiy was to oversee the creation of a sprawling mega-agency under one roof with powers and responsibilities far beyond anything INSA's early founders had ever imagined.[8] The jewel in the crown was a new Artificial Intelligence Institute, answerable directly to the prime minister, established with the express purpose of spying on Ethiopian citizens. Indeed, when Abiy later took visitors on tours of INSA's new office building in Addis Ababa, he was seen to proudly demonstrate his government's ability to eavesdrop on private communications—including on phone calls.

* * *

For a young Oromo with strong ties to EPRDF leaders, the second half of the 2000s was a propitious time to be rising up the ranks of Ethiopia's expanding security apparatus. For a few years, in the 1990s, political freedoms had briefly flourished. By the following decade, however, whatever hopes remained for a democratic future were fading, and nowhere more than in Oromia. The OLF's low-level but persistent insurgency in the years after its exit from the transitional government in

1992 had given the now politically unrivalled EPRDF a perfect excuse to crack down on opposition of all stripes there.[9] Tens of thousands of Oromos, mostly young men accused of working for the OLF, had been slung behind bars. By as early as 2001, some 25,000 OLF-sympathetic Oromos were reportedly in jail. When Seeye Abraha, the Tigrayan defence minister who fell out with Meles after the Ethio-Eritrean war, emerged from six years of imprisonment in 2007, he memorably observed that "the prison speaks Oromiffa [Afan Oromo]."[10] Having ruthlessly consolidated power in the aftermath of the TPLF's 2001 split by purging or imprisoning rivals like Seeye on charges of corruption, Meles had in the meantime become almost unassailable. The EPRDF's vaunted tradition of 'internal democracy' was cast aside, as power became concentrated in the hands of the prime minister and his most trusted allies.

The elections of 2005 briefly seemed to offer the chance of a reset. Confident that after more than a decade in power its position was now firmly assured, the EPRDF decided to permit its opponents something resembling a free, if not exactly fair, run at the polls. In turn, several opposition parties, with the notable exception of the OLF, decided not to boycott as they had done in both 1995 and 2000. The result was the most competitive general election in Ethiopian history, with the EPRDF shocking both itself and its opponents by winning less than 60 percent of seats in parliament (though the ruling coalition did notably well in most Muslim majority areas, including Abiy's home district). In Oromia, even its then president, Junedin Sado, and Abadula, the OPDO chairman, lost their seats. Most surprising of all, though, were the enormous gains made by a four-party Ethiopianist grouping, the Coalition for Unity and Democracy (CUD), which managed to take all of Addis Ababa's seats in the federal parliament, as well as all but one seat in the capital's own council.

It was a sharp rebuke to the EPRDF, and a salutary lesson that its hold over diverse urban areas, where Amharas and Ethiopianists were still most populous, remained particularly wobbly. Over the next few years, the coalition would attempt to redress this by paying greater attention to urban development, especially in Addis Ababa, and rolling out mass housing programmes, micro-financing, subsidised commodities like sugar and job schemes for the urban poor.[11] But the election was also a reminder just how much Ethiopian politics continued to be animated by both the faces and the themes—above all, the vexatious 'national question'—of the student movement three decades earlier.[12] At the heart of the CUD's campaign against the EPRDF was its critique of the 1995 constitution, which it argued had balkanised Ethiopia along ethnic lines. Other lines of attack drew on debates dating back to the 1970s as well. On the matter of Eritrean independence, which many former student radicals had fiercely opposed, the CUD argued that Ethiopia should at least have taken back the crucial Eritrean port town of Assab. Against the EPRDF's policy of continued state-ownership of land, the CUD advocated privatisation.

Most damaging of all, though, was the campaign's focus on the then overbearing dominance of Tigrayans and the TPLF across politics, business and the security apparatus. Over the course of an especially bilious campaign, which foreshadowed some of the rhetoric of the Tigray War fifteen years later, an SMS campaign called on residents to take action against their Tigrayan neighbours. A newspaper owned by the prominent Ethiopianist journalist-activist Eskinder Nega, who was later thrown in prison, issued a chilling appeal for a German-style national struggle against the Tigrayan "Judah". The TPLF, for its part, evoked memories of the aerial bombardment of Tigrayan civilians by the Derg as warning of what was to come should the opposition take power. Meles, in accusing the opposition of fomenting ethnic hatred against Tigrayans, drew parallels with the Rwandan genocide.[13]

In the event, the 2005 election would come to count among the most significant turning points of all the EPRDF years—but for all the wrong reasons. The opposition, led by the CUD, claimed that it had, in reality, won the election overall, and called for mass demonstrations and a boycott of the results. When the new parliament opened in October, most of the newly elected opposition MPs at first refused to take up their seats. Violent protests in Addis Ababa the following month led to the deaths of 193 civilians (and seven policemen). Tens of thousands were arrested; 131 people including a number of CUD leaders—among them the future chair of Abiy's national electoral board, Birtukan Mideksa— were charged with a range of crimes including genocide, high treason and outrages against the constitution.[14] Meanwhile, mostly out of sight of the foreign embassies and media in the capital, much of Oromia also erupted. Organised by the OLF, which was by then operating over the border in an Eritrea increasingly hostile to Ethiopia, students and young people across the region turned out onto the streets for some 205 days of anti-government protests. For weeks at a time large swathes of the region were rendered effectively ungovernable. More than 15,000 people were detained and eighty reportedly killed.[15] The OLF dubbed it the "Revolt against Subjugation".

The election's messy fallout gave the EPRDF licence to further tighten its grip. Having already discarded much of the democratic rhetoric it had briefly espoused in the early 1990s, the coalition now doubled down on the more avowedly anti-liberal implications of its signature doctrine, 'Revolutionary Democracy'. Once described by Meles as representing a "coalition with the people", a form of mass participatory democracy better suited than liberalism to an agrarian society, this was a concept as slippery as it was opaque.[16] By combining a Leninist disdain for pluralism with the engrained authoritarianism of Ethiopia's own political culture, it had always offered, at least implicitly, an ideological rationale for expanded state power. After 2005, it gave the EPRDF an added intellectual justification for a renewed assault on both political opposition and civil society.

Over the following years independent media houses and NGOs were smashed. In 2009, the government rolled out its infamous anti-terror legislation, which expanded the definition of terrorism so dramatically that even a protest march that caused a traffic jam might theoretically violate it. The new law would soon ensnare hundreds, perhaps thousands, of Oromo and other dissidents.[17] In 2014, the government would go even as far as to arrest, torture and charge members of a critical, if hardly insurrectionist, blogging group in Addis Ababa, known as Zone 9.

But the ruling coalition also sought to extend its reach deeper, and wider, into Ethiopian society. Following the example of the Chinese Communist Party, which became an increasingly important ally and inspiration in these years, the EPRDF dramatically grew its party ranks, transforming itself from a self-proclaimed 'vanguard party', in which a few enlightened elites led the majority, into a mass movement. In just three years its membership was said to have risen from around 760,000 to six million, making it by far Africa's largest party.[18] In ways which many of its leaders would later come to regret, the governing coalition was now to be fused so tightly with the apparatus of the state that it would come to resemble, in the words of one foreign observer, a "party-business-nongovernment-organization-military-mass-organization-state, where the lines among all of these different facets of the EPRDF overlap and are blurred by design".[19] Hundreds of thousands of young men and women were recruited into new party-linked youth leagues. Those who joined could expect special access to jobs, land, agricultural inputs like fertilisers, and micro-credit. Those who refused risked being tarred with the stigma of association with the OLF or other opposition groups.

Nowhere was this expansion of the ruling party more striking than in Oromia, then under the leadership of Abadula, the most consequential regional president of the entire EPRDF years. Partly as a direct response to the mass protests over the course of that year, and partly to act as a counterweight to the Amhara and Ethiopianist politicians then flexing their muscles in Addis Ababa, Meles had given his lieutenant in Oromia licence to tilt the OPDO in a more openly Oromo nationalist direction. On a symbolic level, this involved, among other things, building an Oromo cultural centre in the heart of Addis Ababa. A graphic and controversial memorial for victims of Menelik II's imperial wars of the late nineteenth century, the first of its kind, was also erected in the Oromo district of Arsi.

More substantively, though, the new approach involved a radical overhaul of the OPDO's membership base. "Intellectual Oromos had been seen, categorically, as the enemy of the OPDO: they were labelled OLF. We decided this had to change," recalled one of Abadula's close allies from this time. "The only way out was to recruit better citizens. And so we started recruiting students, university professors and teachers." It was in precisely these years that Abadula and his allies enlisted many of the young, relatively well-educated cadres—some of whom had even been organisers of the protests only a year or so earlier—who would go on to dominate Abiy's administration. The results, though, were ambiguous. The rising generation were not obviously any more honest or more capable than their predecessors; in fact, given the rapid expansion of the party-state, many had clearly joined out of self-interested, mercantile motives. But at the same time, the Oromo ruling party gradually became, in important respects, ideologically less distinct from the OLF than it ever had been previously: more openly ethno-nationalist (though not secessionist), more outspoken on matters like Oromo representation in Addis Ababa, and, crucially, more critical of the TPLF.

To join the governing coalition also meant becoming part of an ever-growing infrastructure of surveillance and control. At the national level, this was an expansion from which both INSA and NISS stood to benefit: despite lagging quite far behind most other countries in Africa when it came to digital communications, not least internet connectivity, sizeable investments over these years had given Ethiopia's government many more tools to monitor their citizens. By 2014, according to *Human Rights Watch*, Ethiopia had acquired some of the world's most advanced surveillance technologies. Thanks to its complete monopoly of the rapidly growing telecoms sector, through the state-owned operator, Ethio Telecom, the EPRDF thus had arguably greater capacity for state surveillance than any other government in Africa. The absence of strong legislative and judicial oversight to protect citizens' privacy also gave cyber-intelligence officials like Abiy virtually unfettered investigative power.[20]

But it was not only the infrastructure of digital surveillance which was being expanded. All over the country, even in its farthest and most disconnected reaches, networks of informants and systems of grassroots surveillance were increasing their footprint. From 2011, in villages throughout Ethiopia, new party members were assigned to monitor five peers in their schools, universities, businesses and prisons—even, sometimes, in their own households.[21] Alongside these so-called 'one-to-five' networks, the lowest rung of Ethiopia's surveillance state, were 'development armies', 'women's armies' and 'model farmers'.[22] Ostensibly responsible for mobilising the public towards development goals such as reducing maternal mortality, all were also tasked with snooping, and could be involved in anything from tax collection to forcing their neighbours to attend meetings and vote for the ruling coalition. The result was an omnipresent, if not completely omniscient, federal state. Such was the reach of the EPRDF in these years that shortly before his death in 2012 Meles would be able to boast that, for the first time in Ethiopian history, the state's "writ runs in every village".[23] By the time the EPRDF's final national elections rolled around in 2015, the ruling coalition and its affiliates in the lowland peripheries found they could win every single seat in parliament almost without trying.

It was in the years after 2005, too, that Ethiopia became something of a poster child for what is often called 'authoritarian development': a Chinese-style trade-off in which civil and individual liberties are downgraded in exchange for stability and rapid economic growth. Under Meles, and inspired by the 'Asian Tiger' economies of Singapore, South Korea and Taiwan, as well as China, the ruling coalition in the 2000s had officially done away with doctrinaire socialism. In its place had come a form of state-led vanguard capitalism popularly known as the 'developmental state', in which parts of the economy were opened to private business while certain 'strategic' sectors—notably telecoms, banking and logistics—were kept under state control. Over the course of the 2000s, it also entailed a gradual shift in focus away from smallholder farmers—long the EPRDF's core constituency—towards large-scale commercial agricultural and industrialisation, a turn which some on the coalition's left denounced as a capitulation to 'neoliberalism' and foreign capital. Coercive and often violent expropriation of land from peasant farmers for private firms, both local and foreign, became increasingly commonplace.

Compared to most other countries on the continent, though, the state's role in the economy remained substantial. Party-owned conglomerates, most notably EFFORT—the TPLF's Endowment Fund for the Rehabilitation of Tigray—acquired stakes in everything from banking and shipping to metals, travel and cement, enriching a new class of Tigrayan businessmen in the process. With the expansion of the military-industrial sector in the 2010s, and the establishment of the military-run Metals & Engineering Corp (METEC), the state would also take over much of the civil engineering and construction sectors. As late as 2013, as much as 80 percent of ostensibly private firms, by one estimate, were still controlled by the ERPDF.[24]

Moreover, the EPRDF generally remained suspicious of private business.[25] Meles, famed for his resistance to IMF and World Bank diktat, postponed the privatisation of land, and much else.[26] He also kept Ethiopia firmly outside the World Trade Organization, in part because joining it would likely entail opening the financial sector to foreign competition. From the 2000s, economic development was cast as an existential threat, a matter of national survival on par with war—requiring, the EPRDF argued, mass mobilisation, state control and rigid conformity.[27] "We were obsessed with development and obsessed with growth," a former senior EPRDF minister recalled. "And, for many, many years, the economy grew and the growth was inclusive." The goal was to achieve 'middle-income' status by 2025.

Broadly speaking, the results were impressive. According to the government, GDP grew at an average of more than 10 percent a year from 2003 to 2018, among the very fastest rates anywhere on earth. GDP per capita, a somewhat better measure of general prosperity, likewise tripled.[28] Experts tended to assume that the official figures were probably overstated by a percentage point or two.[29] But the growth, from a low base, was unquestionably swift. Powered by a recipe of state spending, cheap credit underpinned by 'financial repression', and Africa's grandest programme of infrastructure building—roads, dams, housing and industrial parks were all stacked up at a dizzying rate—the EPRDF could, by the early 2010s, plausibly claim to be running the most rapidly transforming big economy in Africa.[30] Excitable commentators began to speak of an "Ethiopian miracle", while the EPRDF proclaimed Ethiopia's coming "renaissance". From 2011 to 2017, foreign direct investment roughly quadrupled—so much of it from China, the most important foreign investor in these years, that some dubbed Ethiopia the "China of Africa".[31] Rapid industrialisation was thought to be imminent.

Gains could be seen across a range of measures. Extreme poverty was slashed.[32] Child and infant mortality sank. Farming output rose. Famine, the enduring scourge of the Ethiopian highlands, seemed finally to have been consigned to history.[33] Even the country's transport infrastructure no longer seemed quite so creaky and backward. Ethiopian Airlines, the state-owned national carrier, became Africa's largest and most profitable airline, while, for the first time, the country started to open itself up for mainstream international tourism. Three days after my arrival in Ethiopia in 2016, the government inaugurated the continent's first electrified cross-border railway—a shimmering, £2.5bn line from Addis Ababa to the coast of Djibouti. Running alongside it, 80 kilometres eastwards, was Ethiopia's first expressway. Both were built by China.

* * *

But the ramifications of 2005 were no less significant for the opposition camp. On the Ethiopianist side, the arrest of the CUD's leaders, and the refusal of many of its MPs to take up their seats, had splintered the movement. With many now convinced there was no path to power via the ballot box, thoughts had increasingly turned to armed rebellion. Key to this pivot was Berhanu Nega, an unflinchingly self-assured economics professor at America's Bucknell University who had run for Addis Ababa's mayoralty, only to be imprisoned for twenty-one months in the wake of the post-election violence when he refused to take up his post.[34] In 2008, following his release and return to America, Berhanu established Ginbot 7, a new armed opposition movement named for the date of the elections he believed had been stolen. Among his fellow founders were Andargachew Tsige, a deceptively mild-mannered British citizen who had studied philosophy in London and written his doctoral thesis on Immanuel Kant, and Neamin Zeleke, a restless exile who had arrived in Virginia from Addis Ababa as a teenager in 1986 and spent the next two decades at the coal face of anti-TPLF activism. All three would go on to play influential and controversial roles back in Ethiopia before and during the Tigray War.

Ginbot 7, which like the OLF was to be based out of Eritrea, was driven by a special animosity towards both the TPLF and the 1995 constitution. Though Berhanu was from Gurage in the south, Ginbot 7 was—like the CUD before it—associated primarily with Amharas and urban Ethiopians. In 2009, Andargachew and Berhanu, along with twelve others, were convicted in absentia of plotting a coup d'état in Addis Ababa. Six years later Andargachew was seized in Yemen's national airport en route to Eritrea and extradited to Ethiopia, where he faced a death sentence which transformed his case into an international cause célèbre.

In 2010, Ginbot 7 established Ethiopian Satellite Television (ESAT), a satellite news network headquartered in Washington.[35] Neamin was to become its first executive director, and the Eritrean government, ever keen to weaken the EPRDF, was to provide financial support.[36] The network hosted provocative, often incendiary talk shows, and 24-hour rolling news coverage led by exiled journalists, many of whom had fled Ethiopia in the crackdown which followed the 2005 election. "Our policy was that anything and everything which erodes the legitimacy of the government, any popular movement for justice, needs to be supported," Neamin later argued. ESAT's reporting was invariably critical of the government, and focused relentlessly on the TPLF. Helped along by the proliferation of household satellite dishes in Ethiopia in the early 2010s, and later social media, ESAT quickly became the country's most widely watched—and arguably most controversial—satellite channel.[37] It was to be INSA's job to hack the emails of ESAT's employees, plant spyware on their computers and block the outlet's website and satellite signals.[38]

Meanwhile, a younger generation of Oromo opposition activists had taken their own lessons from the 2005 defeat. Among them was Jawar Mohammed, then a fresh-faced Stanford undergraduate with Afro hair and a voice like an accelerated cassette tape. Though, like many others, he considered the mass protests of late 2005 and 2006 to be a promising model for civil disobedience, he was notably contemptuous of the role played in them by the OLF. Still in his mid-twenties, and a co-founder of the International Oromo Youth Association, Jawar was to spark the first of what would be many controversies in 2009 with the publication of an essay stingingly critical of the Oromo old guard. Describing the august liberation movement as "damaged beyond repair", he chastised it for its failure to deliver not even "an inch of Oromo land" over the past two decades. Thanks to "weak, undisciplined and incompetent leadership [...]

and a cult-like outdated organisational tradition," he wrote, the OLF had "brought about its own demise."[39]

For Oromo nationalists in the diaspora, raised on the myth of OLF as the unimpeachable custodian of their national cause, this was sacrilege. "The whole diaspora was set on fire," remembered a former OLF fighter. But for Jawar and his growing band of like-minded activists, the real lesson from 2005 and its aftermath had been that they could no longer rely on the OLF to deliver the political change they sought back home. "I realised that, for the Oromos to be liberated from the EPRDF, they needed to be liberated from the OLF first," he later recalled. Most consequentially, he began to make the novel argument that to overthrow the TPLF, and to put Oromos in the driving seat of Ethiopian politics for the first time, they would need first to enter into a tacit alliance with the OPDO— the Oromo ruling party itself. "Although I was never convinced to join the OPDO," he later explained, "talking to them every summer when I returned home made me realise that there were actually some Oromos within the state who could be utilised toward the struggle." By the early 2010s, Jawar was fast on his way to becoming the pre-eminent figure in the Oromo opposition. Along with many of his colleagues, that meant he would soon find himself among the key targets of INSA's overseas digital espionage.

* * *

All this, though, was to come. In 2009, Teklebrhan set off to London for a master's programme, leaving Abiy in charge of INSA. It was a contentious choice: employees of a higher military rank, or with more academic qualifications, were known to be unhappy about it. But for those already familiar with Abiy's strategy for self-advancement it wasn't surprising. This was, after all, a move he'd had a direct hand in engineering; indeed, the very idea of putting Teklebrhan on study leave seems to have largely originated with him. From almost the moment INSA was established, colleagues recalled, Abiy had been pushing for his boss to go abroad, even taking it upon himself to raise the idea with some of his superiors. When the time came for Teklebrhan to go, another senior department head—Sisay Tola, an Oromo who would continue to be one of Abiy's most trusted allies—was also studying overseas. Abiy, whose relationship with both Teklebrhan and Meles was at this point warm and trusting, put himself forward to hold the fort while his boss was away. Teklebrhan was receptive. "It was not surprising; they were close friends," said one of their colleagues. "Abiy was loved by most people back then, including by Teklebrhan. He was so motivational."

But Abiy's year in charge of INSA would in fact turn out to be among the most controversial aspects of his rise to power. Laying the seeds for the TPLF's opposition to his premiership, it would ultimately contribute to the catastrophic fallout between them which led to war. At the heart of the matter was Abiy's thrusting political ambition, which now became common knowledge for the first time, and his increasingly transparent attempts to leverage his position in INSA for career advantage. "He became too popular and he made his ambition for power too public," said a friend at INSA. "In the EPRDF tradition, this was taboo. Power was believed to be an assignment, not an achievement. But Abiy had told everyone he'd be prime minister, and that the Lord had told him so."[40]

The period also provided the first glimpses into Abiy's distinctive style of governing. Subordinates of his, both then and since, have consistently commented on his restless energy—while noting, as well, a fierce appetite for change and disruption. The speed and scope of his activity in just over one year at the helm of INSA strikingly prefigured his first year in office as prime minister. "He's like a corporate CEO, sleeping three hours a night," said one who later worked with Abiy in the Prime Minister's Office. "This guy is very dynamic, very focused, gets things done."

Equally evident was the influence of a particular strand of Silicon Valley thinking on his emerging worldview. One of his first changes as acting director, for instance, involved renovating INSA's offices by bringing in massage chairs, coffee machines and open-plan furniture—an early example of the 'ergonomics' into which his administration would later plough so much political and financial capital across Addis Ababa. He also sent staff off for training in a variety of 'positive thinking' and 'mindset' practices, including, among others, a course on psychological profiling in China. "Things which could enhance the human mind were all welcome at INSA," explained a former senior staff member. To this end, Abiy and two colleagues themselves jetted off for a month of 'mindfulness' training in San Francisco (though the future prime minister himself, one recalled, absconded to Los Angeles after just a week). Techno-optimistic thinking, which sees the human mind as programmable like a computer, was likewise to become a running theme of Abiy's future administration, with its special focus on artificial intelligence.[41] (Tellingly, he later claimed that his favourite book was *Sapiens*, by the self-described 'post-humanist'

Israeli historian Yuval Noah Harari.[42]) "Abiy doesn't have any patience for nuance, and I don't think he has any intellectual depth," said another future colleague. "But he's good with technology, and he can Google something, read about it on Wikipedia, and then turn it into a PowerPoint presentation."

It was also around this time that Abiy's future political mantra, "*medemer*"—an Amharic word roughly equivalent to "synergy"—first surfaced. "*Medemer*", too, evoked the ethos of a tech start-up. "It was a positive word for all of us," a friend recalled. "Just like teamwork. But for him it was like a magic word. He used to put it in almost every statement he made." In a documentary released after Abiy became prime minister, the then acting director of INSA could be seen lecturing his employees about the importance of "mindset", "*medemer*", and the technologies of the future. He could also be heard advising them that individual flourishing required a healthy body as much as a healthy mind—further early evidence of the cod philosophy of workplace 'wellness' which would infuse his administration. "A massage every day boosts our energy and mental alertness," Abiy explained to his colleagues. "We must support ourselves to access the creative and subconscious mind."[43]

Some also alleged that Abiy undertook initiatives which were mercantile, or procedurally improper to the point of being corrupt. "He turned INSA into a business," complained a former officer in military intelligence. Money supposedly paid to INSA by Oromia's government, for instance, to digitise some of their bureaucracy, allegedly went missing. Land in Oromia, several former employees have alleged, was bought and sold under INSA's name. Of particular concern in this regard were two large plots of land on the outskirts of Addis Ababa, which were intended for building apartments for INSA employees and were acquired through Abiy's connections in the Oromia government.[44] Some of the money INSA paid allegedly went unaccounted for later. "He operates by quid pro quo: you do something for him, he'll do something for you," said a former colleague. "But once you do, then you can't get out, because he has the leverage." Similar allegations would later dog his time as prime minister.

Much of Abiy's more controversial activity that year, however, was simply political. "Everyone knew him at this time," a friend recalled. "He became politically-connected, left the army, re-joined the OPDO and became a member of parliament all in one year." Though it was not prohibited back then for the head of a security agency to be an MP (it would later become so), it was frowned on all the same. Having resigned his military commission that year in order to stand for parliament in his home district of Agaro—an election in which the EPRDF won 499 out of 547 parliamentary seats, with all but two others going to EPRDF-allied parties—Abiy was determined to leave no stone unturned. Senior OPDO officials as well as local notables from Agaro were invited to Addis Ababa for special tours of INSA's offices. INSA's duty-free privileges were allegedly used to import materials to build a high school in his hometown.[45] Camera crews, meanwhile, were invited to INSA's offices to bolster his image.

On arriving back in Ethiopia in 2010, Teklebrhan was furious, and accused Abiy of brazenly abusing his position to launch his political career. The INSA housing project was suspended, pending an investigation into its legality. Over the course of a bruising internal evaluation which lasted two weeks—an EPRDF practice known as "*gimgema*"—Abiy was excoriated. According to friends and critics within the agency alike, his response to the censure was bitter. "Abiy was intolerant of criticism or any form of dialogue," said a colleague who was otherwise admiring of him. On the final day of the evaluation, another colleague recalled, Abiy warned he would return one day as their boss. Meles, on receiving Teklebrhan's feedback, ordered him to be fired. "There was big dissatisfaction from Meles' side about his behaviour and actions," a senior INSA official recalled. One morning in mid-September 2010, Abiy was summoned to his boss's office at INSA and informed that after four years at the agency his time was up.[46] In response, the future prime minister is said to have broken down in tears. Abiy later claimed that in the months which followed he had feared for his life.[47]

5

"OROMO FIRST"

THE ADDIS ABABA QUESTION AND THE RISE OF OROMO NATIONALISM

To make sense of Ethiopia's changing capital, I used to take my car and drive east from the city centre, along the new metro line and past the scruffy hotels which sit on either side of it. The traffic-choked thoroughfare begins at Meskel Square—once Addis Ababa's imperial, Orthodox heart—and passes, often in neatly chronological order, each stage of the city's development: the ramshackle public housing of the Derg years; the drab, Chinese-erected shopping malls of the EPRDF ones; and the gaudy, Dubai-conjured high-rises of the Abiy era. By the time one reaches the suburb of Ayat, founded on land which had consisted of *teff* fields and cattle pastures less than a decade earlier, new Italianate family villas jostle for space with cows and breezeblock sheds. Thereafter the city begins to stretch and unwind, the buildings fewer and further between, the road gradually less noisy and frenetic. And then, all of a sudden, comes the gorge of a river—and Addis Ababa's eastwards march draws abruptly to a halt.

From there, across the river, everything is Oromia: rolling countryside peppered with round *tukul* homes and scraggly oxen. The river seems to form a natural border. At one point, on the western bank, vast new apartment blocks teeter almost to the cliff edge. Yet quite where that border should be—or, indeed, whether there should even be a border at all—is the heart of the so-called 'Addis Ababa question'. For much of the 2010s it was perhaps the most divisive issue of all Ethiopian politics.

Known by Oromos as "*Finfinnee*," Ethiopia's capital—whose Amharic name, Addis Ababa, means 'New Flower' and was purportedly given by Menelik II's wife, Empress Taitu—lies in the fertile Shewan borderlands between Amharic-speaking highlanders and the Oromo clans to their south.[1] In some ways it has always been a melting pot, a common territory for trade, religious exchange and inter-marriage, where Oromos and Amharas have long mingled and their cultures blended.[2] But these are also history's bloodlands, the shifting frontiers of the kingdoms and empires whose authority waxed and waned over centuries. As Oromo nationalists would later note, it was Oromos from the Tulama clans who had resided in the area when Menelik's army arrived and dispossessed them in the late nineteenth century.[3] But Amharas, too, can plausibly claim some ancient connection to it. Etched into the hillside northwest of Ayat, for instance, are the remains of a twelfth-century monastery built in the style of the rock-hewn churches constructed around the same time, some 700 kilometres north, in the mountains around Lalibela in what is now Amhara. Also nearby lie the ruins of the fabled city of Barara, a cosmopolitan mediaeval trading centre.[4] The sediments of these histories underscore just how recent a project the modern capital is. But they also complicate Oromo nationalist claims to eternal, natural rights to its territory.

Oromos in the twentieth century were nevertheless on firm ground when they complained of their peripheral status in the new imperial capital. Like many other southern towns, modern-day Addis Ababa began as a military garrison built for northern soldiers and their families.[5] As it slowly expanded in the reign of Haile Selassie, the city had attracted settlers from the north, who spoke Amharic and went on to dominate urban commerce and the state bureaucracy. Oromos and other southerners, save for a few assimilated elites, were perpetual outsiders. The divisions between an Amharic-speaking urban core and the indigenous hinterlands—a pattern found in much of the former imperial south—would become one of the defining features of Ethiopia's political economy for much of the next century.[6] The rapid urbanisation of the post-2005 period, in particular, would bring them into even sharper relief.

The EPRDF's early attempt to correct the imbalances had involved ceding to Oromia a vaguely defined provision in the 1995 constitution which guaranteed the region a 'special interest' over the affairs of the federal capital. It had been only partially successful.[7] On the one hand, Oromos in the decades after 1991 acquired a greater stake in the city's wealth than they had ever had previously. As Addis Ababa's population exploded in the 2010s—it was projected to double over the course of the decade—rural Oromos flocked there like never before.[8] Satellite towns along its rim, such as Abiy's mother's birthplace of Burayu, were transformed into the country's emerging industrial heartlands.

But the old sense of ethnic exclusion still lingered. Addis Ababa remained, in essence, a city for Amharic speakers and, with the TPLF at the helm of the ruling coalition, one whose expanding economy was widely believed to privilege politically connected Tigrayan insiders. Although the 1995 constitution still granted free plots to farmers, a legacy of the student movement's demand for 'land to the tiller', in practice there had never been strong protections against forced or even arbitrary eviction. As the city continued its march into the surrounding countryside in the 2010s, it was overwhelmingly Oromo farmers who were uprooted.[9] Calls for Oromos to be restored to their place as the capital's rightful 'owners', thus clarifying their constitutional 'special interest' over its affairs and resources, grew louder and became—as so often the case when material grievances sharpen—sometimes much more extreme.

They did so just at the moment when pressures on Ethiopia's economy were beginning to overwhelm the rapid gains won by the boom of the 2000s. Shortage of rural land had long been a problem in the highlands. An exploding population, compounded by subtle changes to the system of rural land tenure in the 2000s which were intended to favour more productive farmers by granting them more secure rights, had sharply exacerbated it.[10] By the 2010s, a whole generation had been effectively cut out of access to state-distributed land. Meanwhile, just as urbanisation took off, much of the countryside had begun to stagnate.[11] Despite the recent spread of factories, industrial parks and commercial farms, especially around Addis Ababa, there remained far too few jobs to absorb the landless youth who flocked to towns in search of work.[12] Nor were there enough for the millions who had begun to emerge from the more than thirty public universities which had been rapidly built over the previous decade.[13] Between 2014 and 2016, precisely the period in which protests in Oromia erupted, the share of graduates in the pool of the unemployed jumped.[14]

Around this time, too, headline economic statistics started to deteriorate. The growth rate, having soared for the best part of a decade, tapered slightly as Ethiopia's debt burden ballooned and exports foundered. Having peaked at nearly 40 percent in 2010, annual export growth had already begun to shrink just five years later.[15] Meanwhile, local investors who had acquired large tracts of land for flagship commercial farms in Ethiopia's peripheries steadily began to default, having systematically failed to cultivate their leases and produce crops for export. By the second half of the decade, according to one estimate, less than three percent of the 90,000 hectares leased to investors in several districts in the far south near the Kenyan border was actually being farmed.[16]

Some have attributed the slowdown to certain failures of economic policymaking in this period, with the shift towards attracting private foreign investment into manufacturing and commercial agriculture coming in for particular criticism. Indeed, it has even been suggested that after 2012 a distracted EPRDF simply wasn't as focused on boosting export growth as it once had been.[17] But how much the Ethiopian government really was to blame for all these sagging economic indicators is an open question. Ethiopia was far from alone, after all, among African economies in encountering setbacks from the mid-2010s. Global headwinds included the spillovers from the slowdown in China and the 2014–17 commodities price slump. Moreover, around the world it was becoming much harder for developing countries to break into ultra-competitive global manufacturing value chains at a time when much of the labour in low-skill industrial production was increasingly automated. Many high-profile economists were beginning to wonder if it would even be possible for countries like Ethiopia to pull off the sort of developmental miracles which South Korea, Taiwan and, more recently, China had in earlier eras.[18]

It was against this ominous backdrop that Addis Ababa's municipal authorities unveiled a new master plan for the city in 2014. Its stated aim was anodyne, that of developing the farmland around the capital and bringing the surrounding villages into an integrated urban sphere of 'transport corridors' and 'industrial zones'. Foreign urban development experts generally spoke of it approvingly, regarding it as broadly sensible and technocratically sound. But as Jawar later put it to me, Oromo activists had been "looking for a trigger" for a revolt against the TPLF. In the master plan, to the great surprise of its architects, they had found it. For whatever the EPRDF's leaders might have insisted to the contrary, it wasn't hard to see how the plan might be perceived as a blueprint for further urban expansion. What was more, having been foisted on them without consultation, it was always likely to cement the already entrenched perception among many ordinary Oromos that urbanisation was something which always happened *to* them, *for* the benefit of others.[19]

Oromia, increasingly a powder-keg of frustrated rural youth and under-employed graduates, exploded. Whereas in the past, the focus of Oromo grievance had been Amhara landlords, now it was Tigrayans.

Oromo activists, who actively sought to drive a wedge between the OPDO and the TPLF, painted the master plan as the imposition of a corrupt, and overwhelmingly Tigrayan, elite which had to be resisted. "We wanted to make the OPDO cadres jealous of the Tigrayans," Jawar later explained. "So we told them: you are not the problem. You are made to be the problem. The problem is your masters. Why don't we get rid of the masters together, and make you the masters?" OPDO officials, particularly those of the younger generation brought in by Abadula after the 2005 election, began to break rank. A few, in what was a watershed moment in the history of the EPRDF, started speaking out publicly against the master plan. In a bid to ease tensions, the government suspended it in January 2016. By then, though, it was too late. The campaign of mass protests which would ultimately sweep the TPLF out of power and Abiy into the palace four years later had begun.

* * *

Abiy's ignominious departure from INSA in 2010 had cast him briefly into the political wilderness. Though he was by now an MP, his reputation among the EPRDF top brass, including with Meles himself, had collapsed. Abadula remained friendly, but inside the EPRDF leadership even his influence was waning. In the aftermath of the 2010 election, in what was billed by Meles as a changing of the guard to allow a younger generation to step forward (yet widely seen by Oromos as a power-grab), the generally popular Abadula had been removed from his post as president of Oromia. Some of his and Abiy's more openly Oromo nationalist acolytes, among them another rising star called Lemma Megersa, had also been fired or demoted. For the next six years they would be left waiting in the wings as power in the OPDO consolidated around a faction of the party considered less nationalistic and more reliably loyal to Meles.

To make matters worse for Abiy, his conduct at INSA had by now put him firmly on the radar of NISS, the spy agency, and of its mighty and secretive Tigrayan executive, Getachew Assefa.[20] "He was in trouble with the NISS guys," recalled a friend from INSA. "There was continuous physical surveillance." To some extent this may have been simply part of the agencies' ongoing turf war: Teklebrhan's own relations with Getachew Assefa were little better, and the INSA director had himself tried to protect Abiy from NISS's surveillance in the past. "It was a very ugly rivalry," said another former INSA official. "Sometimes you'd wonder: are these guys really working for the same cause? It was personal ego, nothing else." But in fact, in Abiy's case there was a more specific, and rather more understandable, concern: that in a failed attempt to save an OLF commander, Legesse Wegi, from being assassinated by Ethiopian security forces in 2008, he had leaked intelligence to the rebels.

Why exactly Abiy did this is among the more puzzling enigmas from the years before he became prime minister. Given his personal history with the OLF, and their torrid future relationship, it would always seem strangely anomalous. "I could never understand why he tried to save Legesse," a former OLF member later mused. One possible explanation, later put forward by a one-time Oromo colleague, was that it was a "tactical" move—"a card he could use down the road." Perhaps, Abiy had simply been among those inside the intelligence services at the time who had favoured a softer, more conciliatory approach to the OLF. But the fact that he didn't make the story public until 2019, when his relationship with Oromo nationalists was falling apart and he needed to reassure them of his commitment to their cause, gives some credence to the notion that his motives were more opportunistic.[21] Indeed, it isn't the only example of double-dealing of precisely this kind. According to Ginbot 7's Andargachew Tsige, Abiy had shared intelligence with him and his Ethiopianist allies on at least two occasions not long after that.[22] In 2012, Abiy had told Berhane Kidanemariam, who was then head of the Ethiopian Broadcasting Corporation, that he had established a website which shared information from inside the government with the opposition.[23] A few years later, as the master plan protests gathered speed, he was also known to occasionally leak sensitive audio recordings and information about his internal party rivals to Jawar and other Oromo activists in the diaspora, a practice in which several of his party colleagues also indulged as part of efforts to gain leverage over the TPLF or their internal OPDO opponents. "Everything is calculated," a close OPDO colleague later explained. "Abiy doesn't give a penny unless it's for some kind of political gain."

But whether this was also the reason why, in early 2012, his wife Zinash and their three children moved to America is less clear. After becoming prime minister, Abiy would claim he had sent them there for their safety, because of his strong defence of Oromo interests and, perhaps, his ties to the OLF. (Though he also claimed, on another occasion, that it was because of his advocacy on behalf of a controversial Amhara dissident, Asaminew Tsige).[24] Several sources, by contrast, have pointed to this period as simply a rough patch in their marriage, and suggested that

Zinash took her children abroad out of frustration. Settling in Denver, Colorado, where a sister of hers already lived, and where there was a sizeable Ethiopian population, she would end up staying there until after her husband became prime minister six years later. Soon after arriving she applied for asylum.

The course of these years were, by all accounts, hard on her and the family. Zinash and their three daughters lived hand-to-mouth in low-cost public housing. Working as the driver of a bus for disabled children, Zinash relied on social security and the support of a local Ethiopian Pentecostal church. Abiy would visit them sporadically, sometimes in the company of Pastor Gemechis Buba Desta—his Pente businessman friend, whose private business school in Addis Ababa, the Leadstar College of Business and Management, Abiy had enrolled in for a master's in business administration in 2012. (Though there was no public evidence of Abiy having acquired a bachelor's degree, despite his later claims, INSA had already paid for him to take a part-time master's in "transformational leadership" at a college affiliated with London's Greenwich University a year earlier.*) In Denver, he spent much of his time at Zinash's church, where Pastor Gemechis would occasionally show up to preach. Few of the Ethiopians he encountered there had any idea of his work or reputation back home. "He'd roam around the city freely; saying hello to people; going to cell phone shops, barber shops … he was very friendly, very engaging. But the people here didn't know anything about him—not at all," recalled a diaspora churchman. "Ethiopian government officials are very secretive in that way."

There was one person in Denver, however, who knew exactly who the visiting EPRDF man was: Tamrat Layne, Ethiopia's prime minister for four years during the transitional government of the early 1990s. An erstwhile Marxist guerrilla, who had led the Ethiopian People's

---

* When Abiy came to power, his official biography—including on Wikipedia and as read out in Parliament during his swearing-in ceremony in 2018—stated that he had received his first degree from MicroLink Information Technology College in 2001. But Microlink was not accredited to grant degrees until 2003. What is more, Abiy is recorded as having enrolled for his final year (Grade 12) at a high school in Addis Ababa in 2003 (a course for which INSA would have paid, as it did for other EPRDF officials who hadn't completed their secondary education). Abiy's official biography was later changed, with the date of his graduation from MicroLink moved to 2009. It is unclear whether he passed his Grade 12 examinations and received his high school leaving certificate, without which, in theory, he couldn't formally enrol in a legally accredited degree course.

Democratic Movement (later ANDM, the Amhara wing of the EPRDF) which fought alongside the TPLF before 1991, Tamrat had spent twelve years in prison in Ethiopia on corruption charges before emerging, in 2008, as a born-again Christian. By the time he and Abiy met in Denver he had transformed into something of an icon among Ethiopian Pentes, a champion of the idea of an Ethiopian renaissance which would come only through Christian renewal.[25] In the young Oromo official, Tamrat thought he saw a moral and spiritual comrade. "We talked a lot about religion, and the bible," Tamrat later recalled. "That was the main reason I was introduced to him. Generally, I looked upon him as a religious person." At that time, Tamrat had long been out of Ethiopian politics, and Abiy's open political ambitions were of only secondary interest. "He told me he'd be PM, and that he'd told this to Meles and others. I didn't take it too seriously."

But then, on 20 August 2012, after a short illness, Meles died. Abiy, who said he had been in America when he first heard the news, later told journalists from the *Financial Times* that friends back in Ethiopia urged him to return home to campaign to succeed him as prime minister. "I said no," Abiy recalled. "Now is not the time for the king." Abiy, however, is an unreliable narrator of his own biography, and it is unlikely many—or even any—Ethiopians at the time seriously advised him to run to be Meles's successor. But it is nevertheless clear that he was now actively plotting his way forward. Over the subsequent years, Tamrat would substantially alter his assessment of the young politician. "Abiy used to tell me what was happening, about the sort of problems they were encountering [inside the EPRDF]. And I could tell he'd done his homework. I realised he was up to something."

* * *

The orderly transition of power which followed Meles's sudden death, after twenty-one years at the top, took many observers and opponents alike by surprise. When Hailemariam, Meles's technocratic but politically inept deputy from the south, succeeded him as prime minister a month later, barely a whisper of internal ruction broke to the surface. There was no unrest and no defections. "Instead of chaos, an eerie calm now hangs over the country," *The Economist* wrote at the time.[26] For a few hazy months it seemed as though the EPRDF's juggernaut was simply rolling on an autopilot that Meles had left running.

In reality, though, the EPRDF had been quickly engulfed in crisis. "As long as Meles was alive nobody else was thinking," recalled one well-placed Ethiopian observer. "With him gone, there was no manual, no road map." The EPRDF's programme swiftly stalled. Hailemariam's cautious attempts to loosen the system ran aground. Policies for which the new prime minister personally advocated—a little economic liberalisation, for instance, or some proportional representation in the electoral system to give opposition parties more say—soon ran into internal opposition and were delayed or axed. Plans for EPRDF veterans to gradually make way for a younger generation over the course of the parliament, injecting new blood into the leadership and correcting some of its more egregious ethnic imbalances, meanwhile foundered. Influential members of the old guard who had been due to retire—such as Bereket Simon on the Amhara side, or Abay Tsehaye from the TPLF—quietly stayed on.

Hailemariam, an unassuming civil engineer from a small and politically insignificant community in the south, the Wolaita, struggled to impose himself. "There was no coherence, no clear direction," recalled a senior cabinet minister. "It became apparent there were really two or three centres of power." Out of public sight, factionalism and feuding reigned. As the economy slowed, resentments of the TPLF's perceived outsized sway over government policy—previously kept in check by dint of Meles's charisma and force of intellect—broke into the open. Among Oromo and Amhara members in particular, the EPRDF's model of 'one nation, one vote', which gave each of the four organisations the same number of party votes, regardless of population size, came under fresh scrutiny. Before too long the idea that Hailemariam was no more than a puppet of the TPLF, or, even more ominously, of spy chief Getachew Assefa, had cemented in the public imagination.

There was certainly a kernel of truth to the claims. In the security sector, there had been a gradual diminution of Tigrayan dominance over the preceding decades thanks to the policy of affirmative action of which Abiy himself was a notable beneficiary. But Tigrayans did still retain considerable clout, especially in the upper echelons.[27] During the Hailemariam years, both the military and NISS also became increasingly powerful and autonomous as institutions, with their Tigrayan leaders— Samora Yunis and Getachew Assefa, respectively—at times disdainful of the embattled civilian prime minister's authority.[28] Inside the EPRDF, meanwhile, the OPDO, the ANDM and Hailemariam's own Southern Ethiopian People's Democratic Movement (SEPDM), undoubtedly remained junior partners—in intangible terms such as status and esteem, not least—despite the numerical weight of their regions' populations. At least for the EPRDF's first two decades in power, it had been common for non-Tigrayan ministers and executives to defer to TPLF deputies, assistants or advisors, an imbalance which had long been a source of resentment. Though all three junior parties lacked the TPLF's historical prestige and ideological ballast, over time they had become more organisationally coherent and politically ambitious. As a result, senior figures in the OPDO and ANDM, in particular, had become increasingly frustrated with their subordinate position inside the coalition. Coming from the weak and fractious multiethnic SEPDM, Hailemariam was poorly placed to contain them.

That Tigrayan intellectuals and prominent TPLF veterans were also highly influential in the realm of policymaking few could plausibly deny. But a feeling that the TPLF continued to call the shots even after Meles's death was pervasive, not only among ordinary Ethiopians but also non-Tigrayan officials themselves. "The obstacle for Hailemariam was the TPLF," a senior Oromo official in his office told me several years later. "In the short, the TPLF was the problem." Hailemariam himself suggested that Getachew Assefa, in particular, had blocked much of his agenda. "If even Meles was afraid of him, how could I—surrounded by Tigrayans—take him on?" he asked me once. "I had no one." One minister who worked with Hailemariam recalled an occasion when the prime minister was challenged as to why he had failed to arrest a certain friend of Getachew on solid corruption charges; Hailemariam, the minister said, quietly conceded that he "simply dare not go against Getachew."[29]

But how truthful this was in reality is hard to know. Certainly, many non-Tigrayan insiders both then and now have consistently complained that the Tigrayan-dominated security establishment, NISS in particular, wielded far too much political influence. But there are also those in a position to know who reject the idea of the TPLF labouring as a party to undermine or manipulate Hailemariam. An older, and more senior, Oromo official—a former minister and advisor to the prime minister—once insisted to me that the influence of the TPLF was "absolutely miniscule". The truth likely lay somewhere in the middle. But by the middle of the 2010s, the popular stereotype of 'hegemonic' TPLF power had taken on a dangerous life of its own, and in later years insider testimonies would become even trickier to parse, as shifting political calculations—not least the battle for the narrative of the Tigray War—coloured retrospective accounts. Figures like Hailemariam, especially, could doubtless see the advantage of playing victim, especially in light of his own administration's evident shortcomings. Probably far more important to its failures than TPLF sabotage were the various cross-cutting ethnic and ideological rifts—between economic liberalism and 'developmentalism', for instance, or ethno-nationalism and Ethiopianism—as well as the competing political ambitions of individuals, which Hailemariam had proved simply unable to bridge.

Harder for anyone to seriously deny was the indisputable fact that government corruption was worsening. Following the massive expansion of the EPRDF membership roll in the years after 2005, political education had atrophied.[30] Grifters and opportunists had risen through the ranks. Lacking the discipline which characterised its early years, parts of the EPRDF increasingly resembled an oligarchy.[31] "We used to meet all the old TPLF guys in Mekelle before Meles died," recalled an unusually well-informed American businessman. "These guys were never flashy, they basically looked like bums. They were ideologues. Then after Meles died suddenly we'd see them in the Sheraton Hotel smoking cigars and drinking champagne. I don't know what happened. But something definitely changed." Of particular concern in this regard was METEC, the mighty military-industrial conglomerate established by Meles shortly before his death. By securing lucrative state contracts, including for flagship projects such as the Grand Ethiopian Renaissance Dam on the Nile, and several sugar factories in the Omo Valley in the far south, METEC had in the subsequent years grabbed an ever-fattening slice of the national economy. In the process, the army officers in charge, among them several prominent Tigrayans who had been retired from the military early precisely in order to reduce their over-representation in it, were alleged to have enriched themselves.[32] The dam and other key infrastructure projects were increasingly hampered by delays and vastly inflated costs.[33]

The problem was neither confined to METEC, nor to Tigrayans and the TPLF, despite what would later be claimed: the regional government in Oromia, in particular, could hardly claim to be graft-free. In any case, by contrast to other countries in the region corruption in Ethiopia was still relatively contained. Very few Ethiopians appeared, for instance, in the leaked Panama Papers of 2016. But it was nonetheless clearly a mounting threat to the health of the coalition. In 2015, Hailemariam himself warned that they risked being overwhelmed by a wave of unchecked 'rent-seeking'. In October the same year, in a bid to counter persistent allegations of Tigrayan dominance, and to stamp his own authority over the coalition following its thumping re-election victory, he appointed a slate of younger officials, in particular Oromos, to his administration. Among them was Abiy: Ethiopia's new minister of science and technology.

* * *

Abiy's arrival at the ministry had coincided with a resumption in protests against the Addis Ababa master plan across Oromia that November. The immediate issue, this time, was an attempt by the authorities to clear a forest for an investment project near the small town of Ginchi, some 80 kilometres from Addis Ababa in a part of the region renowned for its history of dissent. It was not, at first, a matter with much wider significance. But the local protesters there, part of a network by then commonly known as the *Qeerroo*, had met with local secondary school pupils, and drew a connection between the investment project and the master plan. Soon the pupils, and later farmers, were heard chanting that the plans amounted to a "genocide" against the Oromo. Unrest swiftly billowed through towns far beyond Ginchi. Following a pattern which would recur persistently over the course of the next eleven months, until Hailemariam's government declared a nationwide state of emergency, protesters took over local government buildings and attacked and looted farms and factories.[34] "The immediate goal," explained the website *OPride*, "is to uproot all symbols of the regime at the local level."[35] Between November 2015 and February 2016 an average of twenty-six protests took place each week.[36] As the security forces cracked down, brutally and counter-productively, at least 500 people would be killed and tens of thousands detained.[37]

Were it not for the *Qeerroos*—a traditional Oromo term denoting a young bachelor or unmarried man of fighting age—Abiy may never have become prime minister.[38] By drawing on the new power of social media, and working in tandem with Jawar and other Oromo activists abroad, it was these networks of local protest which, by early 2018, had succeeded in making much of Oromia almost ungovernable. Inspired by the peaceful Arab Spring revolts in North Africa and the Middle East, the earliest *Qeerroo* structures had been established as far back as 2011 by the OLF, which had rebranded the 2005 "Revolt against Subjugation" as "*Qeerroo Bilisummaa Oromoo*" (QBO), or "Youth for Oromo Freedom". For several years, the QBO had boasted a central organising committee and a website for announcing coordinated protests and strikes. The early QBO public statements, just like the protesters who demonstrated against the Addis

Ababa master plan after 2015, denounced "land-grabbing" and forced evictions in Oromia, and called for the overthrow of the "TPLF regime". Their immediate impact, though, was negligible, and for the first years of the 2010s the only significant social unrest in Ethiopia was sparked not by Oromo nationalism but by the government's meddling in the affairs of the country's Muslim minority—as part of a cack-handed attempt to staunch a feared rise in Islamic extremism.[39] In fact, it was the Muslim protests of these years, arguably more than anything else, which did most to convince young Oromos that peaceful resistance, rather than armed insurgency, could be a viable approach to challenging the EPRDF. Many of the Muslim protesters, and their diaspora advocates, would later join the *Qeerroo*.

By the time Jawar became the unofficial leader of the movement in the middle of the decade he was a doctoral student at the University of Columbia in New York, and still mostly known among the Ethiopian community abroad as a prominent cheerleader for the Muslim protests. He was also friendly with Ginbot 7 leaders in Washington DC like Neamin Zeleke, and had made occasional guest appearances on their opposition satellite TV station, ESAT, where he was presented as a moderate Oromo critical of the OLF. But speaking to Al Jazeera about the plight of Oromos in June 2013, Jawar had broken dramatically from the Ethiopianist camp. Showing his colours as, above all, an Oromo nationalist, he had declared himself to be "Oromo first", the unwilling subject of an Ethiopian identity which had been forcibly imposed on him.[40] In a vivid demonstration of the intolerance toward alternate identities which had long marked Ethiopian nationalism, Jawar had morphed, almost overnight, into a figure of hate among Ethiopianists in the diaspora. But at the same time, and in direct reaction to the Ethiopianists' outrage, his stock among Oromo nationalists had skyrocketed. Out of the frenzy of the following months, in which Jawar and his friends travelled far and wide through the Oromo diaspora rallying support, came the Oromo Media Network (OMN), a crowd-funded satellite station, modelled on—and as direct rebuke to—Ginbot 7's ESAT. It would be perhaps the most important innovation in almost three decades of overseas Oromo activism. "Oromo first" would become its core mission statement.

Within just a couple of days of OMN's launch in March 2014, its official Facebook account had more than a million followers. Jawar dropped out of his PhD programme and moved to Minneapolis. With unpaid volunteers rushing to pitch in, the channel was soon broadcasting twenty-four hours a day, seven days a week, its burnt-out staff sleeping on the floors of the office to keep the programmes running. Suddenly, there were two stridently anti-government, relentlessly anti-TPLF mass media organisations beaming into Ethiopian homes almost non-stop. Jawar, his influence now vastly magnified by OMN, became the *Qeerroo* movement's loudspeaker. Soon its foot soldiers on the ground in Ethiopia—students, teachers, university lecturers and even civil servants—had begun sharing strategies, videos and photographs of police brutality and other state abuses with OMN's HQ in Minneapolis.

Never before had the Oromo movement possessed a single hub of this kind. Though much of the *Qeerroo*'s activities remained fairly loose and decentralised, even after OMN had muscled in on them, an array of local grievances—the loss of a school football field to an investor, for instance—could increasingly be woven into a wider, pan-Oromo cause. By the middle of 2016, orders for mass demonstrations, region-wide boycotts, or common campaign slogans from the top in Minneapolis were being disseminated through a chain of *Qeerroo* organisers on the ground, right down to the very smallest village.

That year, one particularly controversial slogan, "Down Down *Woyane!*" (a slang term for the TPLF), went viral—and soon became the movement's catchphrase. By then, the protests had long ceased to be about the master plan and had morphed instead into a far broader complaint against ethnic marginalisation, corruption, authoritarianism and, above all, the TPLF. "We were basically doing what Noam Chomsky called 'manufacturing consent'," Jawar later argued. "We were manufacturing narratives." The goal now was not to topple the EPRDF. Jawar and his fellow Oromo activists had learnt lessons from the Arab spring, notably that trying to overthrow the state altogether risked plunging the country into anarchy. What they wanted instead was to work with insiders to reform the EPRDF from within. In a revamped ruling coalition, they hoped, the TPLF would step aside for the OPDO. The OPDO would democratise, and allow space for the Oromo opposition. Nationally, Oromos would finally be on top. That, at least, was the basic strategy. The following year, in 2017, OMN was labelled a terrorist organisation, and Jawar was accused of crimes against the constitution.

* * *

Abiy had, at first, almost no discernible role in the Oromo movement which brought him to power. By now a member of the OPDO executive committee, again largely thanks to his relationship with Abadula, he had little incentive yet to purposefully rock the boat inside the EPRDF. Though some who spoke to him around that time, such as Tamrat Layne, recalled him expressing conventional Oromo nationalist views on the 'Addis Ababa question', Abiy did not—unlike some OPDO colleagues—speak out against the master plan. In fact, one of the future prime minister's colleagues later recalled him even urging them not to criticise it in public. At a time when OMN was beginning to reach out covertly to members of the OPDO in order to forge a common strategy against the TPLF, Abiy was in effect nowhere to be found. Until at least the second half of 2017, barely anybody in the overseas Oromo movement knew who he was at all.

Neither had Abiy made much of a mark on the ministry of science and technology—a post for which, in theory, his interests were particularly well-suited. As it had been at INSA, a key early focus of his at the ministry was less to do with any policy changes than revamping its offices, in particular by knocking down walls to make them open-plan. Apparently frustrated by its sluggish bureaucracy, he had brought in outsiders to staff it. "He is also a good listener, but with a bit of a headstrong attitude towards people who don't deliver," explained one ministry colleague.[41]

Officially, though, Abiy was to spend much of this year researching and writing his PhD on conflict resolution at Addis Ababa University's Institute for Peace and Security Studies. That should, in principle, have absorbed a great deal of his time. In practice, though, it doesn't appear to have involved much work at all, and instead seems to have been pursued primarily to counter claims that, lacking both an academic bachelor's and master's degree, he was unqualified to one day be prime minister. By the 2010s, it was common knowledge that the Institute for Peace and Security Studies, an otherwise quite reputable institution, was expected to make allowances for senior party officials. An exception had therefore been made for the young minister, whose proposed thesis was about the role of 'social capital' in building bridges between Christians and Muslims in his home district of Jimma. It drew, he told examiners in a televised presentation, on his personal experience as a peacebuilder there in the mid-2000s.[42] The final paper, though, was almost certainly not written by him alone: multiple sources from the university and the OPDO have since conceded that Abiy enlisted a friend, or perhaps more than one friend, to help him write it. The resulting thesis was also delivered implausibly fast, in just fourteen months.[43]

Over time, Abiy had managed to draw closer to his boss, Hailemariam. The two were able to bond over prayer, as well as their shared frustrations with the TPLF. But then, in November 2016, allegedly under pressure from senior Tigrayan officials, Hailemariam had fired him. Abiy was furious, and later wrote that he had been sacked so as to "send a message to other daring reformist leaders."[44] "He was so angry," one colleague from the time recalled. But Abiy hadn't been the only one shown the door. By the time I had arrived in Ethiopia the previous month, the whole capital was in lockdown and the EPRDF was on edge. Protests and a deadly stampede at the traditional Oromo *Irreecha* thanksgiving festival in early October had sparked an unprecedently destructive wave of violence throughout Oromia. Unrest had also begun spreading to Amhara, where thousands of ordinary Tigrayans had been the target of ominous pogroms over the summer. Amid a growing sense that the EPRDF, after a quarter of a century in charge, was finally losing its grip, Hailemariam had again reshuffled his administration that November. This time he appointed a team of what were described as more qualified "technocrats". Abiy and several others, including his future battlefield adversary, the Tigrayan communication minister, Getachew Reda, had all been cast out.

The decision to impose a state of emergency that October was about as close as the internally riven EPRDF got to consensus. Tens of thousands of protesters were carted off to camps for ideological indoctrination, where they were taught about the benefits of the "Ethiopian Renaissance" and the dangers of Western-backed "colour revolutions." With both OMN and ESAT banned, police began ripping satellite dishes from the roofs of residential homes. For several months, mobile internet was switched off. Tens of thousands of low-level officials were sacked or reassigned. But actual reforms, such as changes to the electoral system, were punted to the long grass.

By the middle of 2017 a sense of listlessness prevailed. Emergency law was extended for another six months. In a rare move, the coalition congress, scheduled for the autumn, was postponed. So, too, were local elections, as well as the national census, a political hot potato which many worried would aggravate competition between the regions. Internally, a hunt for a new and more dynamic leader, someone who could knock heads together, began to take shape. "I believed that there had to be a new person, a dominant force who could save the country," Hailemariam later recalled. "I also thought that this person should come from Oromia. Otherwise, it would be difficult to stop this."

6

THE STIRRUP AND THE THRONE

OROMARA AND ABIY'S ASCENT TO THE TOP

Shortly after Abiy's departure from Hailemariam's cabinet, a book from a little-known author by the name of "Deraz" was released.[1] *Erkabna Menber*, or *The Stirrup and the Throne*, as it was called, was a 173-page-long Amharic tract on the question of power, and how to acquire and maintain it. Rich in religious imagery, parables and proverbs—with a peculiar bricolage of influences from Václav Havel to the Norwegian peace theorist Johan Galtung—it was above all else a hymn to the importance of strong and wise leadership for the health of a nation. Ethiopia, the author lamented, was blighted by its lack of this. "Our cruel leaders," Deraz wrote, "have enriched themselves with power ... as our people have their shoulders burdened with the yoke of suffering."[2] For anyone who picked up a copy, *The Stirrup and the Throne* might have seemed to be the manifesto of an aspiring national leader.

This was fitting—for the real author was, in fact, none other than Abiy himself. Written in a pique of anger, he later said, after what was to his mind an unjust and premature removal from office, *The Stirrup and the Throne* provided the first sustained glimpse of Abiy's political vision.[3] It was not his first book (nor his last): under the same pseudonym he had already published two works of Pentecostal spiritualism, as well as a historical account of a folk hero from Jimma, *Kedir Setete*, published in 2012. But none was more revealing than *The Stirrup and the Throne*. On some matters, it showed a man who still cleaved to EPRDF orthodoxy: his comments on economics, while insubstantial, were broadly statist and, just as Meles had been, critical of international financial institutions and the 'Washington Consensus'.[4] He also made few positive references to liberal democracy.[5] But in other respects, it read as a clear rebuke to the student radicals of the 1960s and 1970s and their understanding of Ethiopian history and identity.[6] Ethiopia, Abiy wrote, was the product of thousands of years of "glorious history … a nation wherein the dawn of freedom was sparked."[7] Nowhere did he invoke the oppressed state of the many 'nations and nationalities'. Nor did he highlight the federal system for praise of any kind. Instead of imported ideologies like Marxism, Abiy argued, what Ethiopia needed was an integrated philosophy which brought foreign and indigenous thinking into harmony.

But it was the evident fascination with Machiavelli and the darker side of politics which was most striking.[8] The "magic" of power, he wrote, was "mysterious", "bewitching", a "haunting spell". To reach the throne, Abiy suggested, one must be ruthless but also dissembling: like an angel in bright times, but like a devil in dark ones. "An actor who can conceal his interest from others," he explained, will eventually "hold the orb and sceptre."[9] And so, in 2017, as *The Stirrup and the Throne* hit the book stands and Abiy joined the leadership of the Oromia regional government for the first time, this was the approach he would take. Speaking with a local academic that year, Abiy confessed he felt so emboldened by prayer that he was now confident he could take on the EPRDF leadership from the inside. If it was the will of God, he explained, then deliberate disruption would help him succeed. In fact, he later reflected, being fired by Hailemariam was the best thing that could have happened to him.

* * *

Abiy first joined the Oromia regional government as its vice president in October 2016. He was also to become the head of the regional bureau of urban development and planning. The timing, as he later wrote, was exceptionally fortuitous.[10] In the wake of the tragic events at the *Irreecha* festival earlier that month, the Oromo ruling party had embarked on a stunning transformation. By arriving in the vice president's office when he did, Abiy stood to become one of its chief architects—and, in the end, its prime beneficiary.

Days before *Irreecha*, the OPDO had elected a new chairman: Lemma Megersa. He and his new deputy, Workneh Gebeyehu (who was also soon to be Ethiopia's foreign minister), were, like Abiy, both protégés of Abadula. They replaced Muktar Kedir and Aster Mamo, the preeminent hardliners in the party leadership who had been forced out that summer, in part because of their failure to contain the protests in Oromia. Lemma, a young and articulate former chief of regional security, who hailed from the OLF's heartlands in Wollega, western Oromia, had first emerged in the public spotlight in 2015 with a widely-circulated speech rejecting the Addis Ababa master plan.[11] That within only a year he could be elected to the OPDO's top job was testament to the scale of the internal upheaval then underway. For the EPRDF leadership, though, it was also a watershed. Perceived by his colleagues to be among the most strongly opposed to the TPLF's dominance of anyone in the OPDO at the time, Lemma's ascension had thus come without its blessing, tacit or otherwise. Arguably a first in the organisation's more than twenty-five-year history, the move marked the culmination of a process of gradual emancipation from the TPLF's guardianship which had begun with Abadula's overhaul of its membership a decade earlier.

Described by almost everyone who met him as quiet and reserved, and with a self-effacing air reminiscent of a high school maths teacher, Lemma cut a very different figure to the flamboyant and headstrong Abiy. Nor was he, on the whole, inclined to take undue risks. But as president of Oromia, he took the reins convinced that the TPLF would sabotage his administration from the get-go. In particular, he believed that the deadly *Irreecha* protests, in which a niece of his had died, had been deliberately orchestrated by a Tigrayan 'deep state' so as to justify a renewed crackdown in Oromia, thereby nipping his efforts to challenge the TPLF's pre-eminence in the bud. This was a view he shared with most of the Oromo opposition, though not one for which there was ever much concrete evidence, and it seems to have spurred in Lemma a flinty determination to bring the TPLF down from within.[12] "After *Irreecha*, they became totally different," said Milkessa Midega, an opposition-linked academic recruited by Lemma to join his administration not long afterwards. Abiy, once more with the help of Abadula, was brought in to serve as Lemma's right-hand man. "The beginning of the end of the TPLF-led EPRDF regime was the removal of Muktar and Aster," recalled an Oromo businessman and former army officer with ties to various party factions. "That was the beginning of the change."

The two men quickly found common cause in their ambition to supplant the TPLF as the coalition's primus inter pares. Bound, like almost all their closest allies in the new OPDO leadership, by a shared Pentecostal faith, they set about turning the once subservient OPDO into an openly insurgent force—an opposition party, in effect, in all but name. Where once they had tried to stop the *Qeerroo* with force, now the new leaders, soon known by the public affectionately as "Team Lemma", sought to harness the movement's power for their own ends, by adopting much of the opposition's rhetoric and openly promising to make *Qeerroo*'s demands for democracy and justice their own. Protests and strikes, at least those which didn't target private investments or government buildings, were given tacit sanction, with the police ordered to stand back. Thousands of unpopular low-level officials were removed from their posts. With influential *Qeerroo* leaders brought in to replace them, insiders began leaking information to OMN and prominent activists in the diaspora. Ordinary cadres, meanwhile, began quietly sabotaging the day-to-day business of the federal government—impeding the delivery of major infrastructure projects such as the new railway, for instance, or refusing to clear land for construction work.[13]

As the Oromo movement gathered momentum over the course of 2017 on the common platform of removing the TPLF from power and seizing control of the central state, so, for the first time, did it start to overcome the internal divisions which had long bedevilled it. Oromo business elites, opposition activists, government officials, police and even—in some instances—army officers, all now joined forces. "[Officials] gave us information from inside the state; they shared their plans, what they wanted to do, and how they intended to confront the TPLF," recalled another well-connected Oromo businessman and activist. When protests returned with a vengeance upon the lifting of the state of emergency that August, even some of the Oromo police themselves became active participants.

Styling themselves as economic populists, Team Lemma launched what they called an "Oromo Economic Revolution" to tackle youth unemployment and bring the region's legions of disaffected young people onto their side. Plans were drawn up to cancel unproductive investments, with parcels of land earmarked for distribution to the *Qeerroo*. METEC, the controversial military-industrial conglomerate, was stripped of its rights to a failing coal mine; a year later, the site was handed over to a group of Oromo youth. In August 2017, in an unprecedented demonstration of the regional autonomy which, despite being enshrined in the federal constitution, had always been held in check by the EPRDF's leaders in Addis Ababa, the Oromia government refused to provide land to a Chinese manufacturer which had struck a deal with the federal investment commission. Footloose investors who failed to use the land they had leased, or to pay export taxes, were now denounced as "thieves" waging war against Oromia.

Within a few months Lemma had become the most popular OPDO politician in its history. "Lemma receives a hero's welcome wherever he goes," wrote *OPride*, the influential diaspora outlet based in America.[14] Here for the first time, it seemed, a senior party official was brave enough to criticise their own record, and to disavow the EPRDF's most stale, ideologically infused jargon—terms like 'rent-seeking', 'narrow nationalism' or 'chauvinism'—which had long been so alienating for many Ethiopians. By the time I visited Ambo, the epicentre of the Oromo protests, in November 2017, Lemma's face was on the bumper stickers of rickshaws and on posters inside barber shops. "I love him," a local student told me. "He is my life." Songs and prayers were even devoted to him.

Team Lemma and the *Qeerroo* were a generational phenomenon: the product of nearly three decades of nationalist consciousness-building both inside the country and abroad. To an extent, though, they were also a reflection of the EPRDF's achievements over the same period. Oromos of the so-called "*Qubee*" generation which came of age in the 2000s and early 2010s were the most educated, prosperous and assertive in the country's history.[15] They had a state to call their own and, especially after Meles's death, an unprecedented, if still imperfect, degree of political autonomy. "The *Qubee* generation exhibits a pure and unadulterated allegiance to the Oromo question," wrote one of its most influential spokesmen, Mohammed Ademo, in 2016. "[They] can proudly and unapologetically proclaim, 'I am Oromo first and I am proud of it'."[16] Though many also had shared experience of the Ethiopian state's brutality, and the inequities of a political and economic order in which they were—relative to their population size—still fairly marginal, most Oromos of this generation didn't demand wholesale revolution, nor radical changes to the structure of the state. The 1995 constitution was overwhelmingly popular: the *Qeerroo*'s main complaint was merely that the EPRDF had failed to respect it. Meanwhile, the question of Oromo secession, once the presiding concern of the Oromo movement, had been more or less put to bed. None of the key protagonists of Oromo politics in this period had any interest in an independent Oromia. What concerned them—and what united OMN, the *Qeerroo* and Team Lemma—was the goal of capturing the Ethiopian state and remaking it in their own image. "We Oromo have a chance to build an Ethiopia that resembles us, and in which we entrench *Oromummaa* [Oromoness] in every structure," the future president of

Oromia, Shimelis Abdissa, later explained. "We will create the Ethiopia we want."[17] The core elements of their shared agenda included making Afan Oromo the working language of the federal government (alongside Amharic), securing Oromo dominance and control of Addis Ababa, and elevating more Oromos into key positions in federal state structures— from the army to the cabinet to the Prime Minister's Office. They also wanted a much bigger slice of the national economic pie.

Abiy's own relationship to the Oromo movement, however, was more ambiguous. On the one hand, he was now increasingly open about his ambitions to challenge the primacy of the TPLF and secure the pre-eminence of the OPDO. Even when he was still at INSA, one Tigrayan colleague recalled, he had hinted at a desire to cut the TPLF down to size once he reached the top. "It was Oromo nationalism which brought us together," said an official in the Prime Minister's Office who later defected to the opposition in Minneapolis. "I'd say we shared almost everything in common at this time. We had the 100 percent same views in favour of the constitution. And we had the same criticism of the TPLF's dominance." As a leading member of Team Lemma, Abiy would play a key role in, for instance, transforming the Oromia state broadcaster into something almost resembling an opposition outlet, covering previously untouchable subjects such as land grabs and corruption.[18] Moreover, in a particularly audacious U-turn, he took credit for reclaiming the very same land which had been leased by the Oromia government to INSA on his watch in 2010—even going so far as to claim this as a victory for the Oromo people.[19] Though overshadowed in public by Lemma throughout this year, Abiy would also have a critical role behind the scenes, devising many of the tactics Team Lemma were to deploy against the TPLF. "Who should be fired, promoted, what to say—the plans were being devised by Abiy and implemented by Lemma," recalled a former OPDO insider who eventually fell out with Abiy and went into private business. "He had a great role inside the OPDO at the time in creating chaos," said one of the Oromo businessmen working closely with Team Lemma. "He was working hard to become PM. He was very good at causing chaos and destabilising."

But Abiy was hardly a conventional Oromo nationalist. Those who had known him from his INSA days, or even earlier, rarely recalled any particular enthusiasm for the Oromo cause, and certainly never any hint of secessionism. However ethno-nationalist his father, Ahmed Ali, might have been, it was his mother's Ethiopianism—reflecting her Christian

Orthodox and, quite possibly, Amhara background—which seems to have been the greater influence on him. Compared to Lemma, whose upbringing in the Wollega heartlands of Oromo nationalism had marked him with a more critical view of the country's past, Abiy was visibly comfortable with Ethiopia's imperial myths and symbols. Indeed, once he became prime minister, many of his OPDO colleagues would be alarmed to discover that he had friends and allies in Addis Ababa, many of them Amhara, who were passionate Ethiopianists and whose ultimate ambition was the abolition of ethnic federalism.[20]

A degree of subterfuge and deceit had always been part of Abiy's politics. "Every step of the way, he is manipulating," said a senior OPDO colleague. "The key to his mindset is manipulation." Over the coming years, Abiy would flit between Oromo nationalist and Ethiopianist constituencies with sometimes remarkable brazenness, often saying different things to different audiences, or signalling different messages to different members of the same audience through the traditional rhetorical practice of what in Amharic is known as "*samna-warq*", or "wax and gold": the studied use of words for ambiguous purposes. "Politics is all about doing tricks, nothing else," his ultra-loyal disciple Shimelis later admitted. "It's all about how much intrigue you can play."[21]

Yet there was also a certain consistency in some of Abiy's positions. He didn't seem to believe, for instance, that there might be any contradiction between the Ethiopianism and the Oromo nationalism which he simultaneously espoused. Far from being incompatible, he once argued, the two movements might be mutually beneficial, just like the synthesis of opposing ideas, identities and ideologies he later characterised as "*Medemer*" (synergy). "People think that Oromummaa and Oromo nationalism and Ethiopian nationalism can't mix together," he told the Oromia Broadcasting Network in 2019. "But we can strike the balance and make the two move together to become our beauty."[22] The key to this, he argued, was for Oromos to alter their minds and attitudes. They should start, for instance, by seeing themselves as agents—rather than simply victims—of Ethiopian history. Speaking to a gathering of Oromo politicians and academics in the city of Adama in 2017, for example, the new vice president of Oromia presented a paper in which he argued for the rehabilitation of Oromo warriors, like the controversial Ras Gobena Dache, who had fought alongside Menelik II in the wars of the late nineteenth century. Oromos, he argued, had long been part and parcel of Ethiopia's nation-building journey. "His point was that Oromos are the founders of Ethiopia," one of those present recalled. "The message was clear: we led before and we should lead again."

* * *

It was not only in Oromia that Team Lemma were unsettling the established order. At the start of November 2017, on the very same day the TPLF began a historic meeting of their own in Mekelle, the Tigrayan state capital, Lemma and several of his colleagues took their seats at the Blue Nile Resort on the shore of Lake Tana in Bahir Dar, the capital of the Amhara region.[23] The trip had been billed as an opportunity for productive dialogue between the country's two biggest ethnic groups, following a recent spate of violence between them in western Oromia. At first glance, it might not have seemed especially significant. A cheerful jamboree attended by party elites, business leaders and academics in Bahir Dar's convention centre was to be followed by a dinner at the iconic lakeside hotel, under the ostensibly anodyne slogan of "*abironet*" ("togetherness"). Speakers were to deliver warm bromides about brotherly love and national unity as the regions' presidents, Lemma and his Amhara counterpart, Gedu Andargachew, smiled and embraced for the cameras. Under more normal circumstances, it should have been an entirely forgettable affair, the routine application of grease to the machinery of federalism.

Instead, at Abiy's initiative, this seemingly pedestrian forum between OPDO and ANDM party elites was used to cement a budding alliance and to present a common front against Mekelle. From the perspective of the TPLF, which was notably absent, the move could have hardly been more provocative. "Everybody was seeking an ally to topple the TPLF," recalled an Amhara guest. "It was not subtle." In public speeches, delegates including both state presidents made insinuating references to shadowy 'others', and to an unnamed third-party conspiring to keep the two largest ethnic groups divided.[24] Behind closed doors, Team Lemma (bar Abiy, who in the end had remained in Oromia that day) pushed for proportional representation within the EPRDF, a formula which would benefit the more populous Oromos and Amharas at the expense of Tigrayans. They also made the case for the ANDM to join the OPDO in pressing for an Oromo candidate to succeed Hailemariam.

The climax of the public ceremony, though, was almost as important as whatever had transpired in private. In an eloquent speech delivered as the day drew to a close, Lemma played shrewdly to Amhara sensibilities by invoking the old concept of "*Ethiopiawinet*" (Ethiopian-ness), and declaring it to be like an "addiction[...] an identity and a symbol that has kept on being built, one layer over another, over the ages [...] not something that easily breaks or loses its light."[25] It was a historic gesture: never before had an OPDO politician, and an outspoken Oromo nationalist no less, expressed such a lyrical appreciation of the country and its history. Looking back, though, one of those involved recalled that it had been Abiy who had been the driving force behind the idea, even to the point of giving Lemma the specific Amharic words to use in his speech. The result was the defining moment—and, in hindsight, the high-water mark—of the alliance known by then as "Oromara".[26] Almost overnight, Team Lemma became poster-boys in Amhara as well as Oromia. One popular Amharic weekly would go as far as to splash Lemma on its cover as an Ethiopian Moses.

The ANDM's journey to the point of finding common cause with Oromo nationalists was of comparatively recent origin. For many Amharas, Oromo nationalists had always been more dangerous than the TPLF to the Ethiopian 'unity' of which they considered themselves the traditional guardians. Cultural—especially religious—ties also meant that Amharas typically shared closer affinities to Tigrayans than they did most Oromos. As for the ANDM, while clearly a junior partner to the TPLF within the EPRDF, it was still senior to the OPDO. Unlike the latter, the ANDM could draw on at least some historical legitimacy, beginning as it did as a faction of the student movement long active in the armed struggle against the Derg.

The ANDM had also never had a chairman whose legacy compared to Abadula's in terms of building a rank-and-file in his own image. This meant that by the time a new generation of cadres like Abiy and Lemma were climbing the ladder of the OPDO in the late 2000s, turning it into a more openly nationalist front than it had been previously, a similar process was yet to take place inside the ANDM. When the OPDO replaced its two hardline leaders in 2016 with Lemma and his colleagues, the ANDM didn't follow suit. Its most influential veteran, Bereket Simon, had always been much closer to Meles and the TPLF than had Abadula and his colleagues.

Even so, by the time mass protests had gathered steam in Oromia in the mid-2010s, there were signs of a corresponding movement beginning to take off in parts of Amhara. Young Amharas, after all, shared many of the same grievances as their Oromo counterparts: under-employment in the region's expanding towns and cities; injustice at the hands of the EPRDF's authoritarianism, especially in the aftermath of the 2005 election; and a sense of exclusion from a burgeoning, corrupt elite in Addis Ababa. Frustration with playing second fiddle to the TPLF had also long been latent within both the ANDM and the wider Amhara public. When demonstrations began in the faded imperial city of Gondar in the summer of 2016, they were ostensibly in solidarity with the Oromo protests down south.

But Amhara's political culture was very different to that of Oromia, and despite their shared resentment of the TPLF there was to be little to bind the budding protest movements together in the long term. For one thing, their understanding of Ethiopian history was radically different. In the eyes of Oromo nationalists, even more than in those of their Tigrayan counterparts, Amharas figured as colonial overlords and armed settlers. Most Amharas, by contrast, saw their forebears as pioneers of national unification and defenders of the realm over many centuries. Those among them who acknowledged the oppressiveness of the imperial order tended to downplay the particular role of Amharas in it, stressing the equal participation of Tigrayans, Oromos and assimilated elites from the south. Moreover, whereas the goals of the Oromo movement were ultimately limited and reformist—shifting the balance of power from Tigrayans to Oromos while keeping the basic structure of the federation intact—those of its Amhara equivalent were far more revolutionary. In effect, they demanded wholesale change to the constitutional order and an ultimate return to a pre-1991 political dispensation. For the leaders of the EPRDF, and especially the TPLF, the demands of "Amhara Resistance", as it became known, therefore represented a far greater existential threat than the so-called "Oromo Revolution".

Though the protests which erupted in Amhara that summer were ultimately smaller and less widespread than those in Oromia, they were considerably more violent. Protesters there called themselves the "*Fano*", a term with imperial roots evoking the image of a Christian peasant warrior defending the fatherland.[27] Drawing heavily on Amhara's distinctively martial political culture, participants in the demonstrations in Gondar and elsewhere were very often armed, with automatic weapons seen being fired into the air—something unheard of during protests in Oromia. Disparate rebel groups linked in various ways to Ginbot 7 in Eritrea were also found carrying out raids on military installations and government facilities in northern Amhara. In the early months of 2017, they hit a prison and detonated no less than thirteen bombs and grenades targeting government officials.[28]

Protests in Amhara were also more overtly anti-Tigrayan.[29] While violence against Tigrayans had happened before in Oromia—Tigrayan-owned hotels had been targeted in Ambo back in 2014, for instance—demonstrations in Gondar in 2016 were accompanied by evictions and an exodus of the city's sizeable Tigrayan population. Not long after that a chilling broadcast on ESAT's Amhara and Ethiopianist-dominated airwaves urged that Tigray's "sea water" be drained, to get rid of "rotten fish" and end the suffering caused by "5 million against the 95 million people"—a none-too-subtle call for collective punishment of Tigrayan civilians in order to weaken their leaders.[30] By some estimates as many as 100,000 Tigrayans fled Amhara between 2015 and 2018.[31]

Underlying these tendencies was a particular set of grievances. At the heart of them was the 1995 constitution, which was understood very differently in Amhara to much of the rest of the country. For many Ethiopians, not least Oromos, the federal system stood as a guarantee against the return of the old Amhara-centred order. By defining Ethiopia as a multinational entity, it struck at the heart of the assimilationist model of national unity which many considered merely cover for an essentially Amhara 'hegemony'. Among Amharas, by contrast, the federal order was widely seen as directly—perhaps even deliberately—threatening to their interests. Even though the constitution had given them their own region for the first time, it had put the millions of Amharas living as minorities across Oromia and the wider south in a position of distinct vulnerability. Since 1991, Amharas were more likely than any other group to be the target of the ethnic attacks, often precisely because those who, for historical reasons, lived outside Amhara proper were regarded as foreigners on stolen land. 'Ethnic federalism', more than anything else, was thus the unifying grievance for Amharas of all stripes—with Tigrayans and the TPLF ultimately held responsible for it. The idea of a deep historical rivalry between Tigrayans and Amharas, coloured by competing claims to be the true heirs to a primordial Ethiopian lineage reaching as far back as ancient Axum, had been growing stronger and more explicit.[32]

The constitution had also reordered the map of Ethiopia in ways which were perceived as uniquely disadvantageous to Amharas. After 1991, swathes of land, in particular the fertile lowland areas north-east of Gondar known as Wolkait, Humera, Tsegede and Tselemte (in Amharic, the last two are Tegede and Telemte), had been incorporated into the newly constituted Tigray regional state. The reason for this, constitutionally at least, was straightforward. Since Ethiopia's new regional states were to be based on ethno-linguistic criteria, and the ethnically mixed populations of the contested territories in question—which also included Raya to the south of Tigray—had been found in the census of 1994 to be majority Tigrinya-speakers, they were thus to be administered by Tigray and the TPLF.[33] The western part was renamed Western Tigray.

But as elegant as this may have been in constitutional theory, it ran up hard against the emotional power of history and identity in Amhara, and in particular in Gondar. Wolkait, as these territories were often collectively known, had for much of Ethiopia's more recent imperial past been governed from the provincial capital of Gondar.[34] For much of the twentieth century prior to 1991, most of it hadn't been administered, except briefly during the Italian occupation between 1939 and 1941, as part of the old province of Tigray.[35] Though the Amhara region itself was a post-1991 construct, hitherto having never existed as a single political entity, many Amharas regarded the historic border between them and Tigray to be the Tekeze River—making Wolkait a natural part of their own 'ancestral' territory. The TPLF, by this logic, had stolen it.

For most of the post-1991 period the so-called 'Wolkait question' lay dormant. Much of the population of Wolkait were bilingual Amharic and Tigrinya speakers, with a distinct provincial identity of their own, meaning that the question of whether they were administered from Mekelle or Bahir Dar was largely irrelevant. Wealthier landowning families who had lost their farms back in the 1980s, when TPLF fighters had first moved into the area and began implementing land reform, had long since scattered. Some were to be found in Gondar or Addis Ababa, but many had gone further afield to Sudan and eventually Europe and America.[36] Over the following two decades a few had campaigned for the return of the Wolkait from the TPLF, under the umbrella of a rebel movement known as the Patriotic Front, a precursor to Ginbot 7, but with only limited success. After 1991, the TPLF resettled some 25,000 Tigrayan refugees who had been living in camps in Sudan, as well as demobilised TPLF fighters from the struggle, in the fertile lowlands of Wolkait. But, at first, they and the local Amhara and Wolkaites living in the area coexisted relatively peacefully.[37] Though the CUD had made some hay out of the Wolkait issue in the 2005 election, and its successor, Ginbot 7, continued to do so, it was possible even then—and some did—to spend three years studying at Gondar University without the issue registering as a particularly significant one at all. At this time even one of the future leaders of the Wolkait movement, a bilingual army colonel and TPLF veteran from the area called Demeke Zewdu, identified to his comrades as Tigrayan and had no known links to political opposition groups of any kind.[38] In the immediate years after his discharge from the army in 2010, Colonel Demeke's chief goal seems to have been becoming an agricultural investor in Wolkait's lucrative sesame and cotton fields.[39]

The process by which Wolkait irredentism became the defining feature of Amhara opposition to the TPLF was therefore a gradual one. The EPRDF's fierce crackdown on Patriotic Front militants in the 1990s, and, after 2005, Ginbot 7 supporters, undoubtedly had a radicalising effect. So, too, did stories of Amharas in Wolkait being arrested or even killed by the Tigrayan authorities there for expressing opposition to the TPLF. Less obvious, but arguably no less important, was the chronic shortage of productive land in Ethiopia's northern highlands. This was of course nothing new, since population density, compounded by a rigid and inflexible system of tenure, had always been a problem there; indeed, it had been part of the reason for Menelik II's southward expansion in the late nineteenth century.[40] But as population growth exploded after 1991— almost doubling in just two decades—competition for land had become especially acute. In the 2000s, Tigrayan authorities began resettling more farmers from Tigray's densely populated central highlands to Wolkait. Around the same time, with the EPRDF's policy shift in favour of large-scale commercial agriculture, a number of TPLF-affiliated investors, including the TPLF's party-owned conglomerate, EFFORT, also began acquiring large tracts in the area.[41] Among Amharas, and especially those with ties to Wolkait, resentment mounted and accusations of demographic engineering grew louder. In 2014, Tigray's authorities made changes to the regional state's investment laws and land certification processes, which in effect made it harder for those without political connections to acquire more land. Several local Wolkait farmers and civil servants—among them Colonel Demeke—found their land holdings diminished.[42] The following year, the "Committee for the Restoration of the Amhara Identity Wolkait-Tegedé" was formed. Colonel Demeke, who now identified as Amhara, became its leader.[43]

What followed was a textbook example of repression producing the very outcome it was supposed to prevent. The Wolkait Committee didn't, at first, demand that Wolkait become part of Amhara; when its leaders took a petition of 25,000 signatures to Tigray's regional government in Mekelle in 2016, all they asked for was the creation of an autonomous 'Amhara zone' in Western Tigray.[44] The TPLF refused; in July, federal police attempted to arrest Colonel Demeke and his colleagues in Gondar, triggering a wave of protests, riots and—most worryingly—anti-Tigrayan pogroms.[45] The ensuing crackdown, which involved mass arrests and re-education camps, thrust the Wolkait issue to the centre of Amhara politics and turned Colonel Demeke into a martyr. Over the coming years, Amhara media outlets including ESAT would bang the drum of Wolkait irredentism like never before, dusting off old maps and chronicles to demonstrate Amhara's supposed historic claims over the territory.[46] The goal now was full annexation, and any talk of an autonomous 'Amhara zone' inside Tigray had been all but forgotten.

Most significantly, though, the revived Amhara movement eventually succeeded in pulling the ANDM's younger leaders, including the regional president Gedu and Ethiopia's deputy prime minister, Demeke Mekonnen, in their direction. Eager to distinguish themselves in the eyes of the Amhara public from the party's much-loathed old guard—embodied in the figure of Bereket Simon, Meles's right-hand man, whose family roots were popularly denigrated as being more Eritrean than Amhara— the ANDM's younger leaders increasingly sought to bolster their popular credentials by championing irredentism and, implicitly at least, the anti-Tigrayan sentiments which underpinned it. When the federal government sought to bring Colonel Demeke to stand trial in Addis Ababa, the Amhara president resisted and instead kept the protest leader in Gondar, earning him considerable cachet among the young *Fanos*. Two years later, he and his colleagues gave their formal endorsement to the Wolkait Committee's new territorial demands.[47] Just as in Oromia the OPDO had begun to tacitly work with the *Qeerroo*, so by then elements of the ANDM had teamed up with the *Fano*.

* * *

Such was the poison in the air when the EPRDF gathered for the long-awaited crisis meeting of its executive committee in December 2017. The TPLF contingent arrived fresh from their own lengthy self-evaluation in Mekelle, a period of bitter recriminations which had concluded with the replacement of their own leaders and the appointment of Debretsion Gebremichael, a TPLF veteran and then Ethiopia's Minister of Communication and Information Technology, to the position of regional president.[48] The TPLF's anger with their Amhara and Oromo colleagues, whose "Oromara" pact struck in Bahir Dar the previous month could hardly have gone unnoticed, was palpable. The ANDM's young Turks were denounced as 'Amhara chauvinists' pining for the old order, while the OPDO were blamed for presiding over chaos in Oromia. Both were accused of using ethnic nationalism as a means to distract from their own alleged corruption—particularly, in the case of the OPDO, in the context of land administration in the high-value outskirts of Addis Ababa. Both were also accused of doing purposefully little to tamp down unrest.

Amid mounting allegations that they were encouraging an Eastern European-style 'colour revolution' in order to seize power, Abiy and Lemma appear to have been placed under surveillance by NISS. At one point, by many accounts, spy chief Getachew Assefa even threatened to have them arrested.[49] According to the Ethiopian academic who met with Abiy around this time, the future prime minister claimed that he and his colleagues in Team Lemma had recorded a video of themselves in order to document what they were doing in case they wound up dead.[50] "Before we do anything we pray together," he told the academic. "Either we get killed, and become martyrs—or we succeed." Lemma packed his family off to America for safety.

By this point tensions inside the EPRDF were beginning to play out on the ground in the form of spiralling violence between ethnicities and regions. For much of 2017, Oromia's 1,200-kilometre-long border with the neighbouring Somali region had been ablaze with fighting between their respective local militias and 'special police'—a clear indication that the coercive capacity of the federal government was weakening fast, and that the cohesion of the country's political elite was simultaneously fraying. Somali forces, who by most accounts were the initial aggressors, were reported killing Oromo civilians, looting schools, ransacking public offices and seizing land sometimes deep inside Oromo territory.[51] Over the course of the year, several hundred were killed and several hundred thousand displaced, with victims on both sides.

The causes of the conflict were fiercely disputed. They were, from the outset, also somewhat obscured by widespread but unproven allegations from the Oromo side—and, indeed, from some on the Somali side, too—that it was a proxy war: meaning, to the accusers, violence deliberately orchestrated by the TPLF in order to weaken and distract the OPDO from their attempts to take power in Addis Ababa. "The TPLF wanted to make it seem as if the Oromo leaders were waging a genocide against the Somalis," Hailemariam himself later argued, "in order to turn the OPDO into criminals in the eyes of the public." Abiy and Lemma certainly believed that, and, in ways which foreshadowed aspects of the former's premiership, heavily insinuated that the controversial Somali regional president, Abdi Mohamoud Omar, commonly known as Abdi Illey, was doing the TPLF's bidding by sending his forces to attack innocent Oromos along the border and grab their territory. "It is difficult to accept that it is border issues which have caused all these things," Lemma said in a rare interview that September on the revamped OBN. "What we have seen, rather, are organised and trained and well-equipped forces conducting a war."[52]

In part, this was a conflict exacerbated by certain flaws in the federal system. The border between Oromia and the Somali region had been fiercely contested since the 1990s, and, with the carving up of the national map into ethno-regional blocs, local struggles over resources had been increasingly framed in terms of zero-sum ethnic competition.[53] The results of a border referendum in 2004, which saw many districts being transferred to Oromia, had always been disputed by Abdi Illey and his allies. More recently, the federal model's dangers had been magnified by the rapid expansion of regional security forces: since 2009, the Somali region had boasted a 40,000-strong "*Liyu*" (special police) force, answerable primarily to the regional president rather than the federal authorities. Though the *Liyu* had been established for the special purpose of waging a counter-insurgency campaign against separatist rebels in the Somali region in the late 2000s, by 2017 Oromia and other regions had followed suit by building up sizeable forces of their own.[54] Like the Somali "*Liyu*", these were much better trained for war than for ordinary policing, so much so that they were becoming a clear threat to the federal order. Ethiopia's regions had the constitutional right to their own police forces, after all, but not their own paramilitaries. Tensions between regions now posed a significant threat to the federation as a whole. The Somali regional ruling party was not formally part of the EPRDF: like its equivalents in other lowland regions, it was merely 'allied' to the ruling coalition. But in practice its leader, Abdi Illey, was no bystander to its internal frictions. In fact, he was widely understood to be especially close to the TPLF, not least since he owed his position ultimately to Meles. There was certainly no love lost between him and the OPDO.

What is rather less clear is whether he was really doing the TPLF's bidding by launching the border war against Oromia in 2017. It wasn't always obvious, after all, why TPLF strategists in Addis Ababa would pursue a scheme which, by so inflaming Oromo public opinion, was so likely to backfire. Somewhat more plausible, though, was the theory that Tigrayans in the federal military's Eastern Command had some hand in the violence. Given the command's close ties to the Somali state government, as well as, in some cases, its officers' considerable business interests in the region, they might have armed and encouraged the Somali forces. Here, at least, there was a plausible motive. Competition over the smuggling routes which ran through the borderlands (for the lucrative *khat* crop in particular, a trade largely controlled by Somalis), had long been implicated in local conflicts in Ethiopia's eastern badlands. The authorities in Oromia were also anxious to protect and expand their own business interests there. Team Lemma's very public crackdown on contraband passing through the region, and their insistence that additional border districts claimed by Oromia be promptly handed over to them, had recently raised the stakes significantly. Certainly, the Eastern Command didn't do much to stop the fighting, at least in the early days.

But Abiy has also been accused of taking advantage of the violence himself for political ends. "Abiy and his team used [the conflict], flaring it up to mobilise Oromos, taking similar counter actions in order to provoke more," argued a former Oromo officer intimate with both regional officials and activists. "Sustaining that conflict was important at the time, in order to mobilise the Oromo protests. So Abdi initiated it—but Abiy used it." When scores of Ethiopian Somalis were killed in a border town in December neither he, nor Lemma, would publicly condemn it. By the close of 2017, Team Lemma had successfully positioned themselves in the public mind as resolute defenders of Oromo interests against Tigrayan malfeasance.

Over the course of seventeen gruelling days that December the factious EPRDF leadership wrangled over their collective future. Hailemariam presented a paper on "deep renewal", arguing that the party was "lagging behind on democratisation, judicial reform, in respecting human rights, in fighting corruption and embezzlement". Each party responded with broad, albeit vague, commitments to accelerate democratisation. The TPLF proposed a change of leadership at the top, over a gradual timeframe, and pressed the OPDO and the ANDM to sort out their querulous regions and wayward rank-and-file. Most concretely, a decision was reached to release some political prisoners, although with fierce disagreements over who should make the cut. Abiy wanted the most high-profile ones— among them Ginbot 7's Andargachew Tsige—to be the priority. Many in the TPLF objected.[55] According to Hailemariam, there was also a tentative agreement to look again at the 1995 constitution.

Shortly after the meeting concluded, the prime minister announced that the government would release and pardon many of the thousands of political prisoners it held, as part of the twelve-point reform plan which the coalition had finally agreed on. Ethiopia's most notorious torture chamber, Maekelawi, was to be turned into a museum. He also promised a new and genuine commitment to "widen the democratic space".

But it wouldn't be enough to contain the protests, which erupted once again in Oromia just days later. This time the active participation of OPDO bureaucrats was as blatant as it was ubiquitous, and government offices were paralysed. On 15 February 2018, Hailemariam resigned—the first time in modern Ethiopian history that a leader had left office voluntarily. He later told me that he had been so frustrated with the job that he had been thinking about quitting for almost two years. The following day the government declared a state of emergency once again. Abiy, though he had formally supported the decision, was anxious not to alienate his Oromo base. On the day of the vote in parliament to approve it, he was nowhere to be found.

* * *

Abiy's elevation to the chair of the EPRDF, and thus to the Prime Minister's Office, came in hindsight to look almost pre-ordained. The internal rot, six years after Meles's death, was so advanced, and the EPRDF so unpopular, that it would later become hard to see how it could ever have been any other way. Abiy's planning, so apparently meticulous as it was, made him seem like a far-seeing chess-player, moves ahead of his opponents.

But it could have gone other ways. Lemma, after all, was by far the more popular politician of the two at the time. Fortunately for Abiy, however, the state president was a member of the Oromia regional council, not an MP in the federal parliament, so it would have required a time-consuming special by-election before he could become prime minister. Weeks, if not months, before Hailemariam's resignation, the OPDO leadership had agreed that he wouldn't run. Some later claimed it was Abadula, the godfather of the OPDO, who ultimately made the call.

Yet even after Lemma had dropped out there were plausible alternative candidates to Abiy: Workneh Gebeyehu, for instance, Girma Birru—an OPDO old hand who had long harboured prime ministerial ambitions—

or, for a time the most likely candidate, Abadula himself. Compared to all three, Abiy was a far riskier proposition: due to Teklebrhan's testimony he was distrusted by the TPLF and by the federal security establishment. What was more, he lacked popular support among the Oromo diaspora. At least twice in the autumn of 2017 Abiy visited America, partly to visit his family in Denver, but also to lobby influential members of the overseas opposition to back him instead of Lemma, still much their favoured option. "He was in Denver and on the phone non-stop, campaigning and petitioning us," recalled an influential Oromo activist who spoke to the future prime minister for the first time then. Yet not everyone there found his case convincing. "Abiy demonstrated a startling lack of appreciation for the complexity of transition politics," Jawar later wrote of his first meetings with Abiy in America. "I feared that [his] inexperience, excessive personal ambition and lack of appreciation of Ethiopia's complex politics and the required transitional leadership would imperil not only the democratic transition, but also the delicate politics and even the survival of our divided country as it entered its most precarious phase."[56]

Given this it is something of a wonder that Abiy came from behind to ultimately secure his party's nomination. Some have suggested, in part because he was spending so much time in America, that his rise had been somehow engineered by Washington. There is little evidence for this: Abiy was as unknown among Western diplomats at this time as he was among Ethiopians. But it was true that both he and Lemma had reached out to US powerbrokers. In particular, they were in touch with Senator Jim Inhofe, an eccentric Republican Evangelical who had adopted an Ethiopian child and approached America's foreign policy in Africa with the fervour of a colonial missionary. It appears that Inhofe knew a fellow traveller when he saw one, and he had kept in touch with Abiy ever since a meeting in 2016 at a so-called 'leaders' breakfast' of the kind often organised by powerful Evangelical groups in Washington. In subsequent calls and meetings, which on occasion involved Lemma, Hailemariam and Abadula, the pair would pray together. Inhofe would later describe Abiy as the "most highly educated Prime Minister in the history of the continent" on the floor of the Senate.

Established ties to a senior Evangelical Republican would be a boon for Abiy when Donald Trump entered the White House in January 2017, and appointed Inhofe's fellow Evangelical, Mike Pompeo, as his Secretary of State. Christian allies in Washington would also be useful given the widespread misapprehension among Western policymakers at the time which equated Oromo nationalism with Islamic extremism. But Inhofe's endorsement likely had no influence at all on the outcome of the EPRDF's internal election process—a point worth emphasising given the subsequent proliferation of conspiracy theories attributing extraordinary power to American officials over Ethiopian politics. Nor would the presumed support of Donald Yamamoto, the acting Assistant Secretary of State of African Affairs and a former US ambassador in Addis Ababa, who had met with the Oromo diaspora in Minneapolis around this time and was later accused by Abiy's critics of helping to parachute him into the top job, have mattered much. If Abiy was unfit for the EPRDF's highest office, as many would later argue, then the coalition had nobody but itself it could honestly blame.

Many insiders have therefore singled out Lemma for special culpability. "Abiy manipulated him," recalled one. "Lemma is the one who ruined everything." In the weeks and months before the vote, the two men were almost inseparable, praying and working out in the gym together each morning, and, for a while, even living under the same roof in Lemma's home in central Addis Ababa. "Abiy started managing access to Lemma," recalled another Oromo insider friendly with both men at the time. "He was controlling his schedule." According to some of their colleagues, Abiy now used his influence and proximity to turn Lemma against Abadula, persuading him that the former OPDO chairman was too close to the TPLF to be trusted. Assuring friends he would keep Abiy on a tight leash, it was Lemma who then organised an urgent meeting of the OPDO's central committee on 22 February, and urged his colleagues to endorse his deputy for the job.[57] "This was a huge risk," said a member of the OPDO central committee, "but we were ready to gamble."[58]

But Lemma was not solely responsible. Abadula, after all, was himself well-placed to stop Abiy if he had wanted. "Abadula had a much more powerful network in the OPDO than Lemma," Milkessa Midega, a close ally of Lemma, later argued. "But Abiy had Abadula's support to be the prime minister of Ethiopia." The TPLF, too, might have done things differently to alter the outcome. When it came to the vote inside the EPRDF council, the TPLF nominated as an alternative to Abiy the SEPDM's Shiferaw Shigute, a hardline southerner dismissed even by the mild-mannered Hailemariam as the TPLF's "servant". "We all expected the TPLF to nominate Abadula," recalled an Oromo insider close to the former regional president. Had they done so the OPDO vote might have then splintered. "But the TPLF were arrogant and ignorant. They wanted a servant. And nobody was going to vote for Shiferaw."

Abiy would later describe the tortuous deliberations inside the central committee as a week of "stress never before seen in the history of the EPRDF."[59] By this point the gloves had been thrown well and truly off, the old Leninist party principle of 'democratic centralism', which for so many years had kept internal disagreements in check, consigned firmly to the dustbin. During a series of furious private sessions, Abiy's opponents launched a fusillade of criticism—accusing him of, among other things, populism, neoliberalism, incompetence and corruption. The harsh, personalised character of the attacks evidently left a mark on him, feeding resentments and, perhaps, a desire for revenge. Getachew Assefa reportedly told Abiy bluntly he didn't deserve the role.[60] The spy chief would soon become one of the first Tigrayan heavyweights to be shown the door.

The final vote, which took place on 27 March, came down to the wire.[61] For the first time, and with a real sense of novelty, Ethiopians everywhere found themselves glued to their smartphones and their televisions, anxiously awaiting the result of an unprecedentedly competitive party election. The outcome, when it emerged, was even more historic. Abiy won the backing of 108 of his colleagues, from a roughly 170-member council, with just 59 for Shiferaw, his closest rival. Crucially, Demeke Mekonnen, the Amhara candidate—informed by colleagues that he risked losing his position as deputy prime minister if he lost—had withdrawn at the last moment, opening the door for Abiy to clean up the ANDM's votes. The southern bloc split, with some, including Hailemariam, plumping for Abiy instead of their own candidate. And although the majority of the TPLF supported Shiferaw, some insiders reckoned that even a few of its delegates had supported Abiy.[62] It was, in the end, a decisive victory, which showed not just how much the influence of the EPRDF's founding generation had waned, but also the true extent of the coalition's fracturing. Abiy, for all his scheming, had been luckier than he would later admit. The EPRDF had shown itself to be surprisingly vulnerable to capture.

* * *

Exactly why Abiy's candidacy offended so many of his colleagues was not always transparent to observers at the time. Many wrongly imagined that he was more establishment-friendly than Lemma, on account of his time at INSA and his more moderate-sounding Oromo nationalism. But in reality, much of the TPLF and heavyweights like the ANDM's Bereket Simon would have preferred Abiy's former boss. Lemma is "much more predictable", Getachew Reda, the future interim president of Tigray, later told me. On top of the murky stain of his time at INSA, Abiy's self-promoting behaviour raised hackles in a coalition whose culture stressed the collective before the individual. In the months before his election, his public relations operation had gone into overdrive: a Facebook page called "*Sewyew*" ("The Man") was launched to boost his online profile, while a hastily created Wikipedia page described him as a multilingual fitness aficionado with a passion for philosophy.[63] In a strange English-language interview on OBN broadcast a few weeks earlier he gave answers to questions about his geopolitical outlook which had been lifted almost verbatim from an interview with Henry Kissinger in *The Atlantic*, and from an essay in the *New Statesman* by the British comedian Russell Brand.[64] "Abiy was always online, mobilising the public behind him," recalled a close OPDO colleague. Sebhat Nega, the TPLF's most venerated living founder, later claimed that the young hopeful announced in the run-up to the vote that he was qualified not just to be Ethiopia's prime minister, but even the secretary-general of the UN.[65] "He's un-EPRDFite," noted a well-connected political analyst in Addis Ababa at the time. "In every respect he's an anomaly for the party."

In the end, though, the TPLF stood aside for Abiy despite their misgivings. Given its history as a liberation movement which had come to power by the barrel of the gun, this was to the front's credit: no other former liberation army in post-independence Africa had ever stepped aside like this. By some accounts, Getachew Assefa had asked General Samora Yunis to intervene to stop Abiy—a military takeover, in effect. But the Tigrayan head of the army, who had known Abiy for many years, was said to have refused. What transpired instead was, from one angle, a bloodless palace coup; from another, a negotiated climb down from the pinnacle of power for the TPLF. In any case, a relatively smooth transfer of power, between generations and between ethnicities, had seemingly been assured. Were it so it would have been the very first of its kind in modern Ethiopian history.

PART TWO

REFORM

7

ABIYMANIA

THE HONEYMOON WHIRLWIND

Little more than a year later, the new prime minister was to be found planting a tree in the grounds of his palace with Francis Fukuyama. The American political scientist—liberal democracy's intellectual standard bearer and populariser of the infamous 1990s phrase, 'the end of history'—was in town for a conference in the newly unveiled Hyatt Regency Hotel organised by an American liberal think-tank. Earlier that afternoon he had delivered a keynote address in which he criticised Ethiopia's 'developmental state' and appealed to democracy as the only salve for the country's predicaments. Soon after he met with Abiy for a tour of his glossily refurbished office.

Abiy understood well the symbolism of a friendly encounter with the prophet of Western liberalism. It was July 2019 and his administration's reformist zeal was already faltering, buffeted by accusations—from all sides—of autocratic drift and messianic incompetence. The prime minister was keen to reboot his democratic bona fides. "Over the years, I've seen a lot of people that have gotten really good at talking to Westerners, because they know exactly how to hit all the right buttons," Fukuyama later recalled. "He was certainly doing that in his conversation with me. Was he sincere? I have no idea. But he said the right words."

As he typically did in meetings with prominent Westerners, Abiy reiterated the importance of upholding the constitution and the rule of law. When pressed on the matter of the upcoming election, which, though scheduled for 2020, was widely expected to be delayed, Abiy reassured Fukuyama that there was a constitutional deadline he was determined not to miss. In a disarming touch, he also brought out a copy of Fukuyama's 1996 book, *Trust: The Social Virtues and the Creation of Prosperity*, describing it—in a shrewd display of flattery—as his "bible" which he continued to rely on.

The rest of the conversation was otherwise unremarkable, Fukuyama recalled. But then, as it drew to a close, Abiy surprised his guest by asking him whether he ever practised prayer. When Fukuyama replied that he didn't, though he and his wife were both Christians, Abiy appeared suddenly animated. "He went into this long riff about how important prayer was, and then talked a lot about the time he spent in the United States, and how his family had absorbed a lot of American religious and political values there, and so forth," remembered Fukuyama. Soon afterwards the meeting ended, and they moved outside to make a contribution to the prime minister's lofty goal of planting four billion trees in a single year.

* * *

It can be easy to forget, looking back, the power of the spell Abiy briefly cast over Ethiopia and its Western allies. For a few heady, almost delirious months his ascendance seemed to many as though it were divinely ordained, the nation's collective deliverance from years of sacrifice and suffering. In his swearing-in speech, first drafted by a group of his closest Oromo colleagues and delivered to parliament, with his own final touches, on 2 April 2018, the new prime minister apologised for the government's killing of protesters and asked for "forgiveness from the bottom of my heart". He called for national unity and for talks with the opposition, urging for bridges to be built even with Eritrea. "For us, building democracy is today an existential matter," he intoned, "more than it is to any other country." He made no mention of either 'Revolutionary Democracy' or the 'developmental state'.

Ethiopians the country over clapped and cheered before their television screens. "He sounded like Obama," gushed a friend as we drove through the capital to the airport that day. In a juice bar in Adama, a city in Oromia, a middle-aged woman and her family watched the event underneath the large poster of the new prime minister she had pinned to the wall. "There is nobody on earth as happy as me," she said, a T-shirt with his face emblazoned on her chest. Far away in the distant south locals celebrated by slaughtering camels, cows and goats.[1] All around the world, teary-eyed diaspora sang and danced into the night. "I cannot even express how it felt," recalled Gennet Negussie, an Ethiopian in Washington close to Ginbot 7. "When he said 'Ethiopia' … well, that was it for everyone."

More than the policy content, much of which simply reaffirmed what the EPRDF had already announced, it was the way Abiy spoke, and the Amharic he deployed, that bewitched people. To outsiders he might have come across as a little stiff, swaying awkwardly at the lectern, with eyes pinned on his notes. But there was something more to his delivery that struck many Ethiopians: verses spoken with the steady timbre and stirring cadences of a church preacher; the gentle, heart-tugging vocabulary of an understated patriot.

He invoked the inclusive spirit of *Ethiopiawinet* and the Battle of Adwa, the equal contribution of all Ethiopia's ethnic groups; the blood of Amharas, Tigrayans and Oromos, all intermingling in the nation's soil. "We are Ethiopians when we live; when we die, we become Ethiopia," he said, before thanking his wife and his mother, who, he added, represented all Ethiopian mothers. He thanked her for the prophecy she had told him as a boy: that he was always destined to be standing where he was that day. And then, as though an incantation, he delivered his final, once unutterable, words: "God bless Ethiopia, and its people". Like a river breaking its banks, across the country emotion burst forth. One of Abiy's future government appointees, Abebe Abebayehu, told friends afterwards this was the moment he felt that his prayers had finally been answered.

Abiy soon embarked on a whirlwind national tour, welcomed in state capitals from Mekelle to Bahir Dar to Jigjiga by seas of well-wishers and tearful supporters. At mass rallies and town-hall meetings he cut a radically different pose to that of his two most recent predecessors, hugging his fellow politicians, taking selfies with fans, and presenting himself as a clean break from the past. He insisted he would be a friend and ally to the Oromo youth, telling a cheering crowd in Ambo, the movement's epicentre, that the *Qeerroos* were the "shield of the Oromo people", colleagues to work "hand-in-hand" with.[2] It would be in Ambo, he proclaimed, where one day his government would "build the statue of our liberty, our New York." A few months later he was reported to have sold his watch for 5m birr (about $155,000) to kick-start development there.[3]

Even in Mekelle, the Tigrayan capital, the mood was bright. Among some Tigrayans in these early days there was hope that Abiy's ascendance might spell the end of their demonisation, opening a new era in which they were no longer assumed to be the shadowy hand behind every friction, conspiracy or wrongdoing. In the upbeat audience that welcomed him to the city's Martyr's Hall that month, Abiy sat comfortably beside Debretsion Gebremichael, the new regional president; dusting off his

Tigrinya, he flattered the attendees that Tigray was "the motor that runs Ethiopia". At one point he even appeared to dismiss the dispute with Amhara over the Wolkait district as no more than the concoction of out-of-touch diaspora activists.[4]

At first it seemed as though Abiy's contribution to Ethiopia's public discourse might be constructive and lasting. Repeatedly, he appealed for a more tolerant and inclusive political culture, one which did away with the fraught and divisive language of the student movement for a gentler and less exclusionary alternative. Out went some of the worst of the EPRDF's jargon: 'enemies of peace', 'narrow nationalists', 'chauvinists'. Political opponents, the prime minister said, should be seen as "*tefokakariwoch*" (competitors) not "*tekawamiwoch*" (antagonists). "*Andinet*" (unity or assimilation), he indicated, should be reframed as "*medemer*" (synergy or interconnectedness); political change should be seen as "*tehadiso*" (reform) not "*abiyot*" (revolution).

He also seemed, in those days, attuned to the limits of his powers and the dangers of over-inflating expectations. Everywhere he went he was presented with lists of demands and catalogues of grievances: an industrial park here, a contested territory there. But rarely, in truly messianic style, did he present himself as the singular solution or the utopia as imminent. "I am just a son of an ordinary farmer, not a God," he said on one occasion;[5] "Rome was not built overnight," on another.[6] The true measure of leadership, he observed, was not indispensability but simply being able to deliver "qualified successors and make herself or himself redundant."[7] To this end he promised to amend the constitution and introduce term limits for his position. He also pledged to organise a free and fair election and to step down if he lost it. Colleagues were assured in private that he would stay in power for two terms—ten years—maximum.

There were more concrete actions, too, which seemed to give substance to the lofty oratory. Unrestricted internet was swiftly restored, and the state of emergency lifted two months early. Hundreds of websites, blogs and satellite TV channels were unblocked, with even OMN and ESAT invited to come home and set up shop in the capital. Soon, for the first time in thirteen years, there were no journalists in prison; by the following March no fewer than twenty-three publications and six privately owned satellite channels had been granted licences.[8] Such was the climate of free expression in these early months that for a brief while even open political satire, some of which made direct fun of the prime minister himself, was given almost free rein.[9]

Meanwhile, a blanket amnesty was issued for the EPRDF's political opponents, allowing for the return of all those exiled from Ethiopia over the past three decades. The names of rebel groups—the OLF, Ginbot 7 and more—were struck off the terrorist list, while the steady release of political prisoners begun by Hailemariam was accelerated, with even the charges and death sentence facing the controversial Ginbot 7 co-founder and British citizen, Andargachew Tsige, abruptly dropped. Like flowers in spring, the once-banned colours, symbols, and flags of opposition movements blossomed everywhere. All over the streets of Addis Ababa and Amhara could be seen the starless tricolour of Ethiopia's former imperial and Orthodox flag—or occasionally, and rather more troublingly, the face of Mengistu on T-shirts and bumper stickers. Across Oromia, it was the red and green of the OLF.

Rhetorically, at least, reconciliation and forgiveness were now the order of the day. Ethiopia's Orthodox church had been riven since the fall of the Derg between those loyal to a synod-in-exile, led by its former Amhara patriarch, and those allied to the Tigrayan patriarch installed in Addis Ababa when the EPRDF took power. Abiy swiftly set about bridging the divide. In what would count among his most politically consequential early moves, he brought the exiled patriarch, Abune Merkorios, back to Addis Ababa, to govern alongside Abune Mathias until his death in 2021, a feat of mediation which won him the Church's special recognition. Likewise, he helped to reunite the country's two main Muslim factions and, the following year, brought together the various Pente churches to form a single council.[10] (In 2023, he would do so again, forcefully intervening in the affairs of the Pente churches so as to reconcile their bickering factions.) Unlike the EPRDF, whose meddling in religion was often seen as a form of divide-and-rule, Abiy seemed to be taking the opposite approach, promoting religious unity as a tool for consolidating his own authority.[11] In a country as devout as Ethiopia there were few more powerful resources than faith for an ambitious politician to draw on.

Meanwhile, former Derg officials, many with blood on their hands, were being welcomed back. To the dismay of many Ethiopians old enough to remember the days of the Red Terror, a few were granted an audience with the prime minister. In what would turn out to be one of his more ill-judged early ventures, Abiy even asked his predecessor, Hailemariam, to pay a visit to Zimbabwe's capital, Harare, where the former Derg dictator Mengistu Hailemariam had lived in disgraced exile ever since his overthrow in 1991. (Following an outcry, a photo of the two former leaders smiling next to each other was removed from Hailemariam's Facebook page and plans to invite Mengistu back home were hastily dropped.) Such missteps notwithstanding, Ethiopians were soon speaking of "our third revolution", depicting what was already commonly known in Amharic as "*yelewutu gizé*" (the change), and among outsiders as the "transition", as the latest in a string of historical pivots which turned first in 1974 and then again in 1991. Pentecostal churches, meanwhile, declared that Abiy had been sent by God—for his name alluded to the Easter fasting season, and he had risen to power during Lent. So too did senior government officials: both Gedion Timothewos, a widely respected constitutional lawyer who would later become Abiy's justice minister, and even Hailemariam himself, personally told me so.[12] One survey that summer found Abiy's approval rating to be more than 90 percent. As a flurry of Abiy-themed titles hit the bookshelves, young boys on the streets hawked stickers, posters and T-shirts with his face on them. All sold like hotcakes: a street seller told me he had peddled 1,500 Abiy T-shirts in a single day that June. One best-selling book, *Moses*, compared the prime minister to the prophet.[13]

* * *

The rest of the world was catching 'Abiymania' too. In August 2018, the prime minister embarked on a three-city tour of the diaspora in America, visiting Washington, Los Angeles, and Minneapolis in the hope of mending bridges and persuading some of them to return to Ethiopia and invest there. Wherever Abiy went he was welcomed like a rockstar. A crowd of 20,000 people filled out the Walter E. Washington Convention Center, which was bedecked in red, yellow and green, many of them travelling hundreds of miles just to see him.[14] During the public ceremony, which was entitled simply "*Medemer*", the prime minister called one of ESAT's most prominent faces, Tamagn Beyene, onto the stage and embraced him. The audience was ecstatic; some were even seen falling to the floor to kiss his feet. "It was euphoric," recalled Tewodros Tsegaye, a Tigrayan journalist in Washington. "The intellectuals, who were meant to analyse and ask him questions there, were not using their brains. They just were saying, 'Hail Abiy'."

Not everyone was so happy. Indeed, some of the first signs of real tension were evident in Abiy's interactions with the diaspora he encountered in America, and in particular among some of the Oromos and Tigrayans. "He was not interested in serious deliberation," recalled Jawar, who met with the prime minister privately in Minneapolis after the rally. The Oromo activist had laid out a set of concerns he had with the trajectory of the transition, including its apparent lack of a clear road map, which Abiy had breezily brushed away. "He just wanted us to move on," Jawar later wrote.[15]

Some of those Abiy hoped would join his administration were also wary. One high-profile businessperson in Washington, who refused Abiy's offer of a plum ministerial post citing a lack of experience in Ethiopian politics, found the prime minister took the rejection as a personal affront, even suggesting that to refuse his offer was a mark of cowardice. "He accused us diaspora of not thinking about their country," the would-be minister later recounted. "He said he didn't even have $1,000 in his savings account but, like me, he also had young children. I said he didn't know me well enough to talk to me like that."

To most eyes, though, the trip was a triumph. In Washington, Abiy met with Neamin Zeleke, Berhanu Nega and other Ginbot 7 colleagues, successfully winning them over to his side. "He was so bold and courageous to admit the wrongs of the regime," Neamin told me. "That's why, even before we met, we had decided to declare a unilateral ceasefire." The group agreed they would return to Addis Ababa with their fighters in Eritrea at the earliest opportunity. (They declined, though, Abiy's offer to return with him on the same flight.)

High-profile Oromos began rushing home, too, where they were put up in Addis Ababa's top international hotels on the government's dime. Mohammed Ademo, who was so enthused with the changes he agreed to accompany Abiy on his America trip as an informal advisor, wrote in *Al Jazeera* that he had "never been more hopeful about Ethiopia's prospects."[16] Hassen Hussein, a former OLF fighter who was then a leader of the Oromo Democratic Front, another opposition party, told me at the time that he had not a single reservation about either Abiy or Lemma. His colleague, former OLF chairman Lencho Lata, likewise informed me with a satisfied sigh that he could finally retire from politics and spend his remaining days at home and in peace. Even Jawar, upon his triumphant homecoming later that August, put doubts aside and endorsed Abiy at a grand welcoming ceremony in Addis Ababa. In a final symbolic gesture, he handed his MacBook to Lemma on the stage, as if to formally confer ownership of the Oromo struggle to the OPDO duo.

But perhaps nowhere was the collective entrancement more acute than in Western embassies and capitals. The prime minister's liberal democratic rhetoric; his admission in June that the government's violence and human rights violations could be likened to terrorism; his appointment of a gender-equal cabinet and a respected elder stateswoman, Sahle-Work Zewde, as president; his sensible, technocratic-seeming pragmatism—all played marvellously with Western audiences. "It was like they were meeting a rockstar," said a British aid official, recalling the occasions when government ministers would visit Ethiopia. "The joke among the diplomats was 'I hope my minister doesn't ask him for an autograph'."

Michael Raynor, America's wide-eyed ambassador at the time, stood out as the most unabashed cheerleader among the Western diplomatic corps—declaring Abiy to be the "real deal" among colleagues while pointedly refusing to engage at all with any of the prime minister's political rivals. One senior embassy colleague of Raynor told me at the time that the new Ethiopian leadership consisted of "individuals who have service as the driving force in their work and lives". This core principle, the colleague claimed, "keeps this group of leaders focused on what they are there to achieve, versus the power to be gained." Raynor later told a European counterpart in Addis Ababa that Abiy was the "most pro-West leader we're going to get."

Quite what the breezy assessments were based on, given how little Western diplomats actually knew about either Abiy or his colleagues before they came to power, was never clear. But in the absence of firm direction from Washington in the Trump years—the then National Security Advisor, John Bolton, told me he doubted the president had even read his own administration's Africa strategy—the embassy in Addis Ababa was nonetheless given a free hand to cultivate Abiy as it saw fit. In its internal strategy document of 2018, the embassy cheered Abiy's "strongly Western orientation" and argued that his administration represented a "once-in-a-generation opportunity to advance US interests in the region".[17] In practice, America's geostrategic interest as defined by the Trump administration amounted to little more than pulling Ethiopia out of China's orbit. By assuring Washington that Abiy could be an essential African ally for its deepening cold war with Beijing, and with Abiy having signalled privately to the Americans that he regarded the Chinese Communist Party as "godless", Raynor was able to shepherd a flood of development funding in the prime minister's direction.[18] Between 2018 and 2023 America ploughed more than $4.1 billion in aid into Ethiopia, including more than $600 million specifically to support democratic and economic reforms.[19] The embassy drew up plans to embed advisors in Ethiopian government ministries.[20]

The international media was often just as uncritical. In the first few months comparisons of Abiy in the Western press ranged from Barack Obama, Emmanuel Macron and Justin Trudeau to Nelson Mandela, Mikhail Gorbachev and even Che Guevara.[21] It didn't seem to matter that the prime minister assiduously avoided media scrutiny, refusing—with just one exception—to give press conferences, and almost never granting interviews.[22] Within little more than a year in office the prime minister was anointed one of *Time*'s 100 Most Influential People, *Foreign Policy*'s 100 Global Thinkers, as well as laureate of the UNESCO Peace Prize—all before the Nobel Prize. In 2019, the *Financial Times* splashed Abiy on the cover under the headline "Africa's new talisman".[23]

Abiy was himself visibly anxious for Western endorsements, and actively sought to paint himself as a Westerniser at odds with the more China-friendly TPLF. In a star turn at the World Economic Forum in Davos, he informed his audience—flipping on its head the argument which Meles had made to the World Economic Forum just seven years earlier—that it was "not possible to sustain economic growth without democracy. We believe democracy and development are interlinked." With a flash of his winning smile, Abiy boasted that Ethiopia was now one of the few countries in Africa not to imprison reporters. The audience broke into rapturous applause.[24]

He could be extraordinarily charming. When high-profile foreign visitors arrived in Addis Ababa, the prime minister would often meet them at the airport in his own 4x4, taking the steering wheel himself and driving them through the city for a guided tour of the palace and its surroundings. Among those given the red-carpet treatment by Abiy in this way was David Beasley, a former Republican governor of South Carolina—and fellow Pentecostal Christian—who was then chief of the UN's World Food Programme. The two had known each other for about a decade through the National Prayer Breakfast, an influential networking event in Washington run by the Fellowship Foundation, a secretive Christian outfit known for its promotion of anti-LGBT activism both in Congress and in Africa. Abiy and his wife were so friendly with Beasley, who would later describe the Ethiopian prime minister to colleagues as a "brother in Christ", that he had even been to stay on the WFP chief's farm in South Carolina.

Another well-connected admirer was former British prime minister Tony Blair, whose non-profit organisation, the Tony Blair Institute for Global Change, would be closely involved in steering some of the government's liberalising reforms. "This is a remarkable leader," Blair told an audience in Addis Ababa in 2018. "He has the energy. He has the commitment. He has a real sense of purpose. He's got a good mind, but most important of all he's got a good heart… if the future of Ethiopia is in your hands, sir, I'm confident about its future."[25]

The list went on. France's new president, Macron, hailed the prime minister's reforms as "courageous" and promised to bankroll his plans to rebuild Ethiopia's navy.[26] Achim Steiner, the Brazilian chief of the UN Development Programme, emerged from a meeting with the prime minister in 2018 "gushing", recalled a UN colleague, and insisted that UNDP support his reforms "no matter what." Patrick Gaspard, a Democrat politician close to Obama and then president of the Open Society Foundation, a progressive NGO founded by the Hungarian billionaire George Soros, chatted frequently with Abiy over WhatsApp, quickly committing the OSF to spend millions of dollars in support of his legal and justice reforms.

"He's so charismatic that after about three and a half hours I had to stop myself and think: 'you can't just buy whatever this guy is selling'," said an aide to one of Abiy's favoured American guests. "He'd take me to one side, hold my hand … it was kind of shocking, actually, the way he stops talking to your boss and gives you his undivided attention."

Abiy appears to have been genuinely enamoured with the West, and in particular America. In *The Stirrup and the Throne* in 2016, he had described Ethiopia's biggest donor as the "pioneer" of freedom as well as religious and even racial "tolerance".[27] His children, moreover, had been thoroughly assimilated by this time, and on returning to Ethiopia had been sent to the American school in Addis Ababa. The prime minister would later tell Joe Biden, Trump's successor, what he had previously told friends and colleagues: that he wanted his daughters to be educated in the US. Jon Lee Anderson, a reporter for the *New Yorker* who was one of only two foreign journalists to be granted a proper interview with the prime minister in these years, would later be struck by how Abiy became most animated when talking about America and all the time he had spent there.[28] He was, Abiy told Anderson, a "Bay Area kind of guy", and Americans, he insisted, "the most generous people in the world".

"I kept thinking he's more American than he is African," recalled Anderson, who was granted several days in the prime minister's company in 2022. "In the sense of professing to ignore ethnicity, and, of course, in his repeated demonstrations or protestations of affection for America.

He kept talking about how his wife had been in Section Eight housing, and how much he appreciated that. He was quite sophisticated, a sort of seamless, globalised character."

Abiy also began to remodel his own administration along distinctly American lines. He brought in a Chief-of-Staff and a Press Secretary, two West Wing concepts with no real precedent in Ethiopia. The logo of the Prime Minister's Office was redesigned to look similar to that of the White House, while NISS's emblem was revamped to resemble the CIA's.[29] For his wife, Zinash, he established (without parliamentary approval) an Office of the First Lady. An official photographer—another innovation—was hired to shadow him wherever he went.

Meanwhile, old opponents of the EPRDF with public profiles in the West were parachuted into some of the key institutions Abiy said he wanted to reform. One of those was Daniel Bekele, a human rights lawyer with a doctorate from Oxford who had been imprisoned following the 2005 election violence. After several years in top jobs at both Human Rights Watch and Amnesty International, he was plucked from his comfortable life in New York to head the Ethiopian Human Rights Commission. Another was Birtukan Mideksa, a top CUD politician and judge whose sentencing to life imprisonment after the 2005 election had for a while made her the international face of the Ethiopian opposition. After her release in 2007 she had moved to America, where she received a master's degree from Harvard and worked in Washington for the National Endowment for Democracy. Disregarding the process of public consultation which was supposed to be required for such an appointment, Abiy handpicked her to lead the electoral board.

Offices of the new administration were also being staffed by a bevy of Western-educated officials and advisors. Some came on secondment from the World Bank or the Tony Blair Institute. Others had their salaries paid by the UN. Among these youthful 'technocrats', as they were known—and which included Mamo Mihretu, a thirty-something graduate of Harvard's Kennedy School and World Bank staffer who would later become governor of the central bank—were several who were already in Abiy's and Lemma's social orbit, either as members of the same churches, or as fellow frequenters of the pricey Tilla Spa and Fitness club, situated down the road from the UN's headquarters in central Addis Ababa. Insiders dubbed the new team the "Tilla Administration".

It was Western-friendly faces like these who were to smooth the way for Abiy's keen engagement with the IMF and the World Bank, and to deliver the substance of the economic reform agenda which he first unveiled two months after taking office. That plan, as Abiy first announced it, would see the government opening state-owned telecoms, electricity and logistics, as well as the highly profitable national airline, to foreign investors for the first time. It would also allow for the full or partial privatisation of railways, ailing sugar factories, industrial parks, hotels and some manufacturing firms. Ethiopia's application to the World Trade Organization, long stalled due to disagreements over telecoms and financial liberalisation, among others, was to be revived. So-called 'non-concessional' borrowing, meanwhile, was to be put on hold entirely, with restrictions on private banks—such as those which forced them to buy government bonds in order to finance public infrastructure—to be relaxed so that, in theory, private sector investment might at last, in the technical jargon, 'crowd in'. Long-dormant plans to establish Ethiopia's first stock exchange, once dismissed by Meles as a form of legalised gambling, were also to be sped up. The Ethiopian birr was to be aggressively devalued and, eventually, floated.

Gone was the Meles-era suspicion of international financial institutions. Abiy now likened both the World Bank and the IMF to a "mother" because of their generous lending terms, and called on them to guide his government's "Homegrown Economic Reform Agenda"—so-named to counter allegations that it had been written to appease international financial institutions and investors.[30] Comprising a broad programme of market reforms, its goal was to ease the fiscal crisis and invigorate Ethiopia's struggling private sector. The IMF pitched in with a $3 billion loan (which was supposed to be spread over three years) to backstop the central bank's dwindling currency reserves. The World Bank offered $1.2 billion to support the reform efforts.[31] Though 'Abiynomics' retained the EPRDF's focus on industrialisation, it also incorporated the prime minister's pet enthusiasms for Ethiopia's tourism sector and, as would soon become particularly apparent, modish urban development.[32]

Adherents of the 'developmental state' were incensed, denouncing the changes as a neoliberal bonfire and the death of the Meles project. In a sharp break from EPRDF custom, the TPLF publicly criticised the decision, warning in a stinging statement that such "temporary solutions" were not the answer to Ethiopia's problems. But Western investors and many donors, by contrast, were thrilled. What little they had known about Abiy before then had inspired little enthusiasm. Team Lemma's efforts to get foreign factories in Oromia to outsource some of their supply chains to the *Qeerroos* had gone down badly, as had Abiy's first speech to business leaders during a banquet at the Sheraton Hotel, in which he stated the government would "remain in the business sector", while hectoring his audience for buying foreign cars during a foreign exchange crisis.[33] Now the mood among prospective foreign investors was buoyant. "Inbound emails are back," a British investor told me cheerily that June. "Last year was basically dead. It's like night and day compared to that now."

The Homegrown Economic Reform Agenda was not, as its critics often said, simply written by the IMF or American consultants in exchange for debt relief. Both did, however, have a strong influence on it, and there was ultimately not much in the programme for either to disagree with.[34] The Ethiopian officials involved in the draft undoubtedly did believe in the reforms they were pursuing, especially the general push to strengthen the country's struggling private sector. But in any case, even if some questioned the solutions on offer, very few contested that the strains in the economy which had been increasingly visible since the death of Meles had recently become much more urgent. Though Ethiopia's GDP was still growing, albeit more slowly, its foreign exchange reserves continued to shrink, with businesses frequently complaining of having to wait up to a year or even more to receive their allocation from the banks. Public debt, most of which was in foreign currency, had by 2018 hit almost 60 percent of GDP, with a servicing bill approaching an eye-watering $1.6 billion.[35] A spate of previously unheard-of defaults on Chinese loans had also started to ring alarm bells, while several local contractors complained that the government was failing to meet its obligations to them. In some places, factories lay idle simply because their owners could no longer import the raw materials.[36] Foreign direct investment, which had held up reasonably well in the early years of the Oromo protests despite attacks on foreign farms and factories, had fallen sharply since 2017.[37] Never before in the nearly two decades of its existence had Ethiopia's 'developmental state' been under such pressure on so many fronts. The essential question now was whether it would be possible to provide jobs and security for millions of frustrated young Ethiopians while at the same time shrinking or otherwise rewiring it.

Given this parlous inheritance, Abiy's early moves on the economy were arguably less ground-breaking than they were widely seen at the time. In fact, though he was largely credited—or blamed—for them, many of the headline announcements were the product of long-running internal debates dating back at least to the early Hailemarian years, if not earlier. The decision to dislodge the state from part of the economy's commanding heights, for instance, had been broadly agreed by the EPRDF leadership before Abiy took office. Because of recent government splurges on, among other things, multiple new football stadiums, limits to 'non-concessional' borrowing had been in place since 2016. Plans to liberalise the telecoms sector, meanwhile, and expose the state-monopoly Ethiopia Telecom to competition dated back well before that.[38] Even opening up the financial sector to foreign firms, long among the very reddest of the EPRDF's red lines, in part because its leaders feared chaotic bank runs of the sort more familiar to neighbouring Kenya, had been seriously considered even when Meles was still alive.[39] For the first few years, at least, Abiy himself didn't dare touch it; when he did, the initial reforms were fairly cautious.[40] Likewise, plans to partially privatise Ethiopian Airlines and the state-owned shipping and logistics corporation, once floated were put on pause or taken off the table indefinitely.

What was certainly novel, though, was the government's new rhetoric, and the iconoclastic enthusiasm with which the prime minister seemed to embrace the changes. In marked contrast to his predecessors, and even the market scepticism on show in his own 2016 book, Abiy now seemed distinctly at ease with the liberal tilt. It would soon become clear that he viewed free-market capitalism not as a necessary evil but as an aspirational endeavour, perhaps even a moral one, and an imperative were Ethiopia to move as close to America and the West as he intended. "My model is capitalism," he proudly told the *Financial Times* in 2019. "We need the private sector."[41] Nowhere was this more evident than in his willingness to initiate a debate on the state ownership of land, the most sacrosanct of the economic principles the EPRDF had inherited from the student movement. In 2022, Abiy mooted the eventual privatisation of urban plots, arguing that the existing system was riddled with corruption. (Ultimately, though, any such shift required a constitutional amendment, and was therefore postponed.[42]) "He's a marketeer, no question about it. He strongly believes in free markets. Limited government intervention. Private sector being the engine of growth," enthused Gabriel Negatu, a prominent Ethiopianist veteran of the World Bank who met with Abiy privately on occasion after he took office. "It's not a cliché—he genuinely believes that."

8

BRIDGE OF LOVE

ETHIOPIA, ERITREA AND THE TRIPARTITE ALLIANCE

The moment the pilot announced our descent, passengers broke into song and champagne corks whistled over my head. Like a wedding party held more than 30,000 feet in the sky, people danced in the aisles and scattered rose petals over their seats. Behind me a musician strummed away on a *masenqo* lute, his friends clapping and taking selfies on their camera phones. From the window, Asmara's golden, gridiron streets swam into view.

To my left was Asaminew Teshome, an automation engineer born in Asmara in 1978 who hadn't been back in thirty-four years. Next to him sat his elderly mother, impeccably attired in an embroidered white *tilfi*. "We stopped everything when we heard about this flight," Asaminew told me. To my right was Prophet Suraphel Demissie, a popular televangelist whose mother was born on the border between Ethiopia and Eritrea, and whose Ethiopian father had worked in the Eritrean port town of Assab. He had prayed and fasted for forty days, he told me, prophesying that peace between the two neighbours would come weeks before it did.[1] "It was my dream," Suraphel said that day, dressed to the nines in a slick white tuxedo. "I was expecting this all my life." As the plane touched down at Asmara Airport, he wept with joy.

Waved through immigration with no more than a stamp on their passport, Ethiopians flooded into Asmara to a delirious welcome. For the first time in years the city's cool mountain air echoed with the sound of Amharic, as long lost friends chatted away in restaurants and danced to Ethiopian music through the night. Getachew Demeba, who joined my flight in the hope that he might track down friends he had not seen in decades, strolled the streets proudly wearing the commemorative T-shirt which passengers had been given on board. "I talked to every single person

I met," he told me that night. "I didn't care about who he or she was. I used Amharic to say 'hello' to everyone, and they were all so happy." Thomas Tedros, a tour guide who came to the airport to watch the planes land, likened the feeling to a "second independence".

* * *

The surprise peace agreement signed by Abiy and Eritrea's president Isaias Afewerki on 8 July 2018 was an event quite unlike anything before it in the history of the Horn. Almost everyone, Ethiopian and Eritrean officials alike, seemed caught off guard by the speed of the diplomatic thaw. Even observers who had argued that the rise of a new generation of Ethiopian leaders, relatively distant from the TPLF leadership in both age and orientation, might alter Eritrea's calculations, were taken aback by Isaias's apparent willingness to forgo protracted negotiations over ostensibly intractable issues such as the delineation of the international border. It was as though the established assumptions which had governed regional politics ever since the 1998–2000 border war—that the contest between Addis Ababa and Asmara would always be zero-sum; that as long as Isaias was in office Eritrea would seek a weakened Ethiopia—had crumbled overnight. So swift was the shift that when Abiy first arrived in Asmara, greeted by the sight of Ethiopian flags fluttering across the city, an alarmed Eritrean woman called her father to ask if Ethiopia had just invaded. The notoriously aloof Eritrean president, for his part, seemed so taken by his new ally in Addis Ababa that he even took him to meet his grandchildren.

International phone calls between the two countries were restored within hours of the Ethiopian prime minister's arrival in Eritrea, meaning friends and families divided by the stand-off could at last speak, often for the first time in decades. "There is no border between Ethiopia and Eritrea," Abiy declared in a televised address. "Instead, we have built a bridge of love." Direct flights resumed less than two weeks later.[2]

Like the fall of the Berlin Wall, a border which had once seemed impermeable was reduced to a line on a map, a fiction from another era. Tens of thousands of young Eritreans, tasting freedom for the first time, rushed across it.[3] Border guards, for years under orders to shoot anyone fleeing the country, now did nothing to stop them. By the time the year was up, the UN Security Council had voted to lift its almost decade-long arms embargo on Eritrea. Both countries ceased support for each other's rebel movements, the OLF and Ginbot 7 included. Isaias, meanwhile, having declared the whole region to be "entering a new era", restored diplomatic ties with Somalia after fifteen years of animosity. Western diplomats enthused about the prospect of resolving Eritrea's long-standing border dispute with Djibouti. Abiy even mused aloud of uniting the Horn as a single country.[4]

Enemies turned friends; old scores forgotten. To veteran Isaias-watchers, it was barely conceivable. If Abiy was a rule-breaker, an opportunistic maverick whose strength lay in novelty and unpredictability, the Eritrean dictator was his exact inverse: an old hand with prejudices which were fixed, interests which were clear-cut, and methods which were time-worn. Where Abiy preached love, Isaias nurtured resentments. If Abiy styled himself as an optimistic visionary, who imagined that the whole Horn could be brought together as one through goodwill and free trade, Isaias saw a bear pit where there were no permanent friends. If Abiy really thought he could turn a page on the old ways, Isaias, by contrast, believed in the eternal law of might is right, whereby negotiations were for the weak, and arguments settled with arms.

There were, therefore, good reasons to doubt Isaias's sincerity in letting bygones be bygones. Those who knew him well knew a vindictive streak which had been evident almost his entire life. As a shy and awkward student in Asmara in the early 1960s, a former classmate recalled, an American physics teacher had handed him a particularly shoddy mark; the future president had walked calmly to the front of the class and slapped the stunned young man in the face.[5] Not long after that the Eritrean Liberation Front, the EPLF's forerunner, sent the aspiring guerrilla fighter—and Addis Ababa University dropout—to Mao Zedong's China for ideological training. There, in the furnace of the Cultural Revolution, Isaias "learnt all the wrong things," noted China's former ambassador to Eritrea.[6] As leader of the EPLF over the following decades, he treated anyone who dared challenge him with a ruthlessness which would make all but the most hard-bitten of revolutionaries quiver. Dissidents and competitors were denounced as spies and executed. Not even some of his oldest friends were spared.[7]

Unlike Meles, with whom he'd had a long and tempestuous relationship, question marks had always hovered over Isaias's ideological conviction. He had long been dogged by rumours that he once spied for both the CIA and Haile Selassie; though he had grown up in a village just outside Asmara, one of his uncles had been the governor of imperial Ethiopia's

Wollo province. Even Isaias's sternest principles, some later argued, were negotiable if they served to advance his own power. Years later, it was alleged that he had almost sold his colleagues out to the Derg at talks brokered by East Germany in 1978.[8]

When the Derg fell in 1991, it seemed as though the narrow cause of Eritrean independence might have also slipped from his mind; indeed, when the time came for a referendum, he had even appeared to waver.[9] After it was over, and with 99 percent of his fellow citizens having voted in favour of secession, he pondered aloud about eventual political reunion with the motherland.[10] Perhaps, some of his colleagues had begun to wonder, Isaias had never believed strongly in independence at all. Maybe, a few of them suggested, what he had always wanted was not the presidency of a small breakaway nation but rather the throne of Haile Selassie: in other words, unrivalled pre-eminence in the Horn. After all, even in the 1990s, Ethiopia had remained an empire in all but name. Perhaps the real travesty, to Isaias's mind, was that he was not the one who stood atop it. Three decades later, as his troops went to war again in Tigray, lingering questions like these, and doubts about his real motives in the region, would continue to play on many Eritrean and Ethiopian minds.

The Eritrean leader's celebrated opposition to Western imperialism was also, at times, more flexible than his supporters would later remember. When the American journalist Robert Kaplan met him in the bush in the 1980s, for instance, the future Eritrean president had portrayed himself as neither Marxist, nor Maoist, but as a pragmatist who would make a dependable American ally. In the early 2000s, in the wake of the September 11th attacks, and in the hope of boosting his regional standing, Isaias publicly backed America's invasion of Iraq and lobbied for an American military base to be established in Eritrea.[11] "I share the strategic view of the Americans in the region," he told Kaplan. "You need outside powers to keep order here. It may sound colonialist. I am only being realistic."[12]

But by the end of the twenty-first century's first decade, Isaias had retreated into embittered, increasingly booze-soaked isolation.[13] Ethiopia's stubborn refusal to accept the findings of the international boundary commission set up after the war, and the West's indifference, even complicity in this, had infuriated him—as it did many ordinary Eritreans no less. The EPLF's erstwhile vision of a democratic Eritrea had long since been discarded: elections planned for 2001 had been indefinitely postponed. Senior officials and long-standing colleagues had been purged, some left to rot in shipping containers in the desert. Foreign NGOs had been expelled; private media dismantled; local businesses seized. Anti-EPRDF rebel groups from Ethiopia, Ginbot 7 and the OLF included, were hosted, armed and trained on Isaias's dime.

Ever since the outbreak of hostilities in 1998, Eritrea had remained on a permanent war footing. In the years which followed, hundreds of thousands of Eritreans had been either conscripted to the army or into a system of compulsory national service. Originally set up in 1995 to rebuild the newly independent country, citizens were meant to serve in it for just eighteen months. But in 2002 Isaias had made the term indefinite—an arrangement the UN later likened to mass enslavement. Those who tried to escape risked being incarcerated for years in underground prisons.[14]

Over the following decade hundreds of thousands of Eritreans had fled the country. In 2009, Ethiopia backed by America persuaded the UN to impose an arms embargo—ostensibly to stop Asmara from providing support to Al-Shabaab, a Somali militant group also hostile to Addis Ababa. Isaias was stung; many ordinary Eritreans, among whom there was generally little love for either Isaias or the EPRDF, accused the West of double standards in singling out Eritrea as a uniquely bad actor in a region notorious for them. Asmara gradually curdled into being the most anti-American regime on the continent. By the middle of the 2010s, the country was widely, and unpopularly, known as "Africa's North Korea"—a paranoid hermit state frozen in time.[15] Even by the early 2020s there were no ATMs and no mobile internet. "Everything is seen through one glass," an Eritrean working for a foreign embassy in Asmara told me. "And that glass is called security."

For Isaias, who said barely a word in public about the peace deal after it was signed, everything, ultimately, seemed to come back to the TPLF. Not only did he blame its leaders for Eritrea's military humiliation in 2000; he also considered it a perennial existential threat. The animus was personal: Isaias had known the TPLF's leaders since the 1970s and was profoundly distrustful of them. He hated the fact that, despite the lead part played by him and the EPLF in overthrowing the Derg, the West in the 1990s treated Meles and the TPLF as the bigger players.[16] His own Tigrayan roots, on his mother's side, were also said to have been a source of embarrassment for him. But the hostility was also to some degree comprehensible. Many in the TPLF did genuinely believe Isaias's removal from power to be the sine qua non of regional peace and stability. A few, though they were unlikely to have ever been close to a majority, also harboured irredentist ambitions over Eritrean territory, and in particular its Red Sea coastline.

Isaias's fixation on the TPLF seems to have been at least in part ideological, too. He had never approved of ethnic federalism; nor, since the days of the student movement in which he, too, was a pivotal player, the particular interpretation of the 'national question' which had underpinned it. Eritreans, in the EPLF's account, had obviously been colonised—that was, after all, the theoretical basis for their independence bid. Tigrayans, Oromos and other Ethiopian ethnic groups, it was argued, hadn't been. Granting them all self-determination rights was, from this point of view, thus utterly wrong-headed. Since the 1990s, Isaias had rarely missed an opportunity to criticise Ethiopia's 1995 constitution—while refusing adamantly to implement Eritrea's own—and would often recall how he had warned Meles that federalism would ultimately prove devastating to the country's national unity.

Quite why such a prospect mattered to Isaias was never entirely clear: a weaker neighbour posed him, in theory, much less of a threat. Some, though, have argued that he feared the implications of a successful federal experiment for Eritrea's own territorial integrity. Despite the Eritrean government's stress on a single, monolithic national identity, born of a shared experience of Italian colonialism, the country also possessed several disaffected minority groups of its own, especially in the Muslim lowlands. Isaias might also have imagined that by fostering the growth of a strong Tigrayan identity, ethnic federalism would ultimately lead to the emergence of a 'Greater Tigray', powerful enough to swallow up parts of Eritrea itself. In any case, by the 2010s the destruction of the TPLF and ethnic federalism were, for Isaias, two sides of the same coin.

* * *

The first real attempts to mend bridges with Eritrea had begun not with Abiy but with his predecessor, Hailemariam Desalegn. Weakened by the protests in Oromia throughout 2015 and 2016, the EPRDF had been increasingly concerned by Eritrea's ongoing support for the Ethiopian opposition—which took the form not only of training and matériel for Ginbot 7 and the OLF, but of financial support for ESAT, too. Many in the coalition leadership were also frustrated by the conflict's drain on Ethiopia's resources, especially as the economy began to slow in the 2010s, and would have preferred to rebuild economic ties and restore the country's access to Eritrea's ports. By 2017, following months of what was, by some accounts, heated internal debate, Hailemariam's administration had quietly agreed to accept and implement the 2002 border ruling—though it would never make the change of policy public.[17] This was, in their eyes, a generous olive branch, and one intended to unblock the logjam which had prevented the countries moving forward for nearly two decades of so-called 'no peace no war'. In fact, it was no less than that which Abiy would offer Eritrea the following year. "I designed a policy of reconciliation," Hailemariam later argued, "and it was later implemented by Abiy."

Despite strong opposition from sceptical TPLF figures, notably spy chief Getachew Assefa, and an absence of diplomatic engagement from both America and Europe, Hailemariam said he had enlisted Chinese and Russian officials to act as go-betweens. Isaias, he recalled, had initially played along, and, with an economy in dire need of foreign investment, expressed interest in the Ethiopian proposal. This would have involved settling the border issue first—handing over Badme without delay— and then jointly preparing plans to develop the lucrative potash deposits on either side of it as the first in a series of trust-building measures. By the time Hailemariam resigned in early 2018, the EPRDF executive committee itself had, in theory, broadly agreed to all this.[18]

In the end, though, Eritrea declined to pursue the initial offer any further. When push came to shove, Asmara had persisted in its long-standing position that Ethiopia must first withdraw its troops to enable demarcation of the border before any talks about normalisation could start.[19] In part, Isaias's refusal likely sprung from a sense that the embattled EPRDF was on the cusp of unravelling. But doubtless crucial, too, was his firm belief that Hailemariam was simply a tool of the TPLF, a southern smokescreen for Tigrayan power, and therefore fundamentally unreliable. "Isaias didn't trust the TPLF, and he also didn't trust that I had the authority to do this," the former prime minister recalled.

Even so, Isaias was beginning to come under pressure from other directions to break the eighteen-year impasse. In Washington, in particular, the change of guard from the Obama to the Trump administration had, somewhat counter-intuitively, opened space for a revised approach to the decades-old conflict. John Bolton, then Trump's influential national security advisor, had long been sympathetic to Eritrea's position on the border issue, and critical of the UN's failure to force the EPRDF to implement the terms of the 2000 peace agreement. Though, he later stressed to me, neither he nor anyone else senior in the Trump administration took any role in mediating behind-the-scenes, Bolton was nonetheless acutely concerned throughout this period that China be prevented from gaining a firmer foothold in the region. As a result, and part of his broader strategy for great power competition in Africa, Bolton gave Donald Yamamoto, then America's top diplomat on Africa and a former ambassador and chargé d'affaires in Ethiopia and Eritrea, free rein to look into the possibilities for a settlement which might bring both Ethiopia and Eritrea squarely back inside the US orbit. Liberal squeamishness about engaging with a serial human-rights abuser like Isaias was, to Bolton's mind, now an explicitly second or even third-order concern.

And so, shortly after taking up his post in late 2017, Yamamoto gathered Eritrean officials, including foreign minister Osman Saleh, to his home in Washington to discuss the prospects for a deal. The Eritrean delegation, according to senior American diplomats, remained deeply suspicious of the US, and made it clear that their primary concern was not the border issue but rather that Eritrea be taken seriously by the US government. Eritrea under Isaias, they argued, would be a much more reliable security partner for the US than Ethiopia had ever been.

The following April, soon after Abiy took office, the assistant secretary of state made a visit to Asmara—the first of its kind by a top American official in years. Nudged by Hailemariam, who had also met with Yamamoto in Washington some months earlier, the American diplomat's goal was to get Isaias on board with a wider peace process. The Eritrean president quickly professed himself open to the idea. "Isaias just said: 'Don, you get this done, and we will have a good relationship'," Yamamoto later told me after he had left the US government. "He's a straight-shooter. He said: 'But you got to get the Ethiopians on board too'. And you know Isaias has his own angle, but he has always told us that 'you Americans are my most important contact, and I want you to give me the respect that I gave you.' So what he really wanted was to come to Washington. That's what he wanted."

A few days later, Yamamoto visited Abiy in Addis Ababa. "Abiy was looking for an angle to define who he was going to be as prime minister," the diplomat recalled. "So he said to me and Ambassador Raynor: 'What do you want me to do? What does America want me to do?' And I replied: 'Well, what we want you to do is bring a conclusion to the Ethiopia-Eritrea dispute after twenty years.' [...] So that was what we wanted to get out of it—and he did it. He took it. He took the ball."

This was not, however, the whole story. For one thing, it is clear that Abiy had existing plans of his own and was not merely responding to American entreaties. The decision to implement the 2002 border ruling, after all, had been made already by the EPRDF executive committee under Hailemariam. When I met with Abiy's close OPDO ally, Shimelis Abdissa, the day after the prime minister's inaugural address to parliament, and well before Yamamoto's visit, he had made a point of telling me that peace with Eritrea was at the very top of their agenda.[20] "That will be addressed immediately," he said. "And I don't think it will be tricky." Two months later, on 5 June, Abiy announced that Ethiopia would abide by, and fully implement, the UN border ruling without preconditions, firing the starting gun on the process which would lead to the deal.[21]

Isaias, on the other hand, was rather more wary of a hasty rapprochement than American diplomats might have realised. The Eritrean president was as familiar as anyone with Abiy's professional background. As much as the new prime minister's public appeals in Tigrinya, Isaias's mother-tongue, may have taken Ethiopians by surprise, to many Eritreans they were just a reminder of his pedigree as a former member of Ethiopia's Tigrayan-led security establishment. Though some have subsequently suggested that Abiy had pre-existing ties to the Eritrean regime, perhaps dating back to his INSA days, and alleged that he may have even leaked it intelligence in the past, there has never been much strong evidence. Former INSA colleagues rarely recalled any unusually pro-Eritrean sympathies, nor any outspoken conviction of the need for reconciliation with their neighbour. "He wanted Isaias dead," alleged a former friend and colleague in the agency. "He never talked about making peace with Isaias. Eritrea was a designated threat. So, on the contrary, he'd mobilise every resource to spy on it." Moreover, despite possibly having tried, according to some insiders, to reach out to Asmara in secret even before becoming prime minister, Abiy does not appear to have enjoyed much success. Eritrea responded to his early public overtures with two weeks of conspicuous silence. On meeting with Andargachew Tsige, the Ginbot 7 leader who was released from prison that May, the prime minister complained that try as he might to reach out to the Eritreans—through "presidents, kings and sheikhs"—they had so far failed to reply.

Divining exactly what motivated Abiy to pursue a deal with Eritrea is difficult. Some of the short-term gains for him were obvious enough: an agreement should mean an end to Eritrea's support for Ethiopian rebel movements like Ginbot 7 and the OLF. In the longer term, the potential economic benefits of securing access to Eritrea's Red Sea ports were also well-understood by everyone in the EPRDF at the time. Abiy was himself said by colleagues to believe especially strongly that Ethiopia's lack of a Red Sea outlet was a historic injustice, and, even before becoming prime minister, to have mused in private about expanding Ethiopia's borders all the way to the coast. Just two months after taking office he announced plans to revive the country's navy.

But Abiy also seems to have had more personal ambitions in mind. His image of himself as a pathbreaking conciliator was by this point well-formed. As part of his role mediating between Christians and Muslims in Jimma in the mid-2000s, for instance, he had established an intra-religious forum—work which later became central to his official biography, as well as his subsequent PhD. Around the same time, a colleague from INSA recalled, Abiy had floated the idea of 'peace ceremonies' to Meles himself, events in which he envisaged the government and its domestic opponents coming together to break bread and offer each other forgiveness. Securing status and recognition from the West as a forward-thinking peacemaker seems to have been a core ambition of his from very early on—meaning that any agreement with Eritrea, the outlines of which had already been agreed anyway by the EPRDF executive committee under Hailemariam, was low-hanging fruit. Two close colleagues remembered that as early as 2017, while still only vice president of Oromia, Abiy had spoken openly about negotiating with Isaias and winning a Nobel Prize for it. "He was very sure he'd win," one of them recalled.

But he had other reasons, too. Given what transpired later, it is now abundantly clear that on some level what Abiy sought by reaching out to Isaias was not simply a peace agreement, or brotherly relations between two exceptionally inter-woven societies, but rather a political ally: someone to support him in any future confrontation with the TPLF. Indeed, some have speculated that plans to jointly crush the Tigrayans were hatched in their two leaders' very earliest meetings.[22] But the extent to which Abiy was single-mindedly focused on an all-out war against Tigray from the outset of his premiership, at the expense of all other possible outcomes, remains very much an open question. Full details of what the two leaders agreed between themselves, after all, were kept secret from even their closest colleagues; given that neither note-takers nor aides were ever in the room with them, they may never come to light. But what is beyond doubt is that Abiy endeavoured to win Isaias over by stressing precisely these shared interests and mutual enemies. "Abiy is the manipulator-in-chief," noted an

Ethiopian scholar who had several conversations with the prime minister in this period. "What he does is he tries to figure out who you are, what you want in life, and what your interests are." Crucial for this in the case of Isaias would be the fiercely anti-TPLF Andargachew Tsige, who had spent two years living full time in Asmara with Ginbot 7 before his arrest in Yemen in 2014. Andargachew was known to be particularly close to the Eritrean leadership. Top of Abiy's agenda, when he called Andargachew into his office in May 2018, was thus enlisting his help in persuading Isaias to talk. Andargachew stressed to the prime minister that any meaningful alliance with Eritrea would require putting the TPLF out of business once and for all. "More than anything else, what weighed on the minds of the Eritreans was the removal of the TPLF from Ethiopian politics," the veteran dissident later recalled.

Personally convinced by the prime minister's claims to have been the one who had leaked intelligence to him and Ginbot 7 in the late 2000s, and so reassured—for now—that Abiy meant what he said about his hostility to the TPLF, Andargachew eventually agreed to act as middleman. Not long after, while visiting his family back in London, he met with Yemane Gebreab, Isaias's right-hand man, who had flown there specially to meet him. Abiy, the Ethiopian opposition leader told the Eritrean official, was the real deal, a genuine enemy of the TPLF. On hearing this, and further encouraged by Abiy's swift removal of the long-serving Tigrayan heads of the army and national intelligence that June, Isaias now decided—even against the advice of some of his own colleagues—to take a gamble. "We gave Abiy the benefit of the doubt," he later told Andargachew.

And so, on 20 June, the Eritrean president stood in front of members of his party, the People's Front for Democracy and Justice (PFDJ), and announced that he would dispatch a delegation to meet with the new Ethiopian prime minister. In the same breath, he made clear the real meaning of reconciliation, condemning the TPLF as "vultures" whose final demise was imminent. "Game over," he said. "The twenty-five years of lavish consumption are over."[23] Replying via a TV broadcast not long after, Abiy ignored the thinly veiled threat, gliding smoothly over the invective against his coalition colleagues as though nothing were awry. A political alliance, not just a diplomatic entente, had now been formed. Across the border in Mekelle, alarm bells began to ring.

* * *

On the surface Abiy and Isaias couldn't have been less alike. The glossy modernity of Abiy's administration—its use of social media; the press briefings in shiny, refurbished offices; the tech-savvy advisors with MacBooks under their arms—all contributed to an impression of Abiy as a free-wheeling disrupter, wrenching the ageing dictator next door into the twenty-first century. The prime minister evidently thrived on the contrast, consciously playing up the differences in their age and status, kissing the older man's hand in public, and deploying affectionate names of endearment.[24] He assured foreign visitors he could convince Isaias to open up and relax his regime's economic and political control, just as he and his colleagues were then doing in Ethiopia. "He seemed very confident," recalled a visitor from a Western NGO who met Abiy around this time. "He joked that 'these old guys think we are just youngsters.' He said his approach was to show Isaias some respect, and then bring him to Addis Ababa to show him what's possible. He said he expected an opening up in Eritrea soon, but on Isaias's terms."

But the question of where power in their relationship really lay has always been a live one. Abiy doubtless believed he could manipulate the elder statesman, and in the early days worked hard to appear as though he alone called the shots. "He believes people are really gullible, so long as he flatters them," Andargachew later observed. "So he gave Isaias the respect and recognition he craved." Even so, from the outset there were signs that Isaias was also pursuing an agenda of his own. The Eritrean president insisted, for instance, that Abiy remove certain officials who displeased him, notably Ethiopia's long-serving ambassador to the UN in New York. He also dictated who accompanied the prime minister on his trips to Asmara. Even more importantly, it was Isaias who insisted that among the first things the prime minister did on his return to Addis Ababa was formally request that the UN secretary-general, António Guterres, start the process of lifting the international arms embargo on Eritrea. Guterres agreed, reversing Ethiopia's long-standing strategy of containment in almost a single stroke.

Hasty decision-making, devoid of the normal processes of protracted deliberation so characteristic of the EPRDF, was exacerbated by both leaders' demonstrable lack of interest in the formal institutions of regional diplomacy. Prior to his first visit to Asmara in July, Abiy had neglected to inform the foreign ministry, and its seasoned diplomatic corps, of his plans. They were to be left in the dark until well after the peace agreement had been signed, and never made privy to its finer details. Neither the

UN, nor the African Union, nor IGAD, the East African regional bloc, were ever consulted at all—a feature of Abiy's diplomacy which would remain as consistent as it was striking throughout these years.

What both Abiy and Isaias showed, instead, was a marked preference for the personalised diplomacy of a kind more familiar to the two most powerful monarchies across the Red Sea: Saudi Arabia and, to an even greater degree, the United Arab Emirates. Far more than any other outside powers, it was the two Gulf states who would do most to shape the character of the new alliance and determine its fate. In the case of the Saudis, who in the latter part of the decade were actively seeking to bolster their regional clout, real influence was most felt early on in the process, with the kingdom's diplomats expressing an interest in mediating between Ethiopia and Eritrea even before Abiy took office. After the rapprochement had tentatively begun, both they and the Emiratis are believed to have given the process a further fillip by promising Isaias added investment and financial assistance to push him into a deal—though as with all Abiy's and Isaias's dealings, the precise details of this have remained remarkably opaque. Two months after Abiy's trip to Asmara, the leaders met in Jeddah, Saudi Arabia's second city, and signed an additional seventeen-article peace deal in the presence of the Saudi monarch and the UN secretary-general. Nobody knew quite what had really been agreed.

There would be no more consequential geopolitical development for Ethiopia in the 2010s than the expansion of Gulf involvement in the affairs of the Horn. By propping up its regimes in the face of popular unrest, reshaping their relationships with the outside world, and providing weak, poor states with alternatives to their traditional allies in America and Europe, the Gulf countries led by Saudi Arabia and the UAE had, even by the middle of the decade, begun radically altering the balance of power throughout the broader Red Sea region. In an era defined, if not by America's retreat from their part of the world, then at least its waning influence there, these oil-rich 'middle powers', as they were sometimes known, sought to create new spheres of influence to project control and protect their security interests. To this end, the Saudis and Emiratis, in particular, had adopted much more muscular postures in their regional backyard. Through the 2010s, they snapped up ports and bases along the southern rim of the Arabian Peninsula and up the Red Sea, while forcing governments throughout the region to cut ties with Iran, their chief geopolitical rival. A range of Middle Eastern states, including Turkey, had also begun to take a much more active interest in the Horn's natural resources—abundant fertile land, above all—in order to supply their growing domestic markets and mitigate the impact of climate change on their own food security. Saudi firms, in particular, had been behind some of Ethiopia's most controversial agricultural investments ever since the EPRDF had decided to push for large-scale commercial farming in the late 2000s.[25]

In Eritrea, both Saudi Arabia and the UAE had been actively involved for several years already, helping to ease Asmara's chronic shortage of foreign currency and to circumvent the UN's arms embargo. The Gulf allies' war in Yemen, which began in 2015 and was less than 70 miles away from the port of Assab, had also sparked a rush on Eritrean coastal real estate. In order to supply its forces across the waterway, the UAE had leased the port and built a military base and combat drone facilities there. Several hundred Eritrean troops, meanwhile, had fought as part of the Saudi-led coalition in Yemen, in return for which Isaias had received fuel and finance.[26] A skilled Arabic speaker, the Eritrean dictator found the world of Gulf realpolitik much more amenable to his style of politics than that of either the Europeans or Americans, and he had effectively leveraged this to pull himself some way out of international isolation in the few years preceding Abiy's ascent. The PFDJ-owned Red Sea Trading Corporation, for example, an opaque conglomerate with a virtual monopoly on public contracts, and tainted by its use of forced labour, had been given free rein to run its financial dealings out of Dubai.

In Ethiopia, by contrast, Abiy's predecessors had typically been wary of the Arab world. But the new prime minister, keen to take advantage of the changing regional order, was palpably enthused by it. Like many Ethiopians of his generation, Abiy saw much to admire in the glittering, ordered metropolises of Dubai and Abu Dhabi, as well as in the smooth-running model of a strong—if theoretically federal—state which the UAE seemed to represent.[27] For years, he had been a frequent visitor. Berhane Kidanemariam, who was often in Abiy's company in this period, suspected he must have had established business ties there; a close ally of Abiy later told me he suspected the future prime minister must have been in touch with Emirati officials even before 2018. In any case, once in charge, one of Abiy's very first moves was to hire an Emirati firm to renovate his new office. His first overseas visit, meanwhile, was to Saudi Arabia. A few months later, he cut the ribbon on a new real estate project in Addis Ababa called Eagle Hills, the largest and most expensive project of its kind in the city's history. The firm behind it was Emirati.[28]

More significant still was Abiy's personal rapport with Crown Prince Mohammed bin Zayed al Nahayan, the UAE's de facto ruler and, by some counts, the richest person in the world thanks to his control of its enormous sovereign wealth funds. As soon as Abiy took power in April, MbZ, as he is widely known, moved more swiftly than any other world leader to court the new Ethiopian leadership, promising \$3bn in aid and investments, including a \$1bn deposit in the country's central bank. MbZ also positioned the Emiratis as Ethiopia's security partner of choice, helping to upgrade INSA's cyber-surveillance capabilities with some of the most high-tech equipment on the market, as well as to fund and train Abiy's Republican Guard, an elite protection unit reminiscent of Haile Selassie's imperial bodyguard.[29]

Abiy and the camera-shy Emirati autocrat, who had spent much of the preceding decade bankrolling authoritarian rulers throughout the region, at first seemed unlikely bedfellows. "It's a confusing relationship to me because they're very different people," a former senior American diplomat later observed. "First of all, there's nobody more secular on the planet than Mohammed bin Zayed. He's also very self-contained. He's very disciplined. Very methodical. Abiy is none of those things. He's messianic. He's deeply religious. He's not self-contained. He's erratic. But I guess opposites attract or something. I don't really get it, but there's a particular bond there."

Yet there were certain similarities, too. MbZ, who was known to drive around Abu Dhabi at the wheel of his white Nissan Patrol, and show up unannounced in local restaurants, also had a populist touch of sorts. Like Abiy, MbZ had a knack for winning allies in the West. He had burnished his reputation as a social liberal, for instance by making room for women in his cabinet a decade before Abiy would unveil a gender-equal one. More substantially, both leaders also saw themselves as pioneering modernisers. The Emirati ruler shared, for instance, Abiy's interest in futuristic technologies, especially spyware. Indeed, in their different ways, both aimed at reshaping not just their own countries, but the entire Red Sea region, in their image.[30] "They both see themselves as a new generation of leaders trying to bring about a change of approach in their respective countries," observed another top American diplomat who had met both on several occasions.

In Abiy, it seems MbZ had spied something of a comrade-in-arms. Against the advice of some his colleagues, who worried about getting so involved with a country in which the Gulf kingdom had little experience,

MbZ endeavoured to make himself Ethiopia's indispensable foreign ally. At the expense not just of the UAE's main regional foes—Iran, Turkey, and Qatar—but also Saudi Arabia, an ostensible ally which, by the start of the next decade, had begun morphing into something of a strategic competitor as well, MbZ sought to insert the UAE right into the heart of Ethiopian politics. Soon, Emirati petrodollars would become the indispensable grease in the wheels of the political machine which sustained Abiy's grip on power.[31] "The Emiratis don't invest in states," noted Alex Rondos, then the EU's special envoy to the Horn. "They invest in individuals." Like the Sudanese paramilitary leader Muhammad Hamdan Dagalo ('Hemedti'), or the powerful Libyan warlord Khalifa Haftar—both controversial Emirati allies—Abiy was one such individual. So close was their bond that MbZ was rumoured to describe the Ethiopian leader as his brother.

Critics feared Abiy had traded the country's sovereignty for Gulf investment, reducing Ethiopia to little more than a client state powerless to direct its own fate. Such concerns became especially acute in the aftermath of the Tigray War, in which the UAE had rallied strongly in Abiy's defence: a high-profile visit by MbZ to Addis Ababa in 2023 was accompanied by the signing of as many as seventeen co-operation agreements between the countries, across sectors ranging from finance to counterterrorism. But Abiy was never likely to be anyone's lapdog, and he didn't always do MbZ's bidding. In at least one small, but important, respect, both he and Isaias did part ways with their Emirati ally in the wake of the 2018 peace deal: by seeking to bring Somalia's controversial president Mohamed Abdullahi Mohamed (better known to his people as Farmaajo) into their orbit, too.

A fiercely nationalistic, Trump-supporting Somali bureaucrat, who had spent the bulk of an otherwise unremarkable adult life in upstate New York, Farmaajo was not at first glance an obvious match for either Abiy or Isaias. Eritrea had been in a diplomatic tussle with Somalia for a decade and a half, while Ethiopia, under both Meles and Hailemariam, had tended to work more closely and amicably with Somalia's separatist regional states such as Jubaland and Puntland. Farmaajo was also personally unpopular with the Emiratis, having picked a fight with them over their plans to develop a port and build a military base in Somaliland, an internationally unrecognised breakaway region to the north. If MbZ was to embrace the Somali president he would likely need him to ditch Qatar, a key patron and another of the UAE's regional rivals then squarely in the powerful crown prince's crosshairs. Farmaajo, who relied much on Qatari cash, never would.

Abiy and Isaias nonetheless had eyes on their man in Mogadishu. For Abiy, part of the appeal was parochial: Farmaajo was keen to marginalise Ahmed Madobe, a Somali powerbroker in charge of Jubaland, on Ethiopia's south-eastern border, long suspected of close ties to the TPLF. Isaias, meanwhile, shared with Farmaajo an open dislike of both federalism and elections, viewing them as at best an irritant, and at worst the cause of national disintegration. When Farmaajo first visited Asmara in July 2018 to mend bridges, the pair quickly hit it off. Over the course of a three-hour-long meeting, an aide to the Somali president recalled, Isaias waxed lyrical about Somalia, reminiscing about how he used to live there in the 1970s, and about his friendship with Somalia's former dictator Siad Barre, a direct clansman of Farmaajo. "That is what really bonded them," the aide noted. "But they had the same ideas, too, about nationalism and self-sufficiency and things like that."

Swiftly patching up diplomatic ties, Somalia and Eritrea signed a declaration of "brotherly relations and comprehensive cooperation" on 30 July. To Isaias's evident delight, Farmaajo also joined Abiy in calling for UN sanctions on Eritrea to be lifted, without mentioning the unresolved conflict between Djibouti and Eritrea.[32] A few weeks later, Abiy met them in Asmara—the first of several 'tripartite' meetings over the next two years—followed soon after by a reciprocal visit to Ethiopia's Amhara region and yet another joint statement. A little more than a year later, in January 2020, the trio announced a "joint plan of action for 2020", which included cooperation across a wide range of sectors, including security. The three leaders would also attempt to woo South Sudan into their club.

The idea of a new east African axis centred, so it seemed, on Isaias, provoked alarm throughout the region. In part, this was because few leaders in the Horn trusted the Eritrean leader, who had come to blows with almost all his neighbours since the 1990s. Most viewed his budding friendship with the mercurial and still little-known Abiy with suspicion. But it was also because the club seemed to be positioning itself as a rival to the well-established and hitherto reasonably functional IGAD, which Isaias resented as a vehicle for Ethiopian—or more specifically Tigrayan—influence and had long refused to participate in. Few were more unhappy about this than Ismaïl Omar Guelleh, the Djiboutian president, whose tiny coastal enclave was home to IGAD's headquarters, and whose relations with Isaias had been in the deep freeze since 2008, when Eritrean troops had allegedly seized a strip of Djiboutian land. Abiy's decision to reach out to Eritrea without notifying Djibouti first had sharply blindsided him. The prospect of landlocked Ethiopia one day making use of Eritrean ports—a huge potential benefit of the thaw from Addis Ababa's perspective—was also of great concern to the Djiboutian president: since the 2000s, more than 90 percent of Ethiopian trade had flowed through his country's docks. Abiy now made no secret of his ambitions to diversify away from them, and touted an opaque deal he struck with Farmaajo for Ethiopia to make use of four unnamed Somali ports as an alternative. Negotiations were said by insiders to have continued discreetly until Farmaajo left office.

In practice, though, the new tripartite alliance lived up to neither the expectations of its leaders nor the fears of its critics. Abiy's ambitions, on the one hand, knew no limits: not content with negotiating with Farmaajo for use of Somalia's ports, he also continued to speak to colleagues with apparent seriousness of plans to unite Ethiopia and Eritrea, and perhaps one day even Djibouti and Somalia as well, in a single federation.[33] But Farmaajo was simply too weak at home to ever play much of a role in Abiy's dreams, and he spent most of the latter part of his tenure cloistered in Mogadishu, scheming instead to delay the elections which he would go on to lose in 2022. He and Isaias did, in 2019, arrange for some 5,000 Somali troops to be sent secretly to Eritrea for training—with a view, it was said, to return them to Somalia as Farmaajo's Praetorian guard. But their dalliance went little further than this. Foreign diplomats who met with Farmaajo observed how admiringly he spoke of Isaias, and noted that he seemed to look up to the Eritrean veteran as a model of strongman leadership. Yet reports that he later allowed the Somali trainees to fight alongside Ethiopia and Eritrea in Tigray were unsubstantiated, and his influence over both Isaias and Abiy was ultimately negligible.[34] Abiy's acquiescence in the involvement of Ethiopian troops in the abduction of one of the Somali president's political rivals later in 2018 came, in hindsight, to be just as revealing of the Ethiopian prime minister's own attitude toward electoral competition as it was of Farmaajo's.[35]

* * *

Grand declarations of love and magnanimity were Abiy's preferred mode of peace-making. In his early years in office, he tried to broker deals between rival factions in South Sudan—literally pressing the two leaders into an awkward group hug in one instance—mend bridges between Somalia and

Somaliland, and mediate between Somalia and Kenya in a long-standing dispute over their maritime border. In December 2018, he would even publish an open letter to war-torn Yemen, in which he urged—in faulty Arabic—for the warring parties to simply "shake hands and meet each other with hearts full of love".[36] The following year, he would play a walk-on part in mediating between civilian protesters and the military in the Sudanese revolution next door, imparting his message that Sudanese rivals should embrace one another during a brief visit to Khartoum, the capital, before leaving a personal envoy to follow up.[37] In all instances, personal chemistry, individual forgiveness—and a certain collective amnesia—would always take precedence over structured, formal negotiations.

None of these initiatives were successful. Abiy's attempt to fly Farmaajo into Hargeisa, the capital of Somaliland, for instance, actually backfired, prompting the angry intervention of Somaliland's parliament and a subsequent cooling in diplomatic relations between Ethiopia and the breakaway Somali state.[38] In Sudan, meanwhile, Abiy's star appeal may have given the protesters there a brief morale boost. But his intervention contributed little of substance to the talks which would eventually lead to a shaky deal between the Sudanese military and civilian leaders. In 2023, the country collapsed into civil war.

The peace deal he struck with Isaias, moreover, was a demonstration not only of the limits of a peace-building process which prioritised speed over deliberation, and the goodwill of individual leaders over public consultation, but also of the wilful negligence of the international community. No written agreement ever appeared before Ethiopia's parliament for ratification, and for a while there was little sign that either side had thought about the trickier aspects of the rapprochement: trade and tariff regimes, currency conversion, or even physical demarcation of the border. "Abiy told us clearly: 'we never discussed Badme'," recalled a senior British official who met with the prime minister and asked him what had been agreed about the status of the disputed town which had sparked the war in 1998. If there was ever a concrete agreement for Ethiopia to regain tax-free access to Eritrea's ports, it was never shared with the public. (The Ethiopian government did, however, renovate the road to Assab on its side of the border, and provided construction machinery to Eritrea to do the same with the Eritrean section.[39])

Yet few concerns were ever raised by any of the Western governments which, having first failed to enforce implementation of the original peace agreement in 2000, now hailed the new deal as a breakthrough. The absence of anyone senior from the TPLF accompanying Abiy on his trips to Asmara—a telling oversight given Tigray's centrality to the original conflict—was never mentioned. The TPLF's own objections to the peace deal, set against a backdrop of local protests in Badme, were also brushed aside. Though the TPLF had formally welcomed Abiy's announcement on 5 June, a trenchant statement issued by the party a short while later alleged the process had "fundamental flaws". It called, unsuccessfully, for an emergency meeting of the EPRDF. But foreign diplomats, for their part, typically waved away Tigrayan worries as the work of recalcitrant 'spoilers'.

For a short while, it seemed as though everyone outside the TPLF might be happy to overlook the flaws in Abiy's approach to diplomacy—not least his faith in the power of his own charisma to heal rifts—and simply embrace the new order. After all, when it came to the peace agreement, many ordinary Tigrayans had initially sounded elated too. "I never dreamed this would happen," said a Tigrayan friend whose Eritrean father was deported during the border war, and who was later reunited with a long-lost sister. "It's like divine intervention." Ordinary Eritreans, meanwhile, expressed much the same view. In Asmara, in fact, even some government officials sounded convinced that peace was there to stay. "We didn't go through all this hardship and sacrifice to live in hatred—we don't allow that," one of them told me that July. "We didn't allow ourselves to be obsessed with hatred and hostility in 1991, and we won't now."

9

"IT WAS CHAOS"

THE FEDERAL STATE UNRAVELS

Gunshots rang out in the southern town of Kercha the same night Abiy became prime minister. Fired in celebration, not yet in anger, hundreds of young men and women took to the street, beeping their rickshaws' horns in excitement and blasting Oromo music from speakers rigged to pick-up trucks. At first, as he stood watching from the porch of his home, Geremu Woyte, a twenty-eight-year-old coffee farmer who had lived in Kercha all his life, had shrugged off the commotion. Abiy's speech that day had buoyed him: its spirit was inclusive, its appeal to a transcendent Ethiopian identity generous and forgiving. The promise of a future shorn of ethnic difference felt like a new chapter for him. After months of tension between Gedeos and their Guji Oromo neighbours in Kercha, in western Guji, perhaps they could all breathe a little more easily.

Looking back three years later, Geremu remembered watching a crowd gathering on the street in front of him. As it grew, he told me, he had begun to wonder. He had thought back over a series of incidents which had punctuated the previous months: the elderly Gedeo man found dead in a coffee-hulling mill owned by a Guji businessman; the torching of the mill in revenge; the wealthy Gedeo coffee farmer killed by a passing car as he crossed the road. As Geremu had turned these thoughts over in his mind, the sound of chanting had begun to reach him—distant, at first, but gradually drawing closer. "The prime minister is ours", went one of the cries. "This land is ours," went another. Nearby, a group of local policemen watched the crowd in expressionless silence. That night, the first round of beatings and looting began. Over the coming weeks and months hundreds and thousands of Gedeos would flee.[1]

For Pastor Worku Gollo, meanwhile, it was the second time he had found himself caught up in trouble in Kercha. In 1995, he and a group of construction workers had been stopped by a mob and accused of smuggling weapons into the district. As the cheery Pente preacher had patiently explained to his attackers back then, they had been travelling there to build a new church, one of the more than 200 which he and his fellow missionaries from the Kale Hiwot Church would go on to establish across Ethiopia over the following decades. But the mob had seemed incredulous, and were it not for the timely intervention of a local official, appeared almost ready to kill him.

Thirteen years later, on Ethiopian Good Friday, Worku was again driving from Dilla, the Gedeo capital, to Kercha, across copper-tinted rivers shaded by the leaves of towering *enset* plants and wild coffee. It was the day of his monthly church meeting there, and when Worku jumped into his Land Rover that morning the terraced hillsides he passed through were still shrouded in a sleepy mist. "It was a normal day like any other," the pastor later recalled. "If the church leaders in Kercha had informed us that there were problems then we'd have stayed in Dilla, but they told us it's calm, and that everything was okay."

He arrived at the Kale Hiwot Church in Kercha without incident, and proceeded to gather the local elders and congregants for prayer. But at around midday, as the group were wrapping up and preparing to sit down for lunch, two young men entered the compound. Their visit was unannounced, and there was something about their demeanour which Worku found unsettling. "They said they were checking who we were—which was a bit unusual—and then they checked the car," he told me. "They found nothing, so they let us go."

A couple of hours later, though, the same thing happened. On the road out of Kercha a police officer called the pastor's car to a halt and demanded to see his licence. "He knows me, he sees me every time I come," Worku said. "He'd no reason to stop me." As he waited, a group of agitated-looking young men stepped in front of the car and hurled insults in his direction. For a moment, Worku thought they were preparing to pelt stones, and he readied himself for the onslaught. But then a policeman arrived, breaking up the group and—to Worku's astonishment—placing him and nine of his colleagues under arrest. Though it would never be exactly clear to him why, the pastor would spend the next three days in prison. On his release he was escorted back to Dilla by a posse of local security officers.

As word of Worku's detention spread, tensions mounted across the district. The pastor, it was alleged, had been using his church pulpit to call upon the Gedeos living in Kercha to secede from Oromia, meddling in local politics and conspiring to place his Gedeo allies in positions of power. Some of the more sensational allegations even had it that he had been stockpiling arms in his church in order to launch an ethnic pogrom. Among the Guji, calls for his imprisonment grew louder. "They wanted to kill me," Worku recalled. "Because I'm a man who makes things happen: I go and I build and I preach. They believed that I'm the chief of the Gedeo people and that all the Gedeo would listen to me and obey me. So they propagated that Worku Gollo had started a war. They said the church had declared war on Kercha."

The accusations were fanciful. A giant of a man with a kindly face and a great booming laugh, Worku was a father of nine and a devoted servant of the church—hardly a very likely political agitator. But in the frenetic weeks which followed Abiy's ascent he had become a scapegoat, the lightning rod for a set of political and economic anxieties which would soon tear through Kercha's social fabric with breathtaking speed. Within just days of his release from detention, chaos had been unleashed across the district. An untold number of people were killed, often gruesomely; some would be castrated and beheaded, or hacked to death by machetes. Around 21,000 homes, mostly those belonging to Gedeos, were burnt or torn down, according to official numbers.[2] Pentecostal churches were set on fire.

Geremu, who had immediately fled to Dilla on hearing of the pastor's arrest, returned to his home in Kercha days later to find that nearby houses belonging to Gedeos were being set ablaze by armed Guji youth. As he and his wife fled, once again, this time in an Isuzu truck with scores of other Gedeos, they glimpsed bodies lying on the road behind them. Geremu later learnt that his family home had been burnt to the ground, he told me, his *enset* plants uprooted and his coffee trees torn down. One of his neighbours, a local Gedeo official, had been gang-raped, with her body later found strung to a tree so as to appear as if she had hung herself.[3]

These were just a fraction of the underreported and overlooked horrors from the ethnic violence which exploded in Ethiopia's distant south in the days after Abiy came to power. Outsiders largely ignored them because they were inconvenient: a fly in the ointment of 'Abiymania' and a wrinkle in the otherwise uplifting tale of democratic progress which the prime minister and his allies were anxious to promote. But if there was one standout story in 2018, it was that nearly three million Ethiopians had been forced from their homes by conflict in those twelve months alone—more than anywhere else on earth and up to four times as many as in 2017.[4] Hundreds of thousands of Gedeos fled Guji in southern Oromia; tens of thousands of Guji Oromos went the other way—comparable figures to those in Myanmar's Rohingya crisis a year earlier, which had attracted a global outcry and an investigation by the International Criminal Court.[5]

This was social upheaval on a momentous scale. Drop a pin on southern, western, or eastern Ethiopia in 2018 and more likely than not it would have landed in an active conflict zone. To the west, in the Benishangul-Gumuz region, more than 60,000 people—mostly Oromos—were forced to flee the contested border territory known as Kamashi in less than a month between September and October. To the east, 140,000 non-Somalis were expelled from Jigjiga and other parts of the Somali region in just a few days in August. A few months later, on the southern border with Kenya, violence erupted in Moyale leaving another 150,000 homeless. Just a couple of months after the violence in Guji, pogroms targeting ethnic Wolaita took place in Hawassa, the pretty lakeside capital of the Southern Nations, Nationalities and Peoples Region (SNNPR), normally popular with tourists and day trippers from Addis Ababa. More than 2,000 were displaced. By the new standards of the day this was little more than a rounding error.[6]

At the heart of the matter was the state's eroding monopoly on violence, a trend which had first become evident under Hailemariam—exemplified by the conflict between the Somali region and Oromia the previous year—but which accelerated dramatically no sooner had Abiy taken power. In the six months following his ascent, the number of violent incidents was estimated to have increased by nearly 10 percent, with the number of reported fatalities skyrocketing by almost 50 percent.[7] In the security vacuum left by the government, people had begun stockpiling weapons; the price of the most sought-after firearm, a Turkish pistol, jumped threefold in just a few months.[8] Others took to vigilantism. "Every citizen should be a policeman," a *Qeerroo* leader in Shashemene, a town near Hawassa, told me in November 2018. Three months earlier, a crowd there had lynched a man wrongly suspected of carrying a bomb at a rally organised for Jawar's visit to the town.

It was in Oromia that the spectre of state collapse was most acute. Soon after he had returned to Ethiopia that August, Jawar had told local media that the country now effectively had "two governments": one led by Abiy, the other by the *Qeerroo*.[9] While clearly meant as a provocation, it wasn't too great an exaggeration. In parts of western Oromia there were *Qeerroos* who now called themselves "Qeerroo Police" and had taken over responsibility for local security; in some places they manned roadblocks and exhorted "taxes" from local businesses and passers-by. In the eastern city of Harar, residents went without drinking water for nearly a month after *Qeerroos* in the surrounding hinterland shut the supply down and demanded a ransom of 10 million birr (about $180,000); land grabs by local *Qeerroos* were also widely reported throughout the surrounding Hararghe area.[10] In August, the office of an international aid agency in Guji was invaded by armed men who demanded that they take control of the food supplies to hand out to the local population, meaning aid distributions had to be put on hold for a month. With the unexplained murder in May of the country manager of Dangote Cement, a Nigerian-owned multinational, and two of his staff, foreign investor interest in Oromia slumped even further.[11] "Anarchy and state collapse are within the realm of possibility," fretted one federal official at the time. America's deputy ambassador later put it more bluntly: "it was chaos".

But few outsiders paid heed to what that chaos portended. As security deteriorated, few journalists, local or foreign, ever made it to more remote areas. Western diplomats, anxious to save face and reluctant to admit the dark side of the 'democratic transition' they had so enthusiastically cheered, were more often than not inclined to look the other way. When forced to explain why Ethiopia was suddenly more dangerous, more violent, and more turbulent than it had been even at the height of the protests in early 2018, officials often seemed to prefer the comforting illusion that these were isolated incidents; local difficulties to be expected of any transition to democracy, temporary setbacks which would blow over as soon as Abiy found his feet. "We were aware of the existing ethnic tensions—the fact that there was a displacement crisis was not a shock," recalled an American diplomat who served in the embassy at the time. "Whenever there's a sudden decentralisation of power, this is to be expected." Yet this was almost exactly what Abiy himself argued when he waved away inconvenient questions about the matter; it was also much the same flawed logic which the Nobel committee breezily applied, as though an afterthought, when it gave Abiy the peace prize the following year. "Democratisation poses serious challenges in a country with 100 million inhabitants and more than 80 different ethnic groups", it wrote. "In 2019,

Ethiopia, a country with no tradition of free elections and democracy, was still racked by major internal conflicts."

There were undoubtedly elements of truth to this account. An ostensibly similar pattern of communal conflict had gripped Ethiopia in the early 1990s after the EPRDF took power. Then, as in 2018, uncertainty at the centre encouraged local actors to settle old disputes, often violently, or to claim territory they felt was rightfully theirs before the new federal map had been firmly established. Between 1991 and 2005, at a very conservative estimate, several thousand people were killed in this way.[12] Among the many inter-communal conflicts which raged then were large-scale border wars between the Guji and Gedeo. In 1995, over one hundred people were killed; in 1998, by one estimate, up to three thousand were.[13] Many scholars observed that the new system, by creating new ethnocratic elites and new ethnic minorities at the sub-national level, appeared to have simply decentralised communal conflict rather than have eradicated it.[14] This was particularly true in the highly diverse south where relatively mono-ethnic territories were comparatively rare.

The weakness of the central government, and its apparent inability to keep a lid on disorder, also had echoes through earlier periods of Ethiopian history. The French scholar René Lefort, who chronicled the 1974 Revolution, noted that the state paralysis he found in rural Ethiopia in 2018 bore resemblances to what he called the "pencil strikes" of previous eras, when local officials and security officers hung back in order to avoid committing themselves to a weak or unpopular regime. "We come in the morning in the office, stay there doing nothing, and leave in the evening only to get our salary at the end of the month… We don't receive any guideline from the top, we don't send any instruction to the bottom," a civil servant in a rural Amhara district confided in Lefort. "Nobody takes any decision."[15]

But incapacity was this time compounded by complicity. In Oromia, in particular, years of protests had hollowed out local government structures. In many places *Qeerroos* and their sympathisers increasingly occupied local offices, scrambling chains of command and pulling officials between competing loyalties: to the OPDO; to the *Qeerroo*; and, after their return from exile in September 2018, the OLF.[16] In Guji, and especially in Kercha, where tensions between Guji Oromos and Gedeos were already high, the line between the three had almost ceased to exist. Gedeos who fled the area in 2018 often struggled to distinguish one from the other, repeatedly telling me that their attackers were both the OLF and the *Qeerroo* at once.

With lawlessness becoming the norm, and inter-communal violence routine, eyewitnesses consistently emphasised how local officials—who in Kercha were mostly Oromo—had also become witting participants. Some Gedeos, for instance, suspected that Guji officials and businessmen were after their land and coffee. Others, including many Gujis themselves, suggested that corrupt local officials had been using conflict as a way of distracting people from their own misdeeds (to which officials tended to respond by blaming the hidden hand of the TPLF or 'deep state').[17] Oromia's regional police, meanwhile, were seen doing next to nothing to stop the fighting in Guji—a pattern of ethnic solidarity in policing which was by this point endemic throughout much of the country.

Local government complicity of this kind was common to all Ethiopia's myriad ethnic conflicts in this period. Under the federal system, an identity group's access to land was largely a function of administrative control; the 1998 Gedeo-Guji conflict, for instance, had been sparked by competing claims to govern the district of Hagere Mariam. As the supply of land had shrunk in the subsequent years, without a concomitant increase in productivity, such tensions had only increased; by 2018, Gedeo and Guji were among the most densely populated rural areas in all east Africa.[18] To make matters worse, the population of Gedeos, who had first been settled in the contested territory in large numbers by Haile Selassie in the 1960s, was growing at a much faster rate than that of the Gujis—a source of demographic anxiety for the latter which, like in other parts of Ethiopia, worsened as preparations for the much-anticipated (though later indefinitely postponed) national census gathered pace. By 2018, Gedeos were believed to be a majority in the fertile hotspot of Kercha, in part of what Gujis considered their ancestral land, and were increasingly vocal in demanding self-administration rights such as for schooling in the Gedeo language and their own 'special administrative zone'. Because of the way the federal system had bound certain group or 'ethnic' identities, which had once been relatively fluid, to the administrative control of particular territories, it was no coincidence that all the major recorded conflicts between the Gedeo and the Gujis had occurred after the introduction of the federal system in the 1990s. Under the new administrative arrangements, older antagonisms, such as those which had long existed between Gedeo farmers and Guji pastoralists, had been gradually institutionalised. More recently, hate speech had also been fanned by social media. By the time Abiy took power there was a widespread feeling in Guji that the moment had come to deal with the problem of Gedeo 'settlers' once and for all.

When I visited Kercha in 2019, the violence had subsided and most of the refugees had returned to the district. But many of the homes and coffee farms that previously belonged to Gedeos, some of which remained charred ruins on either side of the main road, were still in the hands of their Guji neighbours. One Gedeo man told me over the phone—he had been too afraid to speak freely when I interviewed him earlier in front of prying neighbours and a government minder—that he had returned earlier that year to find his land occupied. He had taken his neighbour to court, but only part of it had been returned to him. A twenty-five-year-old Gedeo woman likewise told me how some of her relatives had returned to Guji only to be told they had to pay their neighbours, who had been living in their home, a "protection" fee to have it back again. They were tactics which would become both more familiar, and more systematic, as violence and ethnic conflict spread over the coming years, above all in Tigray and Amhara.

* * *

Abiy could at least claim, at first with some justification, that his administration was simply refusing to countenance what had been shown to fail so many times before. The army and police, who shot hundreds of people between 2015 and 2017, rarely used lethal force to contain unrest in 2018. In the six months after he assumed office, confrontations between them and protesters declined, according to one estimate, by more than 80 percent.[19]

Some of his early statements on the proper role of the security forces were particularly noteworthy. In a milestone address to parliament in June 2018, Abiy had argued that the authorities had in the past too often behaved unconstitutionally—a pattern of behaviour he likened to terrorism.[20] For at least the first year of his administration, this message seemed to be filtering down the command, with security officers displaying unprecedented reticence in the use of lethal force against civilians.[21] Rather than send in the army to resolve conflicts, Abiy insisted his preference was for dialogue and forgiveness wherever possible. The real problem, he suggested, was one of mindset, and he frequently exhorted the public to rid themselves of selfishness and what he deemed to be unthinking tribalism. To consign ethnic violence to history, he argued, Ethiopians must stop seeing those from other groups as "aliens and outsiders".[22] To this end, he told his office to organise dialogues and "roundtables", so that

Ethiopians from different ideological camps or ethnic communities could exchange views amicably.[23]

Some of his more concrete efforts to rewire the EPRDF's security state and soften its most authoritarian features were broadly welcome. The administration revised certain draconian laws, mostly those dating back to Meles's post-2005 crackdown on civil liberties, such as the notorious anti-terrorism proclamation and restrictions on the operations of local civil society organisations. Plans were also drawn up to scrap arbitrary detention practices. Under the direction of a new Supreme Court head, Meaza Ashenafi, and with financial support from donors, judges were to become a bit more independent, albeit within clearly demarcated limits.[24] At the same time, however, Abiy's rhetorical castigation of the security forces had the side effect of empowering local vigilantes and hastening the state's unravelling: stinging from the public's hatred, and lacking a clear sense of direction in the absence of brute force, many local police chose to sit idle rather than keep order. Some were seen even joining the mayhem.[25]

Less substantively, Abiy established the country's first-ever national reconciliation commission. In theory, a reconciliation commission could have allowed victims of state-sanctioned crimes, or earlier rounds of communal violence, to give public voice to their suffering and find some form of redress, beginning the process of collective healing which Ethiopia so badly needed. In the long run it might even have offered a way out of the cycle of revenge and retribution, a light that could have scattered the dark shadows of historical memory, which underlay so many of the country's conflicts. But the commission's members—all part-time and unpaid—lacked the resources and technical support needed to effectively carry out the body's fact-finding function.[26] Abiy, meanwhile, whose own party allies had blood on their hands, was unwilling to give it the necessary powers to properly pursue either justice or truth—a problem which would later re-emerge when his government was pushed by Western donors into promising a process of 'transitional justice' after the Tigray War. "I'm not sure the commission is fit for purpose," one of its commissioners admitted to me in 2020. Two years later, it was quietly dissolved.

Meanwhile, to resolve the territorial disputes burning in so much of the country, Abiy set up a boundary commission, which was to report directly to him. Given that such matters were supposed to be handled by the House of Federation, the upper chamber of Ethiopia's parliament, the new commission was of dubious constitutional legality. Many MPs, in particular those from the Tigray, voted against it. To make matters worse, Abiy had handpicked its members, in several cases without consulting them before doing so. One of them later told me that the first he had heard about his appointment was on seeing the news on TV. "They were just playing games with those commissions," said an Ethiopian lawyer working as an advisor to the attorney-general's office at the time. "They were there just to save face and kind of say that they were doing the work." In the eyes of many Tigrayans, the boundary commission's purpose was also rather more malignant: a deliberate effort to wrestle the disputed territories of Wolkait and Raya from their control.

But nothing summed up Abiy's domestic peace-making quite like the Ministry of Peace, established in October 2018 and headed by one of his high-profile new female cabinet members, Muferiat Kemal. An emblematically headline-grabbing initiative, the ministry was billed as the prime minister's signature contribution to restoring order in his conflict-racked country by reallocating resources from security operations to peacebuilding. But Muferiat, in reality, was little more than a figurehead whose powers were strictly limited. Over time, it would become clear that Abiy had no intention of allowing her to devise a strategy for national reconciliation independent of his own, one with a distinct emphasis on amnesty and amnesia—characteristically framed in terms of Christian 'forgiveness'—combined with a politically selective approach to accountability.[27]

More to the point, despite the eye-catching name, the ministry of peace was really just an interior ministry, or department of homeland security, staffed by former intelligence officers, including many former colleagues of Abiy from INSA. Agencies which dealt with refugees and humanitarian affairs sat firmly (indeed, literally, once its new office had been unveiled three years later) underneath the very institutions of the security apparatus which Abiy had promised to rein in. After a while, most of the peace ministry was dismembered. Later it was put under the direct control of the Prime Minister's Office, as part of a gradual centralisation of power in Abiy's hands, and a re-securitisation of the federal state, over the coming years.

* * *

By early 2019 Abiy's distinctly hands-off approach to mounting instability was starting to present other problems. This time the trouble in Gedeo was not simply the ongoing conflict itself but the government's response to the humanitarian fallout. Aid workers feared this response was becoming increasingly authoritarian, with little attention being paid to the demands of the victims while also apparently being subservient to the prime minister's whims. For several months, in which few media reported on the violence and many other Ethiopians remained unaware of it, Abiy had acted as if nothing were happening. He pointedly ignored the string of petitions and increasingly desperate pilgrimages to his office made by Gedeo elders and activists. On the rare occasion he did address the displacement crisis, he downplayed its significance, suggesting that the numbers were exaggerated or that most of those evicted had already returned home.[28] In some meetings with senior diplomats, he bluntly denied Ethiopia had any displaced people at all. It was only after a social media and crowdfunding campaign, sparked by some unflattering articles in the Western press, my own among them, that Abiy would make his first and only visit to one of the many camps which had sprung up to shelter those displaced by the conflict.[29] In a televised conversation with the Gedeo community in May 2019, in which he posed for smiling photographs with children who had just recently been violently uprooted from their homes, he suggested misleadingly that his office had only just been made aware of the scale of the crisis.[30]

In fact, Abiy's government had a clear strategy from the outset: to coerce the displaced into going back home. The means to achieve this involved blocking aid from reaching the camps—a major breach of international humanitarian principles as well as a foreshadowing of what was soon to come in Tigray. Federal police, meanwhile, had forced refugees onto buses, sometimes at gunpoint, ferrying them back to areas like Kercha that were not yet safe—with often disastrous results. One furious eighteen-year-old Gedeo woman told me in early 2019 that no sooner had she and her family, at the government's insistence, returned to their home in Kercha, than armed men arrived at the door again. "They took everything the government had given us. They sent us back empty-handed," she told me. The second time this happened, in December 2018, some 15,000 Gedeos had fled anew.[31]

Abiy's approach to mass displacement was revealing. On the one hand, he was mostly consistent in his argument that Ethiopians of any ethnicity evicted from their homes in any part of the country should be returned, with their property restored, as a matter of principle (though international humanitarian norms stipulate that such returns should always be voluntary).[32] In 2023, in the aftermath of the Tigray War, he told Parliament that there should be "no territory in Ethiopia where Ethiopians can't live."[33] But at the same time he hadn't objected when Oromos expelled from the Somali region in 2017 had been given new plots of land and shelter in Oromia by the regional government—many of them on the politically sensitive outskirts of Addis Ababa. Political calculations, it appears, were never far from his mind, and the Oromo remained his core constituency after all—increasing their demographic weight in and around Addis Ababa had long been a key concern of Oromo nationalists. But when it came to the Gedeo crisis, there may well have been other considerations at play: having been nominated for the Nobel Prize in early 2019, Abiy appeared anxious to keep up appearances internationally. The presence of large numbers of internally displaced people living in squalid, under-resourced camps was an especially vivid stain on his early record.

One of the settlements Abiy seems to have particularly wanted cleared by this point was in the village of Gotiti, just over the border from Kercha. When I visited it in February 2019, there were more than 20,000 Gedeo refugees but not a single NGO there. The small handful of aid workers who spoke with me about the camp before I went did so in hushed voices, helping me to pinpoint its location on the map but offering no further assistance. "They are forbidding us from operating," one explained. For more than six months the displaced had languished under makeshift roofs woven from *enset* leaves, hidden in the shadow of churches and schools and the local football stadium. In UN-speak, malnutrition rates were well above 'emergency thresholds'. This meant, in plainer language, that babies were dying of hunger.

But barely a word was ever said about it in public. Once again presaging the dynamics of the Tigray War, influential UN agencies and individuals leading them appeared to have decided to more or less go along with the cover-up. The UN's distinct model of aid distribution in Ethiopia, which had long given the government unusual latitude to politicise the provision of emergency relief, often by simply excluding troublesome populations, was left unreformed.[34] Scrutiny of Abiy's erratic and now evidently counterproductive approach to managing conflict was meanwhile postponed. "We failed Gedeo-Guji," one senior European aid official admitted a few months later. "And I'm afraid we are going to fail again in Ethiopia, but at an even larger scale."

10

"OUR SON-OF-A-BITCH"

THE SOMALI REGION AND THE EMPIRE'S EDGES

At the entrance to the army base in Degehabur were two stucco Abyssinian lions mounted on concrete plinths. Each day, at sunrise and at dusk, a bell would ring, and the Ethiopian flag would rise up the pole between them. Those who passed by the lions at such times, or the nearby police station, were expected to stand still as a mark of respect. Those who didn't risked arrest.

For a century or more, Degehabur was a garrison post, a fortress defending the far-eastern reaches of the Ethiopian empire inhabited mostly by ethnic Somalis, first from British predations, then later—unsuccessfully—from the invading Italians, whose aerial campaign over the town in 1936 involved poison gas and the bombing of a Red Cross facility.[1] During the 1977–8 war with neighbouring Somalia, Degehabur was one of the final strongholds of the Ethiopian army. Less than a year after its fall to a joint force of Somali national troops and local Somali separatists, it was recaptured with the help of Soviet weaponry and a Cuban tank brigade.[2] On the northern side of the town lay the remains of an Ethiopian Airlines passenger plane downed during that war—evidence, in the eyes of the aggrieved local Somali population, who cared little for their imperial highland overlords, that the Ethiopian army had used civilian carriers as part of its campaign there.

By the 2000s, Degehabur was a citadel of the separatist Ogaden National Liberation Front (ONLF), which had been formed in the 1980s to fight on behalf of local Somalis against the Ethiopian state. The ONLF had won control of the new Somali regional government in local elections in 1992, and promptly sought to follow Eritrea's example in demanding an independence referendum. The EPRDF refused, defying both the federal constitution and its own professed belief in self-determination—sparking an insurgency which had rumbled on ever since.[3] In 2007, the ONLF had attacked an oil exploration camp near Degehabur, killing seventy-four workers, including nine Chinese. The Ethiopian army responded with a scorched-earth counter-insurgency campaign so fierce that whole villages were wiped off the map.[4] The Somali region (or 'Region 5' as it was often dismissively called) became an open-air prison. Degehabur was put, in effect, in solitary confinement, with trade to and from the area blocked.[5] Before 2018, the few visitors who made it to the town—foreign journalists were banned—would be stopped and searched at some of the region's strictest checkpoints. Manning them were glowering, well-armed *Liyu*: the notorious Somali 'special police' established under Meles's direction in 2009.

By the time I visited Degehabur in 2021 there were no checkpoints at all. The lions at the gates of the army base, which had been abandoned, were broken and crumbling; one of their faces had been knocked right off. The former barracks were now occupied by the families of *Liyu* officers, who waved at me with friendly smiles as I wandered among the dust-covered relics the military had left behind: rusted, disused artillery; an empty armoured bunker; the concrete replica of an outdated map of Ethiopia, erected on a pedestal with an imposing Amharic slogan—"we are determined to destroy the anti-peace elements"—daubed on the side. Here was a monument to Ethiopian power, reduced to a field of rubble and weeds. For residents of Degehabur, Somalis mostly from the Ogaden clan, the symbolism was hard to miss. No longer was their region the theatre of a war or violent insurgency. And no longer were they living under Ethiopian military rule.

My guide around Degehabur that day was Mohammed Cadare, a former ONLF fighter who for a while had been the round and boyish face of the Ogaden struggle; a photograph of him trudging through the bush with an AK-47 slung over his shoulder had appeared in the *New York Times* in 2008.[6] A decade before, Mohammed had fought gun battles on this very ground, and he could still remember the spot where five of his comrades had been mown down. For four years prior to 2018 he had languished in prison in Addis Ababa. For more than a year he didn't see the face of a single other of his fellow inmates.

Now, though, Mohammed walked the streets of his hometown so freely it was as if nothing had ever happened. At the camp's entrance, I watched as he and a group of *Liyu* police cracked jokes with each other. After a few minutes of warm chatter one of them jumped in the back of our car to show us around. "I really like them," Mohammed grinned. "They're my friends." A few hours later that afternoon we drank tea with them in the courtyard of a building which the *Liyu* had once used to interrogate and torture suspected ONLF sympathisers—Mohammed included. The very same rope which had once been used to hang detainees from a tree in front of the house, he told me, had only just recently been removed.

The peace which came in 2018 to the Somali region, for decades the most ill-treated and inaccessible place in all Ethiopia, was unprecedented. That this stability prevailed at the same time so much of the country was in turmoil made it all the more surprising. But there was no denying the transformation, not even among Somali critics of Abiy and Mustafa Omer, now the federal government's man in Jigjiga, the Somali regional capital. "It's the safest place in Ethiopia," conceded Kamal Hassan, one of many thousands of Ethiopian Somalis who returned to the region from exile in 2019. Not that he expected the calm to last long—very few did. But when we spoke again three years later, he granted Mustafa, the Somali state president, some begrudging respect: "He kept the region more peaceful than the rest of the country. And that is more than I expected of him." Just as war raged in Tigray, the Somali region was enjoying a greater degree of self-rule than it had at almost any point since its annexation to the Ethiopian empire in the late nineteenth century.

* * *

Abiy's relationship with the TPLF didn't fall apart immediately upon his taking office. In fact, one of his very first acts was to pardon and release several officials and businessmen who had been charged with corruption, among whom were several prominent Tigrayans. Debretsion Gebremichael, Tigray's president from early 2018, for his part seemed conciliatory and willing to work with the new administration. At the biennial EPRDF congress, held after repeated delays that October, the two men put on a show of unity, and Debretsion was handed responsibility—though only on paper, it later became clear—for normalising trade ties with Eritrea. The TPLF voted for Abiy to remain party chairman.

But behind the scenes the TPLF's presence across swathes of the Ethiopian state was being concertedly dismantled. Starting in the military and intelligence apparatus—unsurprisingly, given the Tigrayans' established dominance there—scores of senior Tigrayan officers were soon forced into retirement. By the end of the year, one of Abiy's advisers told *Reuters*, 160 army generals had been sacked for actions he said amounted to "state terrorism".[7] In early June 2018, the prime minister had also removed both the head of the military, General Samora Yunis, and the head of NISS, Getachew Assefa—the two most powerful Tigrayan securocrats. "The security officials were a powerful government of their own," he later argued. "They had their own soldiers, media, and businesses. And so we made a decision that it would be impossible to continue working with them, and that they should be removed."[8]

Conscious of the public optics of an indiscriminate Tigrayan purge, Abiy then replaced Samora with Seare Mekonnen, another Tigrayan. But it was cold comfort to those in the TPLF becoming increasingly concerned by the direction of travel. Below the radar, Tigrayans continued to be removed from the civil service, the judiciary, and from state corporations like Ethio Telecom. By 2020, the TPLF would hold no cabinet posts at all. Elsewhere, the TPLF's grip on important sectors of the economy, notably through METEC, the military-industrial conglomerate led by former Tigrayan generals, was being prised open. Within a few months Abiy had broken METEC up, stripped some of its contracts, and appointed new leadership.

A string of unsettling and largely unexplained incidents, meanwhile, was slowly beginning to puncture what remained of the national euphoria sparked by Abiy's ascent. The first of these, a grenade thrown at a mass rally organised in Addis Ababa's Meskel Square by his supporters just two weeks after the removal of the Tigrayan security chiefs, had left one person in the crowd dead, and many more injured. Shortly after the blast, the crowd had erupted into ominous chants of "down down *Woyane*" and "*Woyane* thief", invoking the commonplace nickname for the TPLF. Almost as quickly, the authorities had announced that the bomb had been an attempt on Abiy's life by disgruntled members of the federal security apparatus, including the former spy chief.

The prime minister, appearing grim-faced and sporting a lime-green Nelson Mandela T-shirt on television just moments after, declared the incident a "planned and well-orchestrated" attack by "forces who do not want to see Ethiopia united".[9] Police later arrested thirty people suspected of involvement, among them prominent Tigrayans, as well as nine police officers including the capital's deputy police commissioner. The following month, in one of the earliest signs of a brewing stand-off between Abiy and the TPLF, forty federal police commandos flew unannounced to Mekelle, ostensibly to arrest those Tigrayan suspects who had fled to the region, among them Getachew Assefa himself. After being swiftly apprehended by the Tigrayan authorities, who rejected the legality of their raid, the commandos were placed in detention for several weeks.

Initially the US government had offered to send a team from the FBI, but in the end never did—meaning no independent investigation into the June blast was ever carried out. For its part, though, the federal government offered explanations which were by turns unconvincing and contradictory. For one thing, the plot's amateurishness made it highly unlikely that the spy chief or any other senior securocrats had really had a hand in it. "If it had really been the TPLF or the military," one senior American diplomat noted bluntly, "Abiy would be dead." Indeed, an Oromo government insider alleged to me several years later that the grenade attack had been an inside job carried out by the Oromo special police—in order to boost Abiy's popularity, the insider claimed, and to "build momentum against the TPLF." State media, meanwhile, alternated between calling it a bomb explosion and an assassination attempt. Two years later, by which point blame had been firmly pinned on the TPLF, five non-Tigrayans allegedly connected to the OLF were convicted instead.[10]

Subsequent events thickened the air of conspiratorial intrigue. Barely a month after the June blast, the popular chief engineer of the Grand Ethiopian Renaissance Dam, Simegnew Bekele, had been found slumped at the wheel of his Toyota Land Cruiser with a bullet through his head.[11] Though the police ruled the death as suicide, few Ethiopians believed them, not least because the location was once again Meskel Square, the city's symbolic heart. Tigrayan opponents quickly accused the government of murder. Others reckoned the death was linked to METEC, which was responsible for much of the dam's sluggish construction and was widely believed to have embezzled funds. (In theory, the engineer might have been killed to prevent him becoming a whistle-blower.) Further muddying the picture, though, were the prime minister's own inconsistent and at times strangely tone-deaf responses. "I was with Abiy when he heard the news of his death," a senior opposition figure later recalled. "His reaction? Nothing." Just days before Simegnew's death, Abiy had warned that on current progress it could take another decade to finish the dam, and appeared to talk the project down as if it were just a TPLF white elephant. The prime minister would later be conspicuous in his absence from the engineer's grand public funeral.

* * *

It was against this backdrop that Abiy began mulling how to deal with Abdi Mohamed Omar, popularly known as Abdi Illey ("the one-eyed"), Ethiopia's most controversial regional president. Here the considerations were particularly delicate. On the one hand, any move against the powerful Somali leader was bound to be contentious. For more than a decade he had been a close ally—and reputed drinking companion—of the Tigrayan generals running the Eastern Command. Moreover, it was due to Meles's patronage, back when Abdi had been the region's security chief in charge of the newly formed *Liyu*, that he ultimately owed his current position. When anti-TPLF protests raged in Oromia in 2016, Abdi had organised counterdemonstrations in Jigjiga in a pointed display of public solidarity.

Added to this was the simple, if sensitive, fact that prominent Tigrayans—veterans of the guerrilla war, in particular—were notably well-entrenched in Somali affairs, with a stake not only in the security sector but also the region's wider economy. This was not, by any stretch, a dynamic unique to the Somali region: Ethiopia's resource-rich but politically weak peripheral regions had always been where the outsized influence of Tigrayan, and before that Amhara, elites was most visible.[12] But in the Somali state it was particularly noticeable, with senior Tigrayan generals for instance owning large tracts of fertile land along the Shabelle River, and Tigrayan officials largely in charge of issuing bank permits for exports in the lucrative *khat* trade. The upshot of this was that any attempt to strike at the network of entrenched interests around Abdi was bound to be risky.

But on the other hand, removing the Somali leader would certainly be popular with much of the Ethiopian public. Abdi may have been well-connected, but he was also a thug, whose decade in power—after being catapulted from humble beginnings as a lowly employee of a provincial electricity company—had been stained by the *Liyu*'s campaign of rape, murder and mass imprisonment.[13] "He's a son-of-a-bitch," an Ethiopian political analyst once quipped, likening the relationship between Abdi and the federal authorities in Addis Ababa to the model of outsourced counter-insurgency infamously employed by Putin in Russia's Chechnya province, "but he's our son-of-a-bitch." So miserable was the Somali president's reign that by 2018 it was clear that almost all the local population bar his network of government cadres and patrons in the federal security apparatus—which included some key figures in the TPLF—would be happy to see the back of him.

But prior to August 2018 it was far from a foregone conclusion that Abiy intended to heed them. Regimes in Addis Ababa had long governed Ethiopia's disenchanted peripheries through pliable local puppets, and there was no real reason to imagine the new prime minister intended to do any differently. In fact, for the first few months of his tenure Abiy seems to have calculated that, rather than removing Abdi, his interests would be better served by co-opting the Somali strongman in much the same way as the TPLF-led EPRDF had done before him. When a delegation of Abdi's Somali critics, among them prominent clan elders, descended on Addis Ababa to lobby the new government to remove Abdi, Abiy pointedly refused to see them.

In any event, he could hardly rely on popular pressure to force Abdi out. The ONLF, which—like the OLF and Ginbot 7—had mostly decamped to Eritrea in the 2000s, was weak and divided, with its leaders by now scattered across Europe and America. Ordinary Somalis inside the region, meanwhile, were cowed. Most of those opposed to the regime had long been locked up or driven into exile. Somali opposition figures such as Mustafa, then a UN staffer living in Nairobi and writing critical blogs under a pen name, had given up waiting on a local uprising; in the months after Abiy's appointment only a ripple of small-scale protests broke out. Nothing was ever likely to change in the Somali region without Addis Ababa's say-so.

Exactly why the green light finally came in August 2018 is unclear. On the one hand, the ties Mustafa and other Somali activists had cultivated among influential Oromo figures had certainly helped in their anti-Abdi campaign. Behind the scenes, Jawar and others had been actively pushing for the Somali president's removal, too. As one OPDO colleague of Abiy later recalled, the overwhelming majority of the Oromo public were furious with Abdi following the border conflict the previous year, and were anxious to see him brought down. Lemma, still Oromia's president, was known to be particularly hostile.

But on the other hand there was the matter of Abdi's own increasingly erratic behaviour. Despite the handshakes and smiles, his unhappiness with Abiy's rise was common knowledge; on the day of the prime minister's appointment, he had been spotted looking visibly distressed in Addis Ababa's Sheraton Hotel. In May, several months of uneasy calm along the border with Oromia had been broken by *Liyu* raids on the town of Chinaksen, in which some 250 homes were reportedly razed to the ground. Two months later, apparently in response to a report by Human

Rights Watch which detailed human rights abuses in Jail Ogaden, Abdi had taken to the floor of the state parliament and proclaimed that he had only ever been doing the bidding of NISS chief Getachew Assefa—an unlikely allegation given that rivalries between Ethiopia's intelligence chief and his military counterparts were such that the Somali region was generally considered one of the few places the former had limited clout.[14] A few days later, Abdi warned that if ever he left power, "Jigjiga [would turn] into Mogadishu"—the capital of war-torn Somalia next door.[15]

Either way, the wheels of regime change were firmly in motion by the start of August. Organising for the first time in public to defy the Somali president—undoubtedly with Abiy's blessing—Somali elders, activists and opposition politicians had gathered in a conference hall in the city of Dire Dawa, 150 kilometres west of Jigjiga, in the final days of July. Already waiting in the wings as the most likely candidate to take over from Abdi was Mustafa, by then ensconced in a hotel in Addis Ababa. At the meeting hall in Dire Dawa, congregants posted videos of themselves on social media calling for Abdi's overthrow. Buses were made ready to carry them to Jigjiga in a show of strength. Holed up in his hilltop fortress above the Somali state capital, and sensing the walls closing in on him, Abdi panicked.

What followed over the next few days is hotly disputed. But what is incontestable is that on 4 August Abdi called on his supporters to defend him, unleashing a state-sponsored youth group known as the "*Heego*" to stop the crowd then making their way from Dire Dawa. In the storm of violence which subsequently blew across the city, as well as through smaller towns like Degehabur, shops and businesses owned by Amhara and Oromo minorities were ransacked and churches set ablaze. Scores died, all non-Somalis, with thousands chased from their homes by marauding gangs. Senior *Liyu* officers, sensing the ground beneath them beginning to crack, fled the country.[16]

In a final desperate act, Abdi summoned the state parliament. His plan, it appears, had been to press the nuclear button and trigger secession. In theory, this might have been constitutional, had any of his parliamentary colleagues been willing to go along with it. But before that theory could be tested, Abiy sent in the army. Following two days of fierce fighting on the streets of Jigjiga, Abdi was arrested and flown by helicopter to Addis Ababa, where he was eventually put on trial. When Mustafa later entered the president's palace as Abdi's successor, at Abiy's invitation, he found the whole place had been upturned and looted. Scrawled on the city's walls, likely by factions loyal to Abdi's outgoing regime, were the words "Fuck Abiy".

Some Somalis, including Mustafa, later speculated that the order to mobilise the *Heego* had come not from Abdi himself but from Tigrayan generals or even senior members of the TPLF itself. Abiy, too, later gave credence to this theory, telling parliament shortly after the start of the Tigray War that "the first dream to disintegrate Ethiopia" had begun in the Somali region.[17] But there was again little actual evidence of this, and Abdi's wild and unpredictable behaviour in the weeks leading up to his arrest strongly suggested that the most plausible explanation was simply that he had seen his options dwindling and lashed out.

Whether this then justified the federal government's military intervention was less straightforward: legally speaking, removing a dangerous regional president was the job of the regional parliament, not the army. To many constitutional experts, Abiy's claim that Abdi had posed such an imminent threat to national security that his government was left with no choice but to intervene didn't hold water.[18] Public opinion, though, was a different matter: Abdi's reign had been harsh and unpopular. In any case, nobody really imagined that any of Abiy's predecessors would have deferred to constitutional probity and responded much differently.

But there was one place where all arguments of this kind fell on deaf ears. In Tigray, the overthrow of Abdi was seen as a clear shot across the bows. "The process of destroying the regions began in the Somali region," a veteran Tigrayan diplomat later wrote. "If Abdi Illey's government committed a crime, it should've been held to account legally."[19] Jigjiga, from the TPLF's perspective, was where the new prime minister first showed his disregard for the niceties of the constitution, and his willingness to use force to remove recalcitrant leaders. It wouldn't be forgotten easily.

* * *

For a great number of Somalis, however, the change of regime in Jigjiga was simply a relief. Mustafa, like Abdi himself, had grown up in Degehabur; because of his outspoken activism, a brother of his had been shot dead by the *Liyu* and thrown from a speeding car just a few years earlier. With one of their own at the reins, dissidents and rebels soon began returning in droves. When I visited Jigjiga a year later, former detainees who had previously been too afraid to meet me in public had jobs in government. Jail Ogaden was closed, and within months human rights workers and journalists were being given tours of it. Across the region, thousands of prisoners were freed. A former inmate of Jail Ogaden was put in charge of regional security; a former exile was made his deputy. On their watch the *Liyu* underwent reform, with the most abusive commanders fired and the remainder retrained. Reports of human rights violations fell dramatically.[20] "Killings have stopped; torture and mass arrests have stopped," said the former ONLF fighter, Mohammed Cadare, who was among those released from prison in 2018.

The ONLF, like the OLF and Ginbot 7 before it, returned from Eritrea and elsewhere abroad. When I visited the Somali region in 2019, it was common to see former ONLF fighters like Mohammed walking arm-in-arm with the same *Liyu* police they had once been waging war against. Tensions between the ONLF and Mustafa persisted—the new Somali president held the separatists in very low regard—but they didn't flare into open violence. After a peace agreement had been signed, Mustafa launched a joint committee with the ONLF leadership to manage relations and to oversee the demobilisation, disarmament and reintegration (DDR) of its troops. The ONLF's leaders paid visits to Northern Ireland and Mindanao in the Philippines to take lessons in how to undergo a peaceful transition.

It wasn't all plain sailing. Although the border war with Oromia soon quietened, large-scale fighting at Moyale in the deep south erupted in late 2018 and was only defused once Mustafa—under private pressure from Abiy, and in the face of local opposition—fired the *Liyu* commander responsible for mobilising the Somali forces there. On Mustafa's watch, a simmering conflict along the border with the Afar region also escalated dramatically and continued for several years, peaking in 2021 during the Tigray War. The Somali president's ill-judged and nationalistic decision to pull out of an agreement with Afar struck by his predecessor in 2014 had clearly been a major cause of the fighting.

Over time, Mustafa also built up his own impressive list of enemies. Many of those suspected of ties to either Abdi Illey or the TPLF—his greatest foes—were given short shrift. "He treats everyone who worked for Abdi like they are Hitlers," complained one associate of the former regime. Much like Abiy himself, the new Somali leader tended to blame the TPLF for almost anything which went wrong, often accusing it of trying to incite clan conflicts or religious unrest through its old regional networks of money and patronage. Yet even those with no ties at all to the old regime could on occasion be dealt with harshly. Some of his former allies would later accuse him of ruling dictatorially, and of sending intimidating messages to those who criticised him.

At the heart of his rule, though, was a revealing paradox. On the one hand, though never truly trusted, Mustafa was unquestionably Abiy's man. Although it was the ruling party in the region which elected him (despite his not being a party member), there was never any question that the new president served at Abiy's pleasure. He did so despite the palpable differences between them. While Abiy could be preening and self-aggrandising, Mustafa was typically down-to-earth and generous; when he invited me for dinner in the presidential palace, we ate barefoot on the sofa. But he would never dare speak ill of his boss. "I think most people were relieved by Mustafa's appointment," one ex-detainee told me in 2021. "But at the same time, it was a reality check. They can bring in whoever they want here." If the president displeased the prime minister, he could be summoned to Addis Ababa for a dressing down. On more than one occasion he was nearly fired.

At the same time, though, no leader of the Somali region in recent memory had enjoyed such autonomy. Gone were the days when prospective parliamentary candidates would be screened by officers in the Eastern Command; no longer could federal officials simply ring up the president and tell him to appoint their friends to regional offices. In some ways, it was a bargain between centre and periphery which recalled aspects of Menelik II's empire: so long as Mustafa didn't threaten the federal government or Abiy's hold on power—when he objected to Abiy's establishment of the Prosperity Party in 2019, for instance, he was swiftly put in his place—he was granted the freedom more or less to run the region as he saw fit. It helped that Abiy could rely on Mustafa to be a loyal ally against the TPLF, and it was said that in the fated final meetings of the EPRDF in 2019, nobody was more openly hostile towards the Tigrayan contingent than the Somali president. "He was the attack dog," said a well-placed observer in Addis Ababa. "Abiy would leave the floor to Mustafa." But in return, Abiy generally left his man to his own devices.

The flipside of this was that the Somali region, much like the other peripheral states of Benishangul-Gumuz, Afar and Gambella, remained a bit-player in federal affairs. On one level, ethnic Somalis were more visible in the federal government than they had ever been, and Abiy made much of his efforts to bring them and other marginalised groups to the fore. His influential finance minister, Ahmed Shide, for instance, became perhaps the most powerful Somali politician in recent Ethiopian history.

But on a deeper level, little had changed. Nothing was ever really done to heal the wounds wrought by Ethiopia's rule over the many preceding decades. Old resentments were simply left to fester. Abiy himself often seemed oblivious to them, such as when he suggested—with profoundly ahistorical insensitivity—that he would build a monument at Karamardha mountain in Jigjiga to commemorate Ethiopia's 1978 victory over Somalia there. By reviving the old Ethiopian nationalist narrative of the war, as Abiy did, local Somalis were given a painful reminder that their own demands for self-rule, which long predated the 1977–78 conflict, still meant little to highland Ethiopians. "The region is stable but not peaceful," a former advisor to the president later observed. "We're not yet at peace with ourselves. And we're not yet at peace with the Ethiopian state."

* * *

Abiy continued to shake up the old order elsewhere in the country. After Jigjiga, he moved to replace the leadership of other peripheral states— Gambella, Harar and Afar—all of whom were, rightly or wrongly, seen as tainted by association with the TPLF. In Benishangul-Gumuz, a particularly troubled region towards the far-western border with Sudan, the state president remained in place, giving a rare illusion of continuity. But there, too, the TPLF's influence was fast waning. Over the next couple of years, TPLF 'advisors' seconded to the Benishangul state government— typically Tigrayan intelligence officials—would be replaced, while several major Tigrayan investors would have their licences revoked for failing to develop their agricultural leases. A Tigrayan hotel owner in Assosa, the regional capital, was arrested. Gradually, Tigrayans dropped out of the local bureaucracy, either being fired or leaving their posts for the sanctuary of Tigray—a pattern mirrored in the north-eastern Afar region, where, in 2019, scores of large-scale salt miners affiliated with the TPLF were expropriated, and in some cases thrown in jail.[21] For the most part, Tigrayans on the way out were to be replaced by Amharas or Oromos, the two groups scrambling quickest and most forcefully to fill the vacuum opening up.[22]

As Abiy pressed ahead with consolidating his rule he seemed increasingly anxious about his own security. A mutiny of elite soldiers in October was seized as an opportunity for another photo-op: within a day of their march on his palace, videos were circulating showing the prime minister doing press-ups with the grinning troops. But not everyone was convinced the uprising was a genuine one, with some noting that the soldiers had been able to march all the way across the city without once being stopped. In any case, the incident was followed by a further purge of the army and, a few months later, the establishment of the Emirati-funded and trained Republican Guard—a new elite unit loyal only to the prime minister.[23] Abiy would later claim that by this point he had decided that the TPLF wanted him dead.[24]

At the same time, fears in Mekelle were also mounting. Emboldened by his ostensible success in dismantling the Tigrayan core of the security establishment, Abiy raised the stakes even higher in November by issuing arrest warrants for twenty-seven senior, and predominantly Tigrayan, officials in METEC on charges of corruption—a move so escalatory that one official in the Prime Minister's Office likened it to the nationalisation of land in 1975, the high-water mark of Ethiopia's first revolution.[25] Shortly after came a flurry of warrants for the arrest of senior NISS officers and prison bosses, this time for human rights abuses, including one for the deputy head of intelligence.

The ensuing trial-by-media, which included a controversial documentary broadcast on state TV in which former prisoners described torture at the hands of "Tigrinya-speakers", further inflamed ordinary Tigrayans' fears of persecution.[26] Now, from the TPLF's perspective, a brazen witch-hunt was underway. Selective prosecutions for past crimes, they feared, would soon envelop the entire leadership, leaving them either in prison or penniless.[27] "Every Tom, Dick and Harry wants to blame the TPLF for every bad thing going on in the country," fretted the future Tigray president Getachew Reda that same month. "It's as if the TPLF had supernatural capabilities."

So they dug in their heels. When Abiy's administration made public that it had also issued a warrant for Getachew Assefa, again because of alleged human rights violations, Tigray's regional authorities refused to hand him over. By now the former spy chief had been re-elected to the TPLF politburo, a provocative and unhelpful move likely intended to shield him from prosecution. Other Ethiopians were incensed. (Speaking to a *Reuters* journalist at the time, Getachew Reda claimed he had no idea of his colleague's whereabouts, and suggested he could be in either Israel or Sudan.) In January 2019, the Amhara regional government added further fuel to the fire by arresting one of the EPRDF's founders, Meles's closest ally in Amhara, Bereket Simon, at his home in Addis Ababa, and putting him on trial for questionable corruption charges. He would spend the next four years in prison.

By the start of 2019 whatever remained of goodwill between Abiy and his former Tigrayan colleagues, many of whom had already begun to decamp for the perceived safety of Mekelle, had evaporated. For the first time, Debretsion spoke in public of Tigray's willingness to defend itself.[28] Within only a year he would accuse Abiy's government of working "to destroy the people of Tigray".[29]

In just a few short months the two sides had found themselves locked in a 'security dilemma', in which one's defence was the other's aggression. As Abiy began building up his own security forces, including the Republican Guard, the TPLF bolstered their own. Over the course of the next two years, it would add several thousand troops as well as heavy weapons to its own special police force. Across the country, other regions followed suit.[30] By the middle of 2019 a national arms race would be fully underway.

Meanwhile, the EPRDF limped on. Now no more than a passing ghost of its former self, the parties barely meeting together at all, the chaos and discord inside it increasingly seemed to threaten the very survival of the state. Speaking to a foreign researcher, Sebhat Nega, the TPLF's intellectual godfather, warned that Abiy was leading Ethiopia to the brink of disintegration. "The constitution is negated every day. The elected government is gone. I not only fear—I believe—Ethiopia will no longer exist," he said. "There is no light at the end of the tunnel. In effect, the EPRDF is destroyed."[31]

PART THREE

CRISIS

11

"THEIR PROTECTOR"

ASAMINEW TSIGE AND AMHARA NATIONALISM

Brigadier-General Asaminew Tsige was not a typical army officer. His relatives remembered him as unusually emotional for a soldier, a devout Orthodox Christian who wept passionately at his father's grave after being released from prison in 2018, and who cared little for money or earthly possessions. In the Amhara holy town of Lalibela, where his family lived, he was known as a tireless public servant; as a local administrator there in the early 1990s he had helped to install its first water pipes and electricity. That he could be impulsive, if occasionally reckless, was well known—indeed, it was part of his romantic appeal in his home state. His ill-fated participation in a Ginbot 7 plot to overthrow Meles in 2009, which had landed him in prison for the best part of a decade, was exactly the sort of doomed heroism so venerated in Amhara.[1] When he finally returned home in 2018, the bells of Lalibela's churches rang out and a great crowd welcomed him.

I found Asaminew's younger sister, Desta, in Lalibela in 2022, at the modest family home just off the main square, an earthen bungalow covered by tarpaulin and corrugated iron. Tears fell down Desta's face as we spoke about her late brother, who had been slain in a final shoot-out with the federal army near the state capital Bahir Dar three years earlier. She didn't believe the government's story that Asaminew's fighters had assassinated the Amhara regional president and two more senior officials as part of another coup attempt any more than she had ever trusted Meles's claim a decade earlier that her brother had tried to oust him, too. In the eyes of his relatives and neighbours, Asaminew had been a selfless patriot, so devoted to his fellow countrymen that he barely had any time for his own family. "He was their protector," Desta told me quietly, sitting upright on a rug made of sheep's wool. "He gave more time to others than himself." In the weeks before his death in June 2019, she recalled, Asaminew was so preoccupied with work that he had barely ever been home.

When Asaminew had finally left prison in early 2018, pardoned by the government for his part in the 2009 conspiracy, he emerged bitter and resentful—and not a little unstable. During his imprisonment he had endured torture and solitary confinement; sometimes, it was commonly said, at the hands of Tigrayan prison guards, who beat and insulted him for being Amhara. A voracious reader, Asaminew spent his years on the inside devouring as many books as he could lay his hands on, hardening the political views which, as a member of the military, he was always supposed to have suppressed. Already known for a habit of insubordination, now out of the army he became ever more the political hothead. If once he was the TPLF's comrade-in-arms—in the late 1980s he had joined the Ethiopian People's Democratic Movement, the precursor to the ANDM, and fought against the Derg—now he was their sternest antagonist, an Amhara radical as uncompromising in his hostility to his erstwhile allies as he was unflinching in his conviction that old wrongs must be righted.

Not, some argued at the time, an especially wise choice to lead the security apparatus of a region already coming to blows with its neighbours. But in the quixotic spirit of the moment, blessed by a new amnesty law that exonerated former defectors from the military and officers charged with breaching military discipline, less sober voices prevailed. Asaminew was honourably retired from the army with full pension rights and elected to the central committee of the region's ruling party.[2] Not long afterwards he was picked by Gedu, then still Amhara state president, to head its administration and security bureau—a move mirrored in Oromia when Lemma put a former Oromo general who had previously defected to the OLF in charge of regional security there. Abiy would later claim personal credit for the move.[3]

In the security vacuum which prevailed after Abiy took office, Asaminew became the figurehead for a new form of anxious, revanchist nationalism then sweeping through the Amhara region. Not that he would have ever labelled himself as such: like most Amharas of his generation, Asaminew considered himself an Ethiopian nationalist par excellence and his known political ties were to the avowedly 'pan-Ethiopian' Ginbot 7, soon to be rebranded as the Ethiopian Citizens for Social Justice (Ezema). But in his strident rhetoric there was increasingly little to distinguish Asaminew from the younger firebrands then beginning to coalesce under an unprecedentedly explicit, and unbending, ethno-nationalist agenda. Released from the political shackles which ostensibly bound army officers, the new Amhara security chief transformed himself into a rabble-rouser, delivering tub-thumping speeches in which he inveighed against Amhara's historical enemies—the TPLF and Oromo nationalists—and agitated for the return of the so-called 'ancestral lands' of Wolkait and Raya, formally part of Tigray since 1991.[4] Stretching to breaking point the theory that the best way to contain radical elements was to absorb them, Asaminew was given a free hand to build up Amhara's special police forces in his own image, recruiting rebels returning from Eritrea as well as hardline Amhara former army officers to lead them, and creating new special units that answered directly to him.

Many younger Amharas, who openly embraced their ethnic identity and the nationalist programme which went with it, had always regarded Abiy with scepticism. The Oromo prime minister's disparaging early comments on the matter of the disputed territories, which he had dismissed as mere Amhara "tribalism" and an invention of the diaspora, had gone down particularly badly on university campuses, and among the youth of the region's fast-growing towns of Bahir Dar, Gondar and Dessie. His comments to the diaspora a few months later, in which he invoked the historical place of Oromos in Ethiopia's imperial courts over many centuries, only confirmed the suspicion in their minds that Abiy was, at best, an unreliable ally; at worst, and much more likely, an Oromo nationalist in disguise.

Asaminew, by contrast, had initially trusted the new prime minister. The two men had fought on the same front in the Ethio-Eritrea war two decades earlier; Asaminew in fact remembered them as having been friends at the time. Speaking at a rally organised for the prime minister in Bahir Dar, shortly after he took office, the former general would even go as far as to liken Abiy to Moses, declaring that if the latter had freed the Israelites, then Abiy had "freed Ethiopians".[5] It was only because he believed in Abiy, a relative later recalled, that Asaminew ever agreed to join the government in the first place.

His chilling warning, less than a year later, that the federal government couldn't be trusted to staunch the extermination of Amharas "from the face of the earth" was therefore quite the turnaround.[6] Now the federal government was the enemy, one to be resisted at any cost. Where once the 1995 constitution had been the root of all their troubles—exposing Amharas in other parts of the country to discrimination, harassment or worse—now it was, however contrary to his instincts, the final line of defence. Only in the region's own troops could Amharas put their trust; no other Ethiopians, least of all the Oromos in charge in Addis Ababa, bore their interests at heart. All around were enemies, some even in their midst. If Amharas didn't act first, then they could only expect the worst.

* * *

In traversing the short course from mainstream Ethiopianism to full-bodied Amhara nationalism, Asaminew was an avatar for a region in the midst of a profound ideological shift.[7] Just a few years earlier, for an Ethiopian to proudly identify as Amhara was still frowned upon, and for some it was even a contradiction in terms: for decades there had been many Amharas who had questioned whether there was even such a category at all. To be Amhara was to be Ethiopian; by universalising their culture as the foundation of the nation, they had thus dissolved themselves into it. When Mesfin Woldemariam, an Ethiopianist (and Amhara) academic, debated Meles on the question of the Amhara ethnicity in 1993, he had denied its very existence.[8] Five years later, Tekegne Teka, another academic, gently argued the opposite, while nonetheless conceding that the Amhara possessed neither claims to a common ancestry, territory, or religion— nor indeed, any shared experience at all beyond language.[9] So great was the intellectual resistance to the notion of a distinct Amhara identity that when Muluken Asfaw, one of the most influential Amhara activists of the age, published his first book two decades later, which documented the eviction of Amhara minorities from Oromia and Benishangul-Gumuz, he found that "the very worst reception came from the Amharas themselves."

That by 2018 the debate appeared to have been finally settled—far fewer Amharas outside Addis Ababa now professed themselves simply 'Ethiopian'—did not make the implications any less seismic. For even though the EPRDF had singularly failed to persuade the Amhara public of the merits of the federal system, they had, eventually, achieved a sort of victory in defeat. Back in 1974, the Ethiopianist scholar Donald Levine had described 'Amhara' as less an ethnic category than a "basically aristocratic" cast of mind, a view which would have met with little dissent at the time.[10] The following year Christopher Clapham, another foreign academic, argued that the term Amhara denoted "neither a common consciousness nor a focus for political activity".[11] But once an Amhara "*kilil*" (region) had sprung into existence, with all the trappings of statehood which came with it, a new and powerful sense of collective Amhara identity had begun to gradually take root.

The old provincial identities of Shewa, Gojam, Gondar and Wollo still held some sway. The basic assumption that to be Amhara naturally meant being Orthodox Christian, moreover, still placed several hundred thousand Muslims in the region somewhere outside the fold. But no longer, for ordinary Amharas growing up after 1991, was 'Amhara' simply the word used by others to describe them—an external ascription, even a term of abuse. By 2018, to all but the most convinced Ethiopianists, Amhara was an ethnicity, perhaps—in the language of student movement—even a nation like any other. "The whole historical notion that Ethiopia should continue—that's not what it's about for us anymore," explained Hone Mandefro, a young academic from south Gondar who helped set up the Amhara Association of America, an influential advocacy group, in 2016. "We've found a new ideology, and that ideology is not *Ethiopiawinet*. It's *Amharanet* (Amharaness)."

But for there to be a strong Amhara nation there needed to be a strong Amhara nationalist party to advocate for it. For this the ANDM, which had been renamed the Amhara Democratic Party (ADP) shortly after Abiy took over, was miles from being a suitable contender. Gedu, the Amhara president, had something of a popular following in the region thanks to his newly found irredentist sympathies; his moderate successor, Ambachew Mekonnen, chosen by Abiy in March 2019 (Gedu was made foreign minister), was held in relatively high esteem, too. But the party as a whole was regarded, especially among the Amhara youth, as a haven of sell-outs. The perceived failure of its early leaders—embodied by Bereket Simon, the EPRDF's spokesman during the 2005 election controversy—to stand up for Amharas, and to resist the implementation of the 1995 constitution, made them little better than traitors.[12]

Asaminew's appointment to the ADP's central committee therefore coincided with the establishment of the National Movement of Amhara (NaMA), a new and unapologetically nationalist opposition party. With ties both to the *Fano* which had organised in 2016 to demonstrate against the TPLF, and also to former armed rebels then returning to the region from Eritrea, NaMA could count on a certain popular legitimacy—especially in Gojam and Gondar, the most nationalistic parts of the region, and among an emerging cohort of university students, teachers and educated civil servants. Here, almost for the first time, was a party that spoke directly to the public as Amharas first and Ethiopians second.[13]

By holding the rebranded ADP's feet to the fire, NaMA quickly pulled the region in an ever more nationalist direction. The beating heart of Amhara's political discourse was now at once openly irredentist—the return of 'lost' lands—and defensive, with calls growing ever louder for the region to protect itself and the millions of Amhara citizens scattered across the country from attack by Oromo nationalists to the south and the TPLF to the east. "Ethiopia and Amhara are two sides of the same coin," said Solomon Girmay, a tour guide in Gondar who joined the new party in 2019. "But we in Amhara are being intentionally targeted by a small clique—the TPLF. So we have to defend ourselves."

They had, undoubtedly, grounds for grievance. The TPLF (and their OLF co-authors) may have denied that the spirit of the 1995 constitution was in any way hostile to Amharas as a group, but the supposedly clear distinction drawn in theory between an Amhara ruling class and the ordinary Amhara peasantry was not one easily enforceable in practice. A large number of Amharic-speakers living as minorities outside of the Amhara heartland, a legacy of imperial expansion as well as the Derg's agricultural resettlement schemes, had long been vulnerable, and particularly so when the state was weak. Amharas who had been resettled in Oromia's Bale and Arsi districts under Haile Selassie, for instance, were attacked during the Bale Revolt and the revolutionary fervour of the mid-1970s.[14] The OLF's brief occupation of Assosa, in the far west of what is now Benishangul-Gumuz, in 1988 resulted in a massacre of around three hundred Amhara farmers living there.[15] Similar bouts of bloodshed stained the transition of the early 1990s in parts of Oromia.[16] Amharic-speakers in such places were typically seen as 'settlers', irrespective of how long their families had lived there, and as descendants of Menelik II's "neftegna" (rifle-carriers)—violent agents of imperial control. Their economic dominance of cities and towns in the broader south, an established fact of Ethiopian life, also persisted well into the twenty-first century. They were therefore very often objects of hostility and resentment.

In 2018, familiar patterns repeated themselves. When I visited Bahir Dar in June of that year thousands of Amharas were already making their way there from Benishangul-Gumuz and Oromia, fleeing raids by local gangs who often seemed to have the backing of regional security forces there.[17] A twenty-five-year-old mother of two, for instance, told me how a mob in Benishangul-Gumuz had murdered her husband and chased her and her children from their home. Such incidents were not anomalous: violent pogroms, and armed confrontations between those who claimed 'indigenous' status and those they accused of being 'settlers', would become increasingly widespread over the coming years. Because the regional constitutions of both Oromia and Benishangul-Gumuz, in particular, elevated the rights of longer-standing 'indigenous' ethnic groups over those of highland 'newcomers', Amhara and other minorities often found themselves stranded, with few avenues for protection or redress. Explicitly deemed residents, not citizens, such minorities could vote but—though legally permitted—were in practice inhibited from running for local office. When in 2013 regional authorities in Benishangul-Gumuz drew up a plan to remove 120,000 Amharas and Oromos from the region, on the official pretext of making fertile territory available for commercial leasing, there was almost nothing they could do to stop it.[18] The regional state's constitution had, in effect, made explicit what was only implicit in the federal one: a division between 'natives' and 'outsiders' whose formal rights, in particular to land, were unequal.

That the new Amhara nationalism could spread so fast and wide was due to a large degree to such practices, and to the increasingly strident calls made by Amhara activists at home and abroad to do something about them. Starting with the sensational popularity of Muluken Asfaw's controversial second book, *Amhara Holocaust*, which was published in 2016 and sold some 200,000 copies, the idea that a genocide against Amharas was being committed took a firm hold.[19] Over the coming years social media would be awash with such allegations, as diaspora activists and Facebook groups with names like *"Bete Amhara"* (House of Amhara) launched viral online campaigns, lobbying journalists and calling on foreign governments to intervene. A flurry of new 'Amhara-first' advocacy groups also proliferated.

Amhara politicians embraced often incendiary rhetoric. When I met with Dessalegn Chanie, NaMA's first chairman, in 2019, he described the results of the last national census in 2007, which Amhara nationalists claimed had undercounted their population by some three million people, as a case of "numerical genocide".[20] His successor, Belete Molla, then a lecturer at Addis Ababa University, later alleged that genocide was being committed "on an almost continuous basis, day after day, week after week." Officials in the region's ruling party soon followed suit. In early November 2020, just days before the start of the Tigray War, an Amhara parliamentarian begged the government to end the atrocities in Oromia with allegations previously unheard of on the floor of the house. "An attack which targets one ethnic group—the Amhara—is being undertaken," she warned the upper chamber of parliament, tears streaming down her face. "I understand that such an attack didn't start today, that it is the result of the preaching of a false narrative for many years... but when tolerance surpasses its limit it is inevitable that Ethiopia will become like Syria or Rwanda."[21]

In pushing a narrative of exclusive, or paramount, victimhood, Amhara nationalism was in some ways not too different from its Oromo, Tigrayan, Somali or Eritrean counterparts. Like most nationalisms, it had its own foundational trauma. This was, depending on who one asked, either the introduction of ethnic federalism in the early 1990s or, for those with a longer view, the sixteenth and seventeenth-century period of Oromo and Muslim expansion in the Ethiopian highlands.[22] So, too, did the movement have its own narrative of ancient provenance and exceptionalism. Amhara nationalists, just like Tigrayans and Eritreans, claimed to be the true heirs of the proto-Ethiopian Kingdom of Axum, which had reigned some fourteen centuries previously.[23]

But two aspects of Amhara nationalism made it stand out. Unlike Oromo nationalism, which had to contend with Oromia's religious diversity, or Tigrayan and Eritrean nationalisms, with their modern roots in the secular Marxism of the 1970s student movement, ethno-nationalism in Amhara had strikingly religious underpinnings. Forged in the prophetic tradition of Ethiopian Orthodox Christianity, Amhara activists and *Fanos* often wore symbolic crosses (distinguished by a circle above the horizontal bar) associated with the coming of a new Ethiopian kingdom.[24] The role of the Orthodox clergy was also marked, with their monasteries often used by the *Fanos* as meeting places. Later, during the Tigray War, Amhara Orthodox priests were known to attend the battlefields with prayer and blessings. These years also saw the rise of several fiercely conservative Orthodox movements which championed the historical narratives, and, in particular, the myths of Ethiopian exceptionalism, which underlay Amhara nationalism.[25]

A second distinctive feature was its irredentism. Hardline Oromo nationalists sometimes laid claim to the southern fringes of Benishangul-Gumuz, and even to parts of Wollo in Amhara and Raya in Tigray. But these were not really that movement's core concerns. Amhara nationalists, by contrast, put territorial claims openly at the very centre of their agenda. After all, it wasn't just Wolkait and Raya that they had in their sights. Reclaiming Metekel, a vast and resource-rich expanse in Benishangul-Gumuz, which before 1991 had been administered as part of Gojam, was a key plank of the Amhara nationalist programme. So, too, was the return of al-Fashaga, a slice of fertile farmland inside Sudan where—like in Wolkait—lucrative sesame fields were found. Fights were also brewing with the Oromo, over control of Addis Ababa and other towns where Amharas were numerous, as well as over strategic border territories such as the rail and highway corridor in the Awash Valley to the east. "We will reclaim all our territories and enter Menelik's palace," said the chairman of the Amhara Association of America at a rally in Washington in 2023. "That is the mission of the Amhara movement."

The first real indications of what all this might mean in practice came in 2018, when the *Fano* and Amhara regional forces, by then under Asaminew's direction, focused their resolve on the issue of the Qemant, a small ethnic minority who live near Gondar and had been pushing for political recognition. Though historically Qemant communities spoke a distinctive language and practised a different religion, centuries of assimilationist efforts have meant that many now speak Amharic and practise Orthodox Christianity. When the 2007 census came round, Qemant was removed as an independent identity altogether. This perceived attempt at erasure had triggered a backlash, and tensions spiked in 2017 when a referendum was held on the matter of Qemant self-administration (in seven out of eight districts with a significant Qemant population, voters chose to remain part of Amhara, though both the process and results were contested). Between 2016 and 2017, many Qemant civilians had been attacked and killed.[26] Starting from late 2018, however, violence erupted on a hitherto unprecedented scale, driven by widespread but mostly unsubstantiated fears in Amhara that Qemant activists were being funded and armed by the TPLF to weaken the region. According to ESAT, whose journalists took an especially tough line on the matter, the so-called Qemant Committee had, by 2018, an office in Mekelle. (This was true, though it was tit-for-tat: at the same time, the Wolkait Committee were headquartered in Gondar.) In Amhara nationalist eyes, they were therefore "*bandas*" (traitors), the enemy within to be dealt with accordingly.

In January 2019, according to a report by Amnesty International, at least fifty-eight people were killed by Amhara militias and the *Fanos* in less than twenty-four hours and buried in mass graves.[27] It wouldn't be a one-off. Over the coming years, Qemant villages were razed to the ground, sometimes even with whole families burnt alive. Throughout their heartland along the Shinfa River, lands were stolen and occupied; as late as 2024 much of these remained occupied, according to refugees in Sudan—their former owners—by *Fanos* who were said to have been promised jobs in exchange for holding on to it on behalf of wealthy investors. One by one, Qemant leaders were imprisoned or murdered, their academics fired from university posts, their civil servants purged from local government. At the centre of the violence, which was both ruthless and unremitting, were the *Fanos*, by this point less a protest movement than a paramilitary one. If once they had been antagonists of the government, now they were its allies, with the Amhara officials—Asaminew included—giving them arms, or at least their tacit support. At the hands of the *Fanos*, Qemant-majority towns like Metemnma Yohannes would be effectively ethnically cleansed. It was an ominous portent of what was to come in Tigray just two years later.

By now many observers worried that Ethiopia was starting to resemble Yugoslavia, another fragile multinational federation held together for decades by an authoritarian ruling party and charismatic strongman, on the eve of its bloody break-up in the 1990s.[28] (One particular academic article, on the doomed fate of such 'ethno-federations', was by this point circulating among Ethiopian government officials and associated intellectuals.)[29] If this were so, then the counterpart to the violent Serbian nationalism behind much of the Balkans' misery was most likely found in Amhara. Serbs, much like Amharas in Ethiopia, were scattered in large numbers across the former Yugoslavia, well beyond the Serbian heartland. Just as many Serbian nationalists, who were mostly Orthodox Christians too, had struggled to see Catholics as true Serbs, so were Amhara nationalists often suspicious of Muslims and other 'outsiders' in their ranks.[30] In 2019, in a particularly shocking incident of religious violence, a number of mosques and scores of Muslim businesses in the Amhara town of Mota were attacked and burnt (in revenge for an alleged arson attack on a church there). Three years later, more than twenty Muslims were murdered in a pogrom in Gondar.

However much its more moderate proponents insisted that Amhara nationalism could be an inclusive and democratising force, it therefore rarely seemed that way in these years. Inflamed by the prevailing insecurity of the times, its essential ingredients—like those of Serbian nationalism—were rumour and conspiracy, paranoia and angst. Behind each intrigue, each bloody clash, allegedly lurked the dark hand of the TPLF, or else the OLF. In 2018, a public health researcher visiting a village near Bahir Dar was murdered by a mob, accused of trying to poison the local children. (The allegation reflected years of popular anxieties about a supposed TPLF plot to curb population growth in Amhara.) The next year a rumour spread around Gondar that the water supply had been deliberately poisoned; a regional official blamed "an organised force" seeking to terrorise the Amhara public. When I met with members of the *Fano* in a bar in Gondar that same month, they fretted anxiously about "economic sabotage", "tax sabotage", "demographic sabotage"—all, they said, a plan for weakening Amhara. "The TPLF sponsors every conflict in Ethiopia", a federal minister from the region told a foreign researcher a few months later.[31]

Ethnic 'others' inside the region were seen as fifth columns, nodes in a vast cross-border network of enemies bent on destroying them. Earlier in 2019, some two hundred ethnic Gumuz living just inside the Amhara border—a whole village, in effect—were reportedly massacred by the *Fano*, allegedly in revenge for the killing of Amharas inside Benishangul-Gumuz. Just as he did in the case of the Qemant, Asaminew told his forces not to allow investigators sent by the federal government to do their work.[32] Nor would he permit them to look into what had happened in Kemise, the capital of the self-governing Oromia Special Zone in eastern Amhara, where in April the security chief had dispatched one of his own special police units to crack down harshly on the OLF militants he believed were running amok there. All the while, for months on end, roads leading north and east from Amhara to Tigray were blocked by groups of *Fanos* and other armed youth; a precursor to the siege imposed on Tigray during the war.[33] Asaminew and his special forces would do nothing to prevent them.

* * *

If Amhara nationalism bore more than a passing likeness to Serbian nationalism, then, in his militant calls to defend the homeland and those living beyond its borders from attack, Asaminew was its Slobodan Milošević, the Serbian strongman responsible for ethnic cleansing in Bosnia.[34] Just a few months out of prison and it was evident to anyone who encountered the former general that he was becoming more and more unpredictable. Glued to Facebook, he appeared visibly emotional, allegedly creating fake accounts to go after his enemies. "He was online 24/7," recalled a friend of his who had known him in prison. "He completely lost touch with reality."

The company he kept was also a cause for concern. Among his closest allies at this time were Masresha Sette, a former air force captain who had unsuccessfully tried to escape and join Ginbot 7 in 2015, and was notorious for firing machine guns into the air at weddings, and Zemene Kassie, a glorified arms dealer with a gift for rabble-rousing who had spent several years with Ginbot 7 in Eritrea. Both men had returned to Amhara in 2018 and emerged as commanders of the new *Fano* battalions—irregular forces theoretically outside Asaminew's authority but given his blessing—then under formation. Allegedly funding them was a wealthy Amhara businessman from Gojam called Worku Aytenew, who in addition to his ties to Ethiopia's deputy prime minister, Demeke Mekonnen, was frequently spotted in Asaminew's company in the latter's final months. Worku, who arrived by private helicopter to the rally organised in support of Abiy in Bahir Dar in 2018, and was so flashy he was known for showering cash around at parties, was one of a number of new Amhara oligarchs, often from Gojam, whose murky emergence from obscurity in these years coincided with—and likely helped to finance—the rise of Amhara nationalism. They would later acquire notoriety for their part in the Tigray War.

By early June 2019, Asaminew boasted multiple armed forces directly under his command, including tens of thousands of Amhara militiamen, whose intensive rounds of training were not just military but ideological, too.[35] "Asaminew was trying to build a state within a state," said an Ethiopian academic who had been scheduled to meet with the Amhara security chief just hours before he launched his deadly assault on the office of Ambachew Mekonnen, the regional president. "He was basically building a military to fight his two enemies: Oromia and Tigray. It was frighteningly nationalistic and jingoistic."

In the weeks before the showdown, Ambachew had become increasingly concerned by Asaminew's activities—and told him so directly. But the security chief wouldn't listen, refusing even to take the president's phone calls, and continued his furious drive to recruit more fighters into his ranks. Such was the president's anger he refused to attend the graduation ceremony for them that same month. Meanwhile in Addis Ababa, word of trouble brewing in Amhara was beginning to trickle out. "We all knew a violent confrontation was coming," a well-connected political analyst there later recalled.

What exactly the government knew in advance is unclear, though. Three days before the attack in Bahir Dar, Asaminew attended an internal evaluation in the capital chaired by the deputy prime minister. There they discussed the deteriorating security situation in the Amhara region, the widening rift between Asaminew and the ruling party—and upbraided the regional security chief for his insubordination. The meeting lasted more than fourteen hours, until well into the night. After it finished, Asaminew, who was visibly shaken by the ferocity of the criticism he had received, appears to have decided that rather than wait to be fired he would take matters into his own hands. It is certainly plausible that senior federal officials knew that something was coming and did nothing to stop it—either out of negligence, or because Abiy and Demeke had their own reasons for wanting the increasingly popular Ambachew out of the picture.

In an audio recording allegedly from the day of the attack, 22 June, Asaminew was heard confessing to a journalist in Amhara that he had taken action against the regional leadership because they had sabotaged "the people's demands."[36] Eyewitnesses later reported seeing him shouting frantically over a radio transmitter in a building across the road from the regional state house, apparently directing an armed squadron as it burst into the room where senior officials including Ambachew were discussing how to remove him. In the ensuing gunfight, the president and two of his advisors were killed. Ambachew's body was later found mutilated; Asaminew—evidently the most likely culprit—fled the scene.[37] In a final act which echoed the heroic last stand of Tewodros II, the most revered of the old emperors, Asaminew was gunned down by federal troops two days later. It was an ending fit for a martyr, and, among young Amharas, he duly became one.

That might have been the end of the matter, were it not for a separate— though clearly related—spate of assassinations that rocked Addis Ababa that very same night. Shortly after 9 p.m., at his home in central Addis Ababa just a short walk from my apartment, Ethiopia's Tigrayan army chief of staff, Seare Mekonnen, was shot by his bodyguard. He had been directing the army's response to the violence in Bahir Dar, and was quickly rushed to hospital, where he later passed away. His companion, another retired Tigrayan general who was also hit, died immediately. Seare's widow, the only surviving eyewitness, later told me how she had watched as the bodyguard, an Amhara called Mesafint Tigabu, tried to flee, firing a volley of bullets at the guards in pursuit. Confusing things even further were reports that night of gunfire several kilometres away near the military's headquarters on the western side of the capital. Some would later claim that there had also been a plan to assassinate Shimelis Abdissa, by now Abiy's man in Oromia (he had replaced Lemma as regional president in April; the latter was made federal defence minister, a significant demotion). Jawar would later allege to me that he too had been one of the intended targets.

Conspiracy theories of all kinds quickly spread. Abiy, first out of the gates as he so often was, appeared stony-faced on TV that same night, dressed in army fatigues and pronouncing it an attempted coup. The two incidents in Bahir Dar and Addis Ababa, he claimed, were linked—some of the suspects, he said later, were "trained by people who came from abroad". His press secretary, meanwhile, told journalists that certain "elements", those "whose privileges [had] been eliminated by the reforms" were responsible—a version of events which the American government initially backed, before apparently later changing its mind. Some of those arrested in Addis Ababa, she said, had been found with "planning documents"—all of which, we were told, were "indications of a wider plot".

Over the coming weeks hundreds of Amharas linked to NaMA and also to Balderas, its Addis Ababa-based equivalent led by the controversial journalist and former political prisoner, Eskinder Nega, were arrested on suspicion of involvement in the alleged plot. But in the subsequent months, almost all of them were quietly released. In connection with Seare's assassination, only Mesafint the bodyguard would remain on trial—though any putative links between that incident and the assassinations in Amhara were said to be no longer under consideration. None of the alleged planning documents ever saw the light of day.

Less in doubt was the centrality of Asaminew's role in the killings in Bahir Dar. Even those who hailed him as a hero didn't question it; when I asked the *Fano* in Gondar what they thought, they simply replied that the federal government had killed Asaminew because he was too strong. In Lalibela, his hometown, the general was given a hero's funeral. A year later in Bahir Dar I listened to *Azmari* folk singers paying tribute in verse to their fallen icon's bravery, crowning him as the latest in a pantheon of Amhara saviours of Ethiopia beginning with Tewodros II. The act of violence itself was not much frowned upon.

In the end, the outstanding question was not who killed Ambachew, but rather whether anyone else had played a part in encouraging it. Some blamed oligarchic interests: the fact that all those killed that day were from Gondar fuelled speculation that intra-regional business rivalries may have played a role. Abiy and his Oromo allies, too, might well have had a hand in stoking tensions—it wasn't hard to see how they might benefit from a weakened Amhara leadership inside the ruling coalition. Indeed, a former senior government official from the Oromo side insisted to me in 2023 that Abiy had not only known but actively encouraged Asaminew in his mission for precisely this reason.

Complicating matters was the mysterious killing of the widely respected Tigrayan army chief by his bodyguard. Though it seemed at the time like an impulsive, emotional response to the news from Bahir Dar, it fuelled speculation in Tigray that the general had been removed so as to clear the path for a war against the TPLF (his successor, Adem Mohammed, was an Amhara). That Isaias, Eritrea's president, sent a delegation to Bahir Dar for Ambachew's funeral was to be an added dose of salt to their wounds. The following month the TPLF issued an unprecedentedly hostile statement about its sister party in Amhara, demanding it take responsibility for the events that June.

Subsequent developments seemed to bear the TPLF's fears out. "If Seare had remained the head of the military, there wouldn't have been a war," the same official told me after leaving government. But exactly why Abiy would need to have Seare murdered, when he had the power to remove him peacefully, has never been convincingly explained. The fact that he was able to swiftly fill the Amhara presidency with another ally—an old INSA colleague, Temesgen Tiruneh—and do so again with multiple replacements after that, showed how easy it was for him to appoint loyalists to key positions without the need for conspiracy. Just as likely, perhaps, Abiy had simply seized advantage of the chaos in Amhara, by presenting it as further evidence of his administration's noble struggle against recalcitrant forces. What was never in doubt, after all, was Abiy's opportunism: disorder, as he would later show in Oromia, was the perfect excuse to crack down on rogue elements or potential challengers, and so cement his own authority.[38] Speaking privately to a group of fellow Pente leaders around this time, one of those present recalled Abiy said the death of the Amhara president didn't perturb him much for he had God by his side. He certainly didn't, he informed them, lose any sleep over the matter.[39]

* * *

For many Amharas, however, the death of Asaminew was clear proof for a latent fear: that, beneath the Ethiopianist veneer, Abiy was really an Oromo supremacist. Though many of them still laboured in the belief that the prime minister would one day change the constitution, a tantalising promise which seemed to bear fruit as 2019 turned into 2020, and the EPRDF became the Prosperity Party, his studied ambiguity on the matter would ultimately only strengthen their distrust. His Pentecostalism, moreover, was another source of tension: in a region still overwhelmingly Orthodox and increasingly in the grip of anxieties about the church's relative decline, or even imminent destruction, very few would ever trust him as a custodian of Ethiopia's most august national institution. As accounts of violent attacks on Orthodox churches across the country proliferated over the coming years, with Abiy apparently unable or unwilling to stop them, so would many in Amhara come to see him as even an enemy of the faith. "Thirty-four churches have been burnt in the past year!" a young *Fano* leader in Gondar told me angrily in 2019. "We must get rid of Abiy."

Later, the prime minister would try to win some of them back by presenting himself as a champion of their slain hero, Asaminew. The following year, visibly frustrated as he delivered a speech in the UAE, he hit back against those who accused him of masterminding Asaminew's tragic fate, and insisted that, to the contrary, it had been he who had tried to prevent Asaminew being sent to jail in 2009. This was, he claimed, the real reason he had been fired from INSA a few months later.[40]

This final point was improbable: senior INSA colleagues at the time knew only that Abiy had been an integral part of the operation to arrest Asaminew. (That he had tried to alert their target by sharing intelligence of his coming arrest with Andargachew Tsige and the Ginbot 7 leadership overseas, however, might well have been true.) In any case, among most Amhara nationalists such protestations were never going to fly. Around the same time in early 2020 the government had begun a crackdown on some of the more lawless *Fano* groups then roaming the region. Though they would rally to his cause at the outbreak of the war in Tigray, suspicions in Amhara always ran deep. Large numbers there would never truly trust him. By 2023, many *Fanos* had turned decisively against the federal government and launched an armed rebellion. Ironically, though, down south in his own region many had long felt the same—for precisely the opposite reason.

12

THE HIJACKED REVOLUTION

WOLLEGA AND THE OROMO LIBERATION ARMY

Wollega in western Oromia felt a very long way away from Addis Ababa. When I visited Nekemte, the easternmost of its major towns, in early 2020 there was no way to fly: flights to Dembi Dollo, the only airport in the area, had long been suspended because of security concerns. (Though not only that: Wollega's sole airport—a tin shack beside a bumpy runway—was so dangerous that even Ethiopian Airlines staff were afraid to go there.) There was just one road from Addis Ababa, and much of it unpaved; after Ambo, the smooth tarmac gave way to winding, hair-raising stretches of gravel and craters. By the time I arrived in the city a gruelling ten hours later, there was no longer any internet connection, and phone services cut out completely just a few kilometres from the town centre.

To go any further than Nekemte was almost impossible. When I suggested doing so, my driver fretted I would be shot and killed: "either by the government, who will blame it on the Oromo Liberation Army," he added, "or by the Oromo Liberation Army, who will blame it on the government". When Henning Neuhaus, one of the only Western aid workers to travel any further west in these years, had reached the town of Kake, some 250 kilometres beyond Nekemte, he was expelled less than twenty-four hours later. Not content with kicking him out, the soldiers also tried to seize his jeep and beat up his driver: according to the army, no private cars were allowed in the area. A few months later, as if to underline the point, another car belonging to Neuhaus's German NGO was hijacked by the OLA, the OLF's armed wing, which proceeded to mount a machine-gun on the back and post photos on Facebook claiming they had captured it from the army. After that, basically the only foreigners to regularly venture so far west were a motley group of Chinese and

Afghan gold miners, a British former army officer, the odd Protestant missionary, and a hardened Congolese relief worker. Quite a few wound up being kidnapped.

Wollega was Ethiopia's wild west. Neither foreigners nor many other Ethiopians seemed to care much what happened there. When, in early 2019, the airforce carried out airstrikes against OLA bases, the first instance of an aerial bombardment by the military on Ethiopia's own territory since the days of the Derg, the news barely seemed to register in Addis Ababa. That Wollega (and the southern Oromo areas of Guji and Borana) had been under a so-called 'command post', with the army in charge of security, from as early as 2018 also attracted scant attention. By the time of my visit to Nekemte in 2020, a great expanse of Wollega was a war zone and a telecoms blackout had been in place for several months. "It's a complete black hole to us," admitted a senior European aid official. "We have no idea what's happening."

Nothing new then, many locals would have shrugged. Wollega, after all, had always been isolated and neglected by the Ethiopian state. In exchange for peacefully submitting to Menelik II, and paying him tribute in the form of the gold and ivory in which the territory was abundant, Wollega's traditional Oromo rulers had been mostly—though never entirely—left to their own devices.[1] The region's customs and traditional social structures were kept largely intact.[2] The spread of Orthodox Christianity was relatively limited, and traditional religious practices persisted.[3] The average Wollega peasant, for much of the early twentieth century, would have been only dimly aware of their place in a wider Ethiopian polity.[4]

The process of establishing Ethiopian administration over the territory was pursued more vigorously by Haile Selassie. After his return from exile in 1940, his government increasingly pushed Afan Oromo from the public sphere and disallowed it in print, while overseeing an increase in the number of Amharas in the local administration; the governor-general of Wollega, for instance, was for a while Asserate Kassa, a high-ranking noble and relative of the emperor.[5] By the final years of his reign, a few Wollega Oromos were counted among the more prominent of his senior officials—a measure of their relative, though still limited, integration into the Ethiopian state.[6]

But even then the territory retained a distinctive identity somewhat at odds with the rest of the empire. As part of the so-called 'Free Areas' of the south and west, the doors to Wollega were left open to foreign Protestant missionaries; two of the very first missions in Ethiopia were founded in Nekemte and Dembi Dollo.[7] When the Italians invaded in 1936, some of Wollega's local rulers sought to broker an alliance with them in order to establish the putative Western Oromo Confederation, an ultimately doomed bid for independence.[8] Half a century later, Wollega would become the heartland of Oromo nationalism and the OLF, led by the disaffected and typically Protestant sons of local landowners and administrators.[9]

That spirit lived on in Nekemte in 2020. The first thing I saw on arriving in the lobby of my hotel was a portrait of the early Oromo nationalist Tadesse Birru; across from the window of my room was a billboard of Lemma's face, beneath a slogan proclaiming the ruling party to be the champion of "Oromo Liberation". The streets below, meanwhile, swayed to the chorus of popular struggle songs, as rickshaws emblazoned with bumper stickers of the OLA's new standard-bearer, Kumsa Diriba—better known by his nom de guerre, Jaal Marroo—buzzed by. "Better to die than to live as slaves", one of the stickers read.

* * *

Oromo nationalism was riding high in the early months of Abiy's tenure. For the first time Ethiopia had a leader who seemed proud of his Oromo identity, who could don traditional Oromo white suits for state occasions and put on banquets serving Oromo cuisine for visiting officials.[10] When he hosted Isaias at the palace for the first time, the Eritrean president was gifted a horse, shield and spear—the most prized possessions of a traditional Oromo warrior.

The changes were more than just symbolic, though. Across many measures, Abiy's ascent to high office gave Oromos unprecedented access to state power and economic opportunities. As young Oromos flooded to the capital, Oromo businessmen snapped up contracts, land and property there. In the federal security establishment, too, Oromos filled the upper ranks like never before. By early 2019, the defence minister, spy chief, deputy head of the army, head of the Republican Guard and the attorney-general were all Oromo. By the end of 2020, the army chief of staff would be too.

Down the ladder, Oromos were also on the march: police stations and local government offices in Addis Ababa were widely perceived to have become dominated by them. "It used to be kind of shameful to speak Oromo in the city," said an advisor in the Oromia president's office. "Now

I don't even notice which language I'm speaking." Soon new Oromo restaurants were opening their doors in the capital, as distinctly Oromo songs blared through the night in its bars and clubs. For all but the most committed Oromo nationalist, for whom much could be dismissed as mere cosmetics, this was a profound transformation. In October 2019, *Irreecha* was held for the first time in Addis Ababa's Meskel Square and billed as the festival's triumphant homecoming after more than 150 years in the wilderness.

To many other ethnicities, not least many Amharas, all this was evidence that Abiy was, at heart, an Oromo nationalist—with a project not to unify Ethiopia but rather remould it in his own Oromo image. Nowhere were such anxieties more pervasive than in Addis Ababa. Complaints about local officials speaking only Afan Oromo, for instance, or of government offices favouring Oromos for jobs or services, were so ubiquitous by 2019 that they formed the soundtrack to everyday life. "All Oromos want Addis Ababa—to eat," a taxi driver once told me, making a gesture with hands to suggest the capital was being squeezed to death. Toward the end of that year a popular local weekly would put on its cover a giant boot in the colours of the Oromia flag, stamping on the city.[11]

All this, then, posed a thorny question: how to explain the contrary view simultaneously taking root among many, if not most, Oromo nationalists? For in these circles the prime minister was soon seen in terms almost exactly the inverse of those which prevailed among Amharas: less the architect of an Oromo-led Ethiopia than a traitor so untrustworthy that some started to question whether he was really an Oromo at all.[12] Far from being an Oromo supremacist, they alleged, he was really an Amhara nostalgist, one bent on reviving the old imperial Ethiopia which had trampled Oromo culture and denigrated its history for more than a century. How else, they asked, could one explain the evident fondness for Ethiopia in his inaugural speech to parliament in 2018? Was there any other way to account for his comment, made in a meeting with Amharas in Bahir Dar a few weeks later, that Oromo nationalism had reduced "a great nation" to a "village"? And what to make of Unity Park—the imperial palace and grounds which he had lovingly restored and opened to the public in 2019, and in which the only piece of distinctly Oromo heritage on display was a plastic *Oda* tree?

Abiy's Oromo nationalism, they argued, was an act. As early as July 2018 the Oromo Studies Association had admonished Abiy's embrace of what it called an "Imperial Ethiopianist" narrative that excluded Oromos. Little over a year later, his alleged betrayal of the Oromo cause would be chronicled in an anonymous book called *The Hijacked Revolution*. The suspected author, an Oromo university professor, was arrested; copies of the book were then seized and pulped. But its central thesis was by then conventional wisdom. In a dizzyingly quick reversal, Abiy had gone from being Oromia's most vaunted, celebrated son to—in his Oromo opponents' telling—the modern reincarnation of their imperial oppressors. So bitter was his estrangement from his home constituency that it would lay the ground for a war which would foreshadow, and long outlast, the Tigray one. In its sheer brutality it would at times even equal it.

* * *

In the days before Ginbot 7 and the OLF returned from exile on successive weekends in early September 2018 the Ethiopian capital was awash with colour. As the date drew closer, and the former rebels prepared to touch down from Eritrea, their supporters had gone from street to street, adorning shopfronts with their flags and daubing anything from lampposts to pavements in their respective colours. To any passing visitor, the mood in the capital would have seemed euphoric—vivid testament to the democratic opening which Abiy had ushered in, and to the new freedoms ordinary citizens had embraced. The reality, though, was more troubling. As *Qeerroo* and OLF supporters had rushed into the capital from the countryside, many travelling hundreds of miles from as far afield as Wollega and Borana for the event, residents of Addis Ababa had turned out to confront them. Violence erupted. When tensions between *Qeerroos* and local youth groups degenerated into fighting around the controversial statue of Menelik II in the old city centre, at least twenty-eight people, including many Oromos, were killed. Shortly after, in an act seemingly of spontaneous revenge, scores of non-Oromo minorities were then raped or murdered in the satellite town of Burayu.[13]

There could hardly have been a more chilling vision of the coming battle for control of Ethiopia's future. The flags and colours which had swept over the city represented rival, and ultimately mutually exclusive, claims—not only over Addis Ababa, but over the very essence of Ethiopian nationhood itself. This wasn't simply a fight pitting Amharas against Oromos, or the capital against its hinterland—though on one level, it was both. Above all, it was a struggle which aligned supporters of the existing federal system against those who wanted it radically reformed or even abolished. The central question of Ethiopian politics now increasingly boiled down to whose side Abiy was on.

Over the following weeks relations between Oromo nationalists and residents of Addis Ababa sharply deteriorated. Both groups blamed Abiy and the federal government for not doing enough to defend them. Both also accused the other of having triggered the unrest.[14] In Wollega and many other parts of Oromia, suspicions about Abiy's commitment to the nationalist cause hardened. In Addis Ababa, protesters took to the streets for the first time since Abiy had come to power. Calls for the prime minister to crack down on Oromo nationalism, and the Qeerroo in particular, grew considerably louder.

In fact, given the size of the crowd which turned out to welcome its leaders, the prime minister wouldn't have needed much convincing of the need to take on the OLF. Neither he nor his colleagues in the OPDO had an interest in losing any political ground to it. Trouble between the two Oromo parties had been building even before the returning rebels had crossed the border from Eritrea (and also Kenya) that September. As early as July 2018, just days after its terrorist designation had been removed by parliament, Oromo officials had begun alleging, without evidence, that the OLF group was causing unrest in Wollega by working clandestinely with the TPLF.[15] That same month, the two sides traded blame over a horrific spate of civilian killings in the far west of the region, including that of a pregnant mother murdered in a rickshaw as she travelled to hospital to give birth late one night. In Dembi Dollo, the government deployed soldiers and police after bridges were painted in OLF colours and its flags hung throughout the town. A military truck was later reportedly attacked with a grenade.[16]

Those who had hoped the peace deal in Asmara would soothe tensions were to be quickly disappointed. No sooner had the returning fighters, who numbered just over one thousand, headed home than reports emerged of them being singled out for arrest and police beatings. Some simply disappeared, and were never heard from again. In one especially vivid sign of mistrust between the government and the rebels, some of those who were to be integrated into the regional police forces later complained that they had been poisoned at the military camp to which they had been taken.[17]

In the far west, where many of the returnees had been headed, a few began to enlist with a band of guerrillas led by Kumsa Diriba, better known as Jaal Marroo, an enigmatic OLF fighter who had made his own way back from Eritrea a few years earlier and established a breakaway faction deep in Wollega's forests. Though there had always been a certain absolutism to the harder edge of Oromo nationalism, particularly its secessionist strand, over the years many of its adherents had grown impatient with exile. As the decades wore on, some had drifted away from politics, others had formed their own splinter groups, while a few, looking for an easier life, joined the ruling party. Jaal Marroo, by contrast, was young and idealistic, with the fire of the believer still burning inside him. After being thrown out of Addis Ababa University in the early 2000s on account of his activism, an incident which seems to have marked him with considerable resentment, he had spent the subsequent decade bouncing between Kenya, Uganda and eventually Eritrea. He was scornful of the OLF's ageing veteran leader, Dawud Ibsa, whom he accused of selling out. Instinctively mistrustful, he had little time either for Abiy or Lemma. Having agitated against the peace deal from almost the moment it was signed, he argued that the leadership in Asmara had betrayed the struggle by coming home. Blessed with good looks, and the sort of romantic charisma which often attaches to the committed guerrilla, Jaal Marroo found it easy to rally disillusioned young Oromo men to his side. Within just a few months of the OLF's return, his ragtag band of fewer than one hundred fighters had grown into a force more numerous and more powerful than anything Dawud had managed to mobilise for the best part of three decades.

When I spoke with Jaal Marroo over a crackling phone line several years later, he dismissed the 2018 peace agreement as nothing less than a "surrender". From the forests of Wollega, where he was then hiding, he said he had repeatedly warned his former comrades not to hand over their weapons to the government, reminding them of what had happened to the OLF in the early 1990s at the hands of the TPLF. Neither Abiy nor Lemma, he argued, would ever behave differently. "Abiy was part of the same government we've been fighting for thirty years," he argued. "He was a radio operator in the army, and he was spying on our phones in cyber-intelligence. The slaves have taken the place of the master—nothing else."

If not quite a "surrender", then the agreement struck in Asmara was, nonetheless, certainly not a case study in how to negotiate a lasting peace. To start with, neither side had particularly wanted to talk in the first place: both Abiy and Lemma had needed persuading just to visit Asmara and engage with Dawud. In the end, Abiy kept his distance, and sent Lemma and his foreign minister, Workneh Gebeyehu, to negotiate on his behalf. The OLF's notoriously stubborn chairman, meanwhile, was no less reluctant. By then in his late sixties, and a typically dogmatic product of the student movement, Dawud had spent the best part of his life in the bush or in exile. At first, in the hope it might be able to force the government to keep its word, he had insisted on the involvement of a third-party mediator. But being at the mercy of Isaias, who no longer had any use for the Ethiopian rebels he had hosted for the best part of two decades, Dawud had few bargaining chips at his disposal. In the end, he found he had little choice but to relent.

When the two sides met in Asmara that August, almost nothing of substance was decided beyond the simple premise that the rebels would return to Ethiopia and disarm. Further details of the agreement, whatever they were, were neither written down nor made public. Beyond vague promises to integrate former rebels into the army or the Oromia special police, the process of disarmament, demobilisation and reintegration (DDR) was tackled with so little seriousness that just a few months later Dawud would claim there had never been an agreement to give up their weapons at all. Abiy, for his part, later showed such scant interest in pursuing a DDR programme that those charged with implementing one reported struggling to ever get him to speak with them about it.

Amid the security vacuum, and, in the second half of 2018, a flurry of mutual recriminations, OLF splinter groups refused to hand over their guns. Instead, they returned to the bush, where they coalesced ostensibly under the command of Jaal Marroo. Pursuing a strategy of making Oromia ungovernable so as to force Abiy to the table, rather than capturing and controlling territory, the rebels assassinated local officials and government militias, robbed banks and conducted hit-and-run raids on prisons and local arms stores.[18] In September, regional officials from across the border in Benishangul-Gumuz were killed by gunmen who ambushed their car as they made their way to a meeting with officials in Wollega. The OLF was blamed—an allegation it denied—and over the following days dozens were killed in retaliatory violence in the town of Kamashi in Benishangul-Gumuz.[19] More than 150,000 people, mostly Oromos, soon fled to Wollega for safety. By the end of the year Abiy had sent in the army. But by that point much of the region's disaffected youth, particularly in the far west, were already in open revolt.

Mediation efforts led by Oromo elders as well as Jawar and other opposition leaders, including Bekele Gerba, got underway in early 2019. But they, too, quickly foundered. Jawar's criticisms of the OLF a decade earlier still stung, and he was in any case perceived as too close to the government to be trusted. Jaal Marroo, who resented the way he felt both Abiy and Jawar treated him, refused to cooperate. "It wasn't respectful," he later recalled. "They called us 'boys'. We're not boys. I've spent twenty years of my life fighting for justice. So if someone comes and tells me to disarm, it's very difficult." The day after Jaal Marroo was due to meet with Jawar to discuss disarmament, his camp was hit by a government missile. He and other OLF figures came to believe that Jawar had betrayed them, and severed communication.

Not long afterwards they formally established their own command—announcing themselves as the official Oromo Liberation Army and declaring Dawud and the OLF's political wing in Addis Ababa to be government captives.[20] Fighters who had accepted a government amnesty brokered by the mediators reported returning home only to be singled out for arrest, or to find that their land had been confiscated. At least two former commanders were murdered. Soon, many of those who had given up their arms just months earlier had re-joined the new OLA.[21]

* * *

The insurgency, which gradually gathered strength over the course of 2019, was chaotic and deadly. By the start of 2020, fighting in Guji had forced some 80,000 people from their homes.[22] Less than a year later, almost all the districts in Kellem Wollega, the most westerly territory, were said to be beyond government control, with local officials unable to even travel outside the main towns. So dangerous were the roads that some were known to sleep in their offices rather than travel them at night.

Brother-on-brother; neighbour-on-neighbour. The war in Oromia was, one activist admitted, a conflict in which "you cannot tell who is friend and who is foe." Nobody knew exactly how many fighters the OLA had—perhaps only a few thousand in the early days—but in theory anyone could pick up a gun and claim to be fighting for it. In most places, the insurgency seems to have been less a fully-fledged rebellion than a potpourri of loosely connected militias with only nominal allegiance to a central hierarchy. It was never clear, for instance, exactly how much contact the western command in Wollega, led by Jaal Marroo, had with the southern command in Guji. Some groups in the west, such as one led by a mysterious commander called Fekade Abdissa, claimed to represent the OLA but publicly denied Jaal Marroo's authority over them.[23] A taped phone call between Jaal Marroo and a subordinate, which was either leaked by colleagues or intercepted and published by the government in early 2022, laid bare some of these frictions: Jaal Marroo could be heard complaining that a new commander on the southern front rarely picked up the phone to him and disobeyed his orders.[24]

Discipline among the militants was also lax, and their conduct, in areas where they operated, often brutal. In the same leaked phone call, Jaal Marroo claimed that criminals had infiltrated his ranks and committed atrocities, including looting and raping, in their name. A former OLA fighter from eastern Guji told me in 2022 that many of his comrades considered anyone working for the government to be a legitimate target for reprisal killings. "The civilians are really bearing the brunt," he said. "Because they are always suspected of helping the government." Kept afloat at least in part by revenues from illegal gold mining and the underground coffee trade, as well as continued financial support from the Oromo diaspora, the insurgency soon developed a momentum which was as much economic as it was ideological. Kidnapping for ransom, for instance, was easy money. By 2022, stories of ordinary farmers being abducted for pay-offs as high as 100,000 birr (about $2,000) or more were commonplace.[25] Fekade Abdissa's faction in Wollega's Horo Guduru district was a particularly frequent target of such allegations: frustrated locals, speaking to the *Washington Post* in 2023, described its fighters as gangsters engaged in little more than robbing livestock, killing civilians and battling with other OLA groups.[26]

Jaal Marroo's OLA argued that the government's mass detention of Oromo civilians, and the extortion of their relatives to have them released, was so ubiquitous as to amount to a "commercial enterprise" of its own. It also alleged that Fekade Abdissa and others were working hand-in-glove with government security forces, either because some officials had an interest in seeing the insurgency continue, or in order to tarnish the OLA's image in the eyes of the Oromo public.[27] Given just how fast, and how wide, corruption in the Oromia regional government was said to have spread in the years after Abiy took power, both claims were plausible. It wasn't hard to see, for instance, how some officials might want to use the insurgency for cover as they got their own hands dirty; when local government budgets were shifted from development purposes to security, for instance, they were generally less likely to be audited. Moreover, for anyone opposed to a compromise settlement with the OLA, stories of their atrocities and criminality—their 'terrorism', in effect—were useful as justifications for resisting negotiations with their leaders.

As disorder spread, it was often Amhara minorities in Wollega, especially those who lived near the region's border with the Amhara district of Gojam, who were most vulnerable.[28] Widely seen by Oromos as more sympathetic to Abiy's government than the rest of the local population, they were the target of repeated attacks throughout these years. The numbers were staggering. In late 2019, seventeen Amhara students were kidnapped as they travelled home from university in Wollega. They were never heard from again.[29] In early November 2020, fifty Amhara civilians were dragged from their homes and slaughtered in the village of Gawa Qanqa in West Wollega.[30] In August 2021, 150 or more were reportedly killed in one day in East Wollega.[31] The following June as many as 230 were reported to have been killed in the Wollega village of Tole.[32] Just two weeks later, at least 150 more Amharas were murdered during similar attacks in the neighbouring district of Kellem Wollega.[33]

Investigators and journalists were blocked from visiting the area, which meant that properly establishing what happened, and who was responsible, was close to impossible. Amhara survivors typically blamed the OLA. But many of them also accused local Oromo officials of complicity—both groups were motivated, they argued, by a shared vision of an ethnically homogenous Oromia which had no place for minorities. The OLA rejected the claims, and alleged in return that the killings were further false flag operations intended to undermine the OLA's reputation. Strengthening their defence, in July 2022, was the testimony of an Oromo Prosperity Party MP, who said in a video on Facebook that a group formed by elements in the Oromia government, not the OLA, was behind the massacres of Amharas. He stopped short, though, of accusing Abiy of personal involvement.[34] The following year a former senior Oromo official also alleged in an interview with me that the intelligence services had recruited Fekade early in the conflict, as part of a misguided strategy to encourage the Amhara communities living in Wollega to revolt against the OLA and force it out of the district.

By 2021, the picture in Wollega had become even more complicated, as the Amharas living there armed themselves, and *Fanos* and Amhara militias from across the border joined the fray. The reason, they said, was self-defence. Local Oromos, however, accused them of trying to grab land in Wollega and expand Amhara's territory. Ethnic killings were increasingly reported to go both ways. By 2023, the map of conflict in western Oromia was so fractured, so riven by competing interests and murky allegiances, that nobody could say with confidence who was responsible for anything.

* * *

How serious had Abiy ever been about making peace? In public, the prime minister continued to insist he was open to negotiation with any of his opponents. "It is good for people to solve their issues through discussion, meetings and conversations," he told lawmakers early in 2020.[35] But when it came to the OLA, he seemed especially reticent. His top Oromo allies repeatedly boasted of plans to crush the rebels in days.[36] The future chief of the army staff, Berhanu Jula, later dismissed them as "mentally deranged".[37] When a delegation of Oromo clan elders and activists came to Addis Ababa and camped in the grounds of the palace in the hope of getting an audience with the prime minister, they were rebuffed. Attempts by the council of the *Abba Gaddas*, Oromia's preeminent elders, to engage in dialogue with the government likewise repeatedly hit a brick wall.[38]

Looking back several years later, Jawar believed his own mediation efforts had been purposely sabotaged—either by residual Tigrayan elements within the security apparatus, or, equally likely, Abiy's allies. His colleague, Bekele Gerba, also recalled begging the prime minister to listen to the *Abba Gaddas* and press forward with DDR, but to no avail. "He didn't want all the fighters to come in from the jungle," Bekele argued when we met in Minneapolis in 2022, several months after he had fled Ethiopia. "He rightly thought that the people of Wollega didn't support him. So he wanted an excuse to wage war against them." Deliberately allowing the insurgents to multiply, so this theory went, made it easier to justify cracking down on them. "I don't think Abiy has any intention to democratise," Jawar had argued similarly in early 2019. "And the OLF has become a useful idiot in that game."

Over the course of 2020, newly recruited—and specially indoctrinated—Oromo special police took over from the army in western and southern Oromia. Secret detention sites, which had sprung up in military camps, police stations and even schools across the region, were soon overflowing. In Nekemte, the town's historic palace was turned into a prison. By the middle of the year, Amnesty International reported, some 10,000 people had been thrown behind bars.[39] In 2021 a teenage boy in Dembi Dollo was chained to the railings of the town's central roundabout, where he was murdered in full public view by local security forces; a video of the incident was then posted by the local government on its Facebook page.[40] An Oromia government spokesman later explained that such extrajudicial "measures" were state policy.[41]

Residents of Wollega said the repression was worse—more brazen and more indiscriminate—than under either the Derg or the EPRDF. Homes belonging to family members of suspected OLA members, for instance, including relatives of Jaal Marroo, were burnt down. Not even the revered *Abba Gaddas*, or Oromo elders, were safe. In December 2021, fourteen of them, leaders of the *Karrayyu* clan of eastern Oromia, were taken to the woods and shot in the head. A source in the Ethiopian Human Rights Commission told me around this time of several more public executions in Wollega, on top of the one in Dembi Dollo.

But the OLA, or "*Shane*" as the government insisted on calling it so as to deny them the popular legitimacy of the OLF brand, was not an easy partner for negotiations. The leadership's command-and-control over its forces was substantially weaker than that of the TPLF or the EPLF during the 1980s. Some of its demands, moreover, were unworkable; at one point, for instance, the OLA demanded the establishment of a special police unit under their own command but funded by the government. Others were indistinguishable from those of their opponents. Oromo 'self-rule', autonomy and control of Addis Ababa, in particular, were all goals ostensibly shared by Oromo parties across the spectrum, including Abiy's.[42] Save for the few hardline nationalists still pushing for independence, all wanted more power for Oromos at the federal centre. Plenty of the supporters of the Oromo cause thus overcame whatever misgivings they might have had and supported Abiy, joining his government and splintering the movement. This made it harder for the OLA to convincingly claim to be the true, or sole, representative of Oromo interests.

For many committed Oromo nationalists, though, the problem came down to what they regarded as a fundamental, even irreparable, breach of trust. Before he took office, a member of Team Lemma later recalled, "Abiy had started talking more vociferously about Oromo issues than almost anybody else. Back then, everyone trusted him." But almost as soon as he had won power, he pivoted—ignoring the advice of Oromo intellectuals and turning instead to their ideological and ethnic rivals. The more comfortable Abiy appeared amid the traditional trappings of the Ethiopian state, the more at ease with its history, and the more friendly with their Amhara or Ethiopianist adversaries, the less Oromo nationalists could believe he was really one of them.

Nor did it help that on the rare occasion he directly addressed their concerns he could sound casually dismissive. In public, he often chided ordinary Oromos for what he perceived to be a victim mentality holding them back.[43] In a speech in 2019, for instance, he urged Oromos to be more like American Jews—who, he claimed, "own the media, banks and everything"—and less like African Americans, who he said "complain that the whites beat and oppress them".[44] To many Oromo nationalists, the troubling subtext—beyond the obvious anti-Semitism—was that the prime minister was either blind to or simply unbothered by the structural obstacles which still kept ordinary Oromos down. Abiy's conception of Oromo advancement, many of them argued, was fundamentally individualist: so long as a hard-working Oromo like him could rise to the top of the Ethiopian state, then the status of Oromos as a group was more or less irrelevant.

With both sides holding the other in such contempt, attempts to get them to engage in dialogue consistently foundered. To nobody's great surprise it would take until as late as April 2023 for the first formal negotiations between them to get going. After just a single round of talks in Tanzania, in which the government demanded the OLA disarm entirely, while the OLA insisted on a transitional government in Oromia, they collapsed in acrimony. The government launched yet another all-out military offensive shortly after. A second round of talks in November proved no more successful.

* * *

Oromia was where Abiy's conciliatory mask first slipped, and where the premium he placed on uncontested power was most evident. In part because it was his home region, and thus the bedrock of Abiy's electoral coalition, and perhaps partly because he considered disloyalty there a particular affront, it was in Oromia that the government in Addis Ababa first gave the security forces carte blanche to crush dissent.[45] Just months after taking office, a secret committee of high-level Oromo officials, known as the "*Koree Nageenyaa*", was put in charge of security there. Soon afterwards the committee began ordering extra-judicial killings and arrests.[46] "The Oromia regional state belongs directly to the PM himself," his then colleague, Milkessa Midega, told me in early 2020 while still in government. (The fact that Abiy's brother had been murdered by the

OLF three decades earlier might also have coloured the prime minister's response there.) Two years later, having fled abroad, Milkessa claimed that as early as 2018 Abiy had told party colleagues that the OPDO should learn from the TPLF's decades-long rule in Tigray, and refuse to countenance any rival on its home turf.[47] Since power was what really mattered, Abiy had seemed to suggest, then to maintain their hold they must ensure it remain entirely indivisible—through fair means or foul. "In the past, Oromos were never near power, so we're conditioned primarily to resist the state," another of Abiy's Oromo opponents later argued. "But Abiy is different. He has this instinctive grasp of politics in Ethiopia. He used to tell me all the time: 'it's all about power'."To cede any inch of this power to rebels would therefore be to oversee the ultimate dissolution of his own authority. Here was a line of thought with deep roots in Ethiopia's political culture: the notion that social order could only be guaranteed by squeezing all opposition—and, where needed, through the visible, even spectacular, use of force.[48]

Little more than a year after he had first opened the political space, and only a few months after winning the Nobel Prize in part because of his 'democratisation' efforts, the prime minister had also launched a sweeping crackdown on civil, non-violent opposition in his home region. As the much-anticipated national election approached, party offices belonging to both the OLF and the more moderate OFC across swathes of western and southern Oromia were shut down. "Abiy will leave no stone unturned to win the election," one of the prime minister's government allies told an Ethiopian researcher that year. In the early months of 2020, thousands of opposition supporters were arrested, including nine of the OLF's leaders. Citing insecurity, opposition meetings and public rallies in Wollega and Guji were banned. Meanwhile, as though taken straight from the pages of *The Stirrup and the Throne*—"since people are selfish, take advantage of it"– prominent Oromo opponents were co-opted, either with money or government jobs.[49] "Abiy is the kind of person who thinks he can co-opt anyone," said a former official in the Prime Minister's Office. "He rarely gets a no for his offer."

Among the formal Oromo opposition, despondency set in. In October 2019, fearing the upcoming election could be a bloodbath, the OFC and the official OLF struck an electoral pact with Abiy's OPDO—which, in an early signal of its shifting ideological orientation, had by then been renamed the Oromo Democratic Party (ODP). In theory, the bargain would have meant the parties standing aside for each other in certain districts to limit the competition; it might also have meant the opposition being given control of the regional presidency while Abiy kept hold of the federal government. In December, Jawar formally joined the OFC, and began to hold public rallies in which he called on Oromos to vote against the government. In private, though, he spoke of giving Abiy five or more years as prime minister without attempting to challenge him directly. "We're worried that if anyone runs against him, he will drive the whole thing over the cliff," he told me then. "So I've given up on the transition to democracy. My task is to help Abiy become a benevolent dictator."

13

"MEDEMER"

ADDIS ABABA AND THE PROSPERITY PARTY

On the eve of Ethiopian New Year, in September 2020, a giant billboard appeared on the side of an old high-rise building overlooking Addis Ababa's Meskel Square. The billboard showed Abiy, beaming broadly in a crisp blue suit, surrounded by rows of small figures, clad in various traditional attire, representing the many 'nations and nationalities' of Ethiopia. Above the prime minister, at the top of the billboard, was a banner of text wishing him the best for the year ahead: "The entire people of Ethiopia wish you a peaceful, happy and prosperous New Year".

It was a striking image, in a way redolent of the frontispiece of *Leviathan*, Thomas Hobbes's book of 1651, which, in its famous depiction of almighty power, personified the central state in the figure of the sovereign and his subjects. When I used to drive past this billboard, I would feel Abiy's eyes on me as though he, too, were an all-seeing, all-powerful sovereign— watching, Leviathan-like, over his people. So big was the image it could be seen from almost a kilometre away. The message was simple: the state is Abiy. Abiy is the protective and benevolent state.

This was not the first time such a billboard had appeared at this spot. When Abiy won the Nobel Peace Prize a year earlier, a similar one had been erected which showed his face next to the award's gold medallion. More had cropped up in other parts of the city at various times, each representing the leader in a different guise: Abiy planting a tree; Abiy as the face of the Adwa Day celebrations which marked the defeat of the Italians in 1896; Abiy in a casual jacket and open-collar shirt, unveiling his glitzy Sheger Park; Abiy the philosopher-king, promoting his book of political thought—*Medemer*—when it was published to great fanfare in October 2019. Arguably not since the days of Haile Selassie, whose ubiquitous icon had been on coins, stamps, postcards, statues and more, had a leader sought to be the personification of the Ethiopian state in quite such a way. "He's reduced the entire party and government to one person," said a disillusioned former Oromo activist. "He's like a pre-modern king."

Abiy's project to remake Ethiopia in his own image began on his doorstep. On his first day as prime minister, he had ordered a shiny, modernist makeover of his own office by an Emirati architecture firm, transforming the staid and stuffy workspace of his predecessors with white-washed walls bedecked by glossy photographs and flat-screen TV monitors.[1] Next were the palace grounds, their renovation funded by the UAE. Then, across the road, with Chinese cash, a large plot of land which had previously belonged to the nearby Sheraton Hotel was turned into a public park complete with an artificial lake and dazzling water fountains. A little further down the hill from the palace, a public library opened in 2022; next door to it was the science museum and a new amphitheatre. "If you can change Addis", Abiy explained in a rare interview with a foreign journalist in 2019, "definitely you can change Ethiopia".[2] Government offices and ministries were renovated and revamped in a fresh minimalist style, corporate in aesthetic and international in orientation.

Almost nothing appeared to consume Abiy's time and resources more than the capital's facelift. A plan known as "Beautifying Sheger", after the city's nickname, to transform the capital's filthy riverbanks into footpaths, bicycle lanes and waterside terraces was projected to cost $1bn over three years. A pleasure park on nearby Mount Entoto, which boasted hiking trails, adventure sports, boutique restaurants and a luxury resort, cost a reported $51m. Meskel Square was lavishly refurbished to the tune of more than $73m by official estimates.[3] Keeping close tabs on their progress, Abiy was known to visit construction sites sometimes late into the night, micromanaging project delivery right down to the smallest of details. (He would later explain to Jon Lee Anderson of the *New Yorker* that when restoring the palace he trusted Italians with the finer decorative work, Chinese with the heavy lifting.[4]) When David Pilling, the *Financial Times*'s Africa editor, was offered unprecedented access to the prime minister in 2019, he and its then editor-in-chief, Lionel Barber, were treated to such an exhaustive lecture about the choice of decoration in his revamped office that they began to worry Abiy wouldn't talk to them about anything else. "He explained how it was cleaner, more transparent, more modern," Pilling recalled. "And the message behind it was that this was what he planned to do with Ethiopia—just watch."[5]

For Abiy, refashioning Addis Ababa was not just an aesthetic venture. Nor was it merely an economic one, for boosting tourism and growth. It was, more than anything, a political project. If earlier large-scale public investments, notably the EPRDF's vast programme of functionalist, constructivist-style social housing, had borne the imprint of the official ideology of that era—the 'developmental state'—then the new wave of *grands projets* in the capital similarly provided a keyhole into Abiy's worldview and governing style.[6] "Abiy believes that public spaces and monuments create the image of the Ethiopian state which he wants to project to his citizens and to the world," explained a former official. Rooted in the theology of Prosperity Gospel from which Abiy drew inspiration, this was an outlook in which earthly splendour and divine favour were understood to be intimately entwined. Like King Solomon's biblical Jerusalem, a clean and shiny Addis Ababa was but one step on the road both to heaven and a prosperous Ethiopia. The new-look Addis Ababa was, to Abiy's mind, the future nation in miniature.

And it was a future in which the prime minister was to be both its avatar and its architect. Posters and billboards bearing his likeness bespoke not just a cult of personality—though there were strong signs of that, too—but his own centrality to the national transformation he sought to engineer. By successfully rising from rural poverty to the pinnacle of power in just four decades Abiy was, he believed, the embodiment of the spirit of renaissance he envisaged for Ethiopia as a whole—one which, he often claimed, would propel Ethiopia into the ranks of the most powerful countries on earth in just a single generation. As he told a convention of young Ethiopians—fittingly titled "I am the New Ethiopia"—shortly after he became prime minister, any "dreamer" that put their mind to it could make it to the top. All it took, he explained, were willpower and hard work.[7]

This was a worldview that put men and their visions at the centre of history. Great nations, Abiy told audiences, were the work of great and charismatic leaders. From Moses to Nelson Mandela to Park Chung-Hee, he wrote in *The Stirrup and the Throne*, a country's fate turned on the moral and intellectual capacity of the individuals leading it. (Despite his ostensible commitment to gender equality in government, no women leaders appeared in any of his writings.) And there was no doubting his conviction that he, too, was endowed with such qualities. Not only did he repeatedly invoke the story of his mother's prophecy, he also made it clear to anyone he spoke with that he saw himself as singularly responsible for the trajectory of Ethiopia's transformation. In *The Stirrup and the Throne*, after all, he had also hinted that Ethiopia's next leader would play the role of Moses in wresting his people from Pharaoh's tyranny. "I have done so many great things compared to many leaders," he told the *Financial Times* in 2019. "But I didn't do 1 per cent of what I am dreaming."[8] A year earlier, when pressed by members of the diaspora in America to establish a transitional government to steward the country towards democracy, he replied that he alone would be their shepherd: "I will transition you," he said.[9]

By framing success and failure in this way Abiy sought to overturn the decades-old consensus that Ethiopia's under-development was a product of entrenched structural factors—the legacy of feudalism, say, or the paucity of natural resources besides land—rather than individual or psychological ones. Poverty and powerlessness, the new prime minister argued, were a state of mind, the result of negative thinking or defeatist instincts. He implored his fellow citizens to rid themselves of such mind-forged manacles. "Too many of you reiterate the word 'poverty' repeatedly in your speeches," he admonished ruling party officials in a televised lecture in 2020. "We don't want poverty and we abhor it. [But] we shouldn't write or talk about poverty; rather, we eradicate it by paying our attention to thoughts and deeds of prosperity."[10]

The office of the prime minister was to be turned into a pulpit, a vehicle for reshaping the very minds of his subjects. "We don't advise him," said one of his advisors. "Rather, he comes in and advises us what to think." To correct backwards mindsets in government, Abiy gave televised 'trainings' to generals and cabinet ministers and told them that "attitude problems" were holding the country back. To bolster patriotic commitment, and instil a stronger work ethic among the public, he initiated national street-cleaning days and a nationwide tree-planting programme. Dutiful Ethiopian citizens, Abiy argued, should take pride in their physical environment: "a mind which doesn't see a good thing," he explained, "will not create a good thing".[11] By elevating both their bodies and their minds, together they could remake Ethiopia itself from the inside out. "He wants to literally change everything about our minds, our inner being, our spiritual life," said another former advisor. "It's like a mediaeval king. He's obsessed with social re-engineering. It's not about politics, or laws, or federalism."

With its emphasis on personal salvation, 'self-help' ideology, as it was sometimes known, overlapped significantly with the theology of

Prosperity Gospel. Indeed, one of Abiy's most influential advisors—Mehret Debebe, a popular TV psychologist and the country's most famous positive-thinking guru—was also a Pente preacher. Together the two men would sermonise on the need for mental and spiritual renewal as the basis for national prosperity. As with Prosperity Gospel, and the associated 'name-it-and-claim-it' theology, theirs was a positive-thinking doctrine which stressed the creative power of words, and man's capacity to change the world for the better through sheer force of will. So all-encompassing was this outlook, suggested one Ethiopian critic, that Abiy and his acolytes seemed to genuinely believe "the problem of poverty, ill-health and illiteracy [could all] be overcome by harnessing the power of man to create his own reality through the power of positive affirmation (confession) or by imploring God to shower us with the blessings."[12] Nothing, accordingly, was beyond the reach of human agency. All it took was discipline, motivation, and faith in God. "I've never seen anyone as influenced by Prosperity Gospel as him," Jawar once argued. "Forget anyone in South America or elsewhere in Africa: Abiy's doing the literal application of it."

Styling himself as a politician-preacher, Abiy showed few qualms about transgressing the boundary between church and state which the EPRDF had once sought to erect. In September 2019, he shared a stage with one of the country's many new Pente 'prophets', awarding him a gold necklace and a large financial donation to his organisation. Standing before the congregants he declared that God had blessed Ethiopia with early rains—defying the scientists who had predicted an El Niño-linked drought—and prophesied that, thanks to God's goodness, Ethiopia would be one of the top five economies in Africa by 2030.[13] Two years later, at the height of the Tigray War, he would predict that Ethiopia would be one of two great superpowers in the world by 2050 (a prophesy which exactly echoed one made by his Pente spiritual guide, Belina Sarka, two decades earlier).[14] The following year, as the war continued to rage, he promised in a single speech that wheat production would double by 2023; that exports would double in four years; that Ethiopia would be a net food exporter within a decade and among the top twenty economies in the world by 2050.[15]

Such fervent Christian providentialism just as often shaded into beliefs which, to the secular eye, might have seemed little more than pseudoscience: for instance, the conviction that illness or a natural disaster could be caused simply by the utterance of negative words. "At first I was on board with [the positive thinking], if it helped drive expectations, because my view is that discourse creates reality," recalled Abadir Ibrahim, a human rights scholar at Harvard University who headed Abiy's newly appointed Legal and Justice Affairs Advisory Council early in the transition. "But with the Prime Minister's Office it was the Prosperity Gospel version of that: i.e. don't say bad things, only good things [...] So when I said the words 'state collapse', it was like 'Shh shh don't say that!' It was like just by saying state collapse you will create state collapse."

The distinctively individualist ethos which underlay both Prosperity Gospel and its secular equivalent, 'self-help', also helped furnish the prime minister with an ostensible justification for autocratic rule. As the self-anointed embodiment of the change he sought to see in Ethiopia, and its singular steward, Abiy was able to breezily cast aside the checks and balances which might have constrained him. With the notable exception of economic policy, which he mostly delegated to trusted advisors, key decisions pertaining to the core of his statecraft—and the renovation of the capital, as well as several large-scale luxury tourism projects elsewhere, were all intrinsic to it—were his alone to make. "He decides everything," said a former cabinet member. "No discussion, no questions; cabinet meetings complete in thirty minutes, maximum. He decides everything." Broader consultation and deliberation were deemed unnecessary. It was in this way, for instance, that the landmark deal to develop the area of downtown Addis Ababa known as La Gare, which involved the government handing over 36 hectares of prime city real estate free of charge, was struck by Abiy and the Emirati royal court without the Ethiopian prime minister even notifying the city's planning office in advance. (Though the terms of the deal technically breached Ethiopian law, a simple order to override any irregularities came in the form of a letter direct from the Prime Minister's Office.) The renovation of Meskel Square was carried out in similarly regal fashion. "Projects like this are personal projects through and through," remarked a former official in the Prime Minister's Office. "These are Abiy's projects."

Also rendered redundant were the normal processes of public procurement and parliamentary accountability. When the prime minister was asked by MPs to explain the source of the money behind "Beautifying Sheger", for instance, he replied that since it had not come from them, but rather from private donations or overseas patrons such as the UAE, he was under no obligation to divulge details.[16] Major construction contracts for the city's mega-projects, meanwhile, routinely went to favoured firms without open tenders.[17] In the new parks and public spaces

Fig. 1: Abiy and Isaias Afewerki exchange smiles at the reopening of the Embassy of Eritrea in Addis Ababa, a week after signing their historic peace deal in July 2018.

Fig. 2: Abiy takes the president of the European Commission, Ursula von der Leyen, for a drive around the capital in December 2019.

Fig. 3: The new Addis Ababa skyline as seen from the prime minister's office in late 2019.

Fig. 4: The Ethio-Djibouti Railway, seen here at the Oromia town of Adama in 2018, was the crown jewel of the EPRDF's "developmental state".

Fig. 5: *Qeerroos* arriving in Addis Ababa to welcome the returning leaders of the OLF in September 2018.

Fig. 6: Supporters of the prime minister gather in Addis Ababa's Meskel Square during the height of "Abiymania" in 2018.

Fig. 7: Supporters of Ginbot 7 welcome the rebel movement's returning leaders for a rally in Addis Ababa in September 2018.

Fig. 8: Joyful OLF supporters gather for a rally in Meskel Square in September 2018.

Fig. 9: Jawar Mohammed, seen here at an Oromo Federal Congress meeting in early 2020, was Abiy's most prominent political rival.

Fig. 10: Meret Sisay (second from right, front row), 18, was forced to flee her home in West Guji twice in 2018. She and thousands of other Gedeos were sheltering in the village of Gotiti in early 2019.

Fig. 11: Getachew Reda, seen here in Mekelle in March 2020, was the TPLF's chief spokesman during the Tigray War, and became interim president of the region in 2023.

Fig. 12: People stand next to an exploded tank near the village of Mezezo, Amhara, in December 2021. The area was on the frontline of the Tigray War for a week.

Fig. 13: Amhara militiamen pose at their base near the village of Wanza in December 2021.

Fig. 14: An Amhara militiaman bows in front of a church near the village of Wanza on 9 December 2021.

Fig. 15: A man welds the window of a shop next to graffiti depicting Abiy in the town of Shewa Robit, Amhara, in December 2021.

Fig. 16: The Epiphany of Saint George celebrations in Lalibela on 26 January 2022. The town had been under TDF control for several months in 2021.

Fig. 17: The battlefields of Adwa in Tigray, seen from the road to Axum in February 2024.

under construction in the capital, businesspeople linked (or in some cases related) to his allies were given privileged access to land for investment, allegedly in exchange for financial donations to the ruling party. This was, in the memorable words of a veteran foreign diplomat, a distinctive form of oligarchic patrimonialism best understood as "a kind of Pentecostal mercantilism"—a crudely effective tool, obscured by religious rhetoric, for buying the loyalty of the country's economic elite. Out of it emerged a new class of business moguls affiliated with the ruling party. Though Abiy would regularly inveigh against corruption, often summoning MPs and cadres for long lectures in which he condemned them for their indolence and graft, the problem worsened perceptibly on his watch. In a system which at times seemed to resemble the crony capitalism of post-Soviet Eastern Europe, corruption would become a feature, not a bug, of the political machine which kept his administration in power.

* * *

At its most basic, Abiy's political coalition in these years combined Oromos and Amharas, Ethiopia's two largest and historically most antagonistic groups. From the beginning, though, the set-up proved highly combustible, with the two sides jockeying to influence Abiy's agenda and fill the gap left by the Tigrayans. For Abiy, successfully appeasing such seemingly irreconcilable interests required often audacious double-crossing. "He used to tell Amharas he wanted to finish Menelik's plan—i.e. to extend Ethiopia's borders all the way to the Red Sea," said one Oromo opposition leader. "And he'd tell Oromos he wanted to expand Oromo influence all across the Horn." Given the two groups' rival claims over Addis Ababa, already by far the most lucrative prize of the Ethiopian economy, investing so much of his political and financial capital in its flashy gentrification did not, on the face of it, make much strategic sense—indeed, it risked aggravating the competition over it.

Under the surface, though, was a tacit—if fragile—bargain between two sets of elites. On one side of it was a rising Oromo class anxious for a bigger stake in the wealth of the capital. They were represented by politicians like Takele Uma, the mayor of Addis Ababa who oversaw much of the city's renovation between 2018 and 2020, and business tycoons like Alemayehu Ketema, a construction contractor close to both Abiy and the Oromo nationalist opposition. For them, Abiy offered unprecedented opportunities for investment and public contracts in an urban economy in which they had always been under-represented. On the other side, however, was Addis Ababa's established elite: predominantly Amhara, or at least Amharic-speaking, and with their own very different orientation towards Ethiopian identity and history. For them, too, Abiy dangled the opportunity to claim an even bigger share of the capital's wealth. But, more than that alone, he also presented them with a chance to restore their former cultural and ideological primacy—in large part by energetically rehabilitating Ethiopia's imperial history: turning Menelik II's palace into a public museum, for instance, or establishing a museum commemorating the Battle of Adwa in the heart of the capital's old Italian district. (That the palace could be used to host glitzy gala dinners to raise some of the funds for his glossiest urban projects was an added bonus.)

Resurrecting the ideological power of Addis Ababa and associated Amhara elites was also achieved by drawing visibly close to Ethiopianist opposition figures popular in the capital. Key among these were Andargachew Tsige, who had recently been released from prison, and Berhanu Nega of Ginbot 7, which had returned home from Eritrea in September 2018 and soon rebranded as the Ethiopian Citizens for Social Justice (Ezema).[18] In the first few years of Abiy's tenure, Andargachew and Berhanu enjoyed such prominence on state media, and such privileged access to the prime minister, that they once claimed to have given him a "road map" for the transition to "unity and democracy".[19] According to Andargachew, Abiy had even gone as far as offering him Ethiopia's ceremonial presidency, during a meeting in France in 2018. In part due to their old links to Isaias and the regime in Asmara, and through influential media platforms like ESAT, both men were among the most influential of those urging Abiy to adopt a more uncompromising approach to the TPLF in the months running up to the Tigray War.

Added to this was the striking ascendance of Ethiopianist hardliners like Daniel Kibret, an Orthodox Amhara deacon and writer notorious for his reactionary nationalism and unqualified admiration for Menelik II's empire-building. A friend, or at least an acquaintance, of Abiy since before he was prime minister—both professed an interest in the arts and claimed to have written screenplays in the past—Daniel had quickly become one of his top advisors. Within little more than a year he had been appointed to the boards of numerous state agencies and commissions, including that of the Ethiopian Press Agency, and transformed himself into Abiy's most influential gatekeeper, policing access to him and aggressively attacking his critics online and on the airwaves. When a group of visitors attending an international hospitality conference were granted a pre-opening tour of Unity Park in 2019, to take just one example, it had been Daniel spotted on site making sure no 'unwanted' faces made it inside. "He has the absolute highest level of clearance to the PM," noted one of Abiy's Oromo nationalist allies, who, like many others, was mystified by his boss's intimacy with such a polarising figure. Over the years, Daniel would help to write many of Abiy's Amharic speeches and statements, providing him with the traditional Orthodox imagery, folklore and metaphors which resonated so powerfully with this crucial constituency. He would also be behind some of the most incendiary rhetoric of the entire Tigray War and after.

Politically, one former advisor recalled, Abiy had aimed to use "every tool in his armoury to win over the Amhara." But on a deeper level, there was more than just ethnicity at play. Courting the country's historic urban elite also allowed Abiy to elevate a particular image of Addis Ababa itself as a model for Ethiopian nation-building. This was a model which defined—and celebrated—the capital as a melting pot, and which was presented as 'non-ethnic' in politics and relatively liberal in economics. To invoke it in this way had major political implications. By putting Addis Ababa at the centre of his political project Abiy was, in effect, upturning the EPRDF's signature approach to coalition-building. For the first time in its nearly thirty-year history, the ruling coalition was no longer to be one devoted, rhetorically at least, to agricultural development and the interests of rural farmers. Instead, the very same urban capitalists who had long been maligned by the ruling coalition as parasitical 'rent-seekers' deleterious to the goal of national development were to be implicitly repositioned as the party's core constituency. Just as important, moreover, by directing his focus to the upwardly mobile citizens of Addis Ababa, and championing them as the collective embodiment of the nation— neither Oromo, nor Amhara, nor specifically any of Ethiopia's 'nations and nationalities'—Abiy's urban politics represented a direct challenge to the fundamental assumptions which undergirded ethnic federalism and the 1995 constitution.[20]

* * *

By the second half of 2019 it was common knowledge, at least among Addis Ababa's political class, that Abiy planned to at last do away with the EPRDF and merge the coalition into a single national organisation under a new name: the Prosperity Party. On the face of it, this wasn't especially controversial. The EPRDF had, after all, been internally divided and ideologically adrift for many years. Moreover, talk of uniting the four constituent 'fronts' into a single party, and incorporating the so-called 'allied' or affiliated organisations of the lowland peripheries, such as the Ethiopian Somali People's Democratic Party, had rumbled off and on even while Meles was still alive. A plan to merge the EPRDF had later been discussed—and even agreed, according to Hailemariam—in the seventeen-day-long meeting of the politburo in November 2017. A commission to study the matter was established in the months before the final EPRDF congress in October the following year.

In theory, the goal was simple: to ensure that all regions, including the historically less powerful ones, had a proper role in national decision-making. Doing away with separate fronts might also allow the federation to run more smoothly and more cohesively. But Abiy's own planned party merger represented a change of a different order entirely to anything the EPRDF had previously considered. For one thing, its very name was an affront to the coalition's ideological foundations, alluding as it did to a certain evangelical orientation and capitalist outlook. The new party's programme was spelled out in Abiy's own book, *Medemer*, published that October, and it took direct—if mostly slapdash—aim at both 'Revolutionary Democracy' and the Marxist-Leninist thinking of the student movement which underpinned it. The new watchword, as laid out in *Medemer*, was "pragmatism"—a term Abiy's advisors used repeatedly—and it suggested a distinct model of 'non-ideological' or even apolitical technocratic development, shorn of the essence which EPRDF stalwarts believed lay behind the coalition's success over the preceding decades. "It is just the 'Third Way'," observed Jawar after reading an early draft of the text. "'Third Way' plus God." Hardly the stuff of revolution, then. But for those in the coalition who had come of age as students in the Marxist-inspired struggle of the 1970s, it was an affront which struck to the very core of their politics.

The model of party centralisation that Abiy proposed also appeared to go well beyond anything previously considered by his colleagues. *Medemer* evoked national 'unity'—itself a term with strong historical resonances, not least for those who had lived through the violent assimilationist politics of the Derg era—and could be traced back to Haile Selassie himself, who had used the term in relation to his own nation-building efforts in the post-Italian occupation era.[21] If Abiy's early invocations of *Medemer* had initially seemed harmless if vacuous to many ears, they now began sounding distinctly ominous. Armed with the newly minted language of unity, the Prosperity Party was to be organised along starkly centralised and hierarchical lines. Abiy, as its president, would be given effective control over the entire party apparatus, with the formal power to appoint and dismiss members and officials right down to the very lowest level. Though power in the EPRDF had also been, whatever its leaders might have insisted otherwise, top-down and centralised, each separate front had been at least formally autonomous. The EPRDF chairman wasn't allowed, in theory, to hire and fire regional presidents (though he often did), and nor could he dictate policy without consulting the members. By contrast, the president of the Prosperity Party had the formal power to do almost anything he wanted.

Relatedly, and most alarmingly from the perspective of Abiy's ethno-nationalist opponents, was the threat the new party appeared to pose to the constitution itself. In principle, of course, there was nothing in the constitution which said that the ruling party could only ever be a multi-ethnic coalition like the EPRDF. Indeed, scrapping ethnic-based parties in favour of mere regional chapters, each of which would theoretically be open to all individuals regardless of ethnicity, might on the surface have looked like a sensible step towards a more inclusive politics—one with a bigger role for civic rather than ethnic nationalism, and in which parties might campaign on concrete economic issues more than intangible cultural ones. But for many Ethiopians, not just the relatively powerful Oromos and Tigrayans but also small and marginalised minorities, there were good reasons for scepticism. Many feared that the advances made over the previous three decades, such as the freedoms they now enjoyed to teach and administer in their own languages rather than Amharic, were fragile and could easily be rolled back. A rushed move towards a single national party, some now argued, might be the thin end of the wedge towards the abandonment of the constitutional provisions—indeed, the very principle of ethnic self-rule—that protected such rights. In a country where the governing coalition and the apparatus of the state were so intrinsically linked, critics warned, the organisation of the former was bound to reflect, and reinforce, the ordering of the latter. "If they dissolve the ethnic parties and merge them into a single party today, it is inevitable that they will destroy ethnic federalism tomorrow," warned Jawar in a TV interview that October.[22]

Abiy never said as much openly, and even in private could seem cagey: Ginbot 7's Andargachew later insisted to me that the prime minister had never been candid with him about his real plans for the constitution. Nonetheless, from almost the day he had taken office Abiy had at least hinted at plans to revise it, above all by diluting its most controversial 'ethnic' or 'multinational' elements. "If we are able to form regional administrations without confusing it with ethnic identities, then there is no question that federalism is the best option for Ethiopia's situation," he had told the EPRDF congress in 2018.[23] A few months later, he had questioned the sovereignty of the regional states, dismissing their boundaries as mere "administrative" constructs.[24] In private, he told some friends and legal experts that his goal was to replace the existing parliamentary system with a presidential one, arguing that a directly elected president would need to transcend ethno-linguistic blocs in order to win. Some of his close allies, meanwhile, proposed following the example of countries like Ghana and banning ethno-nationalist parties altogether.

Supporters of the existing federal system could also point to Abiy's response to ethnic separatist movements in other parts of the country as evidence of his true instincts. In the Southern Nations, Nationalities and Peoples Region (SNNPR), for example, multiple different ethnic groups which had seized on the political opening to push for further autonomy and self-rule had found their path blocked by him. A campaign beginning in 2018 by the Sidama, the country's fifth most populous community, to form their own regional state had been followed by similar popular movements among some thirteen smaller southern groups by early the following year. All of them were either obstructed bureaucratically or physically crushed. Indeed, the referendum on Sidama's statehood was delayed for so many months by the national electoral board under pressure from Abiy that protests in the state capital of Hawassa eventually turned violent. Even after 98.5 percent of its population had at last voted in favour of forming their own state in November 2019, the prime minister sought to delay the poll's implementation.

Over the years, as the multiethnic Southern region buckled under pressure from various separatist movements demanding their own states, Abiy would strong-arm all the rest of them into forming multiethnic regions defined by geographical proximity rather than ethno-linguistic groupings. "The prime minister doesn't believe in this ethnic issue," his close ally Shimelis Abdissa, the future president of Oromia, told me the day after Abiy took office. "He believes in the Oromo cause, the Amhara cause—but his views always go beyond that." The top-down dissolution of the former SNNPR into three broadly 'non-ethnic' regions by the end of 2023—Southwestern Ethiopian Peoples, Southern Ethiopian and Central Ethiopian regions—thus provided as clear a view as any onto his preferred model of federalism. "He wants smaller regions," a former senior colleague explained: Amhara broken into three; Oromia into six; Tigray into two.

So too, for those who read between the lines, did *Medemer*. Widely distributed in schools and government offices nationwide, with profits from the sales supposedly funding more than thirty schools around the country, what the book was not was either a rigid or coherent programme for government. "Nothing more than sophistry," wrote one scathing reviewer. "A hodgepodge of ideas constructed with rhetorical fallacies and delivered with pseudo-intellectual evangelical self-help fervour."[25] Ethiopian intellectuals enlisted to help write the book (which Abiy passed off as entirely his own work) were mostly derisive about it. One scholar later described leafing through its pages as the "turning point" in their relationship: "I realised this man doesn't understand history, he doesn't understand political theory, he doesn't understand economics, he doesn't understand international politics—nothing." So negative was the reception among the country's educated class that the Prime Minister's Office eventually scrapped its plan to translate the book into English.

But the fact that the ideas in *Medemer* were so vague they could be taken to mean almost anything didn't make the book any less controversial. Though there was nothing in it which was unambiguously hostile to the current federal system—nor, indeed, was there in pretty much any of the prime minister's official statements—there was equally little there to reassure those who worried that the prime minister didn't care much for the EPRDF's most deeply-held beliefs. It was clear from the book, for instance, that Abiy didn't consider Ethiopia an essentially modern construct. Nor did he share the ethno-nationalist understanding of Ethiopia's ethnic troubles as the product of a long process of state-building which empowered some groups at the expense of others. In fact, *Medemer* suggested that his entire conception of Ethiopia's recent past stemmed from a belief that its problems were rooted not in Menelik's empire-building, nor Haile Selassie's, but in ideological errors made by the students who came of age in the 1960s and 1970s—in other words, the generation of the EPRDF's founding fathers. For believers in the existing federal order, the implications of this were deeply troubling. If Abiy didn't subscribe to such elementary precepts, how could he be trusted to uphold the system they underpinned?

And so it was that the prospect of a new ruling party founded on the prime minister's new doctrine of *Medemer* morphed into the defining controversy of the pre-war era. For sure, many Amharas and urban Ethiopians with mixed backgrounds who had always been unhappy with the 1995 constitution were generally enthused by it. So too were many Western officials and observers. A diplomat in the US embassy in Addis Ababa, for instance, said privately that America would ultimately support Abiy's attempts to turn Ethiopia into a presidential republic like France. But for his growing number of Oromo critics, many of whom had previously refrained from open confrontation despite their growing misgivings, the creation of the Prosperity Party was the final straw. Awol Allo, a law expert at Britain's Keele University who had once been so taken by Abiy that he had nominated him for the Nobel Peace Prize, now denounced *Medemer* as a "new vocabulary to resurrect and operationalise the old assimilationist, Amharic-centric model of the state."[26] In an impassioned appeal posted on Facebook, the Oromo nationalist scholar warned that if the new party was intended to "solve the crisis of representation and legitimacy that plagues the EPRDF, [then it was] like taking a sledgehammer to crack a nut."[27] He would later say that he and others had positively "begged" the prime minister not to go ahead with it.[28]

Even some of the prime minister's closest allies inside the party were set against the idea. Lemma, still by far the most influential of Abiy's rivals in government, was known to be incandescent by what he perceived to be Abiy's betrayal of the Oromo cause and their personal friendship. For the very first time (and to date, the very last) he spoke out against his boss, telling *Voice of America* in November that he had pleaded with the prime minister to discard the plan and warned it risked further alienating their Oromo base. But the intervention, however high-profile, had no effect. By now Abiy had almost completely sidelined his one-time closest ally, sacking him some seven months earlier in a manner which, according to a former colleague, was as unconstitutional as it was unceremonial. Rarely seen in public, and dogged by persistent rumours of ill-health, Lemma quietly mulled forming a breakaway party of like-minded colleagues. At the same time, he entertained the idea of defecting to Jawar's opposition camp. None of it, though, would come to pass. In the subsequent months, Abiy would cast former the Oromia president far into the political wilderness, eventually placing him under house arrest in Addis Ababa and neutralising him entirely.

Meanwhile the TPLF, in what would turn out to be by far the most fateful legacy of the party merger, was preparing to leave the coalition altogether. For the old custodians of 'Revolutionary Democracy' and other foundational tenets of the EPRDF, the Prosperity Party was an ideological bridge too far. (Moreover, they feared the proposed scrapping of equal voting rights for the four fronts, irrespective of population size, would consign the minority Tigrayans to second-tier status in both the new party and the country.) Little was done to reassure them or bring them on board, and lines of communication between Mekelle and the palace were instead almost completely severed. By this point few among the TPLF's leadership still remained in Addis Ababa; it had been almost a full year since Getachew Reda, the future president of Tigray and one of the final senior TPLF members to remain committed to its role in the federal government, had last been spotted at a bar in the capital in the days before the attorney-general announced the government's sweeping arrests of former Tigrayan officers and officials. Instead of trying to broker a compromise, Abiy's unconvincing last-ditch efforts to get them to join the new party seemed almost purposefully designed merely to inflame their darkest fears. In a meeting held with prominent Tigrayan businessmen, the prime minister was reported to have threatened to cut federal subsidies and other public services—including flights—to the region.[29] "Who wants them to join?" Andargachew later recalled Abiy responding dismissively when the former Ginbot 7 leader had asked whether the TPLF would join the new party. "The TPLF have a deep, entrenched identity," Hailemariam remarked several years later. "They fought for seventeen years. They sacrificed for Tigray's survival [...] Was the TPLF even given the chance to discuss and talk about how to abandon its own identity?" Debretsion, the TPLF's chairman, put it more bluntly: "[Abiy and his allies] betrayed the country and we consider them traitors."[30]

In a country with no real history of power-sharing, and in which party and state had been fused so completely since the fall of Haile Selassie that they were almost indistinguishable, many predicted that the splintering of the ruling coalition might lead to nothing less than the country's unravelling. "The most probable outcome is disintegration," a top TPLF official warned the International Crisis Group.[31] Yet Abiy ploughed ahead. Invigorated, it was said, by his receipt of the Nobel Prize that October—Addis Ababa was now festooned with congratulatory billboards—the prime minister rushed to deliver on his plan with unbending conviction. "Now the name of Ethiopia is glorified everywhere," he proclaimed triumphantly at the launch of *Medemer*. "Because Abiy and Ethiopia are inseparable; two sides of the same coin."[32] Advice from his allies was shunted aside, while growing calls for a so-called 'national dialogue' instead of a rushed party merger were breezily dismissed. "Abiy has been emboldened by the international endorsement," warned an Ethiopian scholar friendly with government officials. "He believes the whole international community, as well as God, are by his side. And with God and the international community by your side, you cannot possibly lose." A low-level ODP member in the city of Adama told me only weeks before the dissolution was finalised that he and his colleagues had been barely informed about it, let alone consulted. By then the merger was, in effect, a fait accompli. Ironically, the EPRDF's own strict Leninist culture of 'democratic centralism', honed over three decades, had served to facilitate its demise. Any further flickering of internal dissent would be ruthlessly quashed.

At one of the last meetings of the Oromo ruling party, Abiy had warned potential troublemakers that he was, despite everything, a "son of Meles Zenawi"—a hard-hearted autocrat. "He threatened everyone," recalled one of those present. To make sure he understood the message that nobody would be allowed to oppose him, Abiy now dispatched a top army general to Lemma's home. Following simple votes in the coalition's politburo and central council, in which Lemma was the only notable absentee, Abiy wrote a hasty letter to the electoral board and declared the EPRDF dissolved. By then anyone who might dare to question the wisdom or legality of it all had been purged; Lemma, the prime minister's most likely potential rival, had been simply shut out. Everyone else fell into line. By 1 December 2019, the EPRDF was no more.

14

"MENGISTU DRIFT"

ASSASSINATING THE TRANSITION

Scrappy, headstrong, and more than a little reckless, there was nobody quite like Hachalu Hundessa. A wiry, mischievous-looking man, Hachalu had swaggered his way around Oromia for the best part of the decade, scornful of authority and temerarious toward the dangers he faced. After his murder, which took place late at night on 29 June 2020, there was almost nobody with a bad word to say about him. From across the political spectrum, politicians and activists rushed to pay tribute to a musician who had captured in his songs the spirit of revolt which had brought Abiy to power more than anyone else. "He was the right eye of the Oromo people," one *Qeerroo* told me. "We have lost our hero," said another.

Hachalu had long known he was a target. "He feared for his life," recalled his brother Sisay. Despite his enormous popularity—his 2014 ballad *"Maalan Jira"* ("What existence is mine") was the undisputed soundtrack to the Addis Ababa master plan protests—by 2020, noted a friend from his hometown of Ambo in western Oromia, "Hachalu made nobody happy".[1] Abiy resented his refusal to endorse the Prosperity Party. Amhara militants hounded him as the embodiment of rising Oromo power in the capital. Hardline Oromo nationalists denounced him as a sell-out to the Oromo cause.

But Hachalu had stuck to his guns. He was a proud Oromo, a *Qeerroo* at heart, and he knew better than anyone what the Ethiopian state was capable of: the EPRDF's courts had sent him to prison for five years on trumped-up charges when he was just seventeen years old. But still, Hachalu had believed in Ethiopia and opposed secession. "He couldn't easily be influenced by any group or any interest," his brother told me. "He wasn't the kind of man you can twist your way." Though he never came out in support of the Prosperity Party, he rarely expressed any particular enthusiasm for the OLA, likening the two groups to different sides of the same coin, with each having infiltrated the other. "He used to say that the problem is the government has people in the OLA, and the OLA has people in the government," the friend from Ambo recalled.

In his final months, Hachalu kept a low profile, avoiding public controversies and carrying a pistol around in case of the worst. On Facebook, he received death threats; Oromo militants who had turned against Abiy accused him of cosying up to the regime for money and business favours. On his phone, he received menacing messages from unknown numbers. "He used to say all the time: 'they're going to kill me'," recalled the friend. "He was like the walking dead," said Birhanu Lenjiso, an academic-turned-government official who had known the musician when he taught at the university in Ambo.

I crossed paths with Hachalu just once, a few months before his killing, in the lobby of Addis Ababa's Ramada Hotel. We shared a mutual acquaintance, a well-known motivational speaker, who, on spotting the pop star at the entrance, broke off our conversation and immediately jumped up to shake his hand. In life as in death: everyone wanted a piece of Hachalu. For as an emblem of the transition's tragic path, and the bloody struggle to control it, nothing quite surpassed Hachalu's assassination. Just as different groups tussled—almost literally—over his body the morning after he was found dead in his car in an Addis Ababa suburb, feuding over where to take it, Ambo or the capital, so did the competing factions of Ethiopian politics vie to establish and enforce a narrative of his murder. Was he slain by professional assassins, perhaps the Eritrean commandos by now said to be prowling the capital at Abiy's request? Or were his killers sent by the TPLF, in a cynical bid to overthrow the federal government by triggering mayhem? Conspiracy theories proliferated; convictions hardened. Nobody had conclusive proof.

The Ethiopian government alleged that Hachalu was murdered by the OLA with the TPLF's collusion, yet no convincing evidence of their involvement was furnished. Abiy, appearing again in military fatigues on national TV the very next day, drew links to the grenade attack in Meskel Square in 2018, as well as the assassination of the Amhara regional president in 2019. Both, he noted, had also occurred in June. Once more, he stated, the assassins' aim was to derail the transition.[2]

But in the minds of Abiy's Oromo and Tigrayan opponents it was the government and its Ethiopianist allies themselves who were behind it. "To fight the TPLF, they need Oromo support. To get Oromo support, they want to say that the TPLF and the OLF killed their icon. So the goal was to get Oromo support for the coming war against the TPLF," warned a veteran *Qeerroo*, with prophetic insight, if not hard evidence, a few weeks later. Others pinpointed Amhara oligarchs and *Fano* mercenaries. A few, however, even suggested it was not a political killing at all but the result of a petty business feud.

Nobody ever delivered a decisive verdict. Even so, by the summer of 2020, one thing, at least, was clear: where one stood on the question of who killed Hachalu determined where one was on an even bigger matter. Who killed the transition?

* * *

The afternoon after Hachalu's murder was wet and grey, the early summer rains casting Addis Ababa's streets in a dank, dispiriting gloom. The first round of protests which had erupted that morning after Hachalu died seemed to have dissipated, so before the sun went down I took my car and drove through the city centre. The roads by then were quiet, eerily so, the emptiness punctuated only occasionally by the odd sullen policeman. Most of the shops and restaurants on the road from the airport to Meskel Square were shuttered; the windows of almost all those in the vicinity around my apartment were freshly smashed. On the pavement lay shards of glass, spattered among soil from the upturned flowerpots which Abiy had recently ordered be arranged along the avenue. A huddle of young men holding wooden sticks stood guard at the gates of a nearby apartment building.

Dawn had barely broken before the carnage was unleashed by news of Hachalu's murder. Grieving and angry, thousands of *Qeerroos* had descended on the capital before most of its residents even understood what was happening—it had only taken a few hours for an agitated Jawar to declare, in an emotional Facebook post shared with his two million followers, that the killing was a "shot in the heart of the Oromo nation". In Lege Tafo, a nearby satellite town in Oromia, trucks arriving from the north were set on fire shortly after sunrise. An Amhara lorry owner who had driven from Bahir Dar the day before told me how he and his driver, accompanied by a frightened police officer, had been chased by a gang of machete-wielding youth. "I ran away and hid under a bridge," he said. "They chase you if you don't speak their language." By the time the protesters had drawn close to my apartment in the centre, clashes between them and the police had spread all through the city as cars and even petrol stations were set alight. In all, at least ten people were killed in Addis Ababa over nearly three days of rioting. Many more were injured. I spent the next two evenings on my balcony listening to the retort of gunfire piercing the summer fog.

In parts of Oromia even worse scenes were unfolding. In the town of Dera, in the district of Arsi, seven people were killed. Mobs on the hunt for minorities went door-to-door, beheading a young Amhara man and leaving his mutilated body in the street. Eyewitnesses later reported that the Oromo special police stationed nearby did nothing to stop it.[3]

The booming entrepôt of Shashemene, some 200 kilometres south along the floor of the Rift Valley, saw fewer deaths but even more arson: young men and women from the surrounding countryside checked identity cards before burning or ransacking property belonging to Christians and non-Oromos. When I visited a few days later all that remained of much of the city centre were looted husks, stray dogs sniffing through the blackened remnants of shopping malls and boarded-up offices. All across town "Hachalu" had been scrawled in graffiti paint. Next to a ravaged hotel owned by the Ethiopian (and Amhara) marathon legend, Haile Gebreselassie, someone had written "Oromo Lives Matter", a pointed reference to the murder by a white American police officer of George Floyd, an African American man in Minneapolis, which just one month earlier had set off large-scale anti-racism protests across America. Big red crosses had been painted over Amharic road signs.

Across Oromia some 123 people died, at a minimum, and at least 500 more were injured: some murdered—often in gruesome circumstances— by gangs of youth; others shot by security forces.[4] Even in Abiy's home district of Jimma, hotels, cars and businesses were set alight. Though much of the violence appeared to be communal, with Amharas or Orthodox Christian Oromos in particular singled out for attack, it was also directly political, with symbols of imperial Ethiopia being the most common target. In Harar, in eastern Oromia, for example, a controversial statue of Ras Mekonnen Wolde Mikael, the former governor and father of Haile Selassie, was toppled. Even in London, where diaspora Oromos demonstrated in solidarity, a bust of the last emperor on Wimbledon Common was torn down. Meanwhile, in Addis Ababa, statues representing the *Abba Gaddas*—the preeminent Oromo elders—were attacked by local youth in reply.

What followed was the most aggressive government crackdown since Abiy had come to power. Among those arrested were Jawar himself, as well as his OFC colleague, Bekele Gerba. The two had been caught up in a stand-off with the police over their ill-fated attempts to take Hachalu's body to the Oromo Cultural Centre in Addis Ababa for a public wake (in the ensuing scuffle, a police officer was reportedly killed by a member of Jawar's security detail). They were later charged with inciting violence against Amharas and Christians, and conspiring to overthrow the government by force. Amongst the many allegations in the charge sheet was the explosive—and ultimately unsupported—claim that Jawar had been training a terror group in Egypt.

Other opponents from across the spectrum were also rounded up. Eskinder Nega, the divisive Amhara activist-journalist imprisoned for several years under the EPRDF and now best known for his trenchant opposition to Oromo expansion in the capital, was arrested and charged with crimes which included training a terror group in Amhara to assassinate Takele Uma, the Addis Ababa mayor. Six others from Eskinder's newly formed Balderas party; one official from Ezema, the main Ethiopianist opposition grouping led by Berhanu Nega; and scores of OLF and OFC officials were also apprehended. The OLF's veteran leader, Dawud Ibsa, was put under house arrest.

Even the irreproachably non-violent leader of the Ethiopian Democratic Party, Lidetu Ayelaw, was detained and charged with attempting to topple the government. Despite Abiy's public insistence that he had no direct hand in deciding who was arrested,[5] insiders said that the order for this had in fact come directly from him. Lidetu's appearance on OMN a few weeks earlier, in which he had sharply criticised Abiy's friendship with Eritrea's president, was said to have particularly provoked his displeasure. In all, more than 7,000 individuals were reportedly arrested in the space of just a few short weeks—the most unequivocal sign yet of what a senior EU diplomat at the time described to me as Abiy's "Mengistu drift".

In public, the prime minister remained adamant that his administration was still committed to democratisation. He insisted that all those arrested were extremists bent on subverting the constitution and seizing power through force. "What we learn from the fledgling democracies of Europe of the 1920s and 1930s is that democracy has to be defended from violent demagogues and mobs," his team wrote to the editor of *The Economist* a couple of months later. "Let there be no ambiguity," they added. "We remain deeply committed to the vision of building an inclusive, multinational, democratic and prosperous Ethiopia."

But among the expanding ranks of sceptical observers, it was becoming self-evident that the only way left for the prime minister now was the ratchet logic of ever more repression. "The problem is that if you are the paranoid narcissist in the palace, you can't just lock up a couple of guys," the EU diplomat remarked. "If you are convinced everyone is out to get you then there is no end to who you must arrest."

* * *

A showdown between Abiy and Jawar, in particular, and the Oromo opposition in general, had been a long time coming. If Jawar had, at first, sought to play a constructive role behind the scenes of the transition, nudging the prime minister towards the free and fair elections which he hoped himself to win, then by the time Abiy had made public his plans to forge the Prosperity Party from the dying embers of the EPRDF the Oromo activist had hurled himself into open opposition.

Jawar, too, now cast Abiy as a would-be emperor, a megalomaniacal reactionary on a path to revive the pre-1974 Christian Empire. His criticisms of Abiy's attempts to rehabilitate Ethiopia's former monarchs were particularly unsparing. "If they keep glorifying Menelik, then we will keep digging out what Menelik did to our people and let the next generation know," he said in a widely watched interview that October.[6] OMN, which was still nominally under Jawar's control, now began reporting aggressively on abuses by the security forces in western and southern Oromia (and also the violence against the Qemant in northern Amhara). That same month Jawar had attended a closed meeting of the Oromo ruling party during which he urged participants to resist Abiy's plan to dissolve the EPRDF. The prime minister responded with a warning that he would steamroll anyone who stood in his way.

The two men had always had an unusual relationship. Abiy, conscious of his indebtedness to Jawar's superior campaigning skills, could be unsubtle in his one-upmanship: when his younger rival had first returned to Ethiopia, the prime minister made a show of personally furnishing the former's new office space with an expensive new desk. Jawar, for his part, was scathing about the prime minister's intellect, and didn't hide his conviction that he was much more qualified for the job than Abiy. His endorsement of the prime minister in 2018 had always been lukewarm.

But he also seemed to enjoy his proximity to power, and made much of Abiy's reliance on him for political advice.

But as the charismatic sons of similarly mixed heritage, Abiy and Jawar were alike in some ways. Both were exercised by the pursuit of power, and both could adjust their positions, and their rhetoric, in the service of it—toggling between different ethnic and political constituencies with an ease which to sympathisers read as pragmatism, but to critics as cynicism. Though Jawar was a far more conventional Oromo nationalist, he also shared with Abiy a disdain for the OLF and the movement's wilder fringes. But unlike the prime minister, he could see the stabilising value in a power-sharing arrangement with them and other Oromo political parties.

In the end, it was perhaps their very likeness which made co-existence so difficult. In Oromia, Abiy's own region, Jawar was less an ordinary opponent than a direct threat to the prime minister's own authority. With mass popular support in almost all corners, he had an unparalleled ability to pull crowds to public rallies right under the nose of the ruling party. On top of this, he was widely believed to wield indirect influence over local institutions in Oromia, such as the police, whose members' loyalties were divided between him and the government. Moreover, thanks to his power over the *Qeerroo*, the movement to whose success he had been pivotal, Jawar also had hard leverage over the government which far surpassed that of any other opposition leader. By contrast, Abiy's concerted efforts to persuade Jawar to stay out of politics—offering various commercial opportunities—had got nowhere. Visibly frustrated, Abiy railed angrily against Jawar, Andargachew would later claim. "The venom in his voice was shocking to me."

And so the tensions spiralled. On 22 October 2019, the prime minister for the first time implicitly threatened Jawar, saying in parliament that he would "take measures" against media owners with foreign passports if they fanned instability. (Jawar was at this time still an American citizen; he would give up his passport a few months later in order to run in the election). On Facebook, Abiy's rival responded that the gloves were off, proclaiming that he and his colleagues had "packed up completely and moved into Oromia to live and die". Yet just a few hours later, he posted another message, this time alleging that unidentified police had tried to remove his government-assigned security detail in the dead of night. This had been resisted, but the intent—or so Jawar implied—was clear: someone wanted him dead.

What happened next presaged the popular reaction to Hachalu's assassination eight months later with striking precision. By nine the next morning, 23 October 2019, a vast crowd of *Qeerroos* from in and around Addis Ababa had gathered on the street outside Jawar's home, pledging to protect him from harm. Elsewhere in Oromia, demonstrators stormed the streets. In some places, copies of *Medemer* were seen being torched; in Ambo, a billboard advertising the prime minister's book was pelted with stones. Over the following days, fierce fighting broke out between Oromos and Amharas, or in some cases between Muslims and Christians, with mosques and churches both coming under attack.[7] In towns like Adama, groups of Amhara youth mobilised to confront the *Qeerroo*, provoking the violence, but in places like Robe, in the predominantly Muslim district of Bale, "it was Oromos on Oromos," as a local later put it to me. In total, at least eighty-six people were killed over the course of the unrest.

Clear battle lines over Ethiopia's future had now been drawn. Jawar, who understood the incident outside his home in the early hours of 23 October to have been an assassination attempt, thought it had been planned by a group of Amhara militants. Having appeared to threaten Jawar in parliament, Abiy then hopped on a plane out of the country to attend the Russia-Africa Summit in Sochi. Just hours later, Oromia unravelled. The prime minister's silence over the coming days did not go unnoticed. Moreover, the armed men who had arrived at Jawar's gates at midnight appeared to have the blessing of the commander in charge of the opposition leader's security detail. Two years later, in an added layer of intrigue, the commander himself would mysteriously wind up dead.

Intra-Oromo divisions thus worsened over the coming months, embodied in the now bitter and open power struggle between the prime minister and Jawar. Regional blocs within Oromia began to take shape. Abiy, and the Oromo leadership of the soon-to-be Prosperity Party, increasingly came to be associated with the Shewa territories of central Oromia around Addis Ababa; Oromia's president, Shimelis Abdissa, for instance, hailed from nearby the West Shewa town of Ambo. Because attitudes towards Ethiopian history in such places were generally more ambivalent than they were in either the OLF's stronghold of Wollega or Jawar's Muslim-majority heartlands of Arsi and Bale in the south-east, the Prosperity Party's centralising, Ethiopianist tendencies were not always seen as quite so toxic there. In towns like Selale or Ambo, many former *Qeerroos* joined the government. Further to the west, by contrast, many more joined the OLA.

But general disillusionment among the Oromo youth, if not always among the older generation, was palpable almost everywhere. Frustrations with Abiy for his apparent reluctance to address some core nationalist demands, such as making Afan Oromo a working language of the federal government, or settling the question of Oromo ownership of the capital, were ubiquitous. "The government hasn't done anything for the *Qeerroo*," said a young man in Adama, in East Shewa, when I visited that month. Others complained that Abiy was more interested in putting waxwork figures of former Ethiopian emperors on display in the palace than in addressing their economic plight. In the following weeks, Abiy would tour Oromia to try and ease tension, asking for their patience and insisting in town-hall meetings that he remained steadfast in his commitment to the Oromo cause. But it was clear that this was a message which was leaving few of them convinced.

Ethiopia's broader ethnic and religious fissures were widening further, too. In Addis Ababa, popular dislike of Jawar—a Muslim as well as an Oromo—was becoming increasingly hard to distinguish from the 'Oromophobia' or 'Islamophobia' which had always been somewhat latent there. Even though the police told the UN privately that they had nothing to implicate Jawar in the ethnic violence in Oromia, few in Addis Ababa questioned the now all-pervasive presumptions of his guilt. The new head of the Ethiopian Human Rights Commission, Daniel Bekele, suggested in a conversation at the time that Jawar might be an Islamic extremist. A friend in Addis Ababa, who argued that "eighty-six people died because of this one man", told me bluntly that there were only two options left to deal with him: "court or kill". In some circles of the capital the old pejorative term for Oromo—"*Galla*"—began to stage a comeback. Meanwhile among some Oromos, Abiy's government had become known as a "*neftegna*" one, an old imperial term denoting a gun-wielding Amhara settler from the north. As tensions between Oromos and Amharas mounted, "*neftegna*" increasingly came to function as an ethnic dog-whistle.[8] Online and on the airwaves, hate speech ran amok.

As competition between ethno-nationalist Oromos and Amharas, and in some places Muslims and Christians, intensified in the media, on the ground it was increasingly playing out in the multiethnic towns and cities of Oromia and the wider south. If Abiy's stress on urban development had, in part, been intended to build for himself a new constituency in support of the Prosperity Party, the unhelpful corollary was that it also served to sharpen pre-existing popular anxieties around urbanisation and demographic change. Such worries were most obvious in Addis Ababa, where fears of 'Oromofication' had been latent even before Abiy took power. Since then, there had been regular reports of city identity cards being illegally distributed to non-resident Oromos, and of homes belonging to Amharas on the capital's outskirts being demolished, in order to alter Addis Ababa's ethnic composition.[9] Lemma's admission, back in February 2019, that his government had resettled more than half a million Oromos around the capital, because "politics in urban areas means 'demography'", had sparked a particularly vocal outcry.[10]

But similar anxieties could be found in smaller towns such as Adama or Shashemene, which had large and established populations of Amharas and Christian Oromos from the north. These groups may have felt politically disempowered following the introduction of ethnic federalism, but they still enjoyed relative economic clout and owned a substantial portion of the major hotels and businesses in the old town centres. As ever more rural Oromos, particularly young people, migrated from the hinterlands, these towns were fast becoming among the most volatile parts of the country. When I interviewed local residents of Adama in 2019 and 2020, for instance, both groups claimed with equal conviction to be a demographic majority there. Both also claimed to be marginalised, economically and politically, and both expressed acute fears of the other taking over at the next election. As the months went by, local competition over economic resources in urban areas increasingly came to be seen through the lens of a wider national struggle for dominance. After Hachalu's murder, violence in these places typically fell along lines which were as stark as they were predictable: inter-ethnic conflict fought over the wealth and resources of the urban economy.

* * *

By early 2020, Abiy's project had also begun to feel the heat on another front: the constitution. By law, Ethiopia's parliament was to reach the end of its five-year term on 5 October. Any attempt to retain power after that without an election would be a constitutional breach without precedent in the federal republic's thirty-year history. But the argument for postponing it was clear enough. Despite considerable financial support from Western donors, for whom a 'free and fair' election which kept Abiy in power would be a satisfying conclusion to the 'democratic transition' they had bankrolled, the electoral board's preparations for the vote were by this point hopelessly behind schedule. What was more, given the parlous state of the country's politics, and an economy which was struggling even before the arrival of the COVID-19 pandemic that March, many Ethiopians were fearful that a competitive election would serve only to aggravate the divides. Anxious talk of electoral violence grew louder.

But, at the same time, few were ready to publicly endorse a simple delay. To do so, from the government's perspective, would be to gift the opposition another line of attack. Once the initial fervour of 'Abiymania' began to fade, after all, it had become increasingly hard to overlook the uncomfortable fact that Abiy didn't have a formal electoral mandate for the radical changes he was undertaking. Nobody had ever voted for *"Medemer"* or the Prosperity Party. But from the opposition's perspective, any slippage in the electoral calendar without a prior agreement for a transitional administration to take the reins in the interim risked making themselves complicit in the consolidation of an unelected dictatorship. Nobody in government, least of all Abiy, had any truck with the idea of a power-sharing transitional administration.

The pandemic, however, upturned many of these assumptions. The new state of emergency, brought in on 8 April to contain the virus's spread, suddenly made a postponement not just defensible on practical grounds but arguably on constitutional ones, too. Abiy's government therefore began reconsidering its options. To most of the prime minister's opponents, it had long been clear that he wished to suspend the vote, perhaps even indefinitely. "Abiy would use anything, including his wife's menstrual cycle, to delay the election," the TPLF's Getachew Reda said to me shortly before the pandemic struck. Yet much as Abiy may have been keen to suspend or postpone voting in areas like Wollega, where the opposition was strongest, there were good reasons to doubt he really wanted to cancel the election altogether. For one thing, there was simply no other way to confer his rule with the formal legitimacy needed to win international recognition. If Abiy wanted Western financial taps to remain on, he needed—at the very least—to show that he was willing to go along with the procedural dance of a semi-competitive election. Moreover, Abiy did appear to genuinely want to be able to claim a popular mandate. One of the many contradictions in his project, after all, was that pretensions of monarchical grandeur co-existed with a desire to appear like a modern, Western-aligned democratic leader.

There were, in any case, crude political incentives for him to push ahead with the election on schedule, in spite of the mounting risks to public health: the weakness of his opponents. With the opposition divided among themselves, disorganised and financially straitened, a prompt poll could well play to the ruling party's favour. (For some time, the party leadership had even wanted to hold the election earlier than its due date.) Indeed, for a while Abiy was so insistent about holding the election on time that friends of Birtukan Mideksa, the head of the electoral board, said she planned to resign if he didn't change course. As the pandemic spread in March, one opposition leader texted me outraged that the Prosperity Party continued to hold its training sessions and campaign rallies even as other parties had been banned from doing so.

In the end, though, Abiy appears to have weighed that his interests were in fact better served by a delayed poll, with the electoral calendar revised in such a way as to still suit the government's interests. "Covid was a pretext only," a senior colleague of Abiy later admitted. Initially, Abiy's preferred new date was August: the peak of the rainy season, when roads would be impassable and the opposition would struggle to get their voters to the polling stations. But with the pandemic showing no signs of dissipating, and countries around the world pushing back their electoral calendars as well, an indefinite delay, of perhaps a year or more, increasingly seemed plausible. After weeks of prevarication, Abiy made his move.

To address the awkward matter of constitutionality, Ethiopia's finest legal minds were invited to pass judgement on the matter. This, though, was merely a formality. The Council of Constitutional Inquiry, headed by the new president of the Supreme Court, Meaza Ashenafi, was only an advisory body to the upper house of parliament, which was itself controlled entirely by the Prosperity Party. There could be no doubt it would decide in the federal government's favour. What was more, the council was composed of lawyers who broadly agreed with the government's stated view on the legality of any postponement.

In the event, though, the judgement announced on 9 June 2020 went further in backing the government's position than even most critics had anticipated. According to Meaza and her colleagues, not only was a postponement constitutionally sound, a contentious though arguably defendable position, but also no regional state could independently organise its own election either. The terms of all the regional governments, like that of the federal one, should simply be extended until such a time that the authorities, i.e. Abiy, decided the pandemic no longer posed a public health risk. The Tigrayan speaker of the upper chamber, Keria Ibrahim, promptly resigned in protest.

Much of the opposition were livid, with the notable exception of Ezema and the broader Ethiopianist camp, who had by this point decided that their interests, in particular reform of the constitution along 'non-ethnic' lines, would be best served by partnering with Abiy and building their strength over the coming months in preparation for the vote. The Oromo nationalist opposition, by contrast, argued instead for an interim caretaker government to take over after October until a timetable for elections could be collectively agreed on. In a bellicose rebuttal a few weeks before, Abiy had dismissed such calls as unconstitutional and warned that any "illegal elections" would "harm the country and the people".[11] Those demanding them, he said, invoking a hateful term for the Ethiopians who collaborated with Italian invaders after 1935, were "*bandas*": traitors conspiring with Ethiopia's enemies in order to weaken it.[12]

By far the loudest objections, though, came from the TPLF, which soon announced that it rejected the government's judgement in its entirety. Since any election delay at all beyond the legal deadline would, it declared, be a fundamental violation of the constitution, the federal government would thereafter simply be illegal. TPLF veteran Asmelash Woldeselassie later told the state broadcaster that after 5 October the region would henceforth cease to comply with any laws, directives or regulations enacted by the federal government. Fatefully, and in brazen defiance of the federal government, Tigray's authorities added that they would be organising their own regional polls that September.

* * *

But domestic troubles were now not Abiy's only headache. Compounding them was a regional diplomatic landscape which, by the time Ethiopia's constitutional crisis had come to a head, looked decidedly less favourable for the prime minister than it had done just a year previously. Nobel laureate though he may now have been, it was clear that the effectiveness of a diplomacy which put goodwill and handshakes ahead of negotiations, treaties and hard-nosed compromises had firm limits. With Ethiopia's efforts to finalise the construction of the Grand Ethiopian Renaissance Dam coming under increasingly vociferous Egyptian and Sudanese opposition, and with neither America nor the African Union doing much to come to Ethiopia's aid, it was a situation in dire need of a deft diplomatic touch.

What the Nile dispute did instead was bring together regional and domestic concerns for Abiy in complex and consequential ways. For downstream Egyptians, for whom the mighty river's life-giving waters were at once the source of their millennia-old civilisation and their national birth right, the Grand Ethiopian Renaissance Dam had been perceived as an existential threat since the very day Meles had unveiled it a decade earlier. Ethiopia's insistence that the purpose of the dam—which, when completed, was to be the largest in Africa—was purely to generate much-needed electricity, and so would not run Egypt's taps dry, had long fallen on deaf ears. In 2013, Egyptian state TV had broadcast a meeting in which senior ministers publicly mulled bombing it, confirming deeply held suspicions among Ethiopians that their northern neighbours were forever conspiring to keep their country down. More recently, following the ousting of Sudan's long-standing dictator, Omar al-Bashir, amid popular protests and an army coup in 2019, its new military leaders had drawn closer to Egypt's strongman president, Abdel-Fattah al-Sisi. Nudged by the Egyptians, Sudan's military authorities increasingly began to echo Cairo's strident views on the dam and to talk down the many benefits, not least extra water consumption and massively expanded agricultural output, which they had once hoped to derive from it. By 2020, the tentative progress resulting from years of patient diplomacy by both Meles and Hailemariam, who had together succeeded in bringing Sudan on side and at least partially allaying Egypt's fears, was beginning to unravel. Despite endless rounds of acrimonious talks, a deal on how Ethiopia would fill and operate the dam was still no closer to being realised. As Abiy's administration began filling its vast reservoir for the first time that July, a moment of enormous symbolic if not immediately tangible significance, relations between the two countries sank to a level not seen since at least the 1990s.

From the outset, Abiy's dam diplomacy had been erratic. Apparently viewing the project as an essentially TPLF one, no doubt in part due to METEC's controversial and allegedly corrupt role in its construction, in 2018 he had dismissed it as a mere political tool. Making public an admission no Ethiopian official had previously dared, Abiy had also suggested the dam could take as long as a whole decade more to complete. Making matters worse, at least from the perspective of the horrified veteran diplomats whom he had sidelined, were his clumsy attempts to sweet-talk and indulge the Egyptians: at his first meeting with al-Sisi in Cairo he was reported to have discarded a planned speech and instead sworn "to God" that Ethiopia would never harm them.[13] At the same meeting, according to Egyptian diplomats, Abiy had also offered to make Cairo a financial partner in the project—a private proposal, made without consulting his foreign ministry, so potentially explosive it was later withdrawn.

If the prime minister had, at first, imagined that Ethiopians would appreciate his candour, or relish his skewering of yet another TPLF shibboleth, he was mistaken. Ethiopians of all stripes, most of whom had acquired a financial stake in the project in the form of individual donations or 'mini bonds' over the preceding decade, were unwavering in their support for the dam. Unmatched as a symbol of national unity, and of economic revolution, it was a cause which in the public's mind permitted little space for compromise. By agreeing, as he did in October 2019, to accept Western mediation in the dispute, Abiy thus again gravely misread the domestic political temperature. As soon as word got out, he faced a popular backlash, with the TPLF's Getachew Reda memorably accusing him of offering the dam as a "sacrificial lamb" to foreign powers.

Equally, though, he had misjudged the geopolitics of the matter. Agreed during a private meeting with al-Sisi in Sochi under the auspices of the Russia-Africa Forum, once again without consulting his own foreign minister, Abiy no doubt imagined that mediators from the US Treasury and the World Bank would look favourably upon a Nobel laureate still then basking in a reputation as a liberal reformer. But President Trump, unabashed in his enthusiasm for al-Sisi, whom he had recently professed his "favourite dictator", had other ideas. Convinced, according to US officials at the time, that he could strong-arm Ethiopia into accepting Egypt's terms in time for him to win his own Nobel Prize before the US presidential election the following year, Trump brazenly tilted the scales in al-Sisi's favour. So unqualified was Trump's preference for Egypt, a country he also considered central to his administration's grandiose ambitions for peace in the Middle East, that he would later openly suggest Cairo "blow up" the dam if the deadlock were not resolved.

By early 2020, sensing the wind wasn't blowing in his favour, and in need of a patriotic issue to rally the public behind him in time for the election, Abiy had reverted to a position which one Egyptian diplomat in Addis Ababa described to me then as characteristically Ethiopian "inflexibility". In January, Ethiopian diplomats failed to show up to talks in Washington. Abiy then rejected out of hand a deal proposed by the

Americans which had both Egyptian and Sudanese backing. Not long after, Ethiopian state broadcasters began comparing the struggle to finish the project to the Battle of Adwa. The head of Ethiopia's military, General Adem Mohammed, said on a visit to the project site that the country's armed forces were preparing to repel attacks against it.

The dam dispute was the first real wrinkle in Abiy's hitherto easy relationship with America. In August 2020, the Trump administration paused $272m in bilateral assistance to Ethiopia on the grounds that it had proven insufficiently flexible in the talks—an imperious and cack-handed move which did much to alienate Abiy, as well as many ordinary Ethiopians, from their previously most reliable foreign ally.[14] American officials may have stayed silent in public about the administration's authoritarian drift, and in private some may even have encouraged his precipitous moves to restructure the ruling coalition. But next to its perceived betrayal on the dam, America's still unwavering support for Abiy at home would soon count for almost nothing. Popular suspicions of malign foreign meddling in the country's 'internal affairs', always a rich seam for beleaguered Ethiopian governments to mine, spiked again, as nationalist pundits rallied in defence of the realm against its external 'enemies'. In the weeks running up to the reservoir's filling, as new billboards in the capital showed Abiy inspecting the dam's progress, canny government officials were spotted distributing T-shirts to Ethiopian journalists with a new viral slogan: #ItsMyDam. Foreshadowing the militant Ethiopian nationalism soon to surge in the Tigray War, domestic political opponents—from the TPLF to the OLA and even Jawar—were increasingly cast as traitors, foreign-backed agents conspiring with Egypt and America to thwart the dam's construction and Ethiopia's destiny.

* * *

By the eve of Hachalu's murder, the torrid politics of the Nile had managed to widen the gulf not only between Ethiopia and its northern neighbours—with whom relations had been fraught over decades if not centuries—but also between the Prosperity Party and its rivals at home. With another round of diplomatic talks in the offing, and Ethiopian nationalist fervour in the air, the mood in the opposition camp was one of dejected fatigue. The state of emergency had made political organising almost impossible, and a flurry of new initiatives in support of a 'national dialogue' had been stymied by the lack of serious or top-level interest from the government, not least Abiy. Among the Oromo opposition, plans for a new round of mass protests gathered momentum. In our last conversation before his arrest, Jawar told me that if the impasse continued much longer then popular unrest was inevitable.

If there was, in the end, any specific trigger, then on the surface it was the storm ignited by Hachalu's appearance on OMN seven days before his murder. According to his interviewer, Guyo Wariyo, the singer's intention in appearing on the show had been to salvage his reputation amid an onslaught of accusations that he was too close to the government. In a heartfelt televised plea, Hachalu expressed his sorrow that Oromia was "dying" and directly criticised the prime minister. Abiy's hands, he said, were "spoiled by Oromo blood". According to the singer's brother, he had also made some critical comments about the Oromo opposition, in particular the OLA, though these had been later cut from the final broadcast.[15] Even so, it was Hachalu's words about Menelik II and the "*neftegna*" which really excited controversy. Denouncing the former emperor as a "thief", he claimed his modern-day imitators were "working day and night to influence Dr Abiy to order his army to kill Jawar or one of the Oromo elites."[16] A friend who spoke to Hachalu on the phone two days later recalled feeling terrified as he watched the interview unfold. Another barrage of death threats—some from militant Amharas—followed soon after.

Whether these comments really were the reason for Hachalu's murder has never been proven. Hachalu's family, for their part, were sceptical. When I asked his brother in 2021 who they believed to be responsible, he said the family knew the killers were Oromo, and that they had someone in mind. Beyond that, though, all he would say then was that "all of them"—the government and opposition groups—had blood on their hands. Two years later, an Oromo politician who at the time had been a senior member of the federal government presented me with a far less ambiguous verdict: "He was killed by the government. If you want to crush Oromo politics, you crush figures like Hachalu."

Very few, in any case, save for Hachalu and others whose lives were ruined in the following days, could claim total innocence. Within moments of news of the murder breaking, and well before any evidence of who was responsible had emerged, senior Oromo opposition leaders jumped to blame either the government or shadowy, ill-defined "*neftegna*". By doing so, they helped fuel the inter-communal violence which followed. That night, OMN itself broadcast members of the public issuing bloodcurdling calls for violence against Amharas (its office in Addis Ababa was shut down shortly after).[17] Hate speech billowed online. Over the coming days, demonstrators in the diaspora would be heard chanting "Down Down Amhara".

Abiy showed himself once more to be unnervingly deft at seizing the ensuing crisis for political advantage. In the following days, senior officials including the prime minister insinuated, sometimes quite explicitly, that the murder was part of a conspiracy devised by Egypt and the TPLF. No evidence for this was ever given.[18] Later, the police arrested and charged three Oromos they said were working for the OLA; two of them, the attorney-general's office claimed, had communicated with each other in Tigrinya. A torrent of nationalist propaganda, much of it aimed directly at the TPLF, flooded the airwaves. No longer just ESAT and its ilk, but state TV, too, were soon awash with it. On 8 July, on state-affiliated Walta TV, a former Derg general issued a fiery call for the government to wage war against the TPLF.[19] In the coming months, pundits on ESAT would continue to press such demands, with some even exhorting the government to suspend basic services to Tigray and, in effect, put the region under siege.[20] Homes in Addis Ababa belonging to wealthy Tigrayans began to be seized by the authorities.

The wider struggle between two visions of Ethiopia's future—Ethiopian nationalist or ethno-nationalist; one nation or a confederation of many—which had rent the transition apart since the day it began now appeared to be tilting decisively in the former's favour. Oromo nationalism was knocked to its knees: in the weeks and months after Hachalu's murder, scores of dissenting officials were purged and banished.[21] Lemma, by then under house arrest, was formally ejected from the ruling party. The following year, at Abiy's request and with the acquiescence of his friend, WFP's executive director David Beasley, the former Oromo president, was shuffled out of the country into a job with the UN in Rome—a humiliating career end for a politician who had handed over the reins of the party less than three years earlier in the sincere belief, he confided to friends, that Abiy would be merely a placeholder. The underground *Qeerroo* networks across Oromia which had brought the prime minister to power were rapidly dismantled.

Western diplomats continued to cling to the idea of a transition to democracy, and to the image of a beleaguered but indispensable leader struggling against the forces of division and reaction. "In our view Abiy is still the only viable option for stability in Ethiopia," the Dutch ambassador told me that August. "So we are strong supporters of this government." But Ethiopia was not on the road to liberal democracy, and Abiy was not simply an agent of reform contending with an intransigent old guard. For those with longer memories Ethiopia was instead reliving the traumas of its past: the cultish violence of the Red Terror four decades earlier, perhaps, or even the anarchic disintegration of the 'Era of Princes' two centuries before that. In the shadow of Abiy's newly glittering capital, old patterns had vigorously reasserted themselves. Opponents were enemies; to triumph was to vanquish, and politics meant war. "People now say we aren't ready for democracy," confessed one friend in the capital. "They want Abiy to go after the TPLF and then be a dictator." More and more people warned of a coming conflict. "Listen to me, Tom: forget about solutions," said Aaron Maasho, a friend and Ethiopian former journalist for *Reuters*. "This is just going to get more and more hideous."

PART FOUR

WAR

15

"GAME OVER"

THE ROAD TO WAR IN TIGRAY

Something didn't feel right. Like sentries made from marble, the armed police lining the road to the airport stood unnervingly still—their faces deadpan and arms stiff, their eyes fixed on the sky. Harvest time was nearing, and the fields of *teff* on the plain above Mekelle shimmered in the early morning breeze. For the past few days in the Tigrayan capital the internet had been unusually slow. Security officers in Addis Ababa had been spotted blocking tourists from boarding flights headed to Tigray. Social media hummed with talk of troop movements near the Eritrean border.

Around mid-morning, as we drove west, the signal on my phone went out. Though the road wound around empty mountainsides, and across landscapes where the only marks of human settlement were Orthodox monasteries teetering on distant crags, it was the first time I had ever struggled for internet or mobile reception for so long there. After several hours without service, I asked my companions what they thought was going on. "Abiy", the Tigrayan driver answered in a beat, chuckling grimly as though it were so obvious it barely merited mention.

It was late October 2020, five days before the start of the war in Tigray, and I was making my way to the holy town of Axum, where clouds of locusts were ravaging fields and desperate farmers were gathering what they could of their crops before they were lost. Just as I was doing so, Brigadier-General Jamal Mohammed, an Oromo previously of Ethiopia's Eastern Command, touched down at Mekelle airport. Newly appointed by Abiy as the deputy head of the Northern Command stationed in Tigray, he had flown from Addis Ababa that morning to assume his new post on a commercial Ethiopian Airlines flight—an unusual move made necessary by the regional authorities' prohibition on military planes landing in the region. Greeting General Jamal on the tarmac that morning, however, was an anti-aircraft gun, and an order from Tigrayan officials to turn around and take the next flight home.

Speaking with a foreign journalist a few hours later, a senior TPLF leader explained that any military appointments or troop movements were considered unacceptable because the regional authorities had determined that Abiy had no mandate for such changes.[1] Nine days earlier, the federal government had announced a restructuring of the army with the establishment of two new commands in Amhara, one which would be stationed near Dessie and another near Gondar.[2] With several of the army's divisions having already been shifted south from Tigray to Amhara, the TPLF—by now acutely concerned about encirclement—said it couldn't countenance any further changes to the Northern Command.[3] The effective result, tweeted a Tigrayan journalist close to the TPLF, was that "Tigray [had taken] over the most heavily armed wing of the military."[4] The unexplained telecoms shutdown lasted the full duration of the general's ill-fated stay at Mekelle airport; Tigrayan officials, however, later put it down to a cut wire at a construction site. For me, though, the blackout was the final canary in the coal mine—before threats became deeds, words became bullets, and the country lurched to war.

* * *

Ethiopia's Tigray War wasn't always inevitable. Strange as it would later seem, the new prime minister was once so popular he had been welcomed even in Tigray for a few short weeks in 2018.[5] Though the TPLF still commanded widespread respect across the region for its pioneering role in the struggle against the Derg, many there had gradually grown disillusioned by its record in office. "We thought this [Abiy's appointment] would be our freedom," recalled a former senior TPLF member who had quit the party a decade earlier. "We felt like he took the throne for us too," remembered a Tigrayan woman who later fled to a refugee camp in Sudan. When Tamrat Gebregiorgis, the veteran editor of *Addis Fortune*, travelled the region in the months after the prime minister took office, not one young Tigrayan he asked said he would fight for the TPLF in a hypothetical war against Abiy. "Everything here has always been here," one young man remarked to the editor, bitterly, gesturing to the fields around them. "The trees. The cows. The donkeys. The villages. Nothing has ever changed, in all my life. The TPLF has been in power for twenty-seven years. What have they done for us?"

When it came to the Ethiopian state, the TPLF's outlook had always been ambiguous, reflecting a dualism rooted deep in the identity of Tigray itself: part highland core, part distant periphery. At the party's heart lay several fundamental tensions—between the aspirations of the radical urban intellectuals who founded it, for instance, and the conservative rural peasantry for which they claimed to be fighting; between its appeals to a Tigrayan nation stretching back uninterrupted to ancient Axum, and the reality of Tigrayan nationalism's much more recent—and more revolutionary—provenance.[6] Ethiopia, to many TPLF minds, was a modern imperial project birthed in blood. But among the leadership, at least, there had never been much desire to break free from it.[7] "The only acceptable outcome is a democratic, united Ethiopia," the party's octogenarian founder, Sebhat Nega, told me just days before the war began. "That's what I want—because that's what we fought for."

Little good, in some sense, did it do them. For while other Ethiopians would denounce the party as a Trojan horse for Tigrayan secessionism, many ordinary Tigrayans conversely accused the TPLF of prioritising the rest of the country at the expense of their homeland. On the eve of Abiy's ascent to power, the party had been besieged by criticism from within its own ranks and among its own constituents. Since at least the TPLF's acrimonious split in 2001, following the war with Eritrea, a certain portion of Tigray had always felt somewhat aggrieved, resentful of leaders they believed had abandoned them for the wealth and glamour of the capital. After the death of Meles, that bitterness erupted in the form of even noisier complaints about corruption and maladministration. Despite the widespread myth that Tigray had received vastly more investment and development than elsewhere over the previous three decades, there had never been much sign of it beyond the champagne-soaked bars and raucous nightclubs of Mekelle. Faced with rising popular anger in 2014 the TPLF had sacked hundreds of low and mid-ranking officials. Thousands more were put on notice.[8]

The TPLF was not a monolith when Abiy took power. Much more so than either the ANDM or the OPDO, the EPRDF's founding party was at war not just with the rest of the ruling coalition but also with itself: between young and old; between those close to the intelligence and those around the army; between the more moderate camp of Debretsion, the president, who showed some willingness to work with Abiy, and the hardline wing of Getachew Assefa, the spy chief, who wanted nothing to do with him; and between the regional cadres in Mekelle and the powerbrokers in the capital. Complicating the internal disarray still further were cleavages along provincial lines. The preponderance of leaders hailing from the party's original birthplace of Adwa, Shire and Axum, for instance—Adwa was to the TPLF what Wollega was to the OLF—had never quite been diluted, even decades later.[9] When a small number of Tigrayan dissidents had chosen to join Abiy's Prosperity Party, an audacious but wildly unpopular move which would later have them marked as traitors, notable among their number were figures from the region's east and south who claimed they had long been inadequately represented in the front's upper ranks.[10]

This was not, in short, the all-seeing eye of popular imagination, and Tigrayans were not all-powerful puppet masters out to sabotage the new administration by inciting chaos at every turn. In fact, there was no lack of divisions among them on which Abiy might have played, or resentments to which he could have pandered, had he really wished to extricate at least part of Tigray from the TPLF's clutches. But within only a few brief months that opportunity had been squandered. First were the spiky comments made during his tour of America that first summer, such as when he appeared to take a jibe at a fallen TPLF liberation hero in front of an audience of Tigrayans.[11] Then there was the sinister phrase, "daytime hyenas"—thieving conspirators "who want to profit by making us fight each other", as he put it—tossed around in his second month in office, which couldn't help but sound to anxious Tigrayan ears like a menacing dog-whistle.[12] To be sure, unlike some of his supporters, the prime minister rarely made it explicit that the saboteurs looming in his mind were Tigrayan. "There is no specific ethnicity which are thieves by nature," he once remarked.[13] But it is definitely plausible that Abiy did harbour a certain animus, not only towards the TPLF but the Tigrayan population as a whole. Indeed, several of those who interacted with him over the years later claimed to have observed in him a particular prickliness in their company. "It was obvious that he was against them," argued the former interim prime minister and ANDM founder, Tamrat Layne, who met with Abiy again shortly after he took office. "It was obvious it was not only the TPLF but also the Tigrayan people. I was trying to advise him from the beginning to handle the TPLF situation in a wise way, not to use force of arms […] but he was always telling me: 'They are nothing'; 'They don't have a place in Ethiopia', things like that […] It was like a revenge thing."

By 2020, even senior allies such as Lemma and Gedu had urged him to reconcile with the TPLF in order to head off a violent conflict. But Abiy had doubled down regardless.

There were doubtless some in the TPLF who wanted to reclaim their lost power in Addis Ababa. But few really seemed to think it was realistic. In the soul-searching years which followed Meles's death in 2012, there had been ever fewer voices in Tigray to be found defending the TPLF's outsized role at the centre of Ethiopian politics. Since 2018, new nationalist parties such as the Tigray Independence Party, Selsay Woyane and the Baitona Party had begun openly championing the cause of independent Tigrayan statehood. Faced with such pressures, the emerging consensus within the TPLF was that the road to political salvation lay not in Addis Ababa but in Mekelle, and in a return to their roots as an avowedly nationalist party focused above all else on Tigray's own interests. Though the cause of secession remained marginal among the TPLF's top leaders, there were few voices left in the years before the war arguing for anything other than enhanced regional autonomy.[14] "We just want to be left alone," the garrulous future Tigray president, Getachew Reda, told me in Mekelle in March 2020. "We want our share of power at the centre but, basically, we want to be left alone. We want to be left alone to develop our own policies, to experiment, and if Abiy thinks we can't afford diversity, he can go fuck himself."

At the same time, however, a feverish bunker mentality had taken hold. Faced with a slew of what they considered to be ethnically targeted prosecutions and hateful propaganda on the airwaves, in particular on ESAT, the TPLF had firmly battened down the hatches. Cooperation with the federal government progressively ceased. In their home state, Tigrayan ex-officials wanted by the federal government for alleged corruption or human rights abuses—most notably the former spy chief and TPLF politburo member, Getachew Assefa—were given shelter and an effective amnesty. (Though his whereabouts were officially unknown, Getachew would be spotted in Mekelle at the start of the war.) Ordinary Tigrayans, meanwhile, fretted about being under siege. For two years, the roads to Addis Ababa through Amhara had either been fully blocked by *Fano* militants, or simply deemed too dangerous for Tigrayans to travel down. Tigrayan media seethed with talk of violent border incursions by Amhara militias to the west.

Underlying the prevailing anxiety about encirclement were special concerns about the intentions of Isaias Afwerki and the Eritreans to the north. Despite the initial optimism which accompanied the peace agreement between Ethiopia and Eritrea, by early 2019 it was clear that this was already a dead letter. Mere months after the world celebrated the opening of the border between the countries, Eritrea had slammed it shut again. By early 2019, an irate Isaias had ceased to speak publicly about the peace process. A draft trade agreement which, among things, raised the vexed question of Ethiopia's use of Eritrea's Red Sea ports, had been sent by Ethiopian officials to Isaias's office for comments, only to be left to gather dust for almost two years. In the twelve months following the peace deal the president had called no more than one meeting of his cabinet.

Meanwhile in Tigray, misgivings about Abiy's relationship with Isaias were increasingly all-consuming. Angry with Abiy for having excluded them from the peace talks, the TPLF were also reluctant to progress with the deal's implementation without securing at least some benefits for Tigray first. (One proposal the Tigrayan leadership had considered involved mutual land swaps at the border.) With this seeming increasingly unlikely, they blocked the transfer of the flashpoint town of Badme back to Eritrea, in theory a key element of the agreement but also among their last remaining points of leverage over Isaias. Abiy's attempts in early January to remove units of the Northern Command stationed near the border with Eritrea as part of the peace process were obstructed by local demonstrators with the TPLF's acquiescence, if not encouragement— an early warning of the coming tussle over the command's substantial heavy weaponry.[15] By early 2020, Tigrayan media was awash with talk of a coming Eritrean invasion. Isaias, for his part, would do little to allay their fears. Warning, in his characteristically Delphic way, that when it came to Ethiopian affairs he would never sit idle, the Eritrean president declared ethnic federalism and the "narrow clique" behind it bankrupt. "In our language, it is called 'game over,'" he said on Eritrean state TV that February. "And Ethiopians have said 'enough'."[16]

Had an alternative path ever been possible? Perhaps. In the first few months after the peace deal, Abiy had at times seemed open to bringing the TPLF on board the rapprochement with Eritrea. He had ostensibly handed responsibility for normalisation to Debretsion at the final EPRDF congress in October 2018. He had also engineered a public handshake between Debretsion and the Eritrean president at the official opening of a border crossing in early January the following year. Given the depth of the ill-will between Isaias and the TPLF, gestures which seemed more concerned with public consumption than with delivering a real breakthrough were never likely on their own to have been enough. Yet had he been willing, Abiy might have done more. Later that month an outwardly optimistic Debretsion told the veteran American journalist Dan Connell that he expected to be in Asmara for reconciliation with Isaias "within weeks". But by the time Connell returned to Mekelle just two months later the Tigrayan president had all but given up. "He was extremely frustrated, because he hadn't gotten anywhere with Isaias," Connell recalled. "And he was furious with Abiy for not stepping in between the two of them. Looking back, Isaias just played everybody and the TPLF went after Abiy for it. They blamed him; they were so humiliated—and after that there was no talking. By mid-2019 the preparations began for war."

Whether Abiy really had been pushed by Isaias into preparing for a military operation in Tigray, more than he took the initiative himself, is almost unknowable. After all, both leaders had their own reasons for seeking a weakened, or dismantled, TPLF. Certainly, by November 2020 Abiy appears to have been discussing military options with colleagues in Addis Ababa for months, if not years, under his own steam. It is also clear that relations between him and the TPLF had broken down well before the EPRDF had been acrimoniously dissolved in late 2019. Covert assignations between Abiy and Isaias, on the other hand, had proceeded apace for many months. Between the middle of 2018 and the start of the war the two leaders met at least fourteen times.[17]

The rare details drip-fed to the Ethiopian and Eritrean public were not subtle. In July 2020, state media broadcast images of Abiy being given a tour of Eritrea's Sawa military training centre—an unprecedented visit for a foreign leader and, in hindsight, an unabashed signal of what might be coming. Three months later Isaias was seen inspecting Ethiopia's air force base Bishoftu. As the conflict drew closer, they would meet at least three times in Addis Ababa entirely in secret: aviation authorities were instructed to keep quiet, according to reporting by the *New York Times*, with an unmarked car dispatched to bring the president to Abiy's palace. On several occasions, Isaias would meet separately with Amhara regional security officials in Bahir Dar and Gondar—preparing the ground, it would later transpire, for the joint military operations in Western Tigray which would become notorious for ethnic cleansing.[18] By 2020, alarmed aid workers in Ethiopia were also noting that the federal government had sought to close camps for Eritrean refugees in Tigray, and had ceased to recognise their automatic right for asylum—the first move of its kind since the border war two decades previously.[19] Eritrean intelligence officials, now widely rumoured to be operating throughout Addis Ababa, were spotted at the international airport; Eritrean refugees later told me how they had seen officers they had known back home interrogating people there.

Back in Eritrea, Isaias was reorganising the Eritrean Defence Forces, stocking up on arms from Russia, digging new trenches and aggressively stepping up conscription. As he did, Eritrean media ramped up anti-TPLF propaganda, accusing it of agitating against the peace agreement in defiance of Ethiopia's federal government. Authorities warned repeatedly that the TPLF planned to invade Eritrea and repeat the horrors of the 1998–2000 war. From the first quarter of 2020, Ethiopian soldiers started to deploy inside Eritrea for military training, according to local Eritrean witnesses, disembarking from cargo planes at the airport in Asmara under the cover of night.[20] Units of the Ethiopian army began taking up positions at key locations near the border with Tigray.[21] "It was widely known and talked about by residents in Asmara that [Ethiopian soldiers] were being unloaded," said an Eritrean officer who fled the country for Addis Ababa shortly before the outbreak of war. "It wasn't something that could be hidden." By early 2020, the defector also recalled, trainees in the Eritrean military had started undergoing intense indoctrination for a coming conflict. At the heart of this programme was the message that Ethiopia was to be cleansed of certain dangerous political practices, and of anyone supporting them—in other words, ethnic federalism and the TPLF: Isaias's twin nemeses. "Isaias is now the mentor of Abiy," Ethiopia's former foreign minister Seyoum Mesfin fumed from his home in Mekelle in late October, days before the war began and just weeks before he was murdered in the Tigrayan bush. "Isaias is not for federalism in Ethiopia. He is scared it will spill over into Eritrea, so he never wants it to succeed here."

Abiy's dealings with Isaias now clearly constituted a mutual security pact in all but name. Fuelling not just existential anxieties in Tigray, which it certainly did, it also compounded deep feelings of betrayal among the Tigrayan elite. From their perspective, Abiy had not just made a deal with the devil without consulting them—a move which, in theory, had been agreed to anyway by the EPRDF politburo before he took office. Rather, he had violated the spirit of the understanding they believed had guided their departure in 2018: a tacit agreement to hasten reforms but leave the fundamentals of the constitution untouched; to pursue national reconciliation not selective accountability; and to strengthen the

EPRDF without jettisoning its ideological essence or repudiating its main achievements. Now, the man they believed they had graciously entrusted with the country's fate was fraternising with their bitterest enemies—and not only with Isaias. To their astonishment, he was also openly consorting with hardliners in Amhara, and even with their once outlawed Ethiopianist opponents such as Andargachew Tsige and Ginbot 7. Seen from Mekelle, it was an alliance assembled for no other reason than to destroy them.[22]

In the final months before the war the TPLF sought to build a coalition of like-minded federalists to stand with them in opposition to this emerging axis. But though some in the Oromo camp were receptive, the TPLF's political instincts were not what they once were, and its leaders typically showed little willingness to reckon properly with their own failings over the preceding decades. "Double digit-growth, non-stop. 30 million farmers lifted above the poverty line. 30 new universities," thundered Seyoum Mesfin that same morning in Mekelle. "We achieved miracles." In place of contrition, the TPLF offered the same parties which they had once vigorously repressed little but a second-tier role in a coalition under its tutelage. Together they were to mount a programme of opposition to the very same forces which these opposition parties had themselves once been accused by the EPRDF of representing: 'chauvinism', 'rent-seeking', and the twin scourges of 'anti-peace' and 'anti-development'.[23] To nobody's great surprise, none of the major opposition parties would ultimately be prepared to take up the offer.[24] As the war drew closer, the TPLF, and therefore Tigray, found itself bereft of allies, vilified at home and isolated abroad. "We're in seriously deep s***," a Tigrayan friend texted me. "Maybe we've reached a stage that's unfixable."

* * *

When I returned to Addis Ababa from my summer holiday in early September 2020 it was clear that something had changed, and that the uneasy calm which had prevailed in the months following Hachalu's murder—fearsome repression of demonstrations against the arrest of Jawar, Bekele Gerba, and their colleagues notwithstanding—couldn't, and wouldn't, last. Most international media coverage remained focused on the turmoil in Oromia, and many Western diplomats appeared broadly indifferent to the brewing crisis in Tigray, where preparations for the regional election were underway. But among the few paying attention there was little doubt that in its belligerent response to the coming vote the government had now set itself firmly on a course which could only end badly.

Where once it was only insinuated, now it was explicit: behind all the country's bloodshed, state media reported, lay the hand of the TPLF.[25] Government officials who might once have shied away from fighting talk now spoke openly of the TPLF as their enemy. "They want it to escalate, they are trying to provoke us," seethed Mamo Mihretu, then an advisor in the Prime Minister's Office. "They are trying to make the government look weak in the eyes of the international community and the Ethiopian public. They are actively fomenting crises." Zadig Abraha, a relative of Getachew Reda who had audaciously quit the TPLF and joined the ANDM in late 2017, later to be rewarded by Abiy for his loyalty with the new-fangled position of "minister in charge of democratisation", was even franker about the impending showdown. "I don't think this will be solved by dialogue," he told me, "because this is a structural problem. This dream of ours—to make Ethiopia a democratic success—is on a collision course with the TPLF and its dream of making itself Ethiopia's perpetual governing elite [...] Dialogue may give time to avoid a confrontation only." Speaking with the *International Crisis Group* a few weeks later Zadig predicted the imminent "liberation" of the disputed Tigrayan territories of Wolkait and Raya.[26] "Overtures for an amicable resolution of differences have been met with scorn time and again," echoed an anonymous government official in the Paris-based *Africa Report*. "Perhaps, it is time to adopt a different approach to make the axis of chaos more amenable to reason."[27]

In a rare interview addressed in Tigrinya directly to the Tigrayan public in July, Abiy had adamantly denied any plan to wage war against Tigray with Eritrean support, or even to cut the federal budget to the region. Moreover, he had implored the TPLF not to spend money holding elections when it could simply wait a year and then do so.[28] Later, his allies would point to these words as proof that the prime minister hadn't sought war, and that provocations had come only from the other side. They would also note that Abiy had sent a delegation of respected elders, religious leaders and celebrities such as the athlete Haile Gebreselassie to Mekelle to mediate five months before the conflict, only for them to be rebuffed by the Tigrayan leadership and sent home empty-handed.

But preparations for war had begun on all sides well before this point. Certainly, by the time the TPLF decided to hold its own election its leaders knew well that war was the most likely outcome. They understood as well as anyone how unlikely Abiy was to welcome such open defiance of central authority, or the prospect of a rival centre of power in the country. No previous Ethiopian leader would have embraced it either.

And armed conflict was an eventuality to which, in any case, they were resolved. By the end of 2019, the region had close to 1,000 retired Tigrayan officers—including several dozen generals, and even more colonels—actively training tens of thousands of special forces and militias made up of fresh recruits and recalled veterans from the 1980s.[29] In the central highlands of Tigray they prepared the ground for a long guerrilla war, establishing bunker commands and hideouts for the troops as well as hidden caches of arms, food and medical supplies. Sure of their own military strength, in spite of Tigray's dangerous encirclement, and steeped in martial values inculcated over decades of revolutionary struggle, the TPLF's top brass saw little reason to back down. "Tigray is the most militarised society in the world, except perhaps the Houthis. Every household is supposed to have a gun," Getachew Reda told me. "Ninety percent of wars against foreign enemies were fought in Tigray. Does that give you a fighting edge? It probably does."

At the same time, the TPLF repeatedly claimed to prefer negotiations to armed force. But in the crucial months before the war, its leaders insisted these involve a national dialogue with all the opposition parties, as well as on the release of opposition leaders from prison. Simply ceding to Abiy's terms, they believed, would amount to nothing less than the dissolution of their party, a wholesale restructuring of the federation, and perhaps their own imprisonment and impoverishment, too. Bilateral negotiations with the Prosperity Party—as the government demanded— were deemed unacceptable.

The TPLF's position was not, in principle, unreasonable. A national dialogue involving all the opposition was no less than what many independent experts had long been pressing on the government to head off violence. But with Abiy by then seeming ever more intent on fighting it out, the TPLF's red lines increasingly began to seem like dangerous brinkmanship.[30] "We as a cabinet knew war was coming," recalled Filsan Abdi, an Ethiopian Somali appointed by Abiy to lead his ministry of women, children and youth earlier that year. "He'd drop it in randomly, for example, in a conversation about gender policy: he'd say, 'there is war coming, so this doesn't matter. TPLF will not stop without war. They are calling us a weak government. We must give them what they want.'" When the TPLF demanded a national dialogue Abiy's response was unyielding: we cannot share power; talks must be bilateral; no release of prisoners.

"Any attempt at conducting a sham election will expose the country and its people to grave danger," he had warned in May. "We wish to make it explicitly clear in advance that we will not tolerate it. We also want it to be known that we are fully prepared for this in all aspects."[31]

As Tigray went to the polls on 9 September 2020, the government declared the vote illegal. Journalists trying to travel there were blocked at the airport; some even had their phones and laptops confiscated. The next day Abiy flexed his muscles with a bellicose military parade in Meskel Square, showing the public for the first time some of his freshly purchased weaponry. Soon after the TPLF had announced it had won 189 of 190 seats in the regional council in Mekelle, the federal parliament voted to sever its ties with the region. The upper chamber made it clear that a federal military intervention would be legally defensible.[32]

* * *

The mood in Addis Ababa plumbed new depths. The small number of prominent Tigrayans who remained there shrank further still; General Tsadkan Gebretensae, the former head of the Ethiopian military who had been fruitlessly trying to mediate between Abiy and his former comrades, had fled for Mekelle in fear for his life. "I feel like a stranger here," a Tigrayan working for Ethio Telecom told me. "I've never felt this way before." For those still employed in the city's bureaucracy and federal institutions there was now little choice but to join the Prosperity Party or leave Addis Ababa altogether. "They were detaining us, arresting us—there were all sorts of different pressures," recalled Gebremeskel Kassa, a Tigrayan official then working in the municipal government who decided to join the ruling party and then later its interim wartime administration in Mekelle.

Firing the war's opening salvos, Abiy ratcheted the economic pressure on Tigray, turning what had for many months already been a loose blockade of the region into a fast-tightening chokehold.[33] Ostensibly to fight corruption, but really to strangle the TPLF's finances, the federal government had already introduced new currency in September, forcing everyone to hand their old money in to the banks.[34] Now it went even further, halting budget payments to Tigray entirely—a move decried by the TPLF as a "declaration of war"—and suspending welfare payments to farmers there. Support for the region's efforts to fight the locusts then decimating Tigrayan agriculture was slashed. Inside the military, Tigrayan soldiers suspected of TPLF sympathies were transferred to divisions far away from Tigray and into positions insignificant for the coming war effort.

As prime minister, Abiy generally kept his true intentions tight to his chest. But talk of the forthcoming operation against the TPLF was surprisingly open. In late October, the prime minister met with officials from the Addis Ababa administration, who had convened to diffuse brewing tensions between the ruling party's Amhara and Oromo wings over control of the capital. According to several of those present, the party's Amhara cohort used the meeting as an opportunity to urge Abiy to remove the TPLF as he had done the Somali regional president two years earlier. Zadig Abraha, recalled one attendee, stood up and assured them that the TPLF, which he likened to a rabies infection, was a spent force soon to "scatter in the wind". After this, on the final day of the meeting, the prime minister himself appeared over video-call and delivered a presentation. After explaining how he had successfully removed Abdi Illey from the Somali state house in just three days, Abiy assured the attendees that the federal military was strong and that the problem of the TPLF was already "over", recalled Gebremeskel, who was also in attendance. All regions and state institutions would, the prime minister indicated, henceforth submit to central authority. "He said that the TPLF were encircled in all directions," Gebremeskel recalled. According to three of those present, Abiy vowed to destroy the TPLF leadership in less than a week.

On 1 November 2020, now just two days shy of the outbreak of fighting, the prime minister met in Addis Ababa with General Abdel Fattah al-Burhan, Sudan's de facto leader since a coup a year earlier, and conveyed much the same message. The mission would take "about a week or so, and would target only ten to fifteen leaders," said the then Sudanese ambassador, who was also in the room at the time. An offer from the Sudanese leader to mediate between Abiy and the TPLF was also curtly dismissed: "Abiy told the president not to bother himself with such a small matter," the ambassador recalled.[35] Among several important issues agreed by the two leaders, which included the Renaissance Dam and Ethiopia's simmering dispute with Sudan over its border with northern Amhara, was something of particular concern to Abiy: Sudan's consent to seal its adjacent border with Tigray so as to prevent the TPLF from resupplying itself.[36]

The final days of my visit to Mekelle also left me in little doubt that war was coming. Tigrayan TV buzzed with talk of it. The day before I met with Seyoum Mesfin, the former foreign minister, he had given an interview to the regional broadcaster in which he alleged that Abiy had made a secret one-day trip to Asmara on 27 October to finalise their preparations. Four days later, as I prepared to return to Addis Ababa, Eritrea's government declared in a statement that the TPLF was "on its deathbed". General Tsadkan, the man who had helped mastermind the EPRDF's march on Addis Ababa in 1991, and was soon to join the Tigrayan forces as one of its top commanders, told me that the Tigrayans would likely move imminently to take the Northern Command's heavy weaponry "out of the equation". Following a politburo meeting that same weekend, Getachew Reda tweeted that the TPLF had taken "historic decisions" to bolster the region's defences "against all forces of reaction from Addis Ababa or Asmara or beyond". On 1 November, shortly before my flight out of Mekelle, Debretsion declared that "if war is imminent, we are prepared not just to resist but to win." On my arrival at Addis Ababa airport, I was detained and interrogated.

Ethiopian federal troops were now moving northwards, with units from areas as far away as the Somali region in the southeast, as well as from Oromia in the far west, taking up positions near the Tigrayan border.[37] Special commandos loaded onto flights at the airport in Hawassa.[38] With the army having vacated key locations in insurgency-racked Wollega, armed men slaughtered more than fifty Amhara women and children in a schoolyard there on 1 November. The circumstances were, as usual, extraordinarily murky: the government swiftly blamed the OLA, backed by the TPLF; the Oromo opposition countered with the accusation that it was a false flag operation designed to clear the path for war.[39] The political temperature in Addis Ababa climbed further still. The next day, Abiy's Amhara allies called on him to finish off the TPLF "once and for all". Parliament suggested for the first time that it would declare it a "terrorist" organisation. Special police, militias and irregular *Fano* forces across northern Amhara picked up their guns and readied themselves to fight.

In the end it was, as General Tsadkan warned, the matter of the Northern Command which proved decisive. Ever since Abiy had taken power both sides had fully understood its import. Traditionally the country's best-armed formation, by November 2020 it was still home to four full divisions, and perhaps some 24,000 soldiers, despite the prime minister's attempts to defang it.[40] A disproportionate number of senior Tigrayan officers remained in place. For the TPLF, the command was simultaneously a potential asset and a threat, and they were loath to let it out from under their thumb. Abiy's preferred choice to lead it, Brigadier-General Belay Seyoum, an ethnic Agaw veteran of the operation to remove Abdi Illey in 2018, was simply a non-starter. On 29 October the TPLF "politely informed" him, as Getachew Reda delicately put it, not to even try and take up his post in Tigray.

If the army is "a copy of society", as Leon Trotsky observed, and "suffers from all its diseases, usually at a higher temperature", then the Northern Command on the eve of the Tigray War was effectively bedridden.[41] Despite decades of indoctrination designed to inoculate it against ethnic division, by 2020 its ranks were riddled from top to bottom in it. Late at night on 3 November it spectacularly splintered.

* * *

Little in all Abiy's time in office would prove more divisive than the TPLF's operation against the Northern Command, which was staged in the first few hours of the fighting. And little did more to cement the popular narrative later pushed by Abiy and his allies that his was a war not of choice but of last resort, one he had been only reluctantly drawn into waging. Much is contested or simply unknown, but a few facts are indisputable: that as Ethiopian, Amhara and Eritrean forces positioned themselves around Tigray, members of the Tigrayan special forces forcibly entered barracks and weapons depots across the region and took control of large caches of heavy weaponry and personnel; that a significant portion of the Northern Command's Tigrayan officer corps defected and joined their Tigrayan comrades in the regional special forces; that gun fights broke out with non-Tigrayan members of the command; and that large numbers of Ethiopian soldiers were disarmed and taken into Tigrayan custody, before being released and sent home via Amhara a few weeks later. Quite how many soldiers split each way is not entirely clear, but though a large portion joined the Tigrayan special forces many others remained loyal, with quite a few of them managing to escape over the border into Eritrea with vehicles and artillery in tow.[42] Much was later made by Abiy and his allies of a surprise Tigrayan attack that first night which had hundreds, perhaps thousands, of unsuspecting Ethiopian soldiers slaughtered in their beds. But given the heightened readiness of the military at the time this was highly improbable. Evidence of a bloodbath on any scale was never presented.[43]

What prompted the Tigrayans to act when they did is also fiercely contested. One widely circulated story had it that they reacted to the unannounced arrival of Ethiopian commandos at Mekelle Airport on the evening of 3 November, part of a planned raid to either capture the TPLF leadership or secure the airport under the pretext of planes delivering new bank notes to the region.[44] Another theory, less widely known, was that the Ethiopian army had planned to instigate hostilities by staging a fake attack by Tigrayan forces on its positions in Mai Kadra in Western Tigray that same night—a move akin to the Gleiwitz incident used by Germany to justify its invasion of Poland in 1939. According to this story, the TPLF got wind of the plan and reacted by accelerating their own one for neutralising the Northern Command, while successfully jamming communication between Mekelle and Addis Ababa with the help of a Tigrayan general still stationed in the national capital.

Neither story was ever fully substantiated, and what stuck instead was the description, made by a TPLF associate on Tigrayan TV a few days later and then widely propagated by Abiy's press team, of the operation as an act of "anticipatory self-defence"—a controversial term of international law subsequently disavowed by the Tigrayan leadership.[45] Despite strong evidence that the federal government had long prepared for a military intervention, it would remain hard for the TPLF to ever fully shake the impression that at the very final moment it was they who moved first. A Tigrayan colonel would put it more frankly, if irreverently, in a conversation with a foreign researcher a few years later: "we started a war".[46]

By the time I'd risen early on the morning of 4 November 2020 to catch the first results of America's presidential election, Abiy had already announced that he had ordered his forces to hit back in response to what he claimed was an unprompted "attack" by the TPLF. "The red line has been crossed," he said in his first public statement of the war. Early reports that morning suggested there had been a heavy exchange of artillery fire around Mekelle and on the border with Amhara. The internet and phone networks in Tigray were cut off. Abiy declared a state of emergency.

Civil war had begun. Over the coming days the first glimpses of its horrors would begin to emerge: refugees streaming into Sudan; columns of Amhara militiamen brandishing rusty Kalashnikovs; wobbly videos of corpses under plastic shrouds. "This is about to get very fucked," a shaken foreign researcher texted me as word of the first massacres reached us. Two weeks in and already tens of thousands of Tigrayans were homeless. Nobody had any idea how many people had been killed.

This was a war of choice for Abiy, as it was for Isaias: both were ready and willing to crush an enemy which each viewed as an obstacle to their power and to their respective political projects. But it was also one for leaders of the TPLF, for whom the prospect of ideological reversal—an Ethiopian state built not in their image but in Abiy's; a more centralised federation in which a querulous Tigray would be forever forced to conform—was impossible to countenance. At multiple junctures along the road they too had raised the bar for compromise.

Yet, at the very end, it was neither cold rationalism nor utilitarian calculation which for them played the decisive part.[47] "Everybody was in this crazy mood," recalled Tessema Fesseha Asghedom, a veteran Tigrayan diplomat who left Mekelle shortly before the fighting began. "Nobody was looking for an out." In the final countdown, Tigrayan leaders demonstrated a strange combination of both fear and hubris. Excessively confident in their ability to defeat two armies on multiple fronts, they were equally conscious of Tigray's unique vulnerabilities and the genuine potential for catastrophic bloodletting, even genocide, if the forces arrayed against them were ever let loose.[48] In the end, they too took a gamble: rolling the dice in the hope that a showdown would bring the prime minister to his senses and force him to concede. "War may not be a bad thing", noted one prominent Tigrayan commentator a few weeks before it began. "War is one method of bringing them to negotiation. We have to shorten the war process by using a pre-emptive strike if we need to."[49]

But Abiy would not, perhaps could not, stop. A man burning in his conviction of manifest destiny, he had by now disposed of any pretensions to pragmatism in matters he viewed as zero-sum questions of victory or defeat. On the eve of war, he was a portrait both of arrogance and anxiety. Evidently fearful for his life, and paranoid about assassination, he was reported to have installed his most loyal commandos on every floor of the palace.[50] At the same time he appeared to be genuinely offended by the Tigrayans' rhetoric, which cast him as both a buffoon and a villain— weak but dictatorial, incompetent yet all-powerful. Certain, so it seemed, of a swift and decisive victory to prove them wrong, he retreated into the militant Christian fold of Daniel Kibret and his Orthodox followers, cheered on by the chest-beating nationalism of ESAT and its Ethiopianist viewers. The possibility that the TPLF still had popular support itself, and that millions of Tigrayans would rather rally to its defence than kneel to his sword, wouldn't register at all.

The rest of the world at last began awakening to the disaster now unfolding. But it was much too late. So slow had Brussels been to take heed of the situation that it had taken a direct call from the EU's ambassador to Ethiopia to the office of Josep Borrell, the union's foreign-policy chief, just to get out a lone statement of concern—one which gently urged the parties to refrain from "provocative military deployments"—by 2 November. America, the only country which might have been able to pull Abiy back from the brink, had by this point vacated the stage entirely. The distraction of a looming presidential election, which took place the same day the war began (perhaps not coincidentally), meant few in Washington were anything but "oblivious", recalled Alex Rondos, then the EU's special envoy to the Horn. When I later asked Tibor Nagy, America's top diplomat for Africa at the time, what he had known about the preparations for war, he replied that, "honest to goodness, up to November the 3rd, we in Washington were absolutely surprised that the turn of events had gone dramatically south." Michael Raynor, the US ambassador in Addis Ababa, simply took Abiy's side. Colleagues back in Washington would later hear him justifying the federal government's actions as no different from how the American government would react were a militia to attack a national guard post in Texas—an argument which drew an implicit, and very favourable, comparison to the bombardment of Fort Sumter in South Carolina which triggered the American Civil War. Behind closed doors, officials in Trump's State Department said there was no longer any moral equivalency between the two sides, and argued that America should simply treat Abiy as a legitimate ruler defending the central state against an armed rebellion. In the final months before Biden took over as US president some would bend backwards to give Abiy and even Isaias cover.[51]

Flattering historical parallels were exactly what Addis Ababa needed, and allies of Abiy would soon go as far as to compare the TPLF to the slave-holding confederates and the prime minister to Abraham Lincoln.[52] But this was misleading. The TPLF were not simply secessionists and Abiy's and Isaias's war against them was not about saving the union or freeing ordinary Tigrayans from bondage. At the conflict's heart was the raw matter of power and the competing forms of law, ideology and identity which configured it. The assault on the Northern Command was thus by itself neither the cause nor even the trigger of the conflict. The roots ran far deeper, back to the questions of identity and nationhood first raised by the student movement fifty years earlier, sanctified by the sweat and sacrifice of revolutionary struggle for decades after that. "It's a bit like telling me that there was a minor fight between some guards at the Polish frontier on August the 30th 1939, and that caused the Second World War," Rondos later remarked. "Give me a break."

16

"JUST WAITING TO DIE"

ETHNIC CLEANSING AND THE WOLKAIT QUESTION

The moment the war reached the family of Lemlem Abraha it tore it apart. The mother of three was at home when the sound of the first gunshots approached; distant at first, echoing across the wide plains from the nearby army base, then closer as the Ethiopian soldiers—accompanied by Amhara militiamen and armed *Fanos*—drew up to her gates the following morning. By then Lemlem and her youngest daughter, eight-year-old Hiyab, had fled into the surrounding countryside, but her two teenage children weren't with her, and nor was her husband, a disabled veteran of the struggle against the Derg then working as a trucker for a nearby farm.

Lemlem later learnt that the two children had escaped for the highlands of central Tigray. But she couldn't track them down by phone because the network had been shut off. Her husband, Fisseha, hadn't been heard from at all. When I met Lemlem two years later, in a dusty refugee camp in eastern Sudan, she was in touch with the older children, but Fisseha was still missing—and by then Hiyab was, too. She didn't know whether either of her loved ones were still alive.

Lemlem was among the very first victims of the campaign of ethnic cleansing which ripped through Western Tigray in the first weeks of the war.[1] Baeker, her hometown, was in the district traditionally known as Wolkait, and its population laid claim to diverse identities in a way which was unusual compared to communities in the surrounding Ethiopian highlands. Most of its inhabitants were Tigrayans, many of whom, like Lemlem and her husband, were veterans of the TPLF's guerrilla war who had been sent there to farm its fertile land in the early 2000s. But they farmed alongside Amharas, too, some of whom were seasonal labourers tilling the nearby sesame fields. The remainder were mostly mixed heritage local 'Wolkaites' who could flit between the two.[2] Looking back, Lemlem would remember her old home as a place where the different groups rubbed along amicably enough, where an Amhara neighbour would look after one of her children as part of the traditional Orthodox baptism ritual, and where they would all come together for feast days, weddings and funerals. "For the past twenty-seven years, we never said to each other 'you are Amhara' or 'you are Tigrayan'," she told me. When the war began some of the Amharas in Baeker would warn their Tigrayan friends to flee before the soldiers arrived. Others would refuse to single out their Tigrayan neighbours to the incoming *Fanos*.

Lemlem's mistake was to return to the town in the days after the Ethiopian and Amhara forces first took control of it in early November, leaving Hiyab in the care of her neighbours. The plan had been to collect supplies from the market, but almost as soon as she had got there, she realised she was stuck, blocked from leaving Baeker by the Ethiopian soldiers manning checkpoints, who interrogated and beat her, and by the *Fanos* then roaming the streets. For three weeks she stayed put in the hope her neighbours would manage to bring Hiyab back safely to her. But later she learnt that they, too, had fled for safety in the highlands, and that they had taken her daughter with them.

As Lemlem waited in Baeker, venturing out only occasionally to go to the shops, the mood in the town soured. Each day she left home she found corpses on the asphalt. One of them, a fourteen-year-old friend of her children called Kalayu Mebrahtom, had been shot dead by federal soldiers and left on the street to be buried by his grandmother. Two years later, while preparing me coffee over a stove in her temporary shelter, Lemlem began to count the names of seventy-five neighbours she said had been killed in those weeks. Twenty-five had been buried or burnt in the grounds of a church; another fifty, she believed, in the compound of a former military hospital. She knew five of them well. All of them, she told me, her voice then cracking, were civilians.

By the end of November, a notice had been pinned on her front door ordering all Tigrayans still left in the town to leave or face the consequences.[3] Lemlem fled. Carrying on her only two dresses, both of which she wore at the same time for warmth, a little money, and her phone, she took a rickshaw belonging to her family and drove north towards Sudan.

On the road she passed Ethiopian soldiers wearing T-shirts with Abiy's face on them. By the time she reached the Tekeze River which marked the border, she had been robbed by a group of *Fanos* and a twenty-two-year-old Tigrayan girl had been gang-raped in front of her so violently that she later died from the injuries. The following morning Lemlem clambered into a rickety boat with twenty-one other refugees. She arrived in Sudan, exhausted, penniless and alone, on 28 November 2020.

* * *

Early in the evening of 3 November, several hours before any fighting was reported in Mekelle or elsewhere, a foreign researcher staying in Soroka, a town in northern Gondar exactly on the border with Western Tigray, received a phone call. The caller, a member of the 'Wolkait Committee'—the organisation leading the campaign for Amhara control of the disputed territories since 2015—told the researcher that the beers they had planned to drink together that evening would have to be cancelled. "I can't make it tonight, something will happen," he said. "Take care of yourself." A few hours later, a few minutes after midnight, the researcher awoke to the sound of heavy gunfire and shelling. "They were fighting everywhere," he later recalled. "Shooting like hell."

The dramatic militarisation of Ethiopian society which preceded the war had been particularly visible in Amhara over the past two years. By early 2020, according to one estimate, the regional special forces throughout the country outnumbered the army; in Amhara, they numbered perhaps as many as 20,000 or more.[4] René Lefort, who had conducted research in the same Amhara district for many years, noted that as the local state apparatus there had weakened after Abiy took power, "the only authority channel which remained effective [was] the one in charge of security affairs."[5] With hostile forces surrounding them from every side, its inhabitants believed, anxiety plagued the region. "There is nobody who can defend us," a *Fano* in Gondar told me around that time. "We must defend ourselves."

But they were not, in fact, completely alone. As the federal war machine cranked into gear over the course of 2020, the influence of Abiy's Amhara allies in the ruling party had been growing significantly. In the months before the war began the federal army had begun giving training and military supplies to the Amhara special forces and, in a move without any recent historical precedent, even to some of the *Fanos* there.[6] Amhara forces had also already been dispatched, without objection from the federal government, to the neighbouring Benishangul-Gumuz region, ostensibly to protect the Amhara minorities then under attack by ethnic Gumuz rebels—an intervention which, by setting a precedent soon to be replicated in Tigray, eerily resembled the actions of Serbian paramilitaries in the early stages of Yugoslavia's civil war in the 1990s. By late October, the researcher in Soroka reported hearing talk of a coming irredentist war for the so-called 'ancestral lands' of Wolkait, Tsegede and Serit-Humera across the border (as well as for the fertile pastures of Raya to the south).[7] "Many were not afraid to say they wanted revenge," he later recalled. On 2 November, the head of a 200 man-strong militia there said they would soon be retrieving the land by force of arms. Two months later Amhara's special police chief would boast to an applauding audience that the regional government had "done its homework" and deployed troops all along Amhara's borders for a war which "started the night after we had completed our preparations".[8]

The assorted Amhara forces arrayed against Tigray consisted of regional special police, volunteer *Fanos*, as well as the ordinary armed militiamen who had been entrusted with local security in highland Ethiopia since time immemorial. When war broke out, they were the very first to rush across the border, leading the cavalry charge from all directions and acting as cannon fodder for the regular army which followed them.[9] "In most battles the human ratio was 20:1," reported a Tigrayan intelligence officer hiding in the mountains at the time. On the frontline in Western Tigray, as it was still officially known, were Amhara irregular volunteers so eager to fight they were seen literally queuing to join the fray, in some cases even having to be held back by more cautious army commanders. In their wake, these forces left a trail of some of the war's most wanton destruction: razed villages, looted hospitals and pillaged fields. As the comparatively small number of Tigrayan special forces stationed there beat a hasty retreat for the central highlands, tens of thousands of civilians were uprooted—many of whom, like Lemlem, would head west over the river into Sudan. In town after town, Tigrinya road signs were replaced with Amharic, as Tigrayan flags were swapped for the imperial Ethiopian tricolour. Tigrayan residents were ordered, en masse, to leave. Before the first month of the war was up, Amhara had annexed the entirety of Western Tigray as well as Raya in the south, cutting the Tigrayans off from their most productive land and, on the western side, from their border with Sudan and thus the outside world. Prisons and police stations bulged with Tigrayan captives, as newly appointed Amhara civil servants took over local administrations. Colonel Demeke Zewdu, the leader of the Wolkait Identity Committee later accused by Human Rights Watch and Amnesty of orchestrating the ethnic cleansing, was put in charge of security in Humera, the district capital.[10] He immediately called upon Amharas living elsewhere in Ethiopia and even abroad to come and resettle the annexed lands.

It had fast become clear that this was no ordinary war. More so than perhaps anything besides the invasion of Eritrean troops shortly afterwards, the mass participation of local militias and regional paramilitaries defined the Tigray conflict—dramatically expanding its scope and mutating a seemingly narrow political fight into a profoundly existential one. In vast and vicious pitched battles, consisting of trench warfare and human waves, it pitted friends and neighbours against each other, turning even brothers on sisters and fathers on sons.[11] By sucking in such an array of armies and armaments it became, in a sense, less a single war than many different ones: multiple overlapping battles at once technologically advanced and rudimentary; both local and international. Over the coming months and years, farmers would fight tanks, guerrillas would jostle with drones, and village militias would share battlefields with two of Africa's largest and most experienced armies. In 2021, the war which began in Tigray and later spread to Amhara and Afar would be ranked the deadliest conflict fought anywhere on earth, easily among the very worst of the twenty-first century so far. By the close of 2022, even after Russia had invaded Ukraine, it would still vie for the top spot.

* * *

Back in Addis Ababa, the fighting was at first widely welcomed. Gripped by jingoism and a palpable mood of righteous revenge, the public enthusiastically rallied to Abiy's defence. Thousands turned out onto the capital's streets to clap and cheer the armed forces; to donate blood for the injured, even to give money for the war effort. It was common, in those days, to hear patriotic songs blast from loudspeakers rigged up on street corners, and rare to hear anyone complain when the city's main thoroughfares were closed—as they often were—for demonstrations and parades in support of the troops. "I am so, so happy, oh my goodness," gushed a friend a few weeks into the war. "TPLF is gone, TPLF is finished. Thanks be to God." Pro-government hashtags, meanwhile, such as #EthiopiaWillPrevail flooded the Ethiopian cyber-sphere.[12]

From the view of the capital back then it was as though the advance of the federal forces was unstoppable and that Abiy's eventual triumph was all but inevitable. Almost everyone seemed to imagine it would be all over by Christmas. As federal and Amhara troops advanced swiftly into Tigray, backed by—we would soon learn—UAE-purchased drones and Eritrean artillery, Western diplomats enthusiastically prepared plans for a post-TPLF future. "We completely bought into the myth of the short war," a senior American defence official later admitted.[13]

The moral case for Abiy's actions also seemed to be strengthened by reports of a grisly slaughter of several hundred Amhara civilians by retreating Tigrayan youth in the town of Mai Kadra in Western Tigray in the first week of the war. For anyone still doubting the TPLF's savagery, the government now argued, here was the proof: mere days into the fighting a cold-blooded massacre had been committed by a youth group under its direct command. Aided by an unusually rushed report by Amnesty,[14] as well as a highly partisan one by the Ethiopian Human Rights Commission,[15] the Mai Kadra massacre quickly became core to the efforts of Abiy and his supporters to justify the war and mobilise the Ethiopian public behind it. "Massacring innocent people; what Amharic word can explain it?" the prime minister asked. "Nothing but political and moral bankruptcy."[16] Over time, however, it became clear that what had occurred there was actually far more complex than this. The so-called 'Samre' youth group, in particular, was not the TPLF-run militia it had been widely made out to be. Nor was there any evidence that TPLF commanders had been involved.[17] On the other hand, after the initial killings hundreds of Tigrayans had been murdered or imprisoned in retaliation. Thousands more living and working in the area had been forcibly expelled.[18]

But this wasn't the time for shades of grey. For Abiy's most jubilant supporters, the sight of the TPLF leadership fleeing Mekelle for the mountains of central Tigray had brought the war's maximalist possibilities tantalisingly within reach. Not only would the victory, symbolised by the federal government's relatively ordered capture of the Tigrayan capital on 28 November, spell the end of the TPLF as a political organisation. It would also put to bed any prospect of a Tigrayan revival in Ethiopian politics. But even more than that, total victory, they believed, would open the door at long last to the complete overhaul of the ethno-federal order for which they had so long been agitating. "After the TPLF is defeated, reform of the constitution has to be done," said Aregawi Berhe, a long-time critic (though a founding member) of the TPLF who by then was a strong ally of the prime minister. "That process will start as soon as the TPLF leadership is defeated." By early December, some said, the attorney-general's office had already begun drawing up constitutional amendments. "The constitution must be torn up—by force," said an Ethiopianist academic at Addis Ababa University who was a vocal supporter of the war effort. "And there is a political theory to support this: it's called democratic militancy".[19]

But, in reality, the outbreak of war would drive the final nail into whatever was left of Ethiopia's fledgling democratic opening. With the first gunshots the whole of Tigray descended into darkness, as telecoms were suspended and travel in and out of the region, including for aid workers, was blocked. This was not, the authorities in Addis Ababa soon made clear, a war for prying eyes, and the public narrative about it was to be forcibly imposed from the top. Like the hapless foreign correspondents satirised by Evelyn Waugh in his novel *Scoop*, who had found themselves stuck for weeks in Addis Ababa awaiting permission to visit the front during the Italian invasion of Ethiopia in 1936, those of us still based in the capital were now locked out of Tigray and barred from travelling there. Ethiopian media outlets were ordered not to quote anybody but the government. Even anonymous aid workers commenting on the humanitarian situation were said to be verboten. "They have basically silenced all independent analysts," said an Ethiopian scholar who abruptly ceased making public statements. Local journalists began to be arrested and beaten by the police again. Those deemed to be 'traitors' were harassed and bullied online.

According to Abiy, the war was no more than a limited "law enforcement operation" to apprehend just a handful of renegade leaders who he now called a "junta". As this framing took hold, and was vigorously promoted by a host of government organs including a new "fact-checking" Twitter account run by the Prime Minister's Office, it became ever harder to contest the official line. To speak of the mounting human toll, for instance, in the face of the prime minister's claim that not a single Tigrayan civilian had been killed by federal forces during the month-long battle for Mekelle,[20] increasingly came to be seen as taboo. To highlight the prime minister's own culpability in bringing about the conflict, moreover, or even to call it a "civil war"—as we did at *The Economist*—now meant being cast as another of Ethiopia's 'enemies', an ally of the TPLF and a conspirator in the country's disintegration. Soon foreign journalists were being publicly denounced as agents of the CIA and MI6, or as pens-for-hire on the TPLF's payroll. In December, a local magazine published a long list of foreign and local journalists it alleged were part of a British conspiracy to overthrow Abiy's government. On a trip with friends in the eastern town of Harar around the same time, the owner of a bar told me one night that because I was British, I must be a journalist—and because I was a British journalist, I must be in the pay of the TPLF. For the rest of my time in Ethiopia I would be prevented from travelling to Tigray or anywhere not under government control.

A state of exception, though not formally declared outside Tigray, was now in effect everywhere. Across the country, ordinary Tigrayans, almost any of whom were liable to be labelled part of the "junta", were rounded up and thrown into informal detention camps. Thousands of Tigrayans in the military and police were put behind bars. Tigrayan businesses were closed, bank accounts frozen and Tigrayan government employees were instructed to stay home. NGOs, businesses and even UN offices and some embassies were ordered to weed out their Tigrayan staff. For the first months of the war anyone with a Tigrayan name could be turned away at the door of the international airport and stopped from leaving the country. When faced with criticism many Ethiopians would respond that the TPLF had nobody to blame but themselves for creating the system which made such blatant ethnic discrimination possible. "They don't text me to say, 'I'm so sorry about your mum, how are you feeling?'," complained a friend whose mother was then trapped in Tigray. "They say, 'well, this is the problem with ethnic federalism'."

The process by which the TPLF, and by extension Tigrayans, were singled out as the sole source of Ethiopia's ills appeared to be reaching a perilous climax. "The TPLF's three-decade rule [was] characterised by egregious violation of human rights, corruption and self-enrichment at a grand scale," said Abiy's office, glossing over the role of its coalition partners and neatly rewriting the EPRDF years as exclusively TPLF ones. A few months later parliament designated both the TPLF and the OLA as terrorist organisations.

Justifying all this was the government's core claim that the TPLF had been engaged in a campaign of national sabotage ever since it had left power. In a documentary broadcast by state media just four days into the conflict it was alleged that the "TPLF [had] not slept for three years in trying to destabilise the country". Police interviewed in the programme said they had apprehended suspects and weapons intended for violent plots "directly assisted at a high level by TPLF officials".[21] Speaking to parliament on 30 November, two days after his forces had captured Mekelle, Abiy went as far as to claim that all of the 113 incidents of violent unrest he said had occurred since he took office had been financed by the TPLF, in order to "give an impression the new administration is weak." Even conflicts in neighbouring countries, he suggested, could be traced back to the TPLF.[22]

The evidence presented never came close to meeting the scale and sweep of the allegations.[23] It beggared belief, for instance, that mass violence between ethnic Gedeos and Guji Oromos in 2018 and 2019 could be somehow explained as the work of TPLF operatives. But the government now insisted that it could be, and relied greatly on the observation that while such conflicts raged, Tigray had remained uniquely—and thus suspiciously—stable. "They were never ashamed to say, 'we are the only peaceful region'," Abiy remarked. "Yes, there is peace there, because there is nobody who disturbs peace there; for it's been them who disturbs the peace here."[24]

But in the angry squall of these months, the absence of stronger evidence was less a hindrance than an asset for the government. With conspiracy theories now officially sanctioned as facts, imaginations ran wild and hatreds were loosed. The TPLF, state media alleged, was "obsessed by necrophilia", a "genocide perpetrator" and—quite specifically—"*tut nekash*" (breast-biter), a term for the TPLF previously used by Mengistu which Abiy and his allies now made their own.[25] "In the end, the Tigrayans have become a bit like the Jews," noted a senior EU diplomat in Addis Ababa. "It's very convenient. They are presented as simultaneously weak and cowardly, running a giant conspiracy, and masterminding everything."

The TPLF's opponents would argue that the language used by Abiy and his allies to describe their enemy—a "cancer" to be excised; a "weed" to be uprooted—was narrowly targeted toward the Tigrayan leadership and not Tigrayans as a whole. They pointed to any number of occasions in which Abiy and other government officials had expressed warm words about ordinary Tigrayans, depicting them as loyal patriots who had merely been abused or led astray by their corrupt and predatory leaders. Also weighing in the federal government's favour were accounts of Ethiopian federal soldiers on occasion intervening to protect Tigrayan civilians from Eritrean troops or *Fanos*.[26] Meanwhile, evidence that Abiy had no personal problem with Tigrayans as a group was to be found in the example of Abraham Belay, a close Tigrayan ally of the prime minister since his INSA days who was made defence minister in 2021.

But such assurances were unconvincing. This was not just because any fair-minded observer could see it was not only the TPLF's leaders who were being rounded up en masse or singled out for attack. It was also because these assurances rested on troubling distinctions between 'good' and 'bad'

Tigrayans; between the supposedly innocent, and typically rural, Tigrayan peasant, and the educated, openly political Tigrayan of the towns and cities associated with the TPLF. Binary oppositions like these were key to the rhetoric of Ethiopian nationalism—indeed, to nationalisms anywhere— and they underpinned some of its most dangerous tendencies. Oromos were similarly sorted into 'good' and 'bad': the devoted Ethiopian, usually a Christian, versus the treacherous "*Shane*", for instance, whose loyalty to the state was always suspect. Moreover, in a country where political and ethnic identities overlapped to such a degree, portraying a particular political grouping as fundamentally alien or in some way 'un-Ethiopian', as both the TPLF and the OLA now were, was exceptionally dangerous. If a whole ethnic group were seen as politically suspect, then any one of them could be a target.

Later, as the government's position weakened and war fever took an even tighter hold, the mask would occasionally slip entirely. Top officials would blur the distinction between the TPLF leadership and the wider Tigrayan public in ways which became increasingly hard for anyone to miss. Abiy's influential advisor, the Orthodox deacon Daniel Kibret, declared in December 2021 that "people like them shouldn't be born in this country ever again." When pressed, Daniel claimed that "people like them" referred to the "TPLF terrorist group". But at no point in his speech, which was given to an applauding audience in Bahir Dar, did he make any distinctions or clarify the target of his invective. What followed, in fact, suggested he had a much wider grouping in mind. "They must be removed not only from the institutional registers but also from the people's minds, hearts and history," Daniel thundered. "They must be erased and eliminated. Their trace shouldn't be left."[27] In a similar vein, Ginbot 7's Andargachew Tsige later urged Ethiopian troops to "do anything necessary without hesitation", and to confront their Tigrayan adversaries with "barbaric cruelty".[28]

Abiy himself sometimes made comparably alarming, even incriminating, statements. In one post on Facebook, later removed by the company for inciting violence, he urged civilians to pick up weapons and "bury the terrorist TPLF". In another, in which he compared the "junta" to a cancer, he warned that the "children of Ethiopia have identified their enemy. And they know what they have to do. And they will do it." On at least one occasion, moreover, the prime minister appeared to have even told a senior European official that he would "wipe out the Tigrayans for 100 years"—apparently making no distinction at all between the party and the population as a whole.[29] When foreign diplomats raised concerns about such language, "he and his advisors would minimise it," recalled Jeffrey Feltman, soon to be appointed as the US special envoy to the Horn. "They'd say, 'we're in a war and we must mobilise people'—and then claim the TPLF said much the same things on their propaganda channels anyway."

But with much of the country united behind his endeavour to rid it of the TPLF, Abiy would face little by way of popular criticism for his rhetoric. For the first few months of the war, his political position was the strongest it had been since the early days of Abiymania. Even in parts of Oromia where his popular support had collapsed over the previous year, his actions against the TPLF were met with considerable approval. "Abiy follows the way of the Bible; we've never had such a nice leader in more than a hundred years," enthused an Oromo hotel employee in the town of Bishoftu. "For more than two years he was soft, but still the TPLF didn't stop, they didn't apologise."

Having consolidated his grip over the ruling party and security apparatus considerably in the preceding months, Abiy now went even further, using the cover of wartime exception to replace the few allies reluctant about the conflict with true loyalists who could be trusted to enthusiastically prosecute it. Gedu, for instance, by then foreign minister and the one figure who, next to Lemma, had done more than any to put Abiy in the Prime Minister's Office, was shuffled off stage. So too was General Adem Mohammed, the army chief and a long-time sceptic of Abiy's war plans, who was said to have been incensed when a controversial decision to launch airstrikes on Mekelle was made in the Prime Minister's Office without his knowledge. The next day he was removed from his post and replaced by his Oromo deputy, Berhanu Jula. Temesgen Tiruneh, Abiy's old INSA friend and at the time his man in the Amhara president's office, was appointed to lead the national intelligence agency, while Demeke Mekonnen, the increasingly strident Amhara deputy prime minister, was given the additional role of foreign minister. Completing the appearance of a hardline Amhara ascendancy was Abebaw Tadesse, an officer known to have been especially resentful of the TPLF's former dominance of the army.[30] One of three retired generals Abiy recalled to active duty at the start of the war, General Tadesse would go on to play a key role in coordinating the Ethiopian military's controversial joint operations with Eritrea.

There was now a real spring in Abiy's step. Even some of those with misgivings found it hard not to be impressed by his address to parliament two days after the army's successful capture of Mekelle. Visibly invigorated, the prime minister spoke confidently and at length, detailing what he described as years of effective imprisonment under the TPLF as though now at last he was free to speak his mind. "Even the key to my house was controlled by these people," he said of the early days of his premiership. "They opened the door, they closed the door, morning and night."[31] It was a stellar performance—however dubious some of his claims were— combining stirring patriotism for the Ethiopianists in the audience with studied displays of humility calculated to appeal to his Oromo base. An Oromo businessman and former close ally recalled receiving a phone call from the prime minister shortly afterwards. "We hadn't spoken for over a year," the source recalled. "He called to say: 'I never betrayed the Oromo cause.'"

Behind the showmanship and extensive self-justification, though, was a clear message. Like Mengistu in 1979, then emboldened by the successful crushing of his opponents, both at home and on the battlefield against Somalia, Abiy was now essentially unassailable. The TPLF had scattered, as he would later put it, "like flour in the wind".[32] Now, he impressed on his audience, was no time for compromise.

* * *

The TPLF had gravely underestimated Abiy, miscalculating his firepower and his willingness to unleash overwhelming force regardless of his international reputation as a peacemaker. "Nobody believed Abiy would kick their asses within two weeks," remarked a former Ethiopian diplomat. But the Tigrayans had also misread their Amhara neighbours. Though they had been under no illusions about the rising militancy next door, the TPLF had continued to look down on Amharas as a fighting force. "Very weak in all aspects. Divided. Poorly trained. Immature," General Tsadkan assured me before the war began. "Tigrayan military leaders discount them."

Similar sentiments had been expressed by Tigrayan leaders over the previous decade with respect to the nature and seriousness of the threat posed by Amhara to their hold on the disputed territories. For years, the TPLF top brass had breezily dismissed the complaints of Wolkait activists. Instead of engaging in public debate about the status of these territories, the Tigrayan authorities there had routinely used force, beating and imprisoning activists, and on occasions even arresting people for speaking Amharic, wearing Gondar football jerseys, or listening to Amharic songs.[33] Efforts to resolve the matter peacefully—and constitutionally—were given short shrift. "They were too arrogant," noted an Ethiopian intellectual who, though not Tigrayan, otherwise supported Tigray's claims to the territories. "They believed that truth comes from power, rather than power stemming from truth." Blind to the real depth of resentment harboured across the border, by 2020 the party's leaders still underestimated the scale of the military threat. "My own sister is a police officer in Amhara," said Getachew Reda, who came from Raya and even had relatives there who identified as Amhara, seven months before the war. "That's why, ultimately, war with Amhara is impossible—and that's why people like Asaminew Tsige do not understand a thing."

With the TPLF now in retreat, its bombast punctured, and swathes of what was once Tigrayan territory under their control, Amhara nationalists were triumphant. "Their day has come," lamented one Tigrayan. "Abiy gave them everything they ever wanted." Amhara irredentism, once a minority pursuit even within Amhara, was now increasingly cheered even among the avowedly 'post-ethnic' Ethiopianists in the capital. Seizing the moment, in particular, was Belete Molla, by then the leader of NaMA, the new nationalist party, who met regularly with the prime minister in these months to stiffen his spine and to advance Amhara's war aims. "The TPLF has to be dismantled for good, there should be no compromise," Bellete told me. "There's no way it should be given a chance to have a role in Ethiopia's future." Bellete would later join the government in Abiy's old job of minister of science and technology.

With the TPLF leadership now in the mountains, fleeing the onslaught of Ethiopia's air force and its newly acquired drones, Abiy appointed a new interim administration for the region made up of Tigrayan critics of the TPLF and outspoken opposition figures. Finding willing participants in the administration was hard, with most Tigrayans, even those who previously opposed the TPLF, by this point firmly behind the regional government and certain that the war underway was an essentially genocidal one. When Mulu Nega, a Tigrayan academic at Addis Ababa University chosen to head the interim administration, met with the prime minister he was told in no uncertain terms that the war was just a "law enforcement operation" which had nothing to do with land grabbing. "He was very clear," Mulu recalled. "He told us he'd manage it, that we'd discuss the issue with the

Amhara region, and there would be no problems." Amhara leaders in both NaMA and the ruling party, though, were having none of it. When a team of Tigrayan interim officials led by Mulu tried to visit Western Tigray, flanked by soldiers from the Ethiopian army, Amhara forces simply barred them from entering. "We were encircled, and they threatened to kill us," recalled Gebremeskel Kassa, who was by then also a member of the interim administration.

Emboldened by success on the battlefield, Amhara nationalists now sought to consolidate their advantage and reap the war's dividends. Across Western Tigray, Amhara businessmen quickly moved to secure control of Wolkait's fertile sesame fields, trucking vast quantities of looted produce out of the territory and taking over factories and farms. By the time a foreign academic managed to visit the district capital of Humera in the middle of 2021, the new administration's core activity had become the distribution of title deeds for land and the licensing of shipments of looted crops. Though there was always more to the Tigray War on both sides than just economic interests—Amhara nationalists no less than the TPLF were motivated above all by intangible questions of pride, history and identity— hardnosed Amhara businessmen would continue to play an outsized role in financing and promoting it, and nowhere more prominently than in Western Tigray.[34] In some instances, warehouses taken over by prominent Amhara business moguls were even to be used as prisons for holding Tigrayan detainees.

Amhara nationalists also sought to further their ambitions on other fronts. As 2020 drew to a close, they grew more insistent in their calls for a stronger military intervention in the large fertile district of Metekel across the border with Benishangul-Gumuz to which they also laid claim. In October, deputy prime minister Demeke Mekonnen called on Amharas in the region to arm themselves. Two months later, an Amhara regional government spokesman warned that if attacks against Amharas and other minorities continued in Metekel then it would begin a "second chapter" of the Tigray War there. On 24 December, Abiy duly agreed to send more federal troops to Metekel.

At the same time, he gave rhetorical support to their claims over al-Fashaga, a slice of fertile farmland over the border with Sudan which had long been contested between local Amhara farmers and their Sudanese counterparts. When the Sudanese army took advantage of Ethiopia's distraction in early November to dramatically expand its presence in al-Fashaga—evicting thousands of Amhara farmers in the process—Abiy backed the Amhara resistance, with the government calling Sudan's actions an invasion and sending in reinforcements backed by units from Eritrea. For the first time in decades, Ethiopia's official position on al-Fashaga, a porous frontier space where neither ownership nor sovereignty had ever been sharply defined, now appeared to be that the territory had always been indisputably Ethiopian. "Only one ethnicity claims these lands," the Sudanese ambassador in Addis Ababa argued, referring to the Amhara. "It's their agenda—it's not an Ethiopian agenda."

By the start of 2021, the Western Tigray question appeared to have been conclusively settled in Amhara's favour. "Oromo triumphalism has now given way decisively to Amhara triumphalism," noted an Ethiopian scholar. Over the coming months hundreds of thousands of Tigrayans in the territory would be systematically evicted or killed. "Let us kill all of them who are older than five," an Amhara policeman told the foreign academic. "And start anew."[35] A video shot on a smartphone showed emptied villages, "*tsedu*" (cleaned)—in the exact words of the Amhara special police who shared the video—of the "junta".[36]

Thousands of Tigrayans, in particular young men, were slung into what were essentially concentration camps: police stations, prisons, warehouses and disused schools hastily repurposed for the needs of mass detention. In the sweltering, malaria-ridden lowlands, a single room could contain several hundred detainees at a time, all severely lacking food, water and medical care. Many of the inmates would remain there until as late as 2023. "You could see the terror in their eyes," recalled a visitor who had found himself briefly detained in the Humera police station. Some would simply be murdered, their bodies dumped in mass graves or tossed in the Tekeze River.[37] But most likely died of hunger or disease. Tesfaye Habtu, a thirty-two-year-old Tigrayan man who spent a year and seven months in a prison in Humera, later recounted how he had been forced to load the bodies of sixteen of his fellow prisoners onto the back of a tractor, where he had laid them, two-by-two, to be carted off and dumped elsewhere. "I never expected to survive," he told me in late 2022, a few months after he had pulled off a daring escape into Sudan. "We were just waiting to die."

Abiy never condemned the ethnic cleansing of Western Tigray. But he also never explicitly condoned the annexations.[38] Though the Amhara government claimed that Abiy's administration had swiftly approved the incorporation of the disputed territories into their region, it never formally did so. Over the coming years, Abiy would continually profess his belief in the need to resolve the question through constitutional means, ideally a referendum, and he repeatedly assured his Oromo allies—as well as the Tigrayans in the interim administration in Mekelle—of his commitment to it.

In the end, Abiy's partnership with irredentist Amhara nationalism was as transparently instrumental and transactional as the alliance with the Oromo nationalists who had brought him to power.[39] Ideologically, their claims over Western Tigray were as irrelevant to him as Oromo nationalist claims over Addis Ababa: what he really wanted, a close colleague later explained, was simply to make Western Tigray a new region all of its own. By greenlighting their invasions, however, he had successfully won Amhara support for his cause at its most decisive moment. Later, when they were no longer needed, he would jettison them: cracking down on the *Fano* and Amhara special forces while hinting that he would hand the disputed territories back to Tigray. By doing so, he would ultimately provoke a full-scale rebellion in Amhara in 2023.

Such was the double-dealing at the heart of Abiy's project. Though neither side of the dispute—neither Amharas nor Tigrayans—ever trusted him, a prolonged disagreement helped keep both dependent on him. At each other's throats, in the end they would have little choice but to turn to the federal government for support. "What I realise today is that he was really deceiving us," Mulu reflected after he had resigned from the interim government and fled abroad. "He said something to us, and something else to them."

17

"DIRTY WAR"

ERITREA ON THE MARCH

First came muffled sobs, gradually growing louder with each new voice that joined the chorus. The elderly woman next to me on the sofa, shrouded in a black shawl, began to wail. Her slight body quivering, she rocked towards the portrait of a smiling young man in the middle of the room. Abraham was thirty-five years old when he was shot, said an older brother who was hosting mourning relatives in his apartment on the outskirts of Addis Ababa. Eritrean soldiers had arrived at the family home in Adwa a few weeks earlier. By then many of the town's residents had fled, but not Abraham, who had a young child and a sick, ageing father. When the gunmen tried to steal two of the family's trucks, Abraham had resisted. He was shot dead on the spot, right in front of their father.

Before the war the TPLF were curiously blasé about the reality of Eritrea's widely expected participation in it. As unlikely as it was that Isaias would ever pass up an opportunity to settle scores with them, the TPLF's leaders seemed genuinely to have believed that Eritrean troops would limit themselves to guarding the border and providing artillery cover, just as they appeared to do in the war's very first days at the border town of Humera. Isaias is "rational", General Tsadkan had assured me days before the conflict: "he knows an adventure inside Ethiopia would be the end of him." When it became clear that Asmara Airport was being used as a staging post for Ethiopian troops, the TPLF fired some of its long-range missiles at it; they also launched some in the direction of Isaias's home, as well as Bahir Dar and Gondar, for good measure. Neither had much impact beyond prompting a rebuke from the otherwise serenely unbothered Mike Pompeo, then America's secretary of state.[1]

The early months of the war were, in short, a disaster for the TPLF. Almost overnight, its once supreme leaders had been reduced in the eyes of much of the Ethiopian public to fugitive criminals on the run from the law. By early January, its founding father, Sebhat Nega, alongside several Tigrayan military officers, had been captured; the humiliating sight of him arriving at the airport in Addis Ababa in handcuffs, wearing a rumpled tracksuit and a single sock, would become one of the war's defining images. Other captives included Abraham Tekeste, Ethiopia's former finance minister, who was apprehended when Ethiopian commandos surrounded senior TPLF leaders, including Debretsion himself, as they slept beside the bed of the Tekeze River that month. "It was really desperate and chaotic... hell on the earth," recalled one of their number. In the first three weeks of January, the Ethiopian military killed or captured at least forty-seven people from a most-wanted list of 167 senior leaders of the TPLF, including four of the party's nine-member executive committee. Also among them was Seyoum Mesfin, the seventy-one-year-old former foreign minister, who was shot in the head while hiding in the mountains. So disorganised was the Tigrayan resistance that when guards working for a chicken farm near Mekelle tried to enlist they would spend a fruitless week searching in the hills with their old rifles before giving up and wandering dejectedly back to the city.

Abiy, in his address to Parliament after the capture of Mekelle, noted that the TPLF had failed to understand the true extent of his military preparedness. He detailed, with evident relish, how he had methodically revamped the air force, bolstered the army and built up his new Republican Guard as part of a careful programme of what he now called "confidential reform".[2] The federal military's loyalty to the centre, moreover, had undoubtedly proved stronger than many Tigrayans expected—so much so that Getachew Reda's suggestion to me, several months before the war, that the army would simply refuse to do Abiy's bidding in hindsight came to look spectacularly negligent.[3] "At the end of the day the top leaders were not prudent enough," one member of the TPLF's central committee later admitted. A Western ambassador recalled the TPLF assuring them before the war that the central governments in both Addis Ababa and Asmara would crumble within just a month of fighting.

Underlying this misplaced confidence was the assumption that Abiy would soon come under strong international pressure to end the war, and that once he did the government would concede so as to avoid censure and isolation. But this was as grave a misreading of the geopolitics of the moment as it was of Abiy's temperament. For one thing, whatever the federal government and its supporters would soon allege to the contrary, the TPLF had few reliable friends left in the world. While officials from Washington and European capitals had always put aside their distaste for the EPRDF's Marxist baggage in their efforts to secure influence and support for counter-terrorism operations in the region, frustrations with its Tigrayan contingent, in particular, had been evident even before Abiy took power. Moreover, many governments in Africa had their own separatist movements to contend with. The bulk now regarded the TPLF simply as rebels waging a secessionist insurgency against a sovereign state.

The African Union's then chairperson, South Africa's president Cyril Ramaphosa, did at first try to send mediators to Addis Ababa. But Abiy immediately rebuffed them. By the time the AU Commission, hemmed in by the fact that its headquarters were in the Ethiopian capital—and so susceptible to the government's pressure—got round to holding formal talks about the conflict, the outcome was a statement in firm support of Abiy's position. It would take a full ten months for it to establish a mediation effort of any kind.[4]

The UN Security Council, meanwhile, was hampered by the obstruction of China and Russia, who both backed Abiy's appeals for them to resist foreign meddling in what he called Ethiopia's 'internal sovereign affairs'. The Security Council would ultimately wait more than eight months—until July 2021—before even agreeing to publicly discuss the matter; even then, it failed to release a joint statement on it. Not once would the war make it on to the council's official agenda.[5] The EU, which suspended direct budget support to Ethiopia's government in January 2021, was a partial exception to the general rule, but was also divided amongst itself.[6] Most member states, not least its two most powerful, France and Germany, were furious with the Commission for halting budget support and would continue to resist any further sanctions against the Ethiopian government for the full duration of the fighting. "Quite a few governments—including the UK's—were literally saying, 'yes, it's awful, but we don't just have a relationship with six million Tigrayans,'" a senior EU diplomat recalled. "The argument was that there are 120 million other Ethiopians that we have to have a relationship with—no matter how the war plays out."

At first, the notable international outlier was Sudan, then chair of the increasingly ineffective IGAD, whose interim prime minister, a mild-mannered and avuncular UN economist called Abdalla Hamdok, was one of the few leaders in the Horn pushing sincerely for an immediate end to the war. When Hamdok rang Abiy early on with an offer to mediate he was firmly rebuffed, said Alex Rondos, then the EU's special envoy to the Horn, who was in regular contact with the Sudanese leader. So strong was Abiy's military and diplomatic position at this moment that he evidently felt no need even to put up a front: Rwanda's president, Paul Kagame—another important exception—was later dealt similar treatment. According to Sudan's ambassador in Addis Ababa, who was close to Hamdok, Abiy had told his Sudanese counterpart that the conflict was a purely internal matter and threatened to pull Ethiopia out of IGAD if it were brought up again. An aide later recalled an irate Hamdok some months after the incident staring at Abiy on television and disparaging him as an "arrogant boy". By then Ethiopia's relationship with Sudan was so frosty—with tensions having worsened over both the dam and the border—that the latter had begun allowing Tigrayan fighters to mobilise and recruit in the refugee camps there. The Sudanese army had also begun to supply the Tigrayans with light arms and ammunition.

* * *

If the TPLF had overestimated the interest of America under Trump in pushing for peace in Ethiopia in these years, then its leaders also underestimated the waning of US influence across Africa and the Middle East at the same time. After all, this was a war fought in the shadow of diminishing American power, and—even before Russia's invasion of Ukraine in 2022—an international security order which was palpably fraying. In the Horn, rival regional powers now held more sway than at any time in living memory. For a country like Ethiopia, which had always sought a diverse and balanced network of allies, and a leader like Abiy, whose leanings were Western but whose allegiances were unfixed, the new era of 'multipolarity' was ripe with opportunities. Even as Ethiopia's relations with America deteriorated with the arrival of the Biden administration in January 2021, Abiy would ultimately find it within his power and wit to withstand its pressure for months on end to cease fighting on anything other than his own terms. Over the course of that year, the prime minister would successfully court diplomatic support, and secure arms, from powers ranging from China and Russia to the UAE, Turkey, Israel and even Iran. Until 2022, he wouldn't make a single significant concession to Western pressure, either to meaningfully open up humanitarian access to Tigray or to start talks with the TPLF.

But no backer was more important to Abiy in this period than the UAE. Ostensibly a staunch ally of America, the Emiratis had in recent years increasingly pursued foreign policy objectives independent of—or even at odds with— those of Washington: propping up Isaias in Eritrea, for instance, or, later, arming Sudanese paramilitary forces and bypassing American sanctions on Russia by processing exports of illicit Sudanese gold. In Ethiopia, Crown Prince Mohammed bin Zayed had helped finance not just the establishment of the Republican Guard, which would play a not insignificant part in the war, but also the controversial drone programme which may have been decisive in it. It was these combat drones, perhaps more than almost anything else, which had taken the TPLF by surprise at the start of the fighting: a veteran Tigrayan diplomat once expressed to me his astonishment that Ethiopia even had the capabilities to pilot them. Ultimately, the technology proved devastating to the TPLF's hold on Mekelle, and soon after that made equally short work of the artillery which they had managed to commandeer from the Northern Command.[7] The UAE's role in this—purchasing Chinese-made drones, fixing them up, and transporting them to Ethiopia in exchange for gold—had been indispensable.[8] "We believed the way Abiy was conducting the war was contributing to instability in Ethiopia," recalled the then US special envoy, Jeffrey Feltman. "But the Emiratis believed that helping Abiy to win the war was the key to stabilising Ethiopia."

As for Isaias, an increasingly multipolar world also promised new avenues for expanding his regional clout, above all in Ethiopia. To this day it has remained unclear exactly what he and Abiy agreed in Asmara before the war began: though it is highly likely that the Eritrean president extracted payment from Ethiopia for his troops' services in Tigray, it has never been definitively proven.[9] Some have suggested that the original plan was for the Eritrean army to advance no further than the territories it had claimed during the original border war, and been subsequently awarded to Asmara by the UN commission. But this, too, is unproven. In any case, whatever had putatively been agreed in advance, it swiftly became clear that what Eritrea had in fact embarked upon was a full-scale invasion, albeit one which (confusingly, from the perspective of international law) took place with the clear consent, if not the formal invitation, of the Ethiopian government. By December 2020, Eritrea had deployed no less than four mechanised divisions, seven infantry divisions and a commando brigade, according to Mesfin Hagos, the former Eritrean defence minister then living in Germany but in touch with sources inside the army back home.[10] Over the course of the war's first six months nearly all Eritrea's divisions—effectively the entirety of its conscript army—would at some point rotate into Tigray.

Exactly how the two armies fought together was never entirely clear. In broad terms, there was never any question that Eritrean and Ethiopian generals at the very highest level were closely coordinating; later in the war, video footage emerged of commanders co-operating on the battlefield.[11] According to the former defence minister, the Eritrean army on the eve of the war was a hollow shell of its former self, meaning Isaias was running the show almost single-handedly. Eritrean unit commanders on the ground received orders directly from the president, who was then said to be based almost entirely at the coastal town of Massawa, while Ethiopian generals communicated with him directly, too. But beyond that, Mesfin conceded, the evidence was "mixed and contradictory". According to his sources in the Eritrean military, units from the two armies were at first merged, with Ethiopian units swallowing up their Eritrean counterparts and with Ethiopian commanders in charge on the battlefield. But over time the commands separated. Once these independent Eritrean units had taken the lead, the battle swung more decisively in their favour. By early 2021 they were said to be the vanguard of the fight against the Tigrayan resistance then gathering strength in the central highlands.

In towns and villages all over Tigray, sometimes together, other times alone, Ethiopian and Eritrean soldiers laid the region to waste. Word reached us in Addis Ababa at first in fragments: over crackling phone lines; in the whispers of returning aid workers; through the grainy videos and murky images which gradually seeped out. But for months the Ethiopian government insisted that normality had mostly returned there. Over time, phone networks were reconnected—though not the internet— and a few foreign journalists were given permission to travel there to see for themselves. Such was the bubble in the capital in those days that many officials seemed genuinely to believe that visitors there would find a grateful region mostly at peace. "The government does not have a magic wand to fix everything immediately, but we are now definitely in the recovery phase," an official in the ministry of peace assured me in March.

But what happened instead was that as more outside eyes reached Tigray, the grim reality of what was happening there simply became more widely understood. As even an Ethiopian general would admit to visiting diplomats in Mekelle in this period, this was a "dirty war": a conflict marked by atrocities to rival anything in Ethiopia's long history of violence. By one count, between 8,000 to 18,000 non-combatants in Tigray were killed by bullets or bombs.[12] By the time it was over, tens or even hundreds of thousands more—nobody ever really knew the precise toll—were thought to have succumbed to death by hunger or disease.[13] By one estimate, the Ethiopian army alone lost up to half a million soldiers. One battlefield survivor later said his abiding memory of the fighting was the stench of several thousand bodies rotting in the fields where he slept.[14]

Though camps which for years had housed tens of thousands of Eritrean refugees were razed to the ground, this was not—on the whole—a conflict characterised by large-scale physical destruction, especially of the larger towns: generals on both sides typically avoided major urban warfare.[15] What marked it instead was plunder. All across the region, hospitals were stripped bare. Monasteries and museums were ransacked. All means of survival were targeted: machinery and equipment looted from factories and mills; ploughs and oxen robbed from the fields. What couldn't be carried was burnt. When aid workers dropped off sacks of emergency food, Eritrean troops were seen slinging them onto the back of stolen trucks and carting them over the border.

When Tigrayans resisted, the occupying armies hit back at civilians. "If I even think of going back there, I can see everything in front of me," said a survivor of perhaps the most infamous massacre—the slaughter of several hundred civilians by Eritrean troops in the holy town of Axum— whose two younger brothers were shot dead in front of him.[16] Two years later, by then a refugee in London, he was haunted by nightmares. "I pass through the bodies again… in every corner, everywhere … some of them screaming, asking for help." Young men of fighting age were overwhelmingly the target, leading UN investigators to later talk of "androcide": the systematic killing of boys and men.[17]

Nothing, though, defined the Tigray War more than the ubiquity of sexual violence, which branded the conflict's name thereafter with a mark of notoriety few others could match. By one estimate some 10,000 Tigrayan women were raped in the course of the conflict; others have suggested—quite plausibly, according to those who dealt with victims and survivors—that the true figure may have been as much as ten times higher.[18] Some of those raped were children; others were grandmothers.[19] One woman described being stabbed and drugged by thirty Eritrean soldiers who raped her for ten days straight.[20] Some had nails, gravel or even hot metal rods forced inside their vaginas.[21] Children and husbands alike reported being forced to watch.

Rape is a war crime as old as war itself. But it is not, contrary to certain popular perceptions, inevitable or somehow unavoidable—an unfortunate consequence of male depravity unleashed by chaos. In some conflicts in other parts of the world, such as those where forced recruitment is rife, scholars have shown how gang rape can be used as a means of building cohesion among the ranks—like a particularly hideous form of 'male-bonding'.[22] This may well have explained some of the dynamics in Tigray, where two national armies, who had been sworn enemies until very recently, suddenly found themselves fighting side by side. Most Eritrean soldiers, moreover, were forced conscripts, which might have explained why they were reported to have perpetrated gang rape more often than their Ethiopian counterparts.

Others argue that sexual violence in war is more often simply opportunistic, with soldiers using insecurity and lawlessness to perpetrate acts that would be considered unacceptable, or at least more difficult to get away with, in peacetime. But that seems unlikely to have been the case in Tigray, where so many women reported being abducted to military camps and raped by multiple soldiers in the presence of their commanders.[23] The obvious conclusion therefore, which was reached by both Human Rights Watch and Amnesty, among many others, was that mass rape in the Tigray War must have been tolerated—maybe, on occasion, even implicitly ordered—by Ethiopian and Eritrean army officers themselves.

But why? For many Tigrayans, the answer was simple: the scale of the sexual violence demonstrated, more vividly than almost anything else, the genocidal nature of the war against them.[24] They could point, convincingly, to parallels with earlier genocides. In the former Yugoslavia in the 1990s, for instance, rape was used strategically by Serbian forces to break apart families and communities, and to 'purify' bloodlines so as to exterminate their adversaries for generations to come.[25] In Tigray, similarly, some women reported that the perpetrators had purposefully killed the unborn babies inside them—to "cleanse the bloodline", they said, and because no "Tigrayan womb should ever give birth".[26] That senior government officials like Daniel Kibret had expressed such similar sentiments on the airwaves was, for almost all Tigrayans, added proof of the genocidal intent.[27]

In the eyes of many other Ethiopians, though, this was special pleading. Of the many crimes committed in the course of the war in Tigray—forced starvation, civilian executions, residential bombardments—few of them, however extreme, were truly without any precedent in Ethiopian history.[28] Sexual violence had been widespread in the 1998–2000 war, with countless Eritrean women having been raped by Ethiopian soldiers.[29] It also accompanied the imperial expansions of the nineteenth century, when thousands of female captives were reported to have been delivered to the emperor and his generals as 'concubines'.[30] That the scale might this time be substantially greater, or that the threat posed to Tigrayans might now be unique, was an argument which never seemed likely to win a sympathetic ear. Many in both Ethiopia and Eritrea felt that the terrorising of Tigray was just the latest in a cycle of mass violence which had gyrated for centuries. "It's karma; they got what they deserve," said a businessman in the Somali state capital of Jigjiga. "What goes around comes around."

* * *

Much like the nameless 'little green men', sent by Putin to invade Crimea in 2014, the Eritrean troops roaming Tigray did so for months under a veil of official silence. Unlike in Ethiopia, where government propaganda had gone into overdrive from the very first day, Eritrean state media barely mentioned the conflict next door. For over a year Isaias refused to publicly acknowledge it, let alone admit his own army was deeply involved.[31] So extreme was the silence that his government failed even to acknowledge the TPLF's missile strikes on Asmara's international airport in the war's opening salvos. When American diplomats met with Isaias in early 2021, "he mostly spoke at us", one of them recalled, "and just lied, denied everything. He just kept on telling us that we'd succumbed to TPLF propaganda." Though the president admitted to them his troops were in Tigray, he stressed repeatedly that that they were there at Abiy's invitation.

Addis Ababa was a different matter, however. When asked about Eritrea's involvement, Ethiopian officials invariably broke into furious denial. From the very first days of the fighting the Prime Minister's Office had actively pre-empted such allegations by claiming that the TPLF had been manufacturing fake Eritrean uniforms to deceive the international community—among the very first recorded instances of concerted disinformation in the entire conflict.[32] In early December, when pressed by the UN secretary-general, António Guterres, Abiy said he could guarantee no Eritrean troops had entered Ethiopian territory. When Mulu Nega, the interim president of Tigray, physically encountered Eritrean troops in the town of Shire in late November, and immediately reported the matter, the prime minister's response was outright denial. "He said: 'No, we told them to stay at the border'," Mulu recalled. Two months later, in a meeting in Addis Ababa with the interim Tigray administration, Abiy's response to emotional pleas for the government to expel the Eritreans from Tigray was to repeat that he wasn't aware of any of them even being there.

By March 2021, though, this had become an almost impossible façade to maintain. When Biden, by then US president, dispatched his close Democrat ally, Senator Chris Coons, to meet Abiy in Addis Ababa, the prime minister for the first time dropped the pretence. In a series of conversations with Coons, in which Abiy described Isaias as mad and unpredictable, he finally acknowledged his troops' presence in Tigray and promised to travel to Asmara and ask the Eritrean president to withdraw them. A few days later, in an address to parliament, the prime minister for the first time admitted in public that Eritrean troops were inside Ethiopian territory (though he still downplayed their atrocities and their full geographical footprint).[33] On 26 March, his office released a statement which claimed that, following a meeting between the two leaders, Eritrea had agreed to pull out its troops.[34] "Coons was very surprised that Abiy followed up in such short order," recalled an aide. "He initially committed to going within a period of weeks, and it ended up being days."

But then nothing happened. "I don't think Abiy was actually interested in forcing them out," noted a senior American official in the Biden administration. "There was no international consensus, and he wasn't under military pressure. At that point the Tigrayans were literally roaming around in the mountains with a single cell phone. There was no internal pressure and no external pressure … why would he compromise?" When Jeffrey Feltman, who was appointed by Biden as the US special envoy to the Horn, met with Abiy a short while later, the prime minister blithely assured them he was able to "manage" Isaias, including by expelling Eritrean troops militarily from Tigray later if necessary.[35]

In any case, few Ethiopians seemed especially bothered by the presence of Eritrean troops on their own country's territory. Government propaganda was generally met with public enthusiasm. Until Abiy made his first admission to parliament, most people seemed ready to either accept the government's denial of Eritrea's involvement, or, if presented with contrary evidence, actively defend its role. "War is brutal," shrugged one Ethiopianist academic at Addis Ababa University. "Most Ethiopians hate the TPLF so much they consider the involvement of Eritrean troops a necessary evil."

At first glance, this might have been surprising: just two years earlier the countries had still nominally been at war. But it was also a reminder that, for many Ethiopians, Eritrea had never really been a foreign country at all. "Each and every Eritrean, if asked, would admit they don't celebrate the day they separated from Ethiopia," said a spokesman for Ethiopia's foreign ministry in a controversial press conference that March. "We are one people, we are one country."[36] The statement was soon retracted following a storm of Eritrean criticism, but it hinted at a deeper truth. For many Ethiopians, Eritrea was indeed just another domestic actor and Isaias just another regional big man—no less a part of the greater *Habesha* polity than, say, Debretsion or Jawar. Whatever Isaias's past sins, alliances in Ethiopia had always been fluid and shifting. With enough time, bygones could be bygones, such that even the man who had done more in the service of dismembering the Ethiopian empire than anyone in its history could be recast as a champion of its territorial integrity. "Isaias is the greatest supporter of Ethiopian unity there is," said Asfa-Wossen Asarate, a relative of Haile Selassie and a prominent member of the Ethiopianist diaspora in Germany. "We owe Eritrea so much."

General insouciance about their involvement was matched by a tolerance for the atrocities Eritrean troops were found to be committing. When Abiy was asked, for instance, about the allegations of mass rape in Tigray, he lamented that just as women in Tigray might have been raped, "our soldiers were also raped by bayonets."[37] Officials and their supporters followed his lead, engaging in a cruel campaign to cast doubt on Tigrayan accusers—arguing that victims' testimonials were false or exaggerated, that rape was already endemic in Tigray, and that many such assaults had actually been committed by Tigrayan criminals who had been released from prison during the fighting. Even documented incidents, such as a video of security forces burning a Tigrayan man alive, were either downplayed or denounced as lies. "Like you make a Hollywood movie by selecting actors, they planned and orchestrated the raping of women," claimed Redwan Hussein, then the national security advisor, in a private briefing with Ethiopian diplomats.[38] General Bacha Debele, an Oromo officer recalled by Abiy for active duty at the start of the war, would later insist that the Ethiopian soldiers executing dozens of young Tigrayan men and throwing them off a cliff near the village of Mahbere Dego—seen in videos shot by the perpetrators themselves—had Tigrayan accents.[39]

Almost no international organisations, officials now alleged, were free from malign Tigrayan influence or TPLF infiltration. Just as they had previously been depicted as the puppeteers behind every violent incident in Ethiopia, now they were accused of masterminding a global influence operation in the service of what Tigrayan activists in the diaspora now called "#TigrayGenocide" but what government supporters deemed an information or propaganda war. "You find them in the WHO, you find them in UNICEF, you find them in NGOs and foreign embassies," alleged an official in the ministry of peace. "You don't find an embassy in Addis without a TPLF-affiliated attaché." Not even the internationally-respected Tigrayan head of the World Health Organization, the former TPLF member and Ethiopian foreign minister Tedros Adhanom Ghebreyesus, was spared: internal government documents leaked after the war revealed the elaborate lengths Abiy's government had gone to smear the global health leader with allegations of embezzlement and sexual misconduct ahead of his reappointment at the WHO in 2022. Tedros later spoke of being trailed by plainclothes Ethiopian agents around his home in Geneva.[40]

Even Ethiopia's supposedly reformed human rights commission appeared to succumb to such thinking. At first, under the leadership of Daniel Bekele, the widely respected veteran of both Human Rights Watch and Amnesty, the new EHRC had looked like it might be different to its EPRDF-era predecessor—more independent and more willing to hold the government to account. As late as February 2021 it had mostly endorsed Amnesty's findings on the recent massacre in Axum (though it still downplayed the scale) and confirmed the presence of Eritrean troops in Tigray at a time when this was still officially denied by the Ethiopian authorities.[41] It also enjoyed more formal autonomy than in the past: its commissioner, for example, was freer to hire independent staff. This was undermined, though, by the increasingly obvious bias of senior employees—and, above all, the commissioner himself—who on several occasions would cast doubt on the testimonies of Tigrayan refugees in Sudan and downplay the scale of atrocities committed against them.[42] "Most of the staff support the war—starting with the commissioner," a disgruntled member of the team confessed in 2021. Ultimately, the commission would fail to acknowledge the ethnic cleansing in Western Tigray and depicted the departure of Tigrayans from the territory as essentially voluntary. "There was a groundswell of goodwill as Daniel set out to overhaul EHRC prior to the outbreak of the war. But what the EHRC leadership did in return was betray its victims," said Aaron Maasho, who was a special advisor to the commission before resigning in 2021. "It never truthfully probed the government's atrocities. Its leaders made plausible excuses and skilfully distorted the picture."

Under pressure from foreign donors, Abiy's government allowed the UN to carry out an investigation in Tigray in 2021 in partnership with the EHRC. But by that time the commission's role had become less about holding the government accountable than helping it stave off further international censure. Daniel "consistently pleaded with foreign delegations to not be too harsh on Abiy," recalled a senior EU diplomat. Efforts to re-investigate the Mai Kadra massacre, to interview Tigrayan refugees in Sudan, or to incorporate in the new joint report with the UN some of the Tigrayan testimonies which it had collected earlier were blocked. In private conversations with the UN high commissioner for human rights, Daniel "made totally unacceptable comments", a frustrated senior UN official involved in the investigation told me at the time. "Sometimes it's very difficult to differentiate the view of the commission from the view of the government."

In private, the UN's investigators admitted that the overwhelming majority of the war crimes in Tigray had been committed by the federal army and its allies. But the final draft of the report, published in November 2021, failed to quantify the scale or proportion committed by either side. The term "massacre" was used only to refer to killings attributed to Tigrayan forces.[43] Abiy welcomed the report, noting that it had presented no evidence that genocide had occurred. But he rejected the UN's call for further international investigations. When the UN Human Rights Council launched another inquiry of its own in December 2021, in the face of fierce Ethiopian opposition, Daniel would write a letter to the high commissioner recommending, in essence, that the UN simply leave the matter of criminal investigation and accountability to the Ethiopian authorities.[44]

By Ethiopian authorities, he meant, in particular, the attorney-general's office (later renamed the justice ministry), which was then under the helm of Gedion Timothewos, another prominent technocrat and once the great hope of liberal reformers both in Ethiopia and abroad. Described by a friend of his as the "finest mind of his generation", Gedion seemed to many the embodiment of the sort of high-flying public servant Abiy's rise had once heralded: cosmopolitan and open-minded, moderate and well-liked by donors. But after an encouraging start as attorney-general—endeavouring, among other things, to curb the increasingly rampant police practice of ignoring judges' orders—he too slid into the role of dutiful party cadre. By now a member of the Prosperity Party, and one of its chief ideologues no less, he would emerge over the course of the war as one of Abiy's most trusted allies, an eloquent defender of his administration on the international airwaves and, in private, a seemingly genuine believer in its God-anointed mission. Though he may, some of his friends suggested, have privately ached at the suffering in Tigray, he gave every impression in public of believing the TPLF to be exclusively responsible for all that had befallen its people. When Filsan Abdi, then minister of women, children and youth, tried enlisting the young lawyer's help in addressing the allegations of mass rape in Tigray, he appeared to dodge her calls and even complained, she said, to the Prime Minister's Office about her conduct. "He simply didn't care," Filsan told me after she had become the sole senior official to resign from the government on account of its failure to hold war criminals to account. "As far as they were all concerned, when it came to rape, it was case closed: the PM had come out and said nothing had happened."

Under pressure, the government eventually put out a statement in the EHRC's name, in which it claimed that 108 rapes had indeed taken place in Tigray.[45] ("They had wanted to say only five," Filsan alleged.) Later, the justice ministry announced that sixty Ethiopian soldiers had been indicted for rapes and murders committed during the war. But few further details were ever made public, neither their identities nor the nature of their crimes, and no senior commander was thought to be among them. By August 2022, twenty-five soldiers were said to have been convicted, one with a life sentence. But no victims appeared to have been consulted, and all the proceedings were kept hidden from the public.[46] Not one Eritrean soldier was ever known to have been prosecuted.

This was not, in the end, any great surprise. As a committed Pente, Abiy could always turn, as he had done in the past, to the idea that God's hand would deliver peace without the need for justice. He could also rest in the knowledge that the Ethiopian state itself had never, in all its history, been held to account for crimes committed in its name. The idea of 'transitional justice', which after the war ended the government claimed it was pursuing, could make sense only in a context in which power had actually changed hands. In keeping with old conceptions of power and statehood in Ethiopia, in which the figure of the sovereign stood high above the law, Abiy's idea of justice was always selective; even before the war, he had shown a striking disinclination to see anyone loyal to him brought to book. The notion that any Ethiopian institution could be trusted to pursue justice fairly, in the wake of a civil war in which he had ultimately prevailed, and which had made a partisan of almost everyone, was little more than a fantasy. "Even the most fair-minded people in Ethiopia have taken sides," an official at the EHRC admitted. "There is no judge among us, no arbiter among Ethiopians anymore."

18

"OUR ADWA MOMENT"

FROM OPERATION ALULA TO #NOMORE

Yellow daisies bloomed, like poppies in Flanders, among the bodies still rotting in the fields. Of their former lives only glimpses remained: a scarf soaked in mud; a torn fragment of uniform; the toe of a plastic sandal poking through the dirt. Some had been buried under stones and leaves. Others had been left to lie in the open, limbs ravaged by dogs, torsos blackened and bloated from the rain.

Not much was known for certain about what happened in Chenna, a village in northern Amhara, in the early days of September 2021. There was certainly a battle, a fearsome one, for the evidence of that was everywhere—in the ransacked homes, the slaughtered cows, the bullet casings and the artillery shells. I had wandered into what remained of the village later that month, in the company of local officials and a couple of other journalists, through woods and across streams, gingerly avoiding the corpses and batting away the swarms of flies which swirled and eddied above us. Across a plunging valley, the kind whose bucolic beauty had once drawn tourists, came the thunder of distant artillery.

Locals had buried at least fifty-six bodies: civilians, they said, murdered by the invading Tigrayans as they beat a panicked retreat. Officials put the number higher still, at nearly 200. Baze Kisade, a farmer, told me that he had come home to find two of his brothers dead, shot in the head, their hands tied behind their backs. Agera Tareke, a priest, said Tigrayan fighters broke into his home and killed his father in front of him. The leader of Chenna village counted an entire family of six among the dead. A subsequent investigation by the UN found that Tigrayan fighters had raped women and girls as young as eleven.[1] When a researcher visited the village three months later, the bodies of the Tigrayan dead remained unburied in the fields.

The giddy and triumphant early days of the war were long gone. Just three months before the fighting in Chenna, the Tigrayans—whose fighters now called themselves the Tigray Defence Forces (TDF)—had swept out of the central highlands and routed the Ethiopian and Eritrean armies, sending them scattering over the Tekeze River and across the open plains of Raya. Amhara fighters had fled Tigray, destroying bridges and looting grain and arms stores as they went. Then, on their tail a few weeks behind, had come the Tigrayans—and the start of a whole new phase of the war.

* * *

Following a string of spectacular victories across central Tigray, reputedly masterminded by the former Ethiopian army chief, General Tsadkan Gebretensae, the TDF had by July 2021 retaken almost all the region. Drawing on decades of experience in mobile guerrilla warfare, and, in particular, the old practice of rural ambushes and hit-and-run raids, it had eventually made short work of the Ethiopian military. Now led almost entirely by non-Tigrayan commanders who knew little about counterinsurgency, and fighting on mostly unfamiliar terrain, Abiy's army had, as one Tigrayan official later put it, bled to death "from a thousand small wounds". Ill-trained and poorly equipped, its infantry fodder came from among the most deprived communities of Ethiopia's far south and west. Morale was low and, as the months had dragged on, desertions spread.

The Tigrayan military leadership, by contrast, had mostly remained intact despite the chaos of the war's first months. They had behind them, too, a sizeable chunk of their pre-war force and some of their arms short of the heaviest weaponry. With the help of the Sudanese military, whose support for the TDF was by now an open secret, they were able to supplement these with supplies, including fuel, from across the border. Arms dealers in Khartoum, the Sudanese capital, had also managed to import artillery pieces and ammunition from munitions factories in Turkey, which were then smuggled into Tigray via entrepreneurial smugglers from—with some irony—Eritrea.

But much more importantly, the Tigrayan commanders had at their disposal tens of thousands of angry fresh recruits.[2] Composed of both men and women, some still in their teens, this new people's army was drawn from all sections of Tigrayan society—from farmers and teachers to lifelong opponents of the TPLF and even diaspora Tigrayans returning from abroad. Unlike the region's ruling party, the TDF enjoyed seemingly unanimous popular support across the entire region. What its troops lacked in professionalism—the Tigrayan generals had managed the remarkable feat of establishing training camps deep in the mountains west of Mekelle just a few months earlier—they more than made up for in determination and grit. Though many in the ranks had no previous love for the TPLF, a great number, perhaps an overwhelming majority, now hated the very idea of Ethiopia and passionately wanted independence. "No More Ethiopian," they scrawled in English on the walls of buildings they occupied, "I Am Tigrayan". All wanted revenge.

Even by the standards of a war whose pendulum would swing as wildly as this one, there would be nothing to match the surprise triumph of what was called "Operation Alula". Named after a nineteenth-century Tigrayan general, it was launched in mid-June—precisely at the moment when Abiy, increasingly worried about the Sudanese border, had begun moving troops from central to Western Tigray in anticipation of a showdown there. Over the following weeks, according to the TDF, as many as half the divisions in the Ethiopian army were destroyed, with some 10,000 soldiers killed.[3] How much this was an exaggeration was hard to know, but what was clear was that the battles had been desperately bloody, perhaps cataclysmically so, with visiting UN officials reporting roads so strewn with bodies that their vehicles had no option but to run right over them. "It looked like an African version of Pompei," shuddered one. On 28 June 2021, Tigrayan forces swept into a rapturous Mekelle with an ease which seemed to even take its own commanders by surprise; according to several sources who spoke to General Tsadkan the night before, he had been hesitant then to try and take the city for fear of destroying it. In the event, the Ethiopian army, as well as officials from the interim administration, evacuated the next morning with the haste of one fleeing a crime scene, pausing only to dismantle telecoms equipment, loot banks and raid a UN office. All that now remained for the triumphant TDF, whose march into Mekelle was trailed by thousands of bedraggled Ethiopian and Eritrean prisoners of war, was the return of Western Tigray and parts of Raya, both still under Amhara control, and the region's northernmost reaches which remained occupied by the Eritreans.

As federal troops scrambled towards the exit, Abiy's government suddenly announced a unilateral ceasefire. The reason, it said, was to give Tigray's war-weary farmers time to plant their crops, a belated if only implicit recognition of the impending famine which aid groups had been warning about for months. In a prickly speech a few days later, Abiy declared victory yet again over the TPLF. Now, he explained, the army's mission had been accomplished: Mekelle was no longer a "centre of gravity" but an ordinary town like any other—no more important even, in military terms, than his hometown of Beshasha. Tigrayans, he pronounced sullenly, should treat it as a period for reflection on the choices they had made.[4] Redwan Hussein, his national security advisor, told colleagues the government would now seal off the region so as to see how much Tigrayans really liked the taste of "freedom".

But the notion that the army's retreat from Tigray had been either orderly or voluntary was implausible. Though it was true, as Abiy himself had noted, that he had raised the material conditions of the troops, boosting their salaries and improving their housing, this could only ever buy him so much loyalty.[5] What the prime minister had really needed was time: to re-indoctrinate the officer corps, to replace the battle-hardened Tigrayan element which he had earlier forced out, and, most importantly, to put the institution as a whole firmly under his heel. This was crucial, for ever since Meles had died, Mao's famous adage—the party must command the gun—had been increasingly honoured only in the breach. Beginning under Hailemariam but continuing under Abiy, its leaders now openly meddled in politics and business. Berhanu Jula, the future chief of staff, flagrantly consorted with Oromo politicians, while his Amhara counterparts were the reputed drinking companions of Amhara nationalists. Though they did, contrary to the enduring belief of the TPLF's leaders, still answer ultimately to Abiy, corruption within their ranks persisted and internal divisions, especially ethnic ones, continued to hobble them right up to the eve of war. "The army was caught in battle at a time when Abiy was still building it in his own image," noted an Ethiopian security expert. However much the government might have insisted its troops were in full control of Tigray, simply mopping up sporadic resistance, the army's collapse had in reality been months, if not years, in the making. For those watching closely it had been all too predictable.

By the time the collapse happened, though, the TPLF was sensing victory. Almost immediately its leaders rejected the government's ceasefire offer. Over the next few weeks, a window which would later come to seem to some diplomats and mediators like a tragically wasted opportunity, the resurgent TDF prepared to continue the war against the Eritreans to the north. It also issued its own maximalist negotiating demands. These included the withdrawal of Eritrean and Amhara forces, with immediate effect, accountability for alleged war crimes and full humanitarian access, and, rather more provocatively, an insistence that Tigray have an effective veto over Ethiopian foreign policy.[6] The federal government refused doggedly to reply. Whatever fleeting opportunity there might have been for a genuine ceasefire and humanitarian opening evaporated. Instead, in the hope that economic ruin would do what military coercion had not, the government tightened the siege.[7]

From the very start of the war, and even before it, humanitarian aid to Tigray had been closely monitored and strictly limited. In late 2020 and early 2021, wheat piled high in Addis Ababa for weeks awaiting government clearances to go north. As Abiy would himself admit, the guiding—albeit erroneous—assumption among many Ethiopians was that the TPLF had won its guerrilla war in the 1980s with the help of international aid agencies, and he would be damned if he made the same mistake again.[8] From July 2021, his government therefore embarked on a new phase in its economic strangulation of Tigray. Now, in imposing what the UN's humanitarian chief would describe as a "de facto blockade", the federal government began restricting the supply not just of food but also life-saving medicines so vigorously that a British diplomat later described having to smuggle HIV drugs inside tampons in order to take them on a humanitarian flight to Mekelle. All communications in Tigray were cut off. The regional border was closed, and Tigrayan civilians were barred from leaving.

Efforts by the UN and America to persuade Abiy to change course were overwhelmingly unsuccessful. The incoming Biden administration, for instance, called on WFP's David Beasley to help them, hoping his old friendship with Abiy might lend him some influence. But on the crucial matter of aid restrictions, the devoutly Christian South Carolinian was notably reluctant to push the prime minister too hard. Top of their agenda when they spoke were God and family, he told frustrated colleagues, not the prosecution of the war: "we don't talk about politics," he admitted. With the WFP chief now effectively leading the international response to the siege of Tigray, the upshot was that whenever a petty bureaucratic restriction on what could enter the region was lifted—a ban on certain communications equipment, for instance, or a handful of essential medicines—this was generally hailed by Western officials as a diplomatic breakthrough. But really Abiy was following an established playbook: ceding a little ground to get the West off his back, while keeping the fundamentals of his military strategy firmly intact.

Given Ethiopia's long and troubled history of famine, there were few allegations more sensitive for the government than that it was using hunger as a 'weapon of war'. But, as UN investigators later concluded, that is exactly what it was doing.[9] For many months, government officials would offer an array of competing justifications for their restrictions: that aid agencies couldn't be trusted because they were biased toward the TPLF; that the TPLF itself was blocking aid convoys in order to reap the political benefits of a famine in Tigray; or that some of the food aid was being redirected in support of the insurgency (which was true, though hardly surprising, and nothing like on the scale the government claimed).[10] In private, though, some in government could be franker. When asked by a foreign researcher in August 2021 what the strategy for defeating Tigray now was, an official in the Prime Minister's Office bluntly replied: "we are going to starve them".

And so, in mid-July 2021, the TDF launched its own invasions. "We gave the international community ample time to respond," General Tsadkan told a British diplomat by way of explanation, "but it didn't." Having been urged by Western officials not to attempt regime change in Asmara, and assessing an offensive on Western Tigray to be too difficult and dangerous, the Tigrayans instead made the fateful decision to strike south into Amhara and east into Afar. The goal, its leaders now said, was to break the government's siege by raiding food and fuel stocks, and perhaps by opening up a supply line from Djibouti. More than that, they argued, only by bringing the heat of war close to him could they finally force Abiy to the table. But what most of them really wanted now, though they might not always admit so in public, was to remove him altogether.[11]

* * *

Abiy's own behaviour, meanwhile, had been growing more erratic. Just as word of atrocities first reached Addis Ababa in early 2021 he had disappeared from public view. Not for the last time, rumours swirled about his health, with some suggesting he had COVID-19. Around the time he finally reappeared at the end of January, looking gaunt and unusually dishevelled, a source inside the Pentecostal community claimed that he had simply been depressed. More cynical observers, however, noted that the studied use of absence to enhance the leader's mystique was a time-worn ruse of Ethiopian emperors. It was also one familiar to close watchers of Isaias.

Either way, he'd had good reason to avoid the limelight for a while. With the arrival of the new US administration that January, Washington's broadly accommodating stance toward his and Isaias's war effort had gone into sharp reverse. Trump and his officials had been fixated on competition with China, and saw the conflict in Ethiopia, if they saw it at all, through a narrowly ideological lens: a chance to deal a blow to Beijing by ridding them of the Chinese proxy in Africa which a handful of Republicans had always imagined the TPLF to be. Biden's team led by Secretary of State Anthony Blinken, by contrast, started out in 2021 with what was, at least at first, a refreshingly hands-on approach to the Tigray War and its seismic humanitarian impact. Even before taking office—and before even the start of the fighting—Blinken had attracted some attention in Ethiopia on account of an unusually strong public warning about the severity of the country's political crisis. Several others in the incoming administration also had significant experience and interest in Ethiopian affairs, and sought to make sure Biden paid them attention.[12] "The President and his advisors understood the significance of what was happening in Ethiopia," argued Payton Knopf, a regional expert appointed to the newly-established Office of the Special Envoy to the Horn of Africa. "And not just in humanitarian terms, but also in terms of what it meant internationally, that it wasn't just a minor war in some forgotten place but something with potentially major geopolitical implications". Now, in place of their predecessors' tacit support for a military solution, which stemmed from the mistaken belief that the federal army would swiftly defeat the TPLF, came a much more single-minded focus on getting the two sides to the negotiating table. (Though this was not, it is worth stressing, ever a concerted drive to remove Abiy from office.) The explicit threat of targeted financial sanctions against his government was intended to be the key tool for achieving it.

Though it wouldn't last the reordering of geopolitical priorities prompted by Russia's invasion of Ukraine the following year, the shift in the approach and tone of US officials was striking nevertheless. In a statement to Congress within weeks of taking office, Blinken shocked Ethiopian officials who had grown used to American coddling with a description of the violence in Western Tigray as "ethnic cleansing"—the very first time a foreign official of any stature had used the term. A few months later, the State Department began investigating allegations of crimes against humanity, with a view to establishing whether a genocide was taking place in Tigray. It also announced visa bans on several unnamed Ethiopian and Eritrean officials until they eased restrictions on humanitarian aid in Tigray and began peace talks with the TPLF—the first ratchet toward a full legal framework for potential sanctions which would be unveiled towards the end of 2021. Meanwhile, the Emiratis were pressured to stop supplying Abiy with drones—which, at first, they did. By June 2021, thanks to American lobbying, Ethiopia's civil war was second only to China on the list of geopolitical headaches to be discussed by Western leaders at the G7 summit in Britain.

Biden, for his part, shunned Abiy, neglecting to even make an official phone call to him until January the following year—a particularly hurtful rebuke for a prime minister keenly sensitive to matters of status and esteem, and who had, moreover, always aspired to make Ethiopia more like America. When Jon Lee Anderson of the *New Yorker* met with the prime minister the following year, Abiy would disparage the Biden administration as "*these* guys", and complain that they had "made the mistake of talking publicly and *down* to me."[13] Officials around him began describing the problem of US policy toward Ethiopia as a specifically Democratic one, drawing comparisons to the Carter administration's decision to break diplomatic relations after the Derg took power in the 1970s.

As Ethiopia's relations with the Biden administration's sank to a comparably low ebb, and Abiy became more and more convinced America was trying to oust him, he responded by reinventing himself as a champion of anti-colonial pan-Africanism.[14] Doing so required some elaborate shape-shifting. After all, the prime minister was not, and had never been, remotely pan-Africanist. In 2018, shortly after taking office, he had skipped his first African Union summit and sent a state minister to represent him instead—a snub unprecedented by any of his predecessors.[15] Nor had he allowed either the African Union or IGAD, the East African regional bloc, any part in mediating his peace agreement with Isaias, preferring to deal with the Emiratis and Saudis. Later, when a group of African leaders offered to mediate in the Tigray War, he bluntly told a senior American official that Ethiopia was a "real country", unlike the rest of the continent, and so wouldn't need their help. "Africans?" he asked the official, outraged. "What do we have to do with Africa?"

Nevertheless, beating the drum of 'African solutions for African problems'—the African Union's cherished mantra—Abiy now railed barefaced against the inequities of the same American-led world order which he had previously lauded. In an extraordinary series of public comments in the middle of 2021, he accused "countries with no history" of conspiring to colonise Ethiopia,[16] and implicitly depicted himself again as an Ethiopian Moses, this time resisting the might of the American Pharaoh.[17] Where once his rhetoric had seemed to challenge the limits of Ethiopia's political discourse—with its strict categories of exclusion and endless construction of 'enemies'—now he doubled down on them. "Just as there were during the Italian invasion, so there are traitors today who still think they will not prosper unless they sell their motherland," he declared, cutting a conventionally populist pose at the inauguration of a sugar factory in April. "We Ethiopians should understand that it is both an obligation and a priority first to eliminate and clean up the internal traitors, and then to struggle against the foreign enemies and stop them".[18]

Soon rallies reminiscent of the Derg era were being staged almost every other week.[19] Crammed into the same stadiums which not long before had been kept empty to staunch the spread of COVID-19, tens of thousands denounced Western imperialism while waving banners which praised Putin and Xi Jinping. Civil servants, in another throwback to the Derg, were ordered to attend. By September, popular support for the war, and anger at foreign criticism of it, had shaded into xenophobia. Private billboards were put up in parts of Addis Ababa calling for "white demons" to leave the country.[20]

Foreign journalists were singled out for particular opprobrium. Gone was the former enthusiasm for the Western press and associated institutions, such as the Committee to Protect Journalists, which had done so much to burnish Abiy's international image. Now it was common to hear government officials talk of a Western media conspiracy against Ethiopia, or of an organised campaign to besmirch the prime minister's name. "In the past it was easy to have an op-ed published in *The Economist* or the *New York Times*," complained Mamo Mihretu, the future central bank governor. "But now it feels like there's been some backroom discussion in the editorial rooms: that if it's from the Ethiopian government then it can't be published."

Even the most liberal or cosmopolitan now sounded fervently nationalistic. "This is our Adwa moment," said a senior Western-educated official involved in plans being drawn up to insulate Ethiopia's economy,

Iran-style, from the impact of future sanctions. "Of course, there will be implications on growth, no question. But if you compromise on your sovereignty for the sake of growth, you'll always be a slave. We've looked at it, line-by-line, putting aside projects we don't need for now. Yes, we have to tighten our belts. But we believe that time is on our side. Sleepy Joe is either going to die or be replaced—it's inevitable. It's a matter of surviving him for a year and a half. And anyway, the attention span of the West is like a three-year-old kid, so they will jump on another crisis soon enough."

Just as the Derg's defence minister had once called for enemies waging anti-Ethiopian propaganda in "prestigious newspapers and the international mass media" to be met with a response, so Abiy's government and its supporters now stepped up campaigns of their own to counter foreign pressure.[21] Across the diaspora, a flurry of new organisations—ostensibly independent but in practice aligned closely with the government in Addis Ababa—took the stage. At the forefront was Neamin Zeleke, who, now spending much of his time in Addis Ababa consorting with senior officials, established a coalition of online advocacy groups under the name of Global Ethiopia Advocacy Nexus (GLEAN) in December 2020.[22] Created with a view to pushing the official narrative of the war, countering Tigrayan allegations of atrocities and lobbying foreign governments against sanctions, GLEAN, in partnership with a series of foreign lobbying firms, would sow the seeds for some of the most organised and influential activism in recent Ethiopian history.

By blurring the line between the state and civil society—a trend personified in Abiy's appointment of a controversial social media pundit to run the Ethiopian Media Authority[23]—the new pro-government advocacy movement excelled at coordinating messaging and building critical mass online. For probably the first time ever, cabinet ministers and activists in the diaspora together exchanged hashtags and campaigning strategies. Abiy's press secretary, Billene Seyoum, played the role of central hub coordinator, ensuring that the government's backers all followed a single script. In a private WhatsApp group for government ministers and advisors established in May 2021, she announced the goal of turning all government institutions into "digital armies". New hashtags such as #TPLFisaTerroristGroup and #UnityforEthiopia were thrust into the Ethiopian cyber-sphere, to be amplified by voices and accounts all over the world.[24]

Over the course of 2021, as the Biden administration began mulling sanctions, these efforts consolidated under the banner of what became known as the #NoMore movement. Ostensibly a campaign against Western intervention and colonialism, the hashtag began trending on Twitter and Facebook around September, and was led by Ethiopianist activists in collaboration with prominent Eritrean supporters of the regime in Asmara. At the heart of its mission was the discrediting of Western media, or critical reporting on the war more broadly, and it made much hay with a handful of publications from opaque think tanks which pushed popular conspiracy theories linking international media organisations to CIA-backed regime change efforts.[25] Ostensibly impartial Western academics were also enlisted to amplify its talking points and to defend Abiy's government.[26]

By certain measures, #NoMore was a huge success. In a single day the movement produced more than 600,000 tweets; at their peak, by contrast, none of the Tigrayan campaigns such as #TigrayGenocide produced more than 250,000 (before quickly dropping off). All over the country, moreover, the movement's narrative of Ethiopia against the world seeped into public consciousness. Towards the end of the year, "#NoMore" in giant plastic lettering would be mounted in the centre of Meskel Square, while drivers in the capital slapped bumper stickers with the slogan over their vehicles. "Dubai is good for Ethiopia. And China is good," a young man in Bishoftu told me that autumn. "But America is like Satan. Why does America tell us to stop?"

Part of the strength of the #NoMore campaign lay in its vagueness. Beyond demanding an end to Western pressure on Abiy and Isaias, #NoMore became a stand-in for a diffuse resentment of 'neo-colonial' meddling, and of perceived double standards towards Africa. While some of these critiques may well have been justified, others were rather less so. In one moment, #NoMore might mean denouncing the French government's support for dictators in its former colonies in West Africa. In another, it meant rejecting defensible American efforts to halt mass atrocities in Tigray. Likewise, while #NoMore's attacks on Western media often spread Kremlin-backed conspiracy theories—many of those boosting the campaign were linked to Russian state-funded media—not all its criticisms of the international coverage of the war were completely unfounded. Foreign reporting was indeed sometimes sloppy. When the TDF drew closer to Addis Ababa in early November 2021, for instance, *CNN*'s rolling news coverage broadcast the wildly erroneous claim that advance units had reached the capital's outskirts. There was similarly never much evidence that thousands of troops from Somalia had participated alongside Eritrean ones in Tigray—a widely circulated allegation picked up by some Western outlets.[27]

#NoMore also tapped into—and skilfully exploited—specific narratives with special purchase in Ethiopia. One was the widespread allegation of Western double standards in its approach to the TPLF. Why, many Ethiopians asked, should they now be expected to take American concerns about human rights violations seriously, when it had so routinely turned a blind eye to them for nearly three decades under the TPLF-led EPRDF? Another was the profound fear many Ethiopians harboured about the very real prospect of state collapse. Rather than helping to avoid this outcome, some argued, by pushing Abiy too hard to the negotiating table the West was in fact making it more likely. "I do not believe Abiy and TPLF will actually make a real negotiated settlement at all," one academic with Ethiopianist sympathies explained to me. "It is not in the culture of the TPLF, nor is it found anywhere in Ethiopia's political history. There has to be a winner." In private conversations, the justice minister, Gedion Timothewos, was said to have put it more succinctly: "The *feranjis* [Westerners] do not understand the importance to our culture of victory and defeat." The power of #NoMore lay in its ability to conflate such anxieties, all the while tying them into an alleged global conspiracy to overthrow Abiy and put the TPLF back on the throne.

* * *

Abiy could be thin-skinned and prickly. He was also liable to crack down on outlets too directly critical of him: in early 2019, for instance, his office had forced a good-humoured satirical TV show off air for having gently mocked him.[28] In fact, it may well have been the TPLF's most personal barbs, in private when Abiy was campaigning to be prime minister, and in public in the months before the war, which did as much as anything to harden his resolve against them. His public speeches had often bristled with coded replies.[29]

On these matters and others, Abiy was not a liberal. Some of those who encountered him before he became prime minister noted a hostility towards the private and, in particular, social media; in his book, *The Stirrup and the Throne*, he had argued that Ethiopian society was not yet ready for "modern journalism".[30] Among his administration's more controversial pre-war measures was a law passed to counter online hate speech and 'disinformation'—one which, though taking aim at a very real problem, did so by criminalising 'fake news' and giving the government the power to define what that was. Unsurprisingly, too, for a Pente with ties to American Evangelicals, he was hostile to LGBTQ rights and, according to the former minister of women, children and youth, could be casually dismissive of feminist concerns. On his watch Ethiopia saw a spike in homophobic attacks, some of which were fanned by government institutions.[31]

Neither was Abiy a Western-style democrat. To be sure, even during the war in Tigray, when his speeches were at their most strident and populist, the extent to which he continued to draw, however counter-intuitively, on liberal democratic tropes could sometimes surprise. In public, his comments were often at odds with those of authoritarian leaders in other parts of the world; he did not, for instance, typically equate autocracies with competence and democracies with chaos. Because of this, he would never quite fit in the category of the modern 'strongman' used by commentators in the West, which usually included more openly anti-democratic figures like Trump, Putin and Brazil's Jair Bolsonaro.[32] Nonetheless, by the time of national elections, which were finally held in June 2021, the gulf between his public pronouncements and actual electoral practice had grown so wide there was no longer any way to reasonably reconcile them.

Reports of Abiy threatening to rig the elections if needed dated back to December 2019, when he was said to have done so in a meeting with several Tigrayan businessmen then mediating between him and the TPLF.[33] But the question of whether he had ever actually made such threats, however plausible, was by 2021 largely immaterial. The elections, once so totemic a matter that they had brought the country to the brink of civil war, were by then broadly inconsequential. The new date had been announced by the electoral board in December, shortly after the war began, but was not of its choosing. Birtukan Mideksa, its chairperson, told me at the time that she was unhappy with a decision which she said the government had foisted on her.[34] By the time the board's preparations gathered pace in early 2021, the dream of the 'free and fair' elections Abiy once promised had faded so much that even she ceased to use the phrase. Now, Birtukan promised, the goal was just to deliver a "different, participatory and representative election", or, as she told American senators, the "most transparent" vote in Ethiopian history. Powerless to influence the factors which really mattered, above all Abiy's imprisonment of his rivals, the board on her watch instead resigned itself to a kind of technocratic proceduralism—hiring more professional staff, for instance, or improving the registration of voters in hard-to-reach areas.[35] When it came to challenging the government for closing offices belonging to opposition parties, as they had done across Oromia, or for restricting the freedom of opposition candidates to campaign, there was little they could do.

Loudly echoed by a sizeable cohort of influential Ethiopianists in Addis Ababa, who continued to credit Abiy with vanquishing the TPLF, the government vaunted the election as the first exercise in genuine democracy in the country's history. But in the genuinely competitive 2005 vote, despite the violent crackdown which followed it, the opposition had won a large number of seats. This time, by contrast, almost the entire Oromo opposition had boycotted the polls. Moreover, due to spiralling insecurity about a fifth of constituencies would not take part at all, including the whole of Tigray as well as districts of Wollega and Benishangul-Gumuz. "It's a very quiet campaign," observed Ezema's candidate for mayor of Addis Ababa, Kebhour Ghenna. "We don't talk about issues; we don't address the issues which need to be addressed."

In the capital, with its relatively well-educated constituents and comparatively strong civil society, election irregularities were rare. In rural Oromia, however, there were stories of officials forcing people to register to vote, for instance by withholding state-subsidised rations of sugar or cooking oil from anyone without a voter card. In Amhara, a NaMA candidate complained that Prosperity Party officials were calling his wife and family and threatening them to stop him from running. When I visited Abiy's home district of Agaro and tried to interview the Ezema candidate running against him, I was made to do so not in his office, but in one belonging to the Prosperity Party—and with an attentive government official taking notes. Later that same day, I wandered into a hall set up for the village of Beshasha's residents to wait in before they cast their vote and found it decked exclusively with bunting celebrating the Prosperity Party. "The people believe in the election," a local official explained. "They want to show their love for the government."

That this was more of a coronation than an election wasn't really much of a surprise. Ethiopia was still run by a fundamentally authoritarian regime. In a society in which there remained few opportunities for advancement outside the party and the state, the ruling party's millions of members had a vested interest in seeing the system perpetuated.[36] Despite promises that the new Prosperity Party would, unlike the EPRDF, separate itself from the state, nothing of the sort had actually happened. By the time of the election almost all the so-called 'technocrats'—Gedion, for instance, or Mamo Mihretu—who had entered Abiy's administration from outside the EPRDF had either joined the new party or else, in a few vanishingly rare cases, resigned their posts. The concept of a sphere occupied by the state, distinct from that of the party, remained one which continued to exist only in the abstract. Once the election period had arrived, state resources were routinely used by the ruling party for its own campaigning purposes.

Compounding structural challenges like these was a leader who had sacrificed democratisation on the altar of a political project built on the premise that he alone was indispensable. Even from late 2020, well before the official campaign period had begun, the coming election was framed as a referendum on the person of Abiy himself. Billboards across Addis Ababa portrayed the vote as a direct and presidential one—"Abiy must go forward"; "Abiy is my choice"—and victory for him as providential approval for his battle against the TPLF. When the results were declared, the Prosperity Party would win more than 90 percent of the seats contested. The only significant opposition gains were in Amhara, and to a lesser extent Addis Ababa; this was, in any case, a reflection of the fact that the only major opposition parties remaining in the elections had been Amhara or Ethiopianist ones. To outflank them during the campaign, Abiy had made sure to run on a ferociously nationalistic and anti-Western ticket. After the results were in, he proceeded to co-opt them. Several nominally independent candidates, notably Daniel Kibret, were nothing of the sort; the Prosperity Party stood nobody against him, and he was later given a formal job in the Prime Minister's Office as Abiy's 'social affairs' advisor. Berhanu Nega, the leader of Ezema, joined Abiy's cabinet as education minister; Belete Molla, chairman of NaMA, was welcomed into the fold as minister of technology and innovation.

* * *

Politically, Abiy emerged from the election stronger and with a tighter grip on his party.[37] Though the event had not demonstrated the widespread public enthusiasm his supporters claimed, it had however provided an effective tool for the regime's own internal consolidation—testing the loyalty of its cadres and enabling it to shuffle political patronage around accordingly. But on the military and diplomatic front Abiy's position had never looked weaker. As election day had approached, the TDF captured a string of towns across Tigray, to which the Ethiopian airforce responded by bombing a marketplace just as vote-counting was underway, and killing scores of civilians. (In their retreat, Ethiopian soldiers also executed three aid workers from Médecins Sans Frontières who were trying to rescue the wounded.[38]) Meanwhile, in a closed meeting of the UN Security Council, Mark Lowcock, then the UN's humanitarian chief, said that parts of Tigray were now suffering famine—a sharp rebuke to the prime minister who, on polling day, would insist in a rare comment to the BBC that there was no hunger there at all. The long-held hope among the prime minister and his allies that a successful election would finally put to bed lingering international doubts about his legitimacy seemed increasingly in vain.

On 11 June, America's State Department said it was "gravely concerned" about the coming election and called on the government to promise talks with the opposition afterwards. By then it had already asked the IMF and World Bank to withhold economic assistance to Ethiopia. The EU, for its part, cancelled its election observation mission, citing bureaucratic obstacles making its work impossible. (Clumsy efforts by Ethiopia's intelligence services to bug its meetings with opposition members and local journalists—taping microphones under the tables— no doubt didn't help matters.) The only high-profile monitoring mission to show up was that of the African Union, which breezily gave the results its seal of approval.

Over the following months Tigrayan fighters would pour into Amhara and Afar, streaming down the mountains and along the main roads south in the direction of Gondar, Bahir Dar, Dessie and—ultimately—Addis Ababa. Within just a few short weeks they would reach the gates of Weldiya on the road through Wollo to the capital. To the west, they would penetrate within just 80 kilometres of Gondar. Where once Addis Ababa had been triumphalist, now it was Mekelle's turn. "Abiy Ahmed's war machine is essentially destroyed," claimed Getachew Reda on 23 July.[39] "If we settle the score, we will become masters of East Africa," a Tigrayan general told his troops.[40] As they marched, the Ethiopian army retreated, abandoning their heavy weapons to their enemies as they did. In the Amhara town of Dessie, where military training camps for thousands of volunteers had recently sprung up, an anxious young policeman confessed to me that the Tigrayans now had the military advantage. Across the road from us lay wounded soldiers, ashen-faced, on stretchers in a makeshift hospital tent.

Across Amhara and Afar, panic spread. Invoking the Battle of Adwa, Abiy called for total war. The president of Amhara ordered all armed residents to mobilise in a "campaign for survival", as the president of Afar called on his people to protect their land "whether by guns, sticks or stones". Under orders from the federal government, other regions including Oromia and the Somali state sent in their special forces.[41] Private businesses including banks were shaken down to raise money for the troops. Videos from Amhara showed truckloads of volunteers armed with little more than sticks, knives and machetes.[42] Such was the feverishness in the air by late July 2021 that within just an hour of my arrival in Dessie, then still some 80 kilometres from the frontline, I had been arrested and assaulted in the back of a police truck as bystanders clapped and jeered. My colleague, whose full name on his ID card was part-Tigrayan, had been accused of being one of the "junta". He was punched and kicked so hard his front teeth nearly came out. Not for the last time, I was accused of working for the TPLF.[43]

This was the mass participation phase of the war, in which ordinary civilians from every side took part and almost nowhere was left unscathed. Like the armies of mediaeval Ethiopia, in which civilians accompanied warlords into battle, providing sustenance to their troops, this expanding 'people's war' meant the line between civilian and combatant increasingly blurred. It also meant that forced recruitment, even sometimes of children, became a troublingly widespread feature. In Chenna, locals showed me a video of a captured Tigrayan boy who looked no older than fifteen. At the same time, though, they told me that their whole community including their own children had been supporting the war effort. "Everybody, including those students in Grade 9, 11 and 12 was fighting with the soldiers," said a middle-aged woman called Misanesh. "It's the same for Chenna as it was in Mai Kadra." Elsewhere in Ethiopia, particularly in Oromia, came reports of young men and women being dragooned onto buses and forced to join the army.

Chenna was not the only place where occupation by the TDF was harsh, and where field executions were routine. If anyone could be a combatant, then anyone might be a target. Similar scenes unfolded in Kobo in Wollo, for instance, where Tigrayan fighters were reported going door-to-door and killing young men and boys.[44] Sexual violence was also widespread. In Chenna, Amnesty found that Tigrayan troops raped dozens of women and girls as young as fifteen, sometimes in gangs and some in front of their children.[45] Meanwhile, in the desert of the Afar region to the east, I met nomadic pastoralists whose homes had been blown apart by Tigrayan shelling. At a hospital in Semera, the region's capital, I interviewed children whose bodies were blistered and charred from the blasts. As town after town fell to the TDF, voices calling for revenge grew louder. "I want to wipe Tigrayans off the face of the earth," said my driver in Chenna. "They are barbaric," Misanesh agreed. "They have no humanity in them. They slaughter priests and infants. They don't even spare the dogs when they kill."

* * *

As the long summer rains faded, and Ethiopia's highland skies cleared, the TDF drew closer to Addis Ababa. Making inroads at the same time, from the other end of the country, was the OLA. The two groups had been formal allies since August 2021, when the OLA's leader Jaal Marroo announced that they had agreed to work together to overthrow the government militarily—"speaking the language they want to be spoken to", as he put it. Fearful that their joint advance could further split the country, and perhaps even collapse it, America and the EU, both in public and in private, called repeatedly on the TDF and the OLA to stop. "We did a lot of diplomatic spade work to make sure Addis Ababa was not attacked and that peace talks could be launched," Payton Knopf, then US deputy special envoy, recalled.

But this did little to alter the now firm belief among many Ethiopians that the West was conspiring against them and had resolved to overthrow Abiy. Barely a week went by now without a statement from a senior official denouncing "foreign enemies", or a new conspiracy theory peddled by state media: that America was supplying Tigrayan fighters with drug-laced biscuits, for example, or that UN agencies were smuggling weapons. In August 2021, the government halted the work of Médecins Sans Frontières and the Norwegian Refugee Council. That same month Abiy ignored a request from Samantha Power, Biden's foreign aid chief and a well-known, if controversial, advocate of liberal interventionism, to meet with him during a high-profile visit to Addis Ababa. Instead, in an unprecedented diplomatic snub, Abiy appeared on television on the very same day at an air base in Afar—inspecting a new fleet of drones made by, of all countries, Iran. (When confronted by US officials, Abiy insisted they came from Azerbaijan.) Two months later his government would expel seven senior UN officials, accusing them of "meddling" in

Ethiopia's affairs—the largest single such expulsion by one country in the organisation's history.

In reality, the top leadership of several of the largest UN agencies in Addis Ababa were broadly supportive of Abiy's government. The leaked audio of an internal meeting in March 2021 on the subject of sexual violence in Tigray, to take one example, demonstrated just how instinctively sympathetic many UN officials were to the arguments of their Ethiopian counterparts.[46] Yet such was the force of official propaganda—and its narrative of Ethiopia alone against the world—that inconvenient facts like these were easily obscured. By the time I visited Chenna in October it had become commonplace to encounter militiamen speaking darkly of "*feranjis*" (Westerners) even fighting alongside the TDF.[47] The next month Abiy claimed in a televised meeting with his officials that "individuals not of Ethiopian descent" had been killed alongside the Tigrayans on the frontline in Amhara.[48]

At the end of October 2021, the TDF captured the strategic towns of Kombolcha and Dessie. Over the course of the next three weeks, they would link up with units of the OLA, advance at lightning speed some 200 kilometres southwards and even come within striking distance of Debre Sina—the last eminently defendable position on the road to Addis Ababa. If there were ever to be a moment when Abiy might actually fall, it appeared now to have arrived. Immediately, the government in Amhara imposed a curfew and shut government offices, saying that all state resources, including government vehicles, should be redirected to the war effort. As panic mounted on 2 November, Abiy declared the first nationwide state of emergency since the war began and urged ordinary citizens to prepare to fight to defend the capital. In Addis Ababa, authorities ordered residents to register their guns and organise by neighbourhoods; over the following weeks, my neighbours would take turns patrolling our street, carrying sticks and donning high-visibility jackets. With recriminations flying, domestic "traitors"—in practice, mostly Tigrayan or Oromo minorities in Amhara—were accused of sharing battlefield intelligence with the enemy. Some in Amhara began pointing fingers at Oromo elements in the army, accusing them of sabotage. In scenes reminiscent of America's hasty evacuation of Afghanistan three months earlier, foreign embassies began packing up and advising their citizens to leave the country. The capital's expatriate population hurriedly emptied.

For Tigrayans living outside Tigray these would be the most dangerous few weeks of the entire war. As the TDF and OLA advanced, calls on social media and diaspora broadcasters like ESAT for the mass internment of Tigrayans—or worse—grew louder and more explicit. On 3 November, following a string of death threats on Facebook, a Tigrayan professor in Bahir Dar University was gunned down outside his home by Amhara special forces. Elsewhere, residents turned on their Tigrayan neighbours, denouncing them to the authorities and calling for their arrest. In parts of Addis Ababa, armed vigilante groups were seen forcing their way into Tigrayan homes. In just a few weeks at least 15,000 Tigrayans, as well as many Oromos, were rounded up and thrown into detention. Though many were kept in police stations and disused schools in the capital, young men in particular—those deemed most dangerous—were bused off to camps into the distant south-west. So squalid were these, and so lacking in food, drinking water and basic medicines, that some detainees would perish from disease in them. Many feared that if the TDF captured Addis Ababa they would all be executed. "There were no files, no evidence," an official in the justice ministry who visited one of the camps told me a few weeks later. "There was no plan to put them through the formal justice process. It was all simply preventative."

For many it seemed as though history were again repeating itself. Within a week of the TPLF capturing Kombolcha and Dessie in 1991, talks between the TPLF and the Derg were in motion and Addis Ababa had fallen.[49] Mengistu had fled the country. Now, it seemed to many Tigrayans, a re-run was just within grasp. "Addis Ababa will submit to the TDF if it reaches the city," one Tigrayan activist overseas assured me. "There will be some resistance, and some of those who have been most vocal will flee. But most people will just adjust." When, on 24 November, Abiy announced that he would be heading to the battlefield himself, a move evidently intended to recall the martial emperors of centuries past, rumours began to fly that he and his family had in fact fled the capital or even the country. Scenting imminent victory, General Tsadkan claimed there was now no need to negotiate with him at all, bluntly telling one American official that it would be up to the West to pick up the pieces if chaos ensued.[50] A handful of analysts in the West declared the TDF's impending triumph to be total; others speculated about a coming army coup. International media outlets began preparing Abiy's obituary.

But Abiy was not Mengistu and this was not 1991. "We are Ethiopians when we live and we become Ethiopia when we die," he told a group of local journalists defiantly on 11 November, repeating words from his very first speech as prime minister. "We have no back-up country to which to run."[51] As the TDF approached Addis Ababa, and as diplomats and even some of his own allies began turning their minds to possible successors, the prime minister made it clear to American officials that his opposition to talks with the TPLF remained absolutely unwavering. "Everything runs up against, basically, the unwillingness of Abiy to engage in anything meaningful," said one senior American official at the time. "The question is really just how to confront the challenge posed by Abiy's enduring belief that he can win militarily."

Now, perhaps more than at any other point in his tenure, it was the sense of messianic certainty which seemed to be driving him. In speeches and public statements laced with Christian allegory, which included invocations of such martyrs as Christ himself, the prime minister cast the war as a fundamentally holy one.[52] All around him were like-minded Pentes who similarly saw the conflict as a cosmic struggle between good and evil. In private conversations, senior officials would cite biblical texts, while cabinet ministers made their way to the palace for private prayer sessions. In the first cabinet meeting after the war began, the former minister Filsan Abdi recalled, the prime minister had ended with a cry of "Hallelujah!"—to which his colleagues had shouted "Amen!" back. "The problem is his epistemology," one of his former advisors complained. "The problem is that when the methodology is religious—unscientific and anti-intellectual—then trials and tribulations are just part of God's plan. So even if things get worse you don't change course, because it is all part of God testing you. It means you externalise everything that goes wrong: there's nothing wrong with the vision, it's all the fault of the resistance. And that's what scares me."

But not all this was an exclusively Pentecostal frame of mind. In Christian Ethiopia, divinely-ordained bloodshed was nothing new: it dated back centuries, perhaps all the way to the ancient Axumite empire, and could be found in the Solomonic mythos of the country's greatest national text, the *Kebre Negast*.[53] In the likes of Daniel Kibret, whose hand was thought to be behind much of his most religiously inspired rhetoric, Abiy had a staunchly Orthodox constituency behind him, too. No less than the Pentes, it was leaders of the Orthodox Church—with the marked exception of its Tigrayan patriarch, Abune Mathias, who was placed under house arrest—who arguably did most to publicly bless the war and sanctify its excesses.[54] Though the church would later apologise for its failure to condemn the fighting, for which it blamed official pressure, the institutional support it lent the government caused great discontent among Tigrayan congregants and would lead eventually to a schism. Whatever private anguish many clergymen may have felt about it, there was no getting around the fact that the church's providentialism, with its deep roots in Ethiopian society, was implicated in the war and had helped inflame it further. "There is no doubt Ethiopia will emerge a winner," Abiy told Orthodox bishops as they blessed his election victory in October. "Ethiopia may face challenges and pay sacrifices, but in the end we will win. Because God is in our company."[55]

Thus, when the news came early in December 2021 that the Ethiopian army had finally turned the TDF back, recapturing a string of important towns in just a few days and forcing the Tigrayans into a humiliating retreat ultimately all the way back to Tigray, it would seem to many Ethiopians a mark unquestionably of God's favour. "The enemy is defeated," a triumphant Abiy said in footage broadcast on state TV on 1 December, wearing military jungle fatigues and scanning the horizon with binoculars near the frontline in Afar. The TPLF replied that this was just a "strategic withdrawal", a repositioning of its forces in order to avoid a bloody battle for Addis Ababa. But few Ethiopians were listening. Victory seemed assured, and like the triumph of Adwa 125 years earlier, so Abiy said, Ethiopia had prevailed. In an echo of previous declarations, the prime minister informed fellow African leaders that the war was all but over. "It wouldn't have been possible had my Creator not been with me," he would tell an audience of cheering diaspora Ethiopians the following month.[56] Now, it seemed, he might never need to compromise.

19

"DO YOU LOVE ME?"

THE ROAD TO PRETORIA

The most important thing, the prime minister insisted, was that nobody find out about the meeting. First, the Americans had suggested it be held at the US naval base in Djibouti—but with a population of just a little more than one million, Ethiopia's Red Sea neighbour was a place where everyone knew everything. If American mediators flew in Ethiopian generals for secret talks, word would surely get out. Nairobi, likewise, was impossible. Nobody trusted loose-lipped Kenyan politicians not to leak. The Tigrayans, meanwhile, were having none of Addis Ababa's preference for the UAE. Norway briefly seemed like a sensible alternative, but the Tigrayan generals no longer had passports and they hadn't been vaccinated against COVID-19. "Abiy didn't want to give them documents because he didn't want people to know," recalled a mediator. "He was very concerned about secrecy."

And so it was that after a "complex dance", as one involved put it, two Tigrayan and two Oromo generals met at a luxury beach resort on an island in the Seychelles in March 2022. Both sides were trepidatious. The two Tigrayans, Tsadkan Gebretensae and Tadesse Wereda, had travelled there side by side with the American mediators. With the war still raging there was no way they were going to risk flying in anything but an American military aircraft with US officials aboard. Until the final hour, it was unclear whether the federal commanders, Berhanu Jula, the chief of staff, and Berhanu Bekele, the trusted head of Abiy's Republican Guard, would actually show up. "Abiy could have pulled the plug at any time," said the mediator. For more than a year the prime minister had been unbending in his refusal to negotiate with the TPLF.[1]

In the event, the first talks to end the war went surprisingly smoothly. The four generals, who had known each other for decades and seemed to get on, had little trouble reaching a basic understanding. For the Tigrayans, the aim was to end the government's blockade of the region, a goal they shared with the American mediators. By early 2022, aid agencies were warning of mass starvation. Eight months since the Ethiopian army had withdrawn from Tigray, less than 10 percent of the food which the UN said was needed had reached Mekelle. No aid of any kind had entered Tigray since mid-December, and almost no medicine at all had been allowed in since June 2021. The region's main hospital in Mekelle was so bereft of life-saving medications that it had begun sending patients home to die.

For the federal government, which by this time easily had the upper hand in the conflict, the immediate aim was more specific: to stop the TDF resupplying itself. Since early February 2022, secret cargo flights, flying low over the Sudanese border so as to avoid radar detection, had been arriving in Mekelle and the northern Tigrayan town of Shire at night. In a meeting with foreign diplomats, Abiy had accused Egypt of transporting weapons and ammunition to the Tigrayans—an allegation which wasn't as far-fetched as it might initially have sounded. "Egypt provided arms and ammunition, via Sudan, including artillery, surface-to-air missiles and vehicles," a Western diplomat with first-hand knowledge later told me. "This is not speculation. It is a statement of fact." Egypt's goal, the diplomat asserted, was to find ways to pressure Abiy on the matter of the Renaissance Dam. TDF sources later said privately that they had bought at least some of these supplies with gold from mines around Shire.

The Seychelles talks were done and dusted within less than forty-eight hours. The two Ethiopian generals agreed to allow a phased reintroduction of aid supplies into Tigray followed by a gradual restoration of services; the Tigrayans promised an end to any external military assistance. Both sides agreed to begin by jointly announcing a cessation of hostilities. The mutual commitments were outlined to the American mediators who had been waiting on the balcony outside the hotel room in which the generals, unbeknownst to other guests, had been secretly negotiating. A few days later, on 24 March 2022, the federal government announced a truce. Clandestine flights into Tigray ceased.

* * *

The Seychelles talks may have been hushed up, but they did not come from nowhere. In the months which followed the TDF's sudden retreat to Tigray in December 2021, the sands of Ethiopian politics had shifted yet again. For the Tigrayans, the failure to reach Addis Ababa and overthrow the government had been a crushing disappointment, and a reminder of just how desperate their predicament really was. Their march on the capital had been remarkable in many ways, but it was also quixotic. Few of its leaders seemed to have any idea how they would stabilise the country in the aftermath of regime change, and few could explain how the still widely loathed TPLF might persuade the bulk of the population to accept its return to power in Addis Ababa. (In conversations with US mediators, they sometimes said the plan had been only to surround the capital until Abiy agreed to negotiate.) At the final hour, Abiy had managed to galvanise considerable popular resistance to the idea of a TPLF-OLA takeover.

Neither had the TPLF's political coalition-building been a great success. The unveiling of an alliance of ostensibly like-minded federalist forces at a signing ceremony in Washington DC that November had sounded to many Ethiopian ears far too much like the coalition of liberation fronts which took power in 1991.[2] If the intent was to signal that the TPLF had a broad church of fellow rebel movements from the peripheries behind it, the effect was rather the opposite. Few of the groups which signed on, with the exception of the OLA, had any more than a few hundred fighters under their command. The veteran founder of the Afar Revolutionary Democratic Unity Front, moreover, insisted to me his group were never a part of the alliance at all. Meanwhile, the OLA had repeatedly oversold its military capabilities, and by the end of the year had failed to deliver the gains in Oromia needed to take the capital.

The TPLF had also been given another reminder of just how isolated internationally Tigray now was. Far from supporting their regime-change bid, Western governments had actively recoiled from the prospect. What was more, Abiy's own efforts to rally foreign allies at the final hour had, by comparison, been remarkably successful. Despite American criticism, the Turks had agreed to furnish his forces with its own Bayraktar TB2 drones (though Turkish officials insisted this was a purely commercial transaction), and, less publicly, with a range of military support including satellite communications, reconnaissance, tanks and artillery. The Emiratis, having initially backed away under pressure from the Biden administration earlier in the year, had also returned to his side. In the final weeks of 2021, cargo flights ferrying, among other supplies, Chinese-made drones, were seen arriving from a military base in the UAE nearly every day.[3] The fleet of combat drones which the Emiratis provided, and which could barrage the TDF's already-stretched logistics with devastating precision, had been particularly potent as the Tigrayans drew closer to Addis Ababa. Perhaps more than anything else, TDF commanders later suggested, it was these last-minute supplies which had ultimately turned the tide of the war in Abiy's favour.

On top of this was the now unequivocal backing of China itself. Anxious about the fate of their investments in Ethiopia—factories, roads and railways, to name a few—the Chinese had spent most of the war hedging their bets, maintaining lines of communication with both sides so as to remain friendly with whichever emerged the winner. But as the TDF approached Addis Ababa they had sprung to Abiy's diplomatic defence. In early December, China's foreign minister made a conspicuously timed visit to Ethiopia—a move widely interpreted as a vote of confidence in Abiy. For the TPLF, with its own long and cherished relationship with the Chinese Communist Party, this was an especially harsh blow. "What we faced was a repeat of the Cold War era," said the Tigrayan former defence minister, Seeye Abraha. "A host of foreign actors were in full gear to destroy us. We were alone."

Abiy's return unscathed from the precipice had meanwhile sent a powerful message to the Ethiopian public. What hope the prime minister's opponents had once placed in toppling him now dissipated. Not only did it seem to confirm, at least for some people, the prophecies which had accompanied his rise, it also stood as a firm rebuke to anyone who underestimated his determination to stay in office. "Abiy's strength is, for me, almost absolute now," said one well-connected critic in the diaspora in early 2022. "I don't see any meaningful force emerging for some time to challenge his power."

His survival also served to give those looking to remove him through force a salutary reminder. The Ethiopian state, as weak and fragmented as it undoubtedly now was, had nonetheless proven sufficiently formidable to ward off challengers. If the TDF, by far the most organised and equipped military force in the country besides—and, perhaps, even including—the federal army itself, had been unable to defeat it, what hope did other rebel groups have? "What makes Abiy strong is not just his acumen, his manipulation or his guile," observed another well-placed Ethiopian analyst. "It comes down to the nature of the Ethiopian state itself: its repressive capacity, its ability to instil fear among its critics and detractors even when it is weak; its propaganda apparatus; the ideological power of Ethiopian nationalism." Abiy's massive recruitment drive in the second half of 2021 was thought to have doubled the federal army's total strength to an estimated 350,000 personnel.[4] "We underestimated the power of the state, that's where we fucked up," one of Abiy's most influential Oromo critics, who by then had returned from Ethiopia to America, later admitted. "We didn't quite understand what it means to be PM in Ethiopia: that there is God, and there's Abiy. People are there to serve him, as if it's God's will."

And so it was that Abiy was able to mark Ethiopian Christmas in January 2022 with a display of magnanimity befitting an emperor: pardoning and freeing his most prominent opponents. Among those released from prison that month were Jawar, Bekele Gerba, Eskinder Nega and—to the particular horror of Abiy's Ethiopianist allies—six TPLF officials including its octogenarian founder, Sebhat Nega.[5] Over the following weeks detention camps holding thousands of Tigrayan civilians were also emptied gradually. "The birth of Christ didn't mean that everything was over," read Abiy's Christmas statement, "but rather that it was a time of mercy."[6]

* * *

But despite a measurable revival in his political fortunes, on the military front Abiy had begun 2022 mulling a change of direction. This was not, it was clear, on account of any popular pressure: there was still no grassroots peace movement in Ethiopia to speak of. When Tariku Gankisa, a popular musician from the south, had spoken out against the war at a government rally in November 2021, he was hounded so ferociously by government officials and state media that just one week later he appeared on TV delivering a tearful apology. But there were nevertheless other factors affecting the prime minister's calculations. For one thing, the UAE, his most important ally, now counselled restraint. Having done their bit to keep the TDF at bay, their support for his military adventures, the Emiratis now emphasised, couldn't be open-ended. Rather than push again into Tigray in a doomed bid to crush the TPLF once and for all, now was the time, they stressed, for a negotiated settlement. It was advice that put the kingdom back, for a short while, on the same page as America and the EU. At the same time, its officials also began to echo their American and

European counterparts in suggesting that the primary obstacle to peace in Ethiopia was Isaias's Eritrea.

But as an internal Prosperity Party document written that December indicated, and some of his colleagues confirmed, opening negotiations with the TPLF was an idea which increasingly seemed to have traction with Abiy himself. "These are the kind of suggestions we made in the last meeting of the executive committee: one, we should re-establish our contact with the West; two, we should start negotiations with the TPLF at some point. We should also release political prisoners," a senior figure in the ruling party pushing for dialogue told me at the time. "The prime minister fully agreed. He seemed to be on board." Plans to advance deeper into Tigray once the TDF had retreated fully inside Tigray's borders were therefore put on hold. Proposals to talk to the TPLF were, for the first time, not ruled out.

Among several other reasons Abiy had to consider changing course was his fraying friendship with Isaias. By this point, according to one senior Western official who met with him at the time, the prime minister was showing obvious "buyer's remorse" over his reliance on his Eritrean counterpart. "He was very explicit," the official recalled. "He said Isaias was 'a threat to everyone'—that you can't speak to him, you can't deal with him. He didn't mince his words." This was not the first time that word of a bust-up had got out: when American officials had met with the Eritrean president the previous year, Isaias had spoken of Abiy as though he were a child, said one of those present, even claiming to have "saved Ethiopia— that if he hadn't intervened when he did, Ethiopia would have collapsed." But if rumours of personal differences had previously been helpful for Abiy (as evidence of Eritrean war crimes had mounted, he may even have done something to encourage them), by the start of 2022 genuine cracks in their relationship seemed to be emerging. In January, the very day after Abiy had released some TPLF leaders from prison, Isaias had given an interview in which he claimed, in effect, the right to intervene in Ethiopia indefinitely in order to eliminate the TPLF's "troublemaking".[7] Abiy said nothing publicly in return; he did, however, make several clandestine visits to Asmara around the same time. As the months went by, and the two leaders' war aims began to diverge further, other signs of a cooling began to appear: sudden roundups of Eritreans living in Addis Ababa, for instance; closer scrutiny of Eritreans passing through Addis Ababa airport; reports (though never confirmed) that the two leaders hadn't spoken for months. Not once between the start of the war and July 2023 were the two seen together in public.[8] By the end of 2023, Abiy had even started to make bellicose noises about Ethiopia's need to take back control of Eritrea's ports—by force if necessary.[9]

What exactly Isaias was really thinking remained, as ever, inscrutable. Abiy's decision—under military duress from the TDF, no doubt—to pull out of Tigray in June 2021 without notifying him seems to have been treated as a personal betrayal. "They [the Eritreans] were hurt," said Andargachew Tsige after meeting with Eritrean officials including Isaias in Asmara two years later. Doubtless Isaias's original goal, at a minimum, had been the end of the TPLF and revenge for Eritrea's defeat in the 1998–2000 war. But it is possible there was always more to his ambitions than this alone. In a private meeting with the UN's special envoy to the region, the Eritrean president claimed that his troops were inside Ethiopia in order to bring about constitutional change—an end to ethnic federalism, in other words—and that they would fight to the last man to deliver it. Though many observers long assumed that Isaias always had a strategic interest in keeping Ethiopia internally divided—the better to minimise any threat to Eritrea it might pose—another plausible theory has it that what he actually wanted was a weak but centralised state which he could more easily influence and dominate. A messy federal structure, according to this theory, would always be much harder to deal with.

Equally, though, there might also have been more immediate concerns at stake for Eritrea: money. Since the 2018 peace deal, Eritrean traders and businessmen linked to Asmara had acquired a substantial foothold in the Ethiopian economy. This included the real estate market in Addis Ababa and the lucrative black market for foreign exchange. By 2021, it likely also included sesame exports from Western Tigray.[10] Leeching off the much larger Ethiopian economy had been Isaias's strategy in the 1990s, and part of what caused the war in 1998. Some now feared this was part of his strategy for survival once again.[11] Either way, few doubted that the alliance with Abiy, whose fight with the TPLF was of comparatively recent origin, and who might therefore be more amenable to compromise, had an expiry date. "It was inevitable that the relationship wouldn't endure," said a veteran Ethiopian diplomat in early 2022. "They came together because of their shared hostility to the TPLF. But the difference between them is structural. Isaias wants the TPLF to be destroyed regardless of the cost to Ethiopia. Abiy needs to have a country left to rule."

Compounding Abiy's worries was the strengthening bilateral relationship between Asmara and Amhara. Like anything involving the Eritrean government, these ties were extraordinarily opaque and generated considerable speculative froth over the years. But there was certainly substance to it. In Western Tigray, where Eritrea shared with Amhara the strategic imperative of keeping the TDF away from the Sudanese border, Eritrean troops had been well-entrenched since the start of the war. Relations between Eritrean officers and Amhara officials there were especially close: when a foreign researcher managed to visit the district capital of Humera in 2021, he saw the latter presenting Eritrean commanders with a portrait of Isaias as a gift. By 2022, reports that Amhara special forces and *Fanos* were receiving training from Eritrean officers were also well-attested.[12] An internal Eritrean strategy document leaked in 2022 stressed the paramount importance of strengthening Amhara's military and intelligence apparatus, and of building closer ties between it and Eritrea.[13]

Militarily, from the point of view of Amhara officials, Eritrean support was essential to prevent the TDF from re-taking Western Tigray. But politically, too, the alliance had its advantages. Amhara mistrust of Abiy had grown exponentially over the course of 2021, in particular since his army had retreated from Tigray and the TDF had invaded Amhara. By the end of that year the popular perception of an Amhara ascendancy established in the wake of the war had decisively flipped. Among many Amharas, the marked preponderance of Oromos in the upper echelons of the federal military apparatus, in particular, as well as their expanding footprint in Addis Ababa, were a source of mounting, at times almost existential, alarm. Fears began to spread of a fast-consolidating Oromo 'hegemony'—an exaggerated claim, but in the realms of business and security, not one without foundation.[14] With recurrent killings of Amharas living in western Oromia throughout 2022, and the increasingly aggressive and expansionist behaviour of *Fano* militants along their shared border, tensions between Amharas and Oromos were only worsening. As they did, many Amhara nationalists came to see Isaias as a more dependable ally than Abiy. In May, as though to confirm their fears, the federal government began arresting thousands of *Fano* leaders and Amhara nationalist critics. Among them was Tefera Mamo, the former head of the Amhara special forces who had publicly called for stronger ties with Asmara and was said to have been meeting secretly with Eritrean officers.

For his part, the prime minister had been growing wary of both his Amhara and Eritrean allies. Releasing Jawar and other Oromo leaders from prison was therefore intended—at least in part—to loosen his dependence on both of these allies and pivot back towards his Oromo nationalist base. Jawar, no longer behind bars but under orders from Berhanu Jula, the army chief, not to challenge the government too directly, had increasingly come to seem like a potential asset for Abiy. For one thing, pardoning him could be presented as a token gesture of conciliation towards the Oromo opposition. What was more, the still influential Oromo activist was also someone the prime minister could work with—tacitly, at least—to put pressure on the Amhara nationalists and businessmen who continued to lobby, either in public or private, for a final offensive against the TPLF. No longer free to criticise the prime minister in public, and, in any case, more inclined after leaving prison to play the role of peacemaker than agitator, Jawar—for now—ceased to be such a sharp thorn in the government's side. Over the coming months and years, he would spend ever less time in Ethiopia, eventually settling in Nairobi. Abiy's own stock among some of his Oromo opponents began ever-so-slightly edging upwards.

Tentatively distancing himself from both Isaias and hardliners in Amhara had the added benefit of helping Abiy mend bridges with the Biden administration. Since taking office in January 2021, Secretary of State Anthony Blinken's team had sought to use the threat of sanctions to push Abiy into talks with the TPLF. But this approach had run into opposition from the US Treasury, which worried that sanctions were being overused as a tool of American foreign policy, and which feared that imposing them on Ethiopia might inadvertently hasten the collapse of the central state. It had taken until that September for Biden to finally issue the executive order which was to pave the legal path for a full sanctions regime. (For similar reasons, the administration withheld the findings of the report it had commissioned to determine whether the Ethiopian government was committing atrocity crimes in Tigray until 2023.)[15] But by the time the executive order had been announced the dynamics of the war in Tigray had significantly altered.

Militarily, Abiy by then was on the backfoot. Politically, too, he had started to come under some pressure internally from certain officials anxious he not alienate Ethiopia's most important foreign ally any further. In May 2021, the prime minister had dispatched a secret delegation to Washington to try to come to terms with the Biden administration. On the surface it hadn't achieved much. Throughout the summer, Ethiopian state media was awash with virulent anti-Americanism, which included targeted campaigns against Blinken, and a particularly vicious one against USAID chief Samantha Power. Behind the scenes, though, the meetings had helped to improve communications between the two governments. The Ethiopian officials who returned to Addis Ababa from Washington went on to play a role in gradually, though not immediately, convincing Abiy not to further worsen relations. Fortunately for the prime minister, this coincided with the appointment, that September, of a new Assistant Secretary of State for African Affairs: Molly Phee, a career diplomat who had previously served as US ambassador to South Sudan and was known for her opposition to financial sanctions.

When it came to actually imposing punitive measures in November 2021, therefore, it was only Eritrean entities that were targeted: Eritrea's ruling party, two affiliate companies including the Red Sea Trading Corporation, the Eritrean Defence Forces, and two senior Eritrean officials. Mooted sanctions against General Abebaw Tadesse, Ethiopia's deputy chief of staff and known point-man for dealings with the Eritrean army, and perhaps some other Ethiopian officials, were put on ice. The decision to target only Eritrean entities was not just about trying to disrupt the illicit economy bankrolling Isaias's military operations—though, by focusing on the Red Sea Trading Corporation, it was partly about that. It also sent a signal to Abiy that the US government ultimately blamed Eritrea more than Ethiopia for the war, and that if America's relationship with Isaias was unfixable, its relationship with him was not. But less widely understood at the time, though no less important, the sanctions sent a message to Abiy's allies in Amhara—and, in particular, the businessmen there known for their links to Eritrea who were widely believed to be helping finance the war. By doing so, recalled Payton Knopf, the deputy US special envoy, "we were also signalling to Abiy that we are willing to do things that will give him political space. And I don't think that was lost on him."

The day before releasing his opponents, Abiy invited Feltman, the US special envoy, to meet with him one-on-one in Addis Ababa. No longer convinced, it seemed, that America was planning to overthrow him, Abiy now informed the envoy that he was ready to talk to the TPLF. In previous meetings that year, Feltman observed, the prime minister's behaviour had been "capricious": on certain occasions charming but on others hostile. Prior commitments regarding, in particular, opening up humanitarian access to Tigray had notably not been fulfilled. "There was always this performative quality to the meetings we had," Feltman recalled. "But this time he conveyed an entirely different approach to what he'd previously conveyed to us." Three days later, on 10 January, the prime minister was rewarded with a personal phone call from Biden himself, something he had been affronted not to have received earlier. "Abiy sees himself in almost mythic terms, as a strong leader bringing Ethiopia into the future, but whom Biden had been ignoring," Feltman argued. "So this was an important reciprocal step from us." The message Abiy conveyed to the US president was much the same as what he had told the special envoy earlier: that he was willing to talk. For the first time, the mediators believed, there might really be a chance to stop the war.

* * *

Having halted the TDF's advance on the capital, Abiy's ambitions were now somewhat more modest. Gone, it seemed, was the conviction that the TPLF could be wiped from the face of the earth. "I think he realised a military victory wouldn't be possible in the end," said one Western diplomat who met with him in this period. "Winning meant killing literally every Tigrayan. And killing six million people is actually hard." What was more, war seemed ultimately to bore him. So did being unpopular with the West. Annette Weber, who took over as the EU's special envoy to the Horn and met with the prime minister in 2021, remarked that Abiy seemed to want to talk about almost anything other than the conflict: his tree-planting campaign; his plans for regional integration; his economic initiatives. Salva Kiir, South Sudan's president, likewise noted that Abiy wasn't much of a war leader because war didn't seem to interest him much.

What Abiy really wanted to talk about were his grand visions for Ethiopia's future: luxury tourism, for instance, or national food self-sufficiency. War was a distraction. After all, as much as Abiy was messianic, fuelled by an unflinching belief in God's purpose for him, he also had a more pragmatic—some would say materialistic—side. Endless war and international isolation spelt ruin for Ethiopia's economy. It also meant that the personal projects to which he was so devoted, not least his new palace in the hills above Addis Ababa, might eventually run aground. "It was really clear that the economic situation was all that got Abiy's attention," observed another US official. "And it wasn't the USAID's development funding that concerned him, but private investment."

Throughout the Tigray War, and long after it, Abiy had remained doggedly boosterish about the state of Ethiopia's economy. In speech after speech, the prime minister painted a relentlessly upbeat portrait of booming exports and expanding agricultural production. His economic advisors, meanwhile, consistently shrugged off the economic impact of the fighting, portraying Tigray's economy as self-contained and largely irrelevant. "Certainly not a big macro-economic issue," Mamo Mihretu, the future central bank governor, told me in early 2021. Officials insisted that year that the economy would grow by eight percent (the IMF expected only two percent). Thanks to the belated sale of a telecoms licence to a consortium led by Safaricom, a Kenyan operator part-owned by the UK's Vodafone, for $850m (another $150m for a mobile money licence was added in 2023), central bank receipts recorded a record FDI inflow in the second quarter of 2021.[16]

But the reality, which by 2022 Abiy surely knew, was that Ethiopia was fast entering a balance-of-payments crisis. Investment—both public and private, foreign and domestic—had collapsed with the first gunshots in the north.[17] Though not immediately felt across the board, with some sectors, such as gold mining, briefly rebounding, by 2022 no amount of 'positive thinking' or statistical chicanery could hide the brute facts of a collapsing economy. GDP growth, already flagging before the onset of COVID-19, had sunk even further. Even by the most optimistic estimates, annual growth had fallen to around six percent. The IMF, by contrast, reckoned it would slow to just 3.8 percent in 2022—partly as a result of the war in Ukraine, which erupted in February, as well as a severe drought in parts of the country. Neither estimate was close to what was needed for a poor country with a population projected to double in just three decades. Analysts now warned that after two decades of expansion Ethiopia's growth 'miracle' had come to an end.[18] By the close of 2022, more than thirty million Ethiopians needed emergency aid—more than anywhere else in the world. In the towns and cities, food price inflation had jumped over thirty percent for the first time in years, an eye-watering level in a country where the average salary earnings had barely budged at around $60 a month. A sense of desperation was everywhere in the air. "I can't survive here," fretted a woman who worked as a cleaner for a house of expatriates in Addis Ababa. "There is no future here."

By May 2022, Ethiopia's foreign currency reserves had, in the dry euphemisms of financial management, reached a "critical level".[19] In private, central bankers would spell out what this meant: enough to cover imports for less than one month.[20] Money which could have been spent on development had been redirected to the war effort. According to the central bank's vice-governor in early 2022, defence spending was $1.5 billion a year more than it had been before the fighting began.

"The economic consequences are beyond what the country can bear," he admitted. So acute was Ethiopia's budgetary crisis that by 2023 there would be reports of civil servants going without their salaries and of government offices being forced to close.

Major international firms now had no choice but to scale down production or mothball their facilities. Pepsi, for instance, stopped manufacturing soft drinks because it didn't have the raw materials; Dangote, Africa's largest cement producer, could no longer get hold of enough foreign currency to import coal. By one estimate, Ethiopia's entire manufacturing sector was operating at below half its capacity. Given this state of affairs, the Biden administration's announcement in November 2021 that it would freeze duty-free access for Ethiopian goods under the African Growth and Opportunity Act—because of human-rights abuses—was merely the final hammer-blow. Just weeks later, PVH, the American clothing company and original multinational to set up shop in the flagship Hawassa Industrial Park, announced it had sold its factory there. By early 2023, business in Hawassa, once one of the great hopes for African industrial development, was "totally dry", according to a factory manager, with firms leaving and workers idle.

For Abiy and his allies, the trouble was the West, and what they believed to be its deliberate efforts to destroy the Ethiopian economy. The country was in dire need of help from the IMF before a $1bn Eurobond payment fell due at the end of 2024. According to the fund's own analysis, Ethiopia would face a financing gap of at least $6 billion until 2026.[21] But by 2022 all that it had received of the much-trumpeted $3bn IMF loan programme signed shortly after Abiy took office were so-called 'special drawing rights' equivalent to no more than about $308 million. Despite his administration's ostensible fealty to IMF-sanctioned reforms, which included implementing sharp spending reductions, which hurt the poor, nothing more had ever been handed over.

This was in large part, as Abiy well knew, because America and other Western donors had since 2021 privately insisted that any loan be contingent on a cessation of hostilities in Tigray. America is the largest shareholder of both the IMF and the World Bank, and wields an effective veto over funding decisions. But there were other reasons, too, behind the delay. Ethiopia's decision to apply for debt relief, under the so-called "Common Framework" established by the G20 a year earlier to help countries battered by the COVID-19 pandemic, had also thrown the whole IMF programme into limbo.[22] This was not, by any stretch, all the

Ethiopian government's fault: getting the financial assurances from all the creditors necessary to secure the IMF loan was complex and time-consuming, and, what was more, the whole framework itself was critically flawed—in part because it pitted China and Western creditors against each other over the matter of debt cancellations and delayed repayments. But it didn't help matters, either, that Ethiopia's negotiators lacked experience in sovereign debt restructurings: posting photos of private negotiations on social media, as they did on occasion, typically went down badly with bondholders. "The Ethiopians are punching above their weight," complained one of the country's debt holders. "They have a lot of fluff but sometimes lack substance."

The IMF, for its part, had also grown increasingly concerned by the government's lack of financial transparency. It remained unclear, for instance, how exactly Abiy was funding his major city projects, including the new palace, since these were 'off-book' and beyond the reach of auditors. Early in 2023, reports emerged of the central bank, in effect, printing money for them.[23] Many reckoned that Abiy's personal projects also enjoyed priority access to scarce foreign exchange, though nobody outside Abiy's close circle seemed to know for sure. His purchase of combat drones during the war, as well as other military supplies, was also notoriously opaque. One senior insider told me these had been paid for with gold exports; others have claimed that large tracts of land in Ethiopia's peripheral regions had been granted to Gulf investors. None of this made negotiating with international creditors any easier.

By appointing Mamo, a World Bank alumnus and tested loyalist, to the central bank in late 2022, Abiy probably intended to reassure the IMF of his government's budgetary probity and steadfast commitment to market reforms. But despite the economically liberal, or to its critics, neoliberal slant of Abiy's administration, the state had never really retreated much from the economy's commanding heights. Since 2018, the reach of the party-owned parastatals, in particular, had if anything grown.[24] So had the public enterprises owned by the regional governments, such as Oromia's Tumsa Development Group, which was notorious for its coercive resource extraction in Oromia. (Getting a job at such firms also typically required being a member of the Prosperity Party.)[25] Abiy's flagship wheat production initiative, which aimed at national self-sufficiency by 2023, was also overwhelmingly state-led. Even METEC, the ERPDF's state-owned military-industrial conglomerate broken up in 2018, was mooted to be resurrected under a new brand and management.[26] Moreover, though the prime minister and his economic advisors were instinctively liberal—with Abiy himself often framing economic problems in terms of individual moral failings—they were generally Ethiopian nationalists first, which meant that when negotiations with the IMF eventually resumed in 2023 they wouldn't be plain sailing. "Abiy is a market liberal person—fundamentally, that is his worldview. But he's constrained by structures," noted one of his former advisors. "You can be a strong liberal market economy or a strong sovereign country. You cannot be both."

The economic liberalisation sought by the IMF, Western donors, Mamo, and in theory Abiy himself, had also been knocked off course by the war. The pace of currency devaluation, for instance, a key IMF concern, had slowed almost to a halt since the fighting began. Responding to crippling dollar shortages, the government had, contrary to IMF orthodoxy, reintroduced import bans on consumer goods deemed unnecessary luxuries, such as cosmetics, chocolate and cigarettes—a move typically exhorted by Abiy as the patriotic duty of individual citizens to obey. (The ministry of industry, meanwhile, pursued a three-year-plan for national self-sufficiency in some ninety-six products including food, beverages and textiles.) On the surface, the reluctance of Abiy's administration to fully liberalise the foreign exchange system was no mystery: a weaker currency would likely fuel further inflation, and perhaps social unrest. But the government also had something of a vested interest in maintaining the existing regime as it was. By 2022, as dollars dried up almost completely, the state was effectively the only entity left in the entire Ethiopian economy which still used the official exchange rate. Whatever donor funding still flowed to government coffers in the wake of the war had therefore become, in effect, an indirect budget subsidy.[27]

The war had also spurred a substantial increase in government corruption.[28] "If the EPRDF was an ordinary hyena," admitted an Oromo official in Addis Ababa, "the Prosperity Party is a hungry hyena." As the cost of living skyrocketed, low-level officials increasingly demanded bribes in exchange for even the most basic of government services. Senior ones were said to hire private planes just to travel the country for routine business. Money-laundering, meanwhile, boomed. "In the past, you entered politics in Ethiopia to improve your social status," observed one opposition leader. "Now people get to power literally just to get rich." Over the course of 2022, gold exports sank by almost two thirds, partly due to smuggling.[29] Public procurement became ever more opaque and graft-riddled. Authorities in Addis Ababa, for instance, were reported to have paid $71m for 200 Chinese-made buses; when the final cost was revealed, it was three times that amount.[30] Later in the year, a low-level employee in NISS, the national intelligence agency, texted me to ask whether I could connect him with "an international mafia group" which wanted to do business in Ethiopia. "We can handle the airport and the security," the text read. "We can prepare everything easily. Just like that." An anti-corruption committee established around the same time declared the problem so acute as to constitute a threat to national security.

But perhaps nowhere was corruption and abuse of power more pervasive than in the burgeoning wheat-growing sector. In order to reduce Ethiopia's import bill and perennial reliance on food aid, and thus its susceptibility to the pressure of foreign donors during the war, Abiy had from 2021 pushed for a massive expansion of state involvement in wheat production. Following a directive to switch to wheat even in those parts of the country that traditionally grew other crops, the government began distributing subsidised fertiliser to farmers, while mandating them to switch away from the more profitable tomatoes, vegetables or onions. According to Abiy, this was an existential imperative, a patriotic endeavour in a time of war. By early 2023 he would boast that it had already met its targets, claiming that Ethiopia was not only self-sufficient in wheat but also exporting it to neighbouring countries.

The reality, though, was much less rosy. Under the cover of the conflict, and the state of exception which still governed it, the wheat import-substitution programme had ultimately ended up resembling a form of violent kleptocracy. Farmers were forced at gunpoint to sell to government co-operatives at well below market prices. Those who refused had their product confiscated, with security forces carrying out house searches and arrests and threatening farmers. To make matters worse, in 2023 it was revealed that government officials and military officers had been involved in systematically syphoning off wheat supplied by donors as food aid, either to sell it on the local market or to export it to meet Abiy's targets. By June of that year, WFP and the US government had got wind of the scheme, and suspended all food aid to Ethiopia for more than six months. US officials later described it as organised theft on an "industrial scale"—perhaps the largest diversion of American aid in history.[31] Bread shortages at bakeries across the country, meanwhile, had worsened—in part thanks to these exports. Food prices surged.

* * *

For three months, by August 2022, the guns in Ethiopia's north had been mostly silent. The Tigrayan forces which had laid waste to much of northern Afar since January, officially in order to secure a buffer zone so that Eritrean forces couldn't use it as a launchpad to attack Mekelle, had withdrawn to Tigray. Eritrean troops had mostly retreated to their own border. Ethiopia's federal army had barely fired a shot since December 2021, with its generals now keeping in regular touch with their Tigrayan counterparts. Abiy's government no longer called the TPLF a "terrorist organisation" in its public statements, insisting instead that it was ready to talk with its leaders—anytime, anywhere. The World Bank had already announced a $300 million grant for post-war reconstruction.

In fact, though, Abiy had been dragging his heels. In the days and weeks which followed the Seychelles talks, the generals' mutual understanding, or what one mediator described as a "gentleman's agreement", had unravelled. Rather than wait to announce a 'cessation of hostilities' together, as agreed, the federal government had gone ahead and done so unilaterally—describing it, as though simply Abiy's gift to bestow, as a "humanitarian truce" without any terms attached. Abiy later hinted to mediators that he couldn't have allowed the Amhara allies on whom he still depended to know he had been secretly negotiating with their enemy. Because nothing had been written down, both sides cried foul.

There was also a lack of clarity to the terms by which the blockade on Tigray was to be lifted, and which the American mediators had notably failed to clear up. The TPLF was insistent that aid had to flow through Afar before its troops could withdraw to Tigray's borders, citing—quite rightly, from the perspective of international humanitarian law—the principle that life-saving aid should flow unhindered, not as a military quid pro quo. But Abiy was not willing to cede his hand yet. For him, no military or political tool was more effective than the control of aid flows and essential services such as banking and telecoms. Hunger was a silent killer: thanks to the communications blackout and a continued ban on journalists visiting Tigray, the outside world was shielded from the true scale of the horrors unfolding there. So long as a little aid trickled in, aid agencies and foreign embassies in Addis Ababa could be trusted to make little noise. Time was on Abiy's side.

He was now engaged in a delicate dance between competing interests. On the one hand, the prime minister appeared to have reached the conclusion that the TPLF couldn't be fully eliminated, at least not without risking total economic collapse and costing his relationship with America.

Though the Biden administration had decided to withhold direct sanctions on Abiy's government, two separate sanctions bills were still winding their way through the US Congress. What was more, it had become clear that the TPLF was no longer the only serious threat requiring his attention. No sooner had he announced the truce in the north, his government had launched a new offensive against the OLA—this time with thousands of federal troops supported from the air by drone strikes and *Fanos* from across the border in Amhara.

At the same time, there was the matter of Isaias, who was firmly set against talks with the TPLF and busy building ties with Amhara officials independently of Addis Ababa. By 2022, the idea that Eritrea might one day also pose him a military threat seems to have firmly lodged in Abiy's mind. In the Seychelles, his generals had for the first time entertained the possibility of future collaboration between the federal army and the TDF *against* Eritrea—a potential reconfiguration of existing alliances so drastic it was scarcely imaginable to most observers at the time. "Abiy wanted to see if there was a way to bring the Tigrayans on board as an asset," recalled an American official with first-hand knowledge. "He needed a balancing asset to counter the Amharas, the OLA and the Eritreans—and counter-intuitively, that balancing party was the Tigrayans."

On the other hand, Abiy still wanted the TPLF neutralised to the point that they no longer posed any threat to his rule. Even as his priorities began to shift, he therefore continued to press his advantage over them. Disregarding what his generals had agreed in the Seychelles, he continued to squeeze what he could out of the siege. It would take several weeks, intense diplomatic shuttling between the parties, and, eventually, a begrudging TDF withdrawal from Afar in April 2022, before aid trucks would begin arriving in Tigray at any kind of scale. Even after that, Abiy would stubbornly refuse to restore any basic services at all. "Abiy never denied the siege of Tigray—there was no denial at all," said a mediator who met with the prime minister then. "We had a very frank exchange of views. He simply demanded the TPLF accept its place in Ethiopia and show it wouldn't go back to war again." Tigrayan civilians had been deemed acceptable collateral.

In the end, though, it was the siege itself that killed the truce. More than 1,000 aid trucks had arrived in Tigray in May, and another 2,500 or so in June, lulling foreign diplomats into yet another bout of complacency. In public, the African Union's top mediator, the former Nigerian president Olusegun Obasanjo, never mentioned the blockade. In mid-July, an official from the World Food Programme told the BBC that famine had been successfully averted. But in fact, the slow strangulation of the region hadn't stopped. The supply of fuel, which the government alleged was being diverted to the TDF, was so tightly throttled that whatever food arrived in Mekelle barely left it. Until as late as June not a single cargo load of seeds or fertiliser for the coming harvest had been dispatched. Starving refugees from the mountains streamed into the capital. When a French documentary team managed to sneak into the region over the border from Afar, they captured footage of emaciated villagers with distended stomachs, gasping for life.[32] By July, the number of trucks arriving had slowed to just 500.

The vacuum had been partly filled by a shadow economy of war profiteers, border smugglers and some TPLF officials themselves, who pilfered aid to sell on the market. As food prices soared, Tigray's social fabric, once renowned for its resilience, began to tear. Word of forced recruitment, one fighter per household, spread—prompting many young Tigrayans to slink over the border to Amhara in the hope of escaping to Kenya. Meanwhile, calls for the TDF to break the siege grew louder. Diplomats and aid workers who visited in these months reported mass mobilisation and military training on a scale, one said, "way beyond anything we've seen before". In April, Debretsion had sent a letter to the UN Secretary-General António Guterres warning that if the siege was not lifted Tigray would be left with no choice but to "resort to other means". On 11 May 2022, he told Tigrayans to prepare for the "final phase of the struggle".[33]

Preparations were also gathering pace across the border. A new military training camp near Asmara opened in March 2022. Two months later, Eritrean state media warned of a coming Tigrayan invasion designed to carve out a "Greater Tigray" with access to the sea.[34] Military round-ups of young Eritreans were intensifying, just as food and fuel rationing were tightened. More and more Eritrean soldiers were defecting across the border to Sudan. Desperate to replenish the ranks of his dwindling army, Isaias's generals began abducting Tigrayan refugees from internal displacement camps inside Ethiopia, taking the unwitting recruits for training in Eritrea. The conscripts were told they would be sent into battle to fight the TPLF themselves. Only a few managed to escape.

Back in Ethiopia, the regional president of Amhara spoke of "wip[ing] out" the "cancers" in Tigray once and for all. Once again, it was unclear whether the euphemism referred to the TPLF or Tigrayans in general.[35]

The federal government continued re-arming. For several weeks in July, Abiy disappeared. Some said he was ill; some that he had been spotted in Abu Dhabi. Others suggested that he was in Asmara, plotting with Isaias to wage another round of war in Tigray.

The official peace process, which he had insisted be led by the Africa Union, stalled. Reiterating its opposition to Obasanjo as the sole official mediator, on the grounds that the Nigerian ex-president (and veteran of Nigeria's own war against Biafran secessionists) was partial to Abiy, the TPLF dug in its heels.[36] An African Union proposal to begin formal talks in Tanzania foundered in part on the prime minister's insistence that they take place in Kenya—which just so happened to be in the midst of a distracting presidential election campaign. A second round of secret talks, in Djibouti in mid-June, again organised by the Americans, ran aground after Abiy again reneged on a commitment to restore basic services to Tigray. Washington, increasingly distracted by the five-month-old war in Ukraine, let it slide. The TPLF argued that negotiating under siege was akin to doing so with a gun to the head. "War is coming," warned a Tigrayan diplomat on 1 August 2022. "Tigray cannot wait." Abiy continued playing for time.

His gamble finally ran out of road on 24 August. A few weeks earlier, the TDF had begun moving west across the Tekeze River, towards occupied Western Tigray and the Sudanese border. On 15 August, the Tigrayans claimed that the Ethiopian army had shelled their positions in the north-west, the first serious violation of the truce since March. In an article published in English on 22 August, Getachew Reda, by then TPLF's chief spokesman, all but declared the African-led peace process dead.[37] Claims of federal and Amhara troops massing at Tigray's borders flooded social media. On 23 August, the federal government suspended all clearances for aid deliveries. In an open letter to the international community the same day, Debretsion said that the Tigrayans approached "the point at which we face death whichever way we turn". The only choice left to them, he warned, was "whether we perish by starvation or die fighting for our rights and our dignity." The very next day the war roared back to life.

For those who had been watching in the days and weeks before 3 November 2020, it felt all too familiar. Nobody was entirely sure who fired the first shot. Both sides blamed the other. A senior source in the OLA, who was in regular contact with the TDF command, later told me that the Tigrayans had planned to resume fighting on 26 August 2022 but had been beaten to it. It was plausible—but so were other explanations, such as the federal army simply waiting for the Tigrayans to make one last go of fighting their way out. What was clear, though, was that an outcome which a few months earlier had been far from inevitable, had—just as in 2020—gradually become so. With both sides increasingly sure of their relative strength after months of preparation, factions in both camps reasoned that less stood to be gained from talking than from a final burst of fighting. Where exactly Abiy stood on the matter was less clear, though it is certainly plausible that he had remained reluctant to go back to active war, and would have preferred to wait out the siege a little while longer.

The result, either way, was the most catastrophic bloodletting of the entire Tigray War. Within days, fighting was raging on as many as thirteen fronts. Perhaps half a million people fled their homes.[38] Armed drones terrorised civilians from the sky—even on one occasion killing children in a kindergarten. Whatever the TDF thought might have been possible—a quick strike into Western Tigray, and over the border into Sudan for supplies—soon seemed fantastical. The next month, Eritrea announced a general mobilisation, calling up all reservists aged 40–65 to fight. Forced conscription intensified. By October 2022, General Tsadkan claimed, some one million soldiers were under arms in northern Ethiopia, of which only about a quarter were Tigrayan. Within just the first month of the renewed fighting, government sources in Addis Ababa suggested, as many soldiers may have been killed as had been in the entirety of the Ethio-Eritrean War of 1998–2000. That might have meant as many as 100,000 lives in just a few weeks. Some reckoned that, in the end, it could have been over three times more.[39]

* * *

The prime minister stared at the sheikh. "But do you love me?" he asked softly. "Do you believe I am your son?" Sheikh Haji Ibrahim, Ethiopia's most senior Muslim cleric, seemed uncertain. He lent tentatively towards the microphone. "Not only me, the entire Muslim community loves you." Abiy bristled. Still staring, a black cap pulled low over a steely gaze, the prime minister repeated the question. The older man hesitated again. "That is clear and public," he replied, evasively. Abiy's voice hardened. "I want to hear it from you now," he repeated, "I want to hear it right now." A pause. "Are you asking if I love you?" the sheikh whispered. "Yes," replied the prime minister. Haji blinked, then quietly assented.

The televised exchange took place in mid-2022, not long after a fresh wave of attacks against Muslims in the northern Amhara city of Gondar had poisoned relations between Abiy's administration and Ethiopia's Muslim community. It was a telling scene in more ways than one. Most obviously, it showed the importance which Abiy placed on the loyalty and obedience of Ethiopia's main religious institutions. Sheikh Haji was the president of the Ethiopian Islamic Affairs Supreme Council, the country's highest Islamic authority, which had been established two years after Abiy came to power. Abiy had since made himself the ultimate arbiter between its bickering factions, just as he had done with the newly formed Evangelical Council and the Orthodox establishment. At the same time, the exchange was also a vivid demonstration of the theatre of Abiy's leadership. Encounters like these—between the prime minister and his subordinates, from generals to ministers to religious leaders—were routinely broadcast live, with Abiy sitting at a desk before his audience so that he could shame, harangue and discipline them in public.

But even more than that, the exchange revealed just how much the foundation of Abiy's power had shifted since 2018. For a while after he became prime minister, it had seemed as though the quest for popularity, for the public's undying devotion, was what consumed him. He appeared desperate to be loved and did little to hide it: he had pulled open the gates of his palace and declared all Ethiopians welcome. But by the middle of 2022, as violence everywhere raged, and anger with his administration grew, Abiy appeared less and less bothered by popular opinion. When news broke that summer of another massacre of Amharas in Wollega, he had shrugged in Parliament that "terrorists are operating all over the world," noting statistics of recent killings in America to put them in perspective. "I should point out that the government has more information than the general public," he added, testily, before reminding his audience of his national tree-planting campaign: "at least the corpses will have shade".[40] The subtext beneath the stand-off between him and Sheikh Haji was, in the end, much the same. Abiy wasn't simply demanding love and affection. He was also issuing a threat.

Abiy's project had never really been a democratic one. 'Democratisation', first and foremost, had always been a tool—for gaining acceptance, at home and abroad, and for consolidating power. It was always expendable. By 2022, it had long outlived its purpose. "People hate him. People hate his guts," said an Amhara businessman in Addis Ababa as the year drew to a close. "People eventually figured out that he never kept his word." Insiders leaked internal documents to embarrass him; Ethiopians online, both at home and abroad—Amharas, Oromos, Tigrayans and more—mocked and lambasted him.[41] That Abiy was delusional and megalomaniacal at times seemed to be the one thing Ethiopians of all stripes could agree on. "It's the nonchalant way he just accepts people dying," observed one member of the diaspora. "That's what upsets people most." A former ally put it more succinctly: "Street-smart, nasty, and selfish. All he cares about is what's in it for him."

But as Machiavelli had written in *The Prince*, and as Abiy had long known, it is far safer to be feared than loved. Officials in the ruling party were kept in line through the suspended, ever-present threat of retaliatory violence, against either them or their loved ones, or through the power of the *kompromat* which Abiy had his intelligence agents place at his disposal. Like an emperor who can never let his courtiers sleep, ministers were reshuffled more frequently by Abiy than they had ever been under his EPRDF predecessors. Those who sought to leave office voluntarily, like the long-serving deputy prime minister Demeke Mekonnen, were denied permission to do so.[42] Overly ambitious rivals were sidelined, put under house arrest or dispatched overseas. Meanwhile, hundreds of thousands of disloyal cadres, the prime minister boasted in June 2023, were simply purged.[43] "Abiy doesn't have allies," said a former senior government official. "You're an ally if you're loyal.... Simple logic."

Just as there is no honour among thieves, there could be no trust among the elites in Abiy's Ethiopia. Disillusioned officials lived in perpetual fear of their colleagues outing them. "They all talk behind his back, all the time," recalled Filsan Abdi, the former minister of women, children and youth. "They don't believe anything he says. They think he's crazy." But besides Filsan herself, there was not one high-level resignation or defection following the outbreak of the Tigray War—a striking measure of the obedience Abiy had instilled in his ranks.[44] "Nobody trusts Abiy Ahmed," an Oromo official in the Addis Ababa city administration told me. "But everyone is afraid, of course. This guy is brutal if you come after his political interests." Abiy could play politics like a populist. But what he wasn't was popular.

* * *

By the close of 2022, the war in Tigray had, at long last, ended—or at least seemed to have done. Abiy, having done more than anyone to start the war, at the final hour became the "ultimate decider", in the words of one mediator, as to how and when it should stop. It was on his insistence that the official talks be led by the African Union, and it was, many insiders suspected, his decision that when they finally began, they did so in South Africa, at a moment more or less of his choosing. Abiy had long seen eye-to-eye on the war with the African Union's top leadership, and in particular its Chadian commissioner, Moussa Faki—so much so that, early in the conflict, Faki had dutifully classified Abiy's offensive as a "legitimate" law enforcement operation. Even after having appointed Obasanjo as a special envoy to mediate, many months passed before the continent's top organisation ensured his office was sufficiently staffed and funded so it could begin its work. By October 2022, the African Union had agreed to establish a "high-level panel" of African mediators, which included Kenya's recently retired president, Uhuru Kenyatta, whom Abiy and the TPLF both trusted, to counter Obasanjo's perceived bias towards the federal government. But in deference to Abiy's anger with the EU, and in particular its outspoken foreign policy chief, Josep Borrell, the African Union had insisted on keeping European mediators outside the negotiation process entirely.

From the resumption of fighting on 24 August, to the day a peace deal was signed in Pretoria, South Africa, on 2 November 2022, Abiy had seemed in no rush. A second round of American-led talks in Djibouti in early September, hidden from the public again at his insistence, had failed. The "parameters of an agreement", as one Western official involved put it, had been more or less thrashed out by the delegates: a cessation of hostilities, an end to the siege. But nothing had been signed off. Abiy's representatives in Djibouti, Gedion Timothewos, the justice minister, and Redwan Hussein, the national security advisor, had returned to Addis Ababa, unable to seal any agreement without their boss's blessing. Crucially, the future status of the disputed territories remained unresolved. So too was the fate of the TDF, which most Tigrayans now saw as their only line of defence against genocide, and were loath to disband.

Most importantly, Abiy was still unready for a deal. Despite their disagreements, he and Isaias remained bound to one another, their respective fates enjoined by the immediate goal of defeating the TPLF. No sooner had the fighting begun, thousands of Ethiopian troops had touched down inside Eritrea to relaunch joint operations against the TDF to the south—an indication that joint war-planning had once again preceded the outbreak of fighting. On 17 October 2022, their forces had together captured the strategic town of Shire, and soon after taken the historic cities of Adwa and Axum. Tigrayan civilians in the surrounding area were subjected to extraordinary, perhaps unprecedented, brutality: over four days in late October, to take just one example, around 300 unarmed villagers in two different locations near the ancient Garima Monastery were butchered in their homes by Eritrean troops.[45] Days later, Abiy proclaimed that victory was nigh. By this point, it seemed that he and Isaias were determined to repeat the trick the TPLF itself pulled off in 1991: to make ongoing peace talks redundant with a decisive military victory. Indeed, insiders said that Abiy's plan now was to install an interim administration in Tigray—again—while hunting down whatever remained of the TPLF's leadership. There were even reports he planned to appoint an Oromo from the Prosperity Party to govern the region.

When at last formal peace talks were scheduled to begin in Pretoria, the South African capital, on 24 October, the delegation sent from Addis Ababa arrived several hours late. Its chief negotiator, Ethiopia's deputy prime minister, never showed up at all. Upon sitting down at the negotiating table, Abiy's team had begun by presenting a single-page document demanding, in effect, the TPLF's total surrender. Up to the eleventh hour they continued to insist that the disputed territories of Western Tigray and Raya remain under Amhara administration. "The government was very rigid," the new US special envoy, Mike Hammer, recalled. "Abiy kept his delegates on a tight leash, and nothing was done without his approval." On the day the deal was signed, his team arrived so late to the official ceremony that diplomats in the room feared the prime minister had, all of a sudden, pulled the plug entirely.

Why then, in the end, did Abiy budge? Because under pressure from both the US and Kenyatta, he ultimately submitted to two key Tigrayan demands. The first was that the disputed territories be settled according to the 1995 constitution. This was to mean, in theory, their return to Tigrayan administration (with the possibility of a referendum on their long-term status in the future). The second, which didn't become fully evident until a second 'road map' implementation agreement was signed by military commanders in Nairobi ten days later, was that the TDF would only demobilise if Eritrean troops withdrew in concert. What Abiy did insist, though, was that in neither agreement Eritrea be mentioned by name.

The TPLF, for their part, had little room for manoeuvre. Barely any aid had entered the region since mid-August. Despite some of its leaders' bravura—"we will definitely take Western Tigray", Getachew Reda had assured me just weeks earlier—the TDF's military position was desperate. Its newly acquired anti-drone equipment had been largely ineffective against the combined onslaught of the Ethiopian air force and the constant barrage of Eritrean rockets over the border. By October 2022, the Tigrayan forces were surrounded, fast running out of guns and ammunition. With a population of little more than six million or so on the eve of war, the region was also running out of people. "We stayed in Pretoria for ten days, as the enemy attacked us from all corners," recalled one of the Tigrayan negotiators. "So, in the end, we blinked first."

But Abiy might have held on longer. The agreement, which was struck just as his forces were bearing down on Mekelle for the second time in two years, was fiercely opposed by Isaias. Eritrea hadn't been invited to participate in the talks; by some accounts, a furious Isaias had instead demanded $1 billion in compensation from Ethiopia for his war losses.[46] Many Amharas opposed the Pretoria talks, too, arguing that Abiy's government didn't represent them, and fearing he might end up striking a deal with the TPLF at their expense. Politically, therefore, any compromise at all was fraught with risks. Moreover, though his troops were dying in unspeakable numbers, and his treasury fast emptying, Abiy still had the military advantage. He might have fought on. In the end, though, "he was able to see the consequences of keeping fighting," the Tigrayan negotiator admitted. Knopf agreed: "The prime minister is not immune to persuasion and compromise. At the end of the day, he changed course." Confounding observers who had predicted he couldn't order a ceasefire because the army was no longer his to command, the guns fell silent in Tigray almost the moment the deal was inked.[47]

To live or to die; to crush or to compromise: these are the gifts of monarchs to bestow. Like an emperor, Abiy had appeared to understand there may be strength in magnanimity. If he had chosen to fight on for total victory, the TPLF's leaders would likely have returned to the hills to wage another insurgency. Instead, they submitted to him. That, for Abiy, was a victory of its own. According to the Pretoria Agreement, the TPLF, in return for having its 'terrorist' designation lifted, was to hand power to an "inclusive" interim administration. Tigray would accept the federal government's "constitutional authority" over it. Both sides committed to safeguarding the country's territorial integrity, which meant, in practice, that the pressure in Tigray for full independence, which had swelled exponentially over the course of the war, was for now to go unheeded.

That too, for Abiy, was a triumph. At a rally on 3 November, he proclaimed his "victory", and crowed that "100 percent" of his side's proposals had made it into the final agreement.[48] Daniel Kibret, his advisor, drew comparisons once again to the Battle of Adwa.[49] "Shock, indignation, denial, condemnation," said a Tigrayan friend of the public reaction in Tigray. "The whole package."

* * *

By the start of 2023, the Ethiopian army and police had made their orderly entrance into the Tigrayan capital. After yet more delays, food and medicine had begun to be delivered to starving civilians. Phone and internet networks had been restored, partially, for the first time in nearly two years. Eritrean troops had left the main Tigrayan towns.

But they hadn't left Tigray. A year later many would still be there, closer towards their border, admittedly, but still deep inside indisputably Ethiopian territory—raping, kidnapping and murdering civilians.[50] The Irob ethnic minority group, which lived near the border, remained under a crushing military occupation. Meanwhile, despite Abiy's private promises that the disputed territories would be returned to Tigray, in accordance with the constitution, by the start of 2024 they still hadn't been. In Western Tigray, ethnic cleansing continued and mass graves there were reported to have been destroyed by Amhara forces.[51]

The TDF, for its part, began to disarm and demobilise, handing most of its heavy weaponry over to the federal military. But by early 2024 it still had, by its own admission, more than 200,000 battle-hardened soldiers under arms.[52] With political alliances having been reconfigured by the Pretoria Agreement, it had become increasingly in Abiy's interest to allow the TDF to remain intact, as a potential bulwark against either Amhara or Eritrea. Fearing a stitch-up which would leave Amhara isolated, vulnerable and unarmed, *Fanos* across the region had revolted against Abiy and the federal government. By the middle of 2023, much of the region had become a warzone.

As for the lofty promises of justice and accountability enshrined in the peace deal, these looked vanishingly unlikely ever to be met. On 5 October 2023, thanks to fierce lobbying by the Ethiopian government, and amid widespread international apathy, the UN allowed the mandate of the sole international war crimes investigation simply to elapse. Just two days earlier, the UN's own investigators had issued a stark warning of further atrocities to come.[53] Yet on the very same day, the EU announced $650 million in development assistance—just the latest in a series of steps by which Abiy was gradually welcomed back into the arms of Western donors. Soon, with a new crisis in the Middle East having erupted on 7 October of that year, Ethiopia and its travails would disappear almost entirely from international headlines and the diplomatic in-trays of Western capitals.

Abiy, for his part, appeared serenely untroubled. In March 2023, Getachew Reda was elected by the TPLF as the president of the interim administration of Tigray. The Prime Minister's Office regally announced that it was Abiy who had appointed him. (This was basically true: the TPLF had at first proposed Debretsion; Abiy had refused.) At a ceremony in Abiy's new Friendship Square in Addis Ababa, in which the former battlefield adversaries exchanged "peace awards" with one another, Getachew addressed the prime minister, in deference, as "Dear PM Abiy". One opposition figure claimed Abiy was now the most powerful Ethiopian leader since Emperor Haile Selassie.

But it was a brittle sort of power, with hard and binding limits. Though Abiy faced no serious contenders for the throne, Ethiopia was a more dangerous, more violent place than it had been in decades. If the central state's writ, under Meles, had once reached every village, now it seemed barely to extend beyond the capital. "Everywhere is anarchy," another NISS official later confessed to me. "Everyone has a gun." Abiy had built a technologically advanced federal security apparatus—the new science museum displayed the Chinese-made 'smart surveillance' kit which officials used to monitor Addis Ababa—and an army and national intelligence service which were now firmly under his thumb. But in the regions, local security forces reigned supreme. When Abiy tried to dismantle the Amhara special police in early 2023, the first step in a planned recentralisation of security under the federal government, its members resisted. Thousands joined the now rebellious *Fanos* in the bush.[54] The economy, meanwhile, lay in tatters: the finance ministry estimated a post-war reconstruction bill of as much as $20 billion, even before the revolt in Amhara. That December, Ethiopia became the latest African country to default on its sovereign debt, having failed to make a $33 million 'coupon' payment on the Eurobond whose issuance a decade earlier had cemented the country's international status as an emerging market star. As for Ethiopian society itself, years of conflict had left it drastically militarised and dangerously radicalised. Many young Ethiopians, believing their lives and futures to be ruined, felt they had no options left to them but exile or the gun. By then almost every prominent government critic had fled the country.

Abiy, his opponents had once believed, was not long for this world. He had repeatedly confounded them. Now, though, his chief object seemed to be little more than manoeuvring to remain in power: a touch of divide-and-rule here, a sprinkle of diversionary nationalism there. "I don't think he cares that Amhara and Oromia are ungovernable," one of his opponents later argued, and many others would echo, "so long as he has Addis Ababa." His dream of remaking Ethiopia in his own image had never seemed more distant; never before had ethnic feeling been so inflamed, the cause of transcendent national unity so improbable. Though he seemed to have a tight grip on the Prosperity Party, despite its ideological incoherence and bitter inter-ethnic divisions, his scope to overhaul the constitution as he wished was now sharply curtailed, not least due to his renewed reliance on Oromo nationalists who wanted nothing to do with it.

According to an old Amharic saying, which Abiy was said to hold dear, the night will darken before the dawn. Ethiopia, the prime minister seemed to have realised, could not be resurrected overnight. It would take time; far longer, maybe, than he had once imagined. But the light, he continued to insist, would inevitably come. What mattered for now, above all else, was that he remain in power until it did—no longer loved, perhaps, but at the very least feared.

EPILOGUE

Zenawi saw no future in Ethiopia. In early 2022, the wiry and God-fearing twenty-six-year-old from Tigray had only narrowly escaped the war. His daring journey over the region's southern border had landed him in a detention centre in Amhara for several weeks, and he was very nearly abducted to a secret military camp in Eritrea. On more than one occasion he had almost been shot. Having made it all the way to the international airport in Addis Ababa, he then only just avoided being stopped from flying to Nairobi by Ethiopian officials at immigration control.

That he had succeeded in making it out of his homeland in one piece was something of a miracle—a sign, Zenawi believed, that despite the hardships God was still listening to his prayers. Like almost every Tigrayan, he had relatives who weren't so fortunate: some of his cousins had been murdered by Eritrean troops early in the war, and an aunt in Mekelle had died a short while after the Pretoria Agreement because she couldn't get the insulin she needed to treat her diabetes. When I first met Zenawi in Nairobi, a few days after he had joined its tight-knit community of Tigrayan refugees in May 2022, he had been planning to move to America to take up an offer of a place at a small university there. But when we met again in early 2024 he was still waiting for a visa appointment at the American embassy. For the past year, he had worked as a content moderator for a company hired by the social media giant TikTok, and was being paid a pittance to wade through a sewage of online videos depicting atrocities and hate crimes back in Ethiopia. By then, Zenawi had all but given up going to college in America, but still he dreamed of a new life in the West. He kept coming up with fresh plans—to go to Uganda, to Britain, then elsewhere. He said he wished to work hard and start a family. But he never wanted to return home.

Since leaving the country in May 2022, I have met many Ethiopians like Zenawi. Some had been lucky enough to have made it to the relative sanctuary of Kenya. But without work permits or settled refugee status many now find themselves in limbo, hustling for odd jobs in order to survive, eyeing up perilous migration routes across the Sahel to Europe or via Djibouti to the Gulf. Others have reached as far afield as Britain or Canada, where they have encountered the cruelty of Western asylum bureaucracies and the immigration rules which make it almost impossible for family members to join them. But they, too, say they can't go back to Ethiopia. Meanwhile, those in the worst predicament of all—refugees from Western Tigray stuck in eastern Sudan—spoke to me of their missing relatives in both the past and present tenses, suspended between moments of tentative hope that their loved ones might still be alive, and an unbearable sense of loss. Though the Tigray War has ended, their nightmare has not. Only once Sudan's own civil war drew closer to the refugee camps in the east in mid-2023 did some of them take the dangerous gamble of returning to Ethiopia.

For those who have remained in Ethiopia all along, feelings of disillusionment are no less acute. By the middle of 2023, much of Amhara had started to resemble the worst parts of western and southern Oromia, with an entrenched insurgency and a lawless government vacuum beyond the major towns. Like Tigrayans and Oromos before them, Amhara civilians now face deadly drone strikes from the sky and house-to-house raids by federal soldiers on the ground. Massacres and mass arrests have become routine. Over WhatsApp, I receive regular messages from friends in different parts of the region asking for help—an invitation letter for a visa to come to Britain, for instance, or for money to help pay for a relative's funeral. "I have to get outside Ethiopia before the stress comes back into my life," texted a tour guide in Lalibela whose brother-in-law had been killed by a drone. "What else can I do?"

Ethiopia in 2024 embodies what has been called the 'polycrisis' of our present age—an entangled web of disparate shocks, political and economic, human and environmental, local and global, cause and effect feeding into one another and pushing solutions out of reach.[1] The sources of the country's plight are, on one level, parochial: the failure of its political leaders—Abiy above all—and their decades-long quest to turn a feudal multinational empire into a modern nation-state. But the causes are also dizzyingly supra-national, born of climate collapse, technological change and widening economic disparities, among our era's many global challenges. Ethiopia, after all, is far from alone today in witnessing an upsurge in armed violence. By one count there were 183 conflicts globally in 2023, the highest in three decades. Though 'Pax Americana' was always grossly overstated—ask any Iraqi, Libyan or Somali—there is no question now that the precipitous unravelling of the established international order is propelling instability not just in the Horn of Africa, but across the continent and beyond.

In Ethiopia, one important consequence of this disorderly world is rampant impunity. By the end of 2023, famine was on the horizon once again across Tigray, with its still decimated farmland, and also in parts of Amhara and Afar, which received their last significant rainfall in the autumn of 2022. Some experts warned that if unchecked the death toll could eventually surpass even that of the 1983–5 famine, when hundreds of thousands starved to death. Yet this time there has been no international response reminiscent of Live Aid or the cross-border relief operations from Sudan of the 1980s. Instead, the US government and the World Food Programme suspended aid deliveries in 2023, accusing both authorities in Tigray and the federal government of conspiring in a vast programme of aid theft. Food operations resumed at the end of the year, following months of grinding negotiations in which American and UN officials tried to force Abiy to cede control over the aid delivery system. But they did so much too late, and at levels far below what was needed. By March 2024, Tigray's regional authorities had counted more than 11,000 hunger-related deaths since Pretoria; overall, nearly 16 million Ethiopians were estimated to be short of food. Abiy himself showed little concern in public about the suffering: in a speech to Parliament in February, he denied any responsibility for food shortages, insisted nobody was dying of hunger, and boasted of what he claimed was the largest grain harvest in Ethiopian history.[2] But those with the power to compel or influence him to act differently didn't appear too troubled either. US lawmakers had cut billions of dollars of funding from WFP the previous year. That June, too, the Biden administration had notified Congress that Ethiopia's government was no longer engaged in a pattern of "gross violations of human rights". And then, in January 2024, the UN's Food and Agriculture Organization awarded Abiy the Agricola Medal, the agency's highest award, for his "contribution to rural and economic development in Ethiopia."

International efforts to stabilise the country have been utterly inadequate. Since the Pretoria Agreement—which, at the time of writing in March 2024, holds, however tenuously—Western and African officials alike have acted as if Ethiopia were a problem solved. It is far from it. For one thing, in the absence of concerted international pressure, Abiy evidently feels no need to implement the deal's most difficult terms. Rather than try to reconcile Amhara and Tigray—and resolve the single most dangerous obstacle to lasting peace, the question of annexed territories—he has played the two groups off each other, privately telling Tigray's leaders to use military force to reclaim Western Tigray, while warning Amhara officials that the still largely intact TDF is planning to attack them. By again threatening to turn east into the orbit of Russia and China, he has also deftly sidestepped the agreement's (admittedly vague) provisions for 'transitional justice' and for further international investigations into atrocities committed during the war. And, many months after the deadline passed, he has continued to dodge promised negotiations over a long-term political settlement to determine the country's future.

Nor does Abiy display any urgency in tackling Ethiopia's other fault lines. The ongoing revolt in Amhara was triggered in large part by the Pretoria Agreement, and a perception among Amharas that the deal served to shore up a tacit new alliance between Tigray and Oromia at their expense. That, in turn, was a consequence of Abiy's insistence on negotiating with the TPLF bilaterally, rather than as part of a broad-based dialogue with all his main opponents. By the middle of 2023, as *Fanos* swept into towns and cities, briefly taking over several of them, Tigrayan officials had begun returning to some of their old posts in the federal security apparatus. Scores of bank accounts belonging to Amhara businessmen had meanwhile been frozen, while young Amhara men were reported to have been blocked from entering Addis Ababa by Oromo policemen. As fears mounted that Ethiopia could yet descend into all-out war between Oromos and Amharas, Abiy did nothing to alleviate them. Instead, he declared martial law in Amhara and made none-too-subtle comments designed to appeal to Oromo nationalists, such as an insinuation in early 2023 that he might back a campaign for an independent Oromo Orthodox Church synod.

So far, there is no sign that Abiy is yet willing to cede anything that might pave the way for a peace process in Amhara, such as allowing for an interim administration to take the reins in the region and reach out to its legions of angry and militarised youth. Negotiations with the OLA in late 2023 failed again for much the same reason; the internal fragmentation of the armed opposition in both Oromia and Amhara also continue to provide Abiy with a convenient excuse to avoid committing seriously to talks. On occasion, the prime minister's vocal new Amhara nationalist and Ethiopianist opponents in the diaspora have claimed that the *Fanos*— some of whom recently coalesced under the umbrella of the Amhara

Popular Front, established by the previously jailed activist Eskinder Nega—are on the brink of overthrowing the federal government and taking charge in Addis Ababa. But in reality, Abiy doesn't appear to feel much heat. On social media he continues to pump out slick videos of new state-built tourist lodges, and boasts of meeting ever-loftier production and exports targets. Clearly, he doesn't much fear being toppled. "It is no longer possible to seize power through the barrel of the gun," he told MPs confidently in February. "The only way is through peace, elections and democracy."[3]

Undeterred by growing popular hostility, Abiy continues his drive to remake Addis Ababa. In the space of a few weeks in early 2024, great swathes of the capital's historic—albeit dilapidated—centre were torn down. Whole neighbourhoods were uprooted and some of its most iconic imperial-era buildings were reduced to rubble, to be replaced by gleaming modern high-rises and manicured green spaces in a Dubai-like downtown. Many Addis Ababa residents have interpreted this eradication of urban heritage in ethnic terms—the latest evidence, they believe, of an Oromo nationalist agenda to wipe away all traces of Ethiopia's imperial past, and the surest sign yet of Abiy's drift away from the broader Ethiopianist (and Amhara) camp. And certainly, it has had the effect of severing what remained of his once carefully cultivated bond with this important constituency—thereby weakening his grip on power, however confident he may appear. But just as noteworthy as his evident willingness to discard erstwhile allies is the underlying consistency in Abiy's politics. He is undoubtedly happy for Oromo nationalists, both inside and outside his party, to believe that by dismantling the capital's imperial heart, he is at last entrenching their control. He is far too canny a political operator not to, and remains unscrupulous in telling different constituencies whatever they want to hear. But at the same time, the vision he is pursuing in the capital is distinctively his own and reflects the essence of his wider project. By doggedly transforming the city in this way Abiy is at once playing the role of an almighty emperor, imposing order on perceived chaos; a future-facing moderniser, scrubbing away an ugly past; a KPI-leading executive, successfully delivering high-end projects; and a righteous prophet, leading his wayward and sinful flock along the winding path to heaven. Though they may protest now, the prime minister seems to believe, Ethiopians will thank him in the end.

* * *

Unrestrained at home, Abiy has also become more provocative abroad. As relations between him and Isaias continued to deteriorate in 2023—and Eritrean troops remained firmly entrenched on Ethiopian soil—he made increasingly belligerent remarks about the need for Ethiopia to regain access to the Red Sea. In a jingoistic broadcast on state TV in October, he declared a new conflict in the region all but inevitable should Ethiopia's decades-old quest for the sea not be answered satisfactorily. For much of the year, rumours swirled of preparations for a coming war against Eritrea—perhaps in alliance with the remainder of the TDF, to drive Eritrean troops out of Tigray and then seize the port of Assab. (Tigrayan leaders claim that, in private, Abiy has suggested almost exactly this.) Such ideas were given added weight by frequent sightings of covert arms deliveries from the UAE, whose alliance with Ethiopia has never appeared so strong.

Of course, Abiy may simply be politicking, resurrecting the cause of Ethiopian irredentism as a way of appealing to disillusioned Amharas and Ethiopianists. But there is also no doubt that the prime minister considers rectifying the loss of Eritrea's Red Sea coastline in 1993 part of his historic mission. The risk of a war between Ethiopia and Eritrea one day is thus considerable, not least given the near-impossibility of two leaders like Abiy and Isaias peacefully coexisting in the same region. Given the military's ongoing commitments in Amhara and Oromia, however, it may not necessarily be imminent.

Abiy retains his appetite for surprise and disruption. On 1 January 2024, he signed a memorandum of understanding to establish an Ethiopian naval base on a 20-kilometre stretch of coastline leased by neighbouring Somaliland, in exchange for Ethiopia becoming the first country in the world to grant the breakaway Somali state formal recognition. The prime minister hailed the move as a diplomatic triumph, the realisation of his promise to restore Ethiopia's direct access to the sea. For Somalilanders, too, it was a historic breakthrough—the first real one, they believe, in their three-decade-long quest for international recognition.

But more than anything, the move was an object lesson in Abiy's maverick brand of regional diplomacy. Taking both local and foreign observers by surprise, it has also infuriated Ethiopia's neighbours, above all Somalia (which claims sovereignty over Somaliland) and Djibouti (which fears commercial competition for Ethiopia's trade flows). Like the controversial Ethio-Eritrea peace agreement of 2018, few had seen it coming. Almost nobody was consulted. Just three days earlier, Somalia's new president, Hassan Sheikh Mohamud, had signed an agreement with Somaliland's leader to resume talks over the internationally unrecognised statelet's disputed constitutional status. Hassan Sheikh says Abiy called to inform him of the Somaliland leader's impending visit to Addis Ababa, but neglected to mention why; in Hassan Sheikh's previous conversations with the Ethiopian prime minister, he vehemently denied any intention of striking a deal with Somaliland for a port on its territory. That previous deal between Somalia and Somaliland is now in tatters.

Behind the scenes, once again, some have spied the hand of the UAE. Mohammed bin Zayed makes little secret of his ambition to secure Emirati influence throughout the southern Red Sea and Arabian peninsula, and like Abiy he has long sought to acquire strategic real estate along this high-value stretch of coast. Emirati officials deny all these allegations, but coming just months after MbZ visited Addis Ababa and signed no fewer than seventeen cooperation agreements with Abiy, it is far from clear why anyone should believe them. "Every step of the way, the UAE is there," one former Ethiopian minister has repeatedly told me. Looking to the future, Abiy's Ethiopia seems set to become the core pillar of an axis of Emirati influence stretching across the Horn and the broader Gulf region.

For now, Somalia argues that Ethiopia has violated its territorial integrity and sovereignty. It has called on the African Union and the UN Security Council to intervene. Perhaps taken aback by the scale of the Somali reaction—President Hassan Sheikh has gone as far as to suggest Somalia might go to war with Ethiopia to prevent the port deal—Abiy has since tried to dial down tensions. He has suggested he might be willing to pause on unilaterally recognising Somaliland statehood, and perhaps back out of the agreement entirely. But such signals could well be bluffs, or short-term tactical readjustments. If the prime minister cannot secure a naval base in Somaliland, his focus will surely return to the even more desirable Red Sea coast of Eritrea. After all, when much more powerful nations freely trample on international law—from Russia and China to America and Israel—it can be hard to see why Abiy should feel much need to respect it. "This is an age where, if you're ruthless and reckless, nobody gets in your way," one veteran Western diplomat has noted. It is a lesson Abiy has long taken to heart.

* * *

Even so, six years of disruption are taking their toll. Abiy's Ethiopia is now seen by its neighbours as a dangerous revisionist power. Former allies, including both Eritrea and Somalia, are lining up against him. Kenya, for decades Ethiopia's most reliable partner, now appears wary. Abiy's word, his fellow leaders have learnt, is not his bond.

Meanwhile, at home, the prime minister's list of enemies grows by the day. His appeals to Ethiopian nationalism, including the promise to turn the country into a Red Sea naval power, fall on increasingly deaf ears. If the economy continues its slide, the supply of rents to keep his remaining loyalists on side will shrink. And if the army continues to be bogged down in wars against its own people, the patience of its leadership could one day snap. Though Ethiopia has no record of military coups since 1974, it would be foolish to rule one out.

Today there are few reasons for optimism. Abiy may secure enough emergency funding from the IMF and the World Bank in 2024 to stave off economic collapse. But with no imminent prospect of a surge in exports and industrial production, further declines in the value of the birr will fuel inflation and possibly further social unrest. Eye-catching wheezes, such as an agreement signed in early 2024 between Ethiopia's sovereign wealth fund and a Hong Kong-based firm to build a $250m data centre for data-mining and artificial intelligence, are hardly long-term solutions. Likewise, privatising land—a radical move said to be on the cards—might well increase agricultural productivity, but it would also lead to a sharp rise in the numbers of landless rural farmers, pushing them into towns and cities which are ill-prepared to absorb them. Fifty years after the Revolution which promised 'land to the tiller', Ethiopia has still to find an answer to the most fundamental of challenges: how to feed an ever-swelling population with insufficiently productive resources. Abiy has yet to seriously grapple with it.

The other central question raised by Ethiopian students five decades ago—what is Ethiopia, and can it hold?—remains as live as ever, too. For now, no region—not even Tigray—is on the brink of declaring independence. Whatever the constitution might say, Abiy clearly won't allow the country to disintegrate without an almighty battle. And as much as Ethiopia shares superficial similarities with Yugoslavia and the Soviet Union, it has a far longer experience of nationhood than any of the former communist federations. But even so, the bonds which bind its constituent pieces appear weaker than they have ever been. According to one recent study, Ethiopians now report lower levels of inter-communal trust than are found even in war-ravaged eastern Congo.[4] Like the flow of traffic through Addis Ababa's roundabouts, where few people trust their fellow drivers enough to follow the rules—causing endless pile-ups—political elites in Ethiopia today are consumed by mutual suspicion. Abiy and his allies, for instance, assume that whatever the TPLF says publicly, the party is always preparing for another round of war. Many TPLF leaders, for their part, take it for granted that Abiy is still plotting to destroy Tigray in its entirety. Neither side is necessarily wrong: the prime minister's persistent lack of concern about starvation in Tigray, for instance, certainly gives grounds for suspicion. But in the absence of basic trust, the danger is that these fears eventually become self-fulfilling. If large-scale war returns to Ethiopia, particularly to Tigray, the country in its current form might not survive much longer. Indeed, for all the relative longevity of nation-states in the Horn, it is also the one region in the world outside the Balkans where in recent decades several of them have broken into pieces.[5] Further fragmentation is not unthinkable. Even much of Amhara, the part which historically identified most strongly with the Ethiopian state, is now up in arms against it.

If there is hope, it will likely be found beyond Ethiopia's fractious elites. Over the course of years reporting on the country's myriad conflicts, it was among ordinary people that I found the most powerful evidence that patches of Ethiopia's social fabric continue to endure. These were the examples of ordinary kindness, and extraordinary bravery, amid horrifying violence and social upheaval: the family of Oromos sheltering the children of their Amhara neighbour from marauding gangs in Shashemene; the Eritrean soldiers protecting Tigrayan women from sexual violence in Western Tigray; the Amhara man who hid a Qemant woman and her children under his bed to prevent them being murdered by a group of *Fanos* near Gondar. Set against a backdrop of sometimes unremitting brutality, it might be tempting to overlook such acts, to dismiss them as minor exceptions to the general rule that Ethiopia's path is a bleak and precipitous one. But of course they do matter. They show that armed conflict is never just inevitable; that even today, the cycle of vengeance can still be broken; and that, despite the machinations of its leaders and the meddling of outsiders, Ethiopia's future can be brighter than its past. Despite everything, it can always be otherwise. I hope it is so.

CHRONOLOGY

2nd century AD	Kingdom of Axum becomes a regional trading power.
4th century	Christianity arrives in Axum and the surrounding highlands.
1520s–40s	Muslim leader Ahmad Gragn overruns much of Ethiopia.
1855	Kassa Hailu, a bandit, becomes Emperor Tewodros II.
1872	Tigrayan chieftain becomes Yohannes IV.
1889	Yohannes IV killed fighting Sudanese forces and is succeeded by the king of Shewa, who becomes Emperor Menelik II.
1889	Menelik II establishes Addis Ababa, Ethiopia's modern capital.
1896	Italian invaders defeated by Ethiopian troops in the Battle of Adwa. Italy recognises Ethiopia's independence but retains control over Eritrea.

* * *

1930	Ras Tafari Makonnen becomes Emperor Haile Selassie I.
1935	Italy invades Ethiopia.
1941	British and Commonwealth troops aided by the Ethiopian 'Patriots' defeat the Italians, and restore Haile Selassie.
1952	United Nations federates Eritrea with Ethiopia.

1962	Haile Selassie annexes Eritrea, which becomes an Ethiopian province.
1973–4	An estimated 200,000 people die from famine in the north.
1974	Mass protests lead to overthrow of Haile Selassie in a military coup.
1976	Birth of Abiy Ahmed in Beshasha in western Ethiopia.
1977–9	Thousands of government opponents die in "Red Terror" orchestrated by Mengistu Hailemariam; Tigrayan People's Liberation Front launches insurgency.
1977	Somalia invades Ethiopia's Ogaden province; Ethiopian troops expel them the following year with help from the Soviet Union and Cuba.
1984–5	Worst famine in a decade hits the north; thousands forcibly resettled in the south and west.

* * *

1991	Ethiopian People's Revolutionary Democratic Front captures Addis Ababa, forcing President Mengistu to flee the country.
1992	Abiy joins the newly formed Oromo People's Democratic Organisation.
1993	Eritrea becomes independent following referendum.
1995	New federal constitution comes into force; Meles Zenawi becomes prime minister.
1998–2000	Ethiopian-Eritrean border war. Up to 100,000 people estimated to have died.
2005	Contested national elections in May spark widespread protests.
2006	Ethiopia invades Somalia to oust Islamists from the capital, Mogadishu.
2010	Abiy enters Ethiopia's federal parliament in national elections.

CHRONOLOGY

2012	Prime Minister Meles dies. Succeeded by Foreign Minister Hailemariam Desalegn.
2016	Government declares state of emergency in October following months of anti-government protests.
2018	Prime Minister Hailemariam resigns in February. Abiy takes over as prime minister in April.

* * *

June 2018	Abiy signs a historic peace deal with Eritrea's president, Isaias Afewerki, declaring nearly decades of cold war between the two countries over.
August 2018	Peace deal signed between the Ethiopian government and the Oromo Liberation Front.
June 2019	Army chief Seare Mekonnen and Amhara regional president Ambachew Mekonnen killed in 'coup' attempt in the Amhara state capital, Bahir Dar.
October 2019	Abiy wins the Nobel Peace Prize.
December 2019	Ethiopian People's Revolutionary Democratic Front dissolved; the Prosperity Party is formed.
June 2020	Assassination of popular musician, Hachalu Hundessa, sparks deadly protests followed by mass arrests across Addis Ababa and Oromia.
November 2020	Tigray War begins.
June 2021	Abiy's Prosperity Party declares thumping victory in national elections.
November 2021	Abiy imposes nationwide state of emergency as Tigrayan forces threaten to storm Addis Ababa.
November 2022	Pretoria Agreement is signed in Pretoria, South Africa, bringing Tigray War to a close.
January 2024	Ethiopia signs historic memorandum of understanding with neighbouring Somaliland; Abiy claims success in restoring Ethiopia's direct access to the sea.

NOTES

1.   "OUR FOREFATHERS"

1.   The refurbishment cost \$170m and was paid for by the United Arab Emirates, a close ally.
2.   Asfa-Wossen Asserate, *King of Kings: the Triumph and Tragedy of Emperor Haile Selassie I of Ethiopia* (2015); Bahru Zewde, *A History of Modern Ethiopia 1855–1991* (1991), p. 137.
3.   The dynasty's claim to an unbroken line of descent was formally enshrined in the 1931 Constitution.
4.   'Did a Nobel Peace Laureate Stoke a Civil War?' *New Yorker*, 26 September 2022.
5.   Ibid.
6.   The restoration of Jubilee Palace was funded by France.
7.   Abiy's address at the inauguration of Unity Park, 10 October 2019: https://www.youtube.com/watch?v=ALYV1dlWe_o
8.   Tadesse Tamrat, *Church and State in Ethiopia 1270–1527* (1972), p. 302.
9.   Tadesse Tamrat noted that Menelik II's imperial expansion closely followed that of Emperor Amda Tseyon (r. 1314–44); ibid.
10.   The archetypal period of disintegration was the so-called Era of Princes (or *Zemana Mesafent*, 1769–1855), in which provincial kings and lords battled for supremacy. It is traditionally said to have come to an end with the rise of Emperor Tewodros II.
11.   Richard Reid, *Frontiers of Violence in North-East Africa* (2011).
12.   Richard Reid, 'Atrocity in Ethiopian History', *Journal of Genocide Research*, 24:1 (2022).
13.   James Baldwin, '*Black English: A Dishonest Argument*,' a speech given at Detroit's Wayne State University in 1980.
14.   Others, including the curators of the central exhibition at Unity Park, have dated the start of modern Ethiopian history to the reign of Emperor Tewodros II (r. 1855–1868).
15.   Christopher Clapham, 'Rewriting Ethiopian History' in *Annales d'Ethiopie*, Vol. 18, 2002, pp. 37–54.
16.   Kjetil Tronvoll, *War and the Politics of Identity in Ethiopia: The Making of Enemies and Allies in the Horn of Africa* (2009), p. 25.
17.   Ibid., p. 13.
18.   Ibid., p. 20.

19. See, for example, Edward Ullendorff, *The Ethiopians* (1960).

20. Thomas Zitelmann, 'Re-Examining the Galla/Oromo Relationship,' in Baxter, Hultin and Triulzi (eds), *Being and Becoming Oromo. Historical and Anthropological Enquiries* (1996), pp. 106–7.

21. Mohammed Hassen, *The Oromo of Ethiopia: A History, 1570–1860* (1990).

22. The most influential proponent of this thesis was Donald Levine. See for example *Greater Ethiopia: The Evolution of a Multiethnic Society* (1974).

23. See, for example, Brian J Yates, *The Other Abyssinians* (2020).

24. Gebru Tareke, *The Ethiopian Revolution* (2009), p. 26.

25. See, for example, Elleni Centime Zeleke, *Ethiopia in Theory* (2019).

26. The most influential of this cohort, Wallelign Mekonnen (himself an Amhara), (in) famously wrote that "Ethiopia is not really one nation. It is made up of a dozen nationalities, with their own languages, ways of dressing, history, social organisation and territorial entity": 'On the Question of Nationalities in Ethiopia', *Struggle* [organ of the University Student Union of Addis Ababa], 17 November 1969.

27. Ian Campbell, *The Addis Ababa Massacre: Italy's National Shame* (2017).

28. Tareke, *The Ethiopian Revolution*, p. 11.

29. In Jimma, for instance, major Amhara landowners such as Mesfin Sileshi were granted large tracts of confiscated land after the Second World War.

30. In 1967, all provincial governors in southern Ethiopia were Amharas from Shewa: cf. Christopher Clapham, 'Centralization and Local Response in Southern Ethiopia,' *African Affairs* 74, no. 294 (1975), pp. 72–81.

31. Teshale Tibebu, *The Making of Modern Ethiopia, 1897–1974* (1995), p. 45.

32. Pierre Guidi, *Éduquer la nation en Éthiopie: École, État et identités dans le Wolaita (1941–1991)* (2020), p. 61.

33. Martin Plaut and Sarah Vaughan, *Understanding Ethiopia's Tigray War* (2023), p. 46.

34. See, for example, Terje Ostebo, *Islam, Ethnicity, and Conflict in Ethiopia* (2020).

35. Both of Haile Selassie's grandfathers had Oromo heritage. His maternal grandmother is generally believed to have been Gurage: cf. Christopher Clapham, *The Horn of Africa* (2017), p. 13.

36. Haggai Erlich, *Greater Tigray and the Mysterious Magnetism of Ethiopia* (2023), pp. 121–3.

37. John Markakis, *Ethnicity and Conflict in the Horn of Africa* (1994), p. 230.

38. Haggai Erlich, *Greater Tigray and the Mysterious Magnetism of Ethiopia* (2023), p. 124.

39. J Hultin, 'Rebounding Nationalism: State and Ethnicity in Wollega 1968–1976,' in *Africa, 73*(3), 2003, pp. 402–26.

40. Clapham, *The Horn of Africa*, pp. 38–41.

41. *Evil Days: Thirty years of war and famine in Ethiopia*, Africa Watch (1991).

42. Ibid.

43. René Lefort, *Ethiopia: An Heretical Revolution?* (1983), p. 174.

44. See in particular, Bahru Zewde, *The Quest for Socialist Utopia* (2014).

45. 'The surprising triumph of "Africa's Kim Jong Un"', *1843*, 28 September 2023.

46. The Oromo scholar Merera Gudina has categorised the three dominant perspectives

on Ethiopian history as: the "nation-building perspective"; the "national oppression perspective"; and the "colonisation" perspective.

47. *Evil Days*, Africa Watch.
48. Atsuko Matsuoka and John Sorenson, *Ghosts and Shadows: Construction of Identity and Community in an African Diaspora* (2001), p. 165.
49. See, for example, Tilahun Yilma, 'The Truth About Ethiopia', *Ethiopia Review* (1996).
50. See, for example, John Markakis, *The Last Two Frontiers* (2011).
51. Christopher Clapham, 'The Ethiopian state's long struggle for reform', in *Ethiopia in the Wake of Political Reforms* (2000), p. 50.

2.   ABIYOT

1.   René Lefort, *Ethiopia: An Heretical Revolution?* (1983).
2.   Herbert S. Lewis, *Jimma Abba Jifar* (1965). Before Menelik's conquests in the late nineteenth century the land around Beshasha had been part of the Kingdom of Gomma, one of the handful of 'Gibe states' incorporated into the Ethiopian empire on terms less favourable than those enjoyed by the Kingdom of Jimma. As in Jimma proper, however, there were fewer Amhara or northern landlords in Beshasha than was characteristic of other parts of the south and west throughout the twentieth century.
3.   Ibid.
4.   Abiy later claimed in an interview with Sheger FM in September 2019 to be his parents' ninth child, though this discrepancy may be because some of them died young: https://www.youtube.com/watch?v=imCTWClFBss
5.   Marina and David Ottaway, *Ethiopia: Empire in Revolution* (1978), p. 73.
6.   Pierre Guidi, *Éduquer la nation en Éthiopie: École, État et identités dans le Wolaita (1941– 1991)* (2020), pp. 303–5.
7.   Christopher Clapham, 'Controlling space in Ethiopia', in James, Donham, Kurimoto and Triulzi (eds), *Remapping Ethiopia: Socialism and After* (2002).
8.   See, for example, Herbert S. Lewis, *Galla Monarchy: Jimma Abba Jifar* (1965). The preponderance of both local Oromo landowners and tenants was also characteristic of western Wollega in this period: Hultin, 'Rebounding Nationalism: State and Ethnicity in Wollega 1968–1976', *Africa*, 73(3) (2003).
9.   Interview with Ahmed Ali (*Lammi*, 17 June 2018). "*Abiy*" in Amharic means "main", and can allude to the "*Abiy tsom*" or "long fast" in the Ethiopian Orthodox calendar: https://youtu.be/wQjYzGObfOw_
10. Kjetil Tronvoll, *War and the Politics of Identity in Ethiopia: The Making of Enemies and Allies in the Horn of Africa* (2009), p. 183.
11. Harold Marcus, *The Life and Times of Menelik II* (1975), pp. 16–17.
12. Ibid.
13. See, for example, Abiy's conference address in December 2019: https://www.youtube.com/watch?v=JtwxQjWVugM

14. E.g. https://www.youtube.com/watch?v=fZATZ5Q-EyE; https://youtu.be/zyQIVgOZ10k

15. Abiy told colleagues in May 2018 that he didn't like having his picture taken because he knew that when he "became king" they would "show it to others and say 'we were together'": https://www.youtube.com/watch?v=LhDoLdIYfyg

16. *Sewyew*, by Mohammed Hassen (2019) includes two low-quality photographs of Abiy during his army days. Mohammed was later appointed by Abiy as CEO of a major state-affiliated media outlet, Walta TV.

17. See, for example, Abiy's July 2020 interview with Oromia Broadcasting Network: https://www.youtube.com/watch?v=fZATZ5Q-EyE

18. Abiy interview with Sheger FM in September 2019: https://www.youtube.com/watch?v=imCTWClFBss

19. Ibid.

20. Abiy Ahmed, *Medemer's Path* (2021), p. 43.

21. Ibid., p. 177.

22. Abiy addressing party colleagues in May 2018: https://www.youtube.com/watch?v=LhDoLdIYfyg

23. Source: Herbert S. Lewis (my interview).

24. Terje Østebø, *Islam, Ethnicity, and Conflict in Ethiopia. The Bale Insurgency, 1963–1970* (2020).

25. See essays in Baxter, Hultin and Triulzi (eds), *Being and Becoming Oromo: Historical and Anthropological Enquiries* (1996).

26. Martin Plaut and Sarah Vaughan, *Understanding Ethiopia's Tigray War* (2023), p. 85.

27. Ibid., p. 86.

28. 'The rise of Abiy "Abiyot" Ahmed', *The Reporter*, 31 March 2018.

29. *Sewyew*, Mohammed Hassen (2019); however, childhood friends interviewed by Mohammed Hassen do not mention the young Abiy's flight to Addis Ababa and instead suggest he joined the OPDO upon their arrival in Jimma.

30. Abiy interview with Sheger FM (September 2019): https://www.youtube.com/watch?v=imCTWClFBss

31. Ibid.

32. Abiy briefly attended high school in Agaro, where he boarded at the home of one of his teachers, but he had dropped out by the time he joined the OPDO. In his 2019 interview with Sheger FM, Abiy said he completed Grade 7: https://youtu.be/zyQIVgOZ10k

33. Abiy addressing party colleagues in May 2018: https://www.youtube.com/watch?v=LhDoLdIYfyg

34. 'The rise of Abiy "Abiyot" Ahmed', *The Reporter*, 31 March 2018.

3. KINGDOM OF GOD

1. 'Ethiopia and Eritrea: War or Peace', International Crisis Group, September 2003.

2. Martin Plaut and Sarah Vaughan, *Understanding Ethiopia's Tigray War* (2023), p. 99.

3. https://wikileaks.org/plusd/cables/08ASMARA543_a.html

4. This was also the conclusion of the UN's Boundary Commission set up after the ceasefire in 2000.

5. See, for example, Richard Reid, *Frontiers of Violence in North-East Africa* (2011).

6. John Markakis, *The Last Two Frontiers* (2011), p. 268.

7. Kjetil Tronvoll, *War and the Politics of Identity in Ethiopia: The Making of Enemies and Allies in the Horn of Africa* (2009).

8. https://twitter.com/AlemayehuGK/status/1399826849732177921

9. The other officer to survive was Zerabruk Tadesse. He died during the Tigray War two decades later.

10. Mohammed Hassen, *Sewyew* (2019).

11. Sheikh Mussa, the imam of Grand Anwar Mosque in Addis Ababa since 1990.

12. Jörg Haustein and Dereje Feyissa, 'The strains of "Pente" politics: Evangelicals and the post-Orthodox state in Ethiopia', in *The Routledge Handbook of the Horn of Africa* (2022).

13. Jörg Haustein, 'Pentecostal and Charismatic Christianity in Ethiopia: A Historical Introduction to a Largely Unexplored Movement,' in *Multidisciplinary Views on the Horn of Africa*, Hatem Eliese (ed.) (2014), p. 116.

14. Jörg Haustein and Terje Østeb, 'EPRDF's Revolutionary Democracy and Religious Plurality: Islam and Christianity in Post-*Derg* Ethiopia', *Journal of Eastern African Studies,* 5(4) (2011), pp. 755–72.

15. Freeman, D., 'Pentecostalism in a Rural Context: Dynamics of Religion and Development in Southwest Ethiopia,' *PentecoStudies*, 12(2) (2013), pp. 231–49.

16. Cities also increase religious diversity, making conversion to Pentecostalism more likely for people from Orthodox or Muslim areas.

17. In an interview with Sheger FM in 2019, Abiy said he had first moved to Addis Ababa, on an on-off basis, following his return from Rwanda: https://www.youtube.com/watch?v=imCTWClFBss

18. Haustein and Feyissa, 'The strains of "Pente" politics…'

19. Emanuele Fantini, 'Go Pente! The Charismatic Renewal of the Evangelical Movement in Ethiopia' in Ficquet and Prunier (eds), *Understanding Contemporary Ethiopia* (2015).

20. https://www.pewresearch.org/short-reads/2017/11/28/ethiopia-is-an-outlier-in-the-orthodox-christian-world/

21. The core of Hailemariam's "Oneness" theology was the rejection of the doctrine of the Trinity.

22. Pastor Bekele Woldekidan described first meeting Abiy in an interview in 2020: https://www.youtube.com/watch?app=desktop&v=ywTGtO8vEE4

23. 'Christian Nationalism Is Tearing Ethiopia Apart', *Foreign Policy*, 18 June 2022.

4. UNDERSTANDING INSA

1. 'U.S. Used Base in Ethiopia to Hunt Al Qaeda', *New York Times*, 23 February 2007.

2. Harry Verhoeven & Michael Woldemariam, 'Who lost Ethiopia? The unmaking of an African anchor state and U.S. foreign policy', *Contemporary Security Policy*, 43:4, 2022, pp. 622–50.

3. 'They Know Everything We Do', Human Rights Watch, March 2014.

4. Abiy Ahmed, *Medemer's Path* (2021), pp. 100–10.

5. 'Did a Nobel Peace Laureate Stoke a Civil War?' *New Yorker*, 26 September 2022.

6. This is the central claim of a hagiographic documentary, *When We Medemer*, about Abiy's leadership of INSA, which included interviews with several former colleagues and was ostensibly leaked in 2019.

7. All email communications were to be gathered, stored and deleted after six months, according to the former senior INSA official. A legal process was in theory supposed to prevent the indiscriminate reading of private emails.

8. INSA and the Artificial Intelligence Institute were in the same building, though formally they were separate institutions.

9. 'Suppressing Dissent', Human Rights Watch, May 2005.

10. 'Because I'm Oromo', Amnesty International, August 2014.

11. Eyob Balcha Gebremariam, 'The politics dominating Addis Ababa, 2005–2018,' in Tom Goodfellow and David Jackson (eds), *Controlling the Capital* (2023).

12. See, for example, Elleni Centime Zeleke, *Ethiopia in Theory* (2019).

13. Martin Plaut and Sarah Vaughan, *Understanding Ethiopia's Tigray War* (2023), p. 110.

14. Patrick Gilkes, 'Election and Politics in Ethiopia, 2005–2010', in Gerard Prunier and Eloi Ficquet (eds), *Understanding Contemporary Ethiopia* (2015), p. 313.

15. Leonardo Arriola, 'Protesting and Policing in a Multiethnic Authoritarian State: Evidence from Ethiopia,' *Comparative Politics*, vol. 45, no. 2, 2013, pp. 147–68.

16. See, for example, Sarah Vaughan, 'Revolutionary democratic state-building: party, state and people in the EPRDF's Ethiopia', *Journal of Eastern African Studies*, 5:4, 2011, pp. 619–40; Jean-Nicolas Bach, '*Abyotawi* democracy: neither revolutionary nor democratic, a critical review of EPRDF's conception of revolutionary democracy in post-1991 Ethiopia', *Journal of Eastern African Studies*, 5:4, 2011, pp. 641–63.

17. 'Terrorism law decimates media,' Human Rights Watch, 3 May 2013.

18. EPRDF official figures.

19. Terrence Lyons, *The Puzzle of Ethiopian Politics* (2020), p. 81.

20. 'They Know Everything We Do', Human Rights Watch, March 2014.

21. M Labzaé & S Planel, '"We Cannot Please Everyone": Contentions over Adjustment in EPRDF Ethiopia (1991–2018)', *International Review of Social History*, 66(S29), 2021, pp. 69–91; '"We Are Everywhere": How Ethiopia Became a Land of Prying Eyes', *New York Times*, 5 November 2017.

22. René Lefort, 'Free Market Economy, 'developmental state' and Party-State Hegemony in Ethiopia: The Case of the 'Model Farmers," *The Journal of Modern African Studies* 50, no. 4, 2012: pp. 681–706.

23. 'Interview with Meles Zenawi', *African Arguments*, 25 May 2012.

24. 'Doing it my way,' *The Economist*, 2 March 2013.

25. Sarah Vaughan, 'Federalism, Democracy and Development', in Gerard Prunier and Eloi Ficquet (eds), *Understanding Contemporary Ethiopia* (2015), p. 307.

26. Joseph Stiglitz, *Globalization and Its Discontents* (2002), pp. 27–30.

27. Fana Gebresenbet, 'Securitisation of development in Ethiopia: the discourse and

politics of developmentalism', *Review of African Political Economy*, 41:sup1, S64–S74, 2014.

28. Tom Lavers, *Ethiopia's Developmental State* (2023), p. 4.

29. A joint assessment made by the World Bank and IMF in 2011 instead estimated "robust growth in the 7–8 per cent range": https://www.imf.org/external/pubs/ft/scr/2011/cr11303.pdf

30. Ethiopia's economic growth model in this period relied on standard instruments of financial repression, including a state-dominated banking sector, mandatory financing of priority projects and directed credit, and strict foreign exchange controls.

31. See, for example, 'Ethiopia is already the "China of Africa"', *Bloomberg*, 29 May 2018.

32. It is worth noting, however, that the Multidimensional Poverty Index of 2011 put Ethiopia just above Niger: https://www.ophi.org.uk/wp-content/uploads/OPHI-MPI-Brief-2011.pdf

33. See, for example, Tom Lavers, *Ethiopia's Developmental State* (2023); Peter Gill, *Famine and Foreigners* (2011).

34. 'Once a Bucknell Professor, Now the Commander of an Ethiopian Rebel Army', *New York Times*, 31 August 2016.

35. Ginbot 7 did not formally admit that it had set up and financed ESAT until 2019: Martin Plaut and Sarah Vaughan, *Understanding Ethiopia's Tigray War* (2023), p. 164.

36. ESAT has never denied that Eritrea provided it with seed funding, and Andargachew Tsige admitted so publicly in 2022: https://twitter.com/meetyoel/status/1562117517732200451

37. See, for example, 'The Voice of Genocide', *Horn Affairs*, 23 August 2017; Endalkachew Chala, 'Diaspora Media, Local Politics: Journalism and the Politics of Homeland among the Ethiopian Opposition in the United States,' PhD thesis, University of Oregon, 2019.

38. 'Champing at the Cyberbit', *Citizen Lab*, December 2017.

39. Jawar Mohammed, 'Failure to Deliver: the journey of the Oromo Liberation Front in the last two decades' (2009).

40. In *Sewyew* (2019), Abiy's biographer also claimed that Abiy's removal from INSA was a result of his well-known political ambitions.

41. "I am so interested in futuristic things. Even now, my focus is on artificial intelligence," Abiy told Sheger FM in 2019: https://www.youtube.com/watch?v=imCTWClFBss

42. Abiy interview with Sheger FM, September 2019: https://www.youtube.com/watch?v=zyQIVgOZ10k

43. *When we Medemer* (2019): https://www.youtube.com/watch?v=5jlGhQwgo5E

44. After the start of the Oromo protests, the Oromia government took back some of the land which had been leased to INSA when Abiy was acting director.

45. Abiy spoke proudly about the high school in an interview with Sheger FM in September 2019: https://www.youtube.com/watch?v=imCTWClFBss

46. In an October 2021 address to his party colleagues, Abiy conversely suggested he hadn't been fired but had rather chosen to leave INSA out of frustration.

47. Abiy said in his 2019 Sheger FM interview that after leaving INSA "stones [were] thrown at my house to shoot me if I came out": https://www.youtube.com/watch?v=imCTWClFBss

5. "OROMO FIRST"

1. Harold Marcus, *The Life of Menelik* (1975).

2. Mohammed Hassen, *The Oromo and the Christian Kingdom of Ethiopia* (2015); Brian J Yates, *The Other Abyssinians* (2020).

3. Getahun Benti, 'A Nation without a City: the Oromo struggle for Addis Ababa' in *Contested Terrain. Essays on Oromo Studies, Ethiopianist Discourse, and Politically Engaged Scholarship* (2009). The Tulama themselves are believed to have arrived in the area during the Oromo 'expansion' of the sixteenth century.

4. Pankhurst Richard, Breternitz Hartwig, 'Barara, the Royal City of the 15th and Early 16th Century (Ethiopia). Mediaeval and Other Early Settlements Between Wechecha Range and Mt Yerer: Results from a Recent Survey' in *Annales d'Ethiopie*, vol. 24, 2009.

5. See, for example, Charles W McClellan, 'State Transformation and Social Reconstitution in Ethiopia: The Allure of the South', *The International Journal of African Historical Studies*, vol. 17, no. 4, 1984.

6. See, for example, John Markakis, *The Last Two Frontiers* (2011).

7. The 'special interest' clause didn't, contrary to the demands of Oromo nationalists at the time, put the city under Oromia's jurisdiction. But it did promise Oromia a share of the city's revenues, as well as some say over the management of social services and natural resources, pledging—in effect—to end the discrimination against Oromos still common there.

8. https://unhabitat.org/the-state-of-addis-ababa-2017-the-addis-ababa-we-want

9. 'Expansion of Ethiopia's first industrial park reopens old wounds', Thomson Reuters Foundation, 1 February 2018.

10. In much of rural Ethiopia between 2011 and 2016, according to a World Bank report in 2020, poverty reduction and consumption growth had stalled: https://documents1.worldbank.org/curated/en/627681605631546436/pdf/Ethiopia-Regional-Poverty-Report-Promoting-Equitable-Growth-for-All-Regions.pdf

11. Tom Lavers, *Ethiopia's Developmental State* (2023), p. 149.

12. See for example, Jonah Wedekind, Davide Chinigò, 'Contract and Control: Agrarian labour mobilisation and resistance under large-scale land investments for biofuel crop production in Ethiopia' in *Annales d'Ethiopie*, vol. 33, 2020.

13. At the turn of the century there were roughly 40,000 students in Ethiopia. Two decades later, there were estimated to be over one million.

14. NW Reda, MT Gebre-Eyesus, 'Graduate Unemployment in Ethiopia: the "Red Flag" and Its Implications', *International Journal of African Higher Education*. 5, 1, February 2019.

15. According to the World Bank, annual real GDP growth from 2003 to 2010 was on average 11.4%, and still high but lower at 10.2% over 2010–15. The general slowdown continued from 2015 to 2019, with an annualised rate of 8.5%. In late 2015, the IMF raised its assessment of Ethiopia's debt risk from low to moderate.

16. 'Why big farms flopped in Ethiopia,' *The Economist*, 8 April 2020.

17. Martin Plaut and Sarah Vaughan, *Understanding Ethiopia's Tigray War* (2023), p. 119.

18. See, for example, Jostein Hauge, *The Future of the Factory* (2023).

19. Officially, it was not a plan to expand the city's administrative boundaries by putting districts in Oromia under Addis Ababa's administration. Nonetheless, by one estimate the city's physical limits would likely expand twenty-fold: 'Ethiopia: a leadership in disarray', *Open Democracy*, 4 July 2014.

20. So secretive was Getachew Asssefa that there exists only one publicly known photo of him.

21. Abiy first told the story in public on 31 October 2019: https://www.youtube.com/watch?v=e6qQGknnNfM

22. One such piece of intelligence concerned the attempted coup by Asaminew Tsige and colleagues in 2009 (see Chapter 11). Andargachew said Abiy revealed, when they met in 2018, that he had been the one who sent the information by email anonymously to him and Ginbot 7 at the time.

23. https://www.goolgule.com/

24. On Abiy's claims about Asaminew Tsige, see Chapter 11; his claim that his family went into exile because of his strong defence of Oromo interests was made to an audience in Haraghe in October 2019: https://www.youtube.com/watch?v=t46Ir2cMqb8&feature=youtu.be

25. Jörg Haustein and Dereje Feyissa, 'The strains of "Pente" politics: Evangelicals and the post-Orthodox state in Ethiopia', in *The Routledge Handbook of the Horn of Africa* (2022).

26. 'Long live the king,' *The Economist*, 16 February 2013.

27. According to ENDF records, proactive promotion of non-Tigrayans across all ranks meant that by 2016 the share of Tigrayans was, in most ranks, below 50 percent. By the start of 2020 non-Tigrayans made up at least 60 percent of generals. Critics, however, have argued that Tigrayan officers continued to wield greater influence irrespective of rank.

28. Michael Woldemariam, '"No war, no peace" in a region in flux: crisis, escalation, and possibility in the Eritrea-Ethiopia rivalry', *Journal of Eastern African Studies*, 2018.

29. Former minister; interview with Patrick Gilkes.

30. Mulugeta Gebrehiwot Berhe, *Laying the Past to Rest* (2020), p. 242.

31. Tefera Negash Gebregziabher & Wil Hout, 'The rise of oligarchy in Ethiopia: the case of wealth creation since 1991', *Review of African Political Economy*, 45:157, 2018.

32. Tefera Negash Gebregziabher, 'Soldiers in business: the pitfalls of METEC's projects in the context of Ethiopia's civil–military relations', *Review of African Political Economy*, 46:160, 2019, pp. 261–78.

33. 'Death on the Nile haunts Ethiopia's rebirth', *Bloomberg*, 2 August 2019.

34. https://www.hrw.org/news/2015/12/18/ethiopia-lethal-force-against-protesters; in October 2016, a general told a foreign farm manager that between December 2015 and the start of October there had already been 103 farm attacks in Oromia.

35. 'The Irreecha massacre explained,' *OPride*, 7 October 2016.

36. https://reliefweb.int/report/ethiopia/acled-country-report-popular-mobilisation-ethiopia-investigation-activity-november

37. 'Ethiopia cracks down on protest', *The Economist*, 15 October 2016.

38. One of the first known Ethiopian chroniclers of Oromo culture, Abba Bahrey, depicted the camps of *Qeerroo* warriors he encountered in his sixteenth century travels as anti-Christian militants. The term was later picked up—and repurposed—by the early Oromo nationalists: Mohammed Hassen, *The Oromo and the Christian Kingdom of Ethiopia* (2015), pp. 237–8.

39. 'Ethiopia's Muslim protests face unfair trial,' Human Rights Watch, 2 April 2013.

40. Jawar on Al Jazeera's *The Stream*, 25 June 2013: https://www.youtube.com/watch?v=uPxBztdKXLw&ab_channel=AnkuarTube

41. '"These changes are unprecedented": how Abiy is upending Ethiopian politics', *Guardian*, 8 July 2018.

42. https://www.youtube.com/watch?v=kE3xKK4N-kU

43. See, for example, https://sites.tufts.edu/reinventingpeace/2022/05/04/abiy-ahmed-phd/

44. Abiy Ahmed, *Medemer's Path* (2021), p. 115.

6.   *THE STIRRUP AND THE THRONE*

1.   *The Stirrup and the Throne* was published in December 2016, though Abiy didn't publicly admit to being its author until November 2019. This was, he said, his fourth book published under the pen-name "Dearaz" (as well as two which were never published)—an anagram formed from the initial letters of the names of his three daughters and wife: https://www.youtube.com/watch?v=8BmG8uKNPiQ&t=98s

2.   Abiy Ahmed, *The Stirrup and the Throne* (2016), p. xviii.

3.   In 2019, Abiy described both *The Stirrup and the Throne* and *Kedir Setete* as "books through which I released the pain that was inside me at that time": https://www.youtube.com/watch?v=8BmG8uKNPiQ&t=98s

4.   Abiy writes, for instance: "Many African countries and countries in Eastern Europe and Asia were led into economic collapse and popular uprising due to the forced imposition of structural adjustment regimes." (p. 144).

5.   On the rare occasion Abiy mentions democracy, his arguments are indistinguishable from EPRDF orthodoxy: "It is imperative that we implement the developmental state by tuning it with democracy. History has shown us that development can be achieved both under a democratic and oppressive government."

6.   For Abiy's criticisms of the student movement, see p. 152.

7.   Ibid., p. 11.

8.   Machiavelli's *The Prince* is rarely cited directly, and in one instance Abiy somewhat counter-intuitively advises Ethiopians to avoid "the path foreshadowed by Machiavelli's ruinous philosophy" (p. 96).

9.   Ibid., pp. 36–9.

10. Abiy Ahmed, *Medemer's Path* (2021), p. 115.

11. 'OPride's Oromo Person of the Year 2017', *OPride*, 31 December 2017.

12. Eyewitnesses reported seeing Tigrayan security agents at the festival, despite assurances from the government that only Oromo regional police would be present. But claims made by Jawar and other activists abroad, that helicopters had fired on protesters from the sky, causing the stampede, were not generally corroborated by those present on the day.

13. Biruk Terefe, *Renaissance Derailed: the politics of infrastructural statecraft in Ethiopia*, PhD thesis, Oxford (forthcoming).

14. 'Is the OPDO the new opposition?' *OPride*, 11 November 2017.

15. Oromos educated in the post-1991 period became known as the "*Qubee* generation", so named for the Latin alphabet adopted for Afan Oromo in the 1990s.

16. 'OPride's Oromo Person of The Year 2016: The Qubee Generation', *OPride*, 31 December 2016.

17. Audio recording of a speech given by Shimelis Abdissa, leaked to the press in August 2020.

18. In 2017, Abiy was the board chairman of the Oromia Broadcasting Network.

19. 'Abiy tests the military,' *Africa Confidential*, 4 May 2018.

20. Notable among these allies were Dr Mehret Debebe and the controversial Orthodox deacon Daniel Kibret.

21. Audio recording of a speech given by Shimelis Abdissa, leaked to the press in August 2020.

22. Abiy interview with OBN, 1 October 2019: https://www.youtube.com/watch?v=Gj-OE3MKNPY

23. Kjetil Tronvoll, 'Falling from Grace: The Collapse of Ethiopia's Ruling Coalition.' *Northeast African Studies*, vol. 21 no. 2, 2021, pp. 11–56.

24. Lemma, for example, said: "We must not allow the 'others' to create unrest. We are the biggest groups and no one can come and tell us what to do." https://www.youtube.com/watch?v=KBa_p6kv724

25. Martin Plaut and Sarah Vaughan, *Understanding Ethiopia's Tigray War* (2023), p. 140.

26. 'The blood in Oromia is our blood too', *African Arguments*, 27 September 2016.

27. See, for example, Tsehai Berhane-Selassie, *Ethiopian Warriorhood* (2018), pp. 13–17.

28. https://reliefweb.int/report/ethiopia/acled-country-report-popular-mobilisation-ethiopia-investigation-activity-november

29. Though there were relatively few examples of Tigrayans being directly attacked or killed by Oromo protesters in this period, it was common for property and businesses associated with the TPLF, or Tigrayans generally, to be targeted, especially during the so-called "week of rage" in October 2016.

30. https://www.youtube.com/watch?v=CXFXaWehyo4.   Nothing   comparable

was broadcast by OMN in this period, though Jawar did on occasion deploy the pejorative stereotype of a money-grubbing Tigrayan—"Hagos"—in his social media posts.

31. 'Keeping Ethiopia's transition on the rails', Crisis Group, 16 December 2019.

32. In *Greater Ethiopia: the Evolution of a Multiethnic Society* (1974), the American sociologist Donald Levine likened the relationship between Tigrayans and Amharas to the rivalry between twins.

33. According to the 1994 census, more than 95% of the population of Wolkait was Tigrayan. Wolkait activists in Gondar alleged to the International Crisis Group in 2020 that when TPLF rebels arrived in the 1980s, they killed and evicted Amhara and took local wives, leading to the demographic shift: 'Bridging Ethiopia's divided north', Crisis Group, 12 June 2020.

34. Jan Nyssen & Biadgilgn Demissie, 'Administrative and ethno-linguistic boundaries of Western Tigray (Ethiopia) since 1683', *Journal of Maps*, 19:1, 2023.

35. In various historical maps of Ethiopia, often produced by colonial cartographers, the territories contested by Amhara and Tigray regional states were sometimes located in Amhara and sometimes in Tigray. But they are of only limited use in determining the "rightful" status of the territories, since they show only political control rather than demographic patterns of language and identity.

36. For example, the family of Tedros Tirfe, the future chairman of the Amhara Association of America, came from Humera in Wolkait, moved to Sudan in the 1970s, and then to America in 1982.

37. Laura Hammond, *This Place Will Become Home: Refugee Repatriation to Ethiopia* (2004).

38. In a 2019 interview, Colonel Demeke's father described his son as Tigrayan: https://www.youtube.com/watch?v=C-cTfNzj03M

39. Plaut and Vaughan, *Understanding Ethiopia's Tigray War* (2023), p. 138.

40. See, for example, Bahru Zewde, *A History of Modern Ethiopia 1855–1991* (1991).

41. Mehdi Labzaé, 'The "Wolqayt question" in Amhara nationalism. Agrarian claims, nationalist mobilization, and violence in the Ethiopian political crisis and civil war (c. 2015–2021)', (2023).

42. Ibid.

43. Many investors who became leading figures of the Wolkait Committee were once TPLF members, according to former administrators of Western Tigray.

44. Labzaé, 'The "Wolqayt question" in Amhara nationalism...' (2023).

45. The former prime minister Hailemariam Desalegn later told me that the order to arrest Colonel Demeke had been given without his approval.

46. See, for example, Achamyeleh Tamiru, *The Wolkait Affairs* (2019).

47. The EPRDF's final congress in Hawassa, October 2018.

48. Among those removed from the TPLF leadership was Azeb Mesfin, Meles's widow and figurehead of a faction considered most loyal to the former prime minister's legacy.

49. Abiy himself claimed in his speech to parliament on 30 November 2020 that he was being tailed during this period. He claimed there was an arrest warrant for his arrest 5–10 days before Hailemariam's resignation. This has never been definitively proven, though it is plausible.

50. Abiy also made reference to this video in his 30 November 2020 speech to Parliament.

51. 'Ethiopia's ethnic federalism is being tested,' *The Economist*, 7 October 2017.

52. Lemma's interview with OBN, 27 September 2017: https://youtu.be/hNR7OmP6KNw

53. Territorial competition between Oromo and Somali clans nonetheless pre-dated the introduction of ethnic federalism, and ethnic identities had already hardened following the 1977–8 Ethiopia-Somali War.

54. Oromia had previously created a version of the *Liyu* to deal with the OLF insurgency in the mid-end of the 1990s: the "*Fetno Derash*" (Rapid Unit). From 2017, however, it was rapidly expanded and upgraded to match the Somali *Liyu*. The "*Adma Bitena*" (Riot Police) was the *Liyu*'s predecessor in the Amhara region.

55. Getachew Reda explained this particular disagreement in an interview in March 2020: "We had our differences from the get-go," he told me.

56. 'How Ethiopia's transition to democracy derailed: reflections by Jawar Mohammed,' *Addis Standard*, 28 October 2020.

57. Milkessa Midega later described Abiy's takeover as a coup d'état, on the grounds that Lemma's removal didn't follow prescribed party procedures.

58. *Addis Standard*: http://addisstandard.com/analysis-dr-abiy-ahmed-becomes-a-prime-minister-the-legacy-eprdf-fought-against-to-the-bitter-end-what-went-behind-closed-doors-and-how-could-that-shape-his-premiership/

59. Abiy to Parliament, 30 November 2020.

60. *Africa Confidential*: https://www.africa-confidential.com/article/id/12312/Abiy_tests_the_military

61. The most exhaustive blow-by-blow account of the vote was published a few days later by *Addis Standard*: http://addisstandard.com/analysis-dr-abiy-ahmed-becomes-a-prime-minister-the-legacy-eprdf-fought-against-to-the-bitter-end-what-went-behind-closed-doors-and-how-could-that-shape-his-premiership/

62. Kjetil Tronvoll, 'Falling from Grace: The Collapse of Ethiopia's Ruling Coalition.' *Northeast African Studies*, vol. 21, no. 2, 2021, pp. 11–56. *Project MUSE*.

63. Abiy's Wikipedia page was opened on 18 February 2018. One of those writing and editing it was Yodahe Zemichael, a former colleague from the ministry of science and technology who would go on to join Abiy in the Prime Minister's Office, and later landed a top job at INSA: https://en.m.wikipedia.org/w/index.php?title=Special:History/Abiy_Ahmed&offset=20180219142508

64. https://www.youtube.com/watch?v=fT96mNqPuRY&ab_channel=CagginooPodcast

65. https://www.youtube.com/watch?v=5J9Rso7IMhU

7.   ABIYMANIA

1. 'Can Abiy Ahmed save Ethiopia?' *Foreign Policy*, 4 April 2018.

2. 'Ethiopia PM asks protesters for patience as he seeks change', *AFP*, 13 April 2018.

3. 'Ethiopia's Ambo city', *BBC*, 12 March 2020.

4. https://youtu.be/OIcYtLwMY6I?si=fAqjWZp5cYDadS25

5. 'The long and daunting journey of Prime Minister Abiy,' *Addis Standard*, 7 June 2018.

6. https://twitter.com/PMEthiopia/status/1066303171109314560

7. https://twitter.com/fitsumaregaa/status/1047413599369670656

8. 'Ink by the barrel in Addis Ababa', *The Economist*, 16 March 2019.

9. Such freedoms did not last long, however; not long after *Min Litazez?* had mocked Abiy personally it was taken off air: 'Wax and gold,' *The Economist*, 23 March 2019.

10. Jörg Haustein and Dereje Feyissa, 'The strains of "Pente" politics: Evangelicals and the post-Orthodox state in Ethiopia', in *The Routledge Handbook of the Horn of Africa* (2022).

11. T Østebø, 'Religious Dynamics and Conflicts in Contemporary Ethiopia: Expansion, Protection, and Reclaiming Space', *African Studies Review*, 1–24, 2023, doi:10.1017/asr.2023.11

12. Hailemariam told me in 2020 that he believed the transition was part of God's plan for Ethiopia. He also said in public the same year that he believed Abiy had been chosen by God to lead a transition which had been planned and ordained by the Almighty himself: https://www.youtube.com/watch?v=tY5XOn-SYXrE

13. 'Ethiopians are going wild for Abiy Ahmed', *The Economist*, 18 August 2018.

14. 'Abiy Ahmed meets the Ethiopian diaspora', *The Atlantic*, 4 August 2018.

15. 'How Ethiopia's transition to democracy derailed: reflections by Jawar Mohammed,' *Addis Standard*, 28 October 2020.

16. 'Why I'm coming back home to Ethiopia after 16 years in exile', Al Jazeera, 30 June 2018.

17. Harry Verhoeven & Michael Woldemariam, 'Who lost Ethiopia? The unmaking of an African anchor state and U.S. foreign policy', *Contemporary Security Policy*, 43:4, 2022, pp. 622–50.

18. Ibid.

19. The total included health, development and security assistance.

20. Ambassador Raynor announced in 2019 that the US government planned to embed "senior US government officials at key Ethiopian economic ministries and operations for a sustained period of time". These plans were dropped following the imposition of legal restrictions on US assistance during the Tigray War.

21. See, for example, 'Ethiopia's new leader is whittling away the old guard's power', *Financial Times*, 12 September 2018.

22. Abiy's first and—at the time of writing in late 2023—only press conference took place on 25 August 2018. He didn't take any questions in English or from foreign reporters.

23. 'Africa's new talisman', *Financial Times*, 20 February 2019.

24. https://www.facebook.com/watch/?v=2154419867957673

25. https://www.youtube.com/watch?v=t4u4bY49jmA&ab_channel=TonyBlairInstituteforGlobalChange

26. 'Abiy Ahmed's 'courageous' reforms hailed in Paris', *Le Point*, 30 October 2018.

27. Abiy Ahmed, *The Stirrup and the Throne* (2016), pp. 11–12.

28. The only other major interview was with the *Financial Times* in 2019. A short, perfunctory interview with the *New York Times* took place between meetings with the Ethiopian diaspora in Los Angeles in August 2018.

29. 'The Americanization of Dr Abiy Ahmed Administration', *Addis Insight*, 23 November 2018; Verhoeven & Woldemariam, 'Who lost Ethiopia?', pp. 622–50.

30. 'Ethiopia signs up for IMF deal: what's in store?' *Addis Fortune*, 21 December 2019.

31. The World Bank extended $1.2 billion ($600 million grant and $600 million credit) from the International Development Association in October 2018.

32. *Ethiopia 2030: Pathway to Prosperity: Ten Years Perspective Development Plan: 2021–23.*

33. 'Ethiopian businesses disappointed by new PM's economic stance', Reuters, 23 April 2018.

34. According to its director, Ricardo Haussmann, and confirmed by a colleague, the Harvard Growth Lab reviewed a draft of the programme and suggested edits, most of which were never incorporated.

35. 'Ethiopia Macroeconomic Handbook', *Cepheus* (2019).

36. 'Ethiopia's new prime minister wants peace and privatisation,' *The Economist*, 7 June 2018.

37. Tom Lavers, *Ethiopia's Developmental State* (2023), p. 286.

38. Ibid., p. 285; see also, 'Ethiopia's football follies,' *The Economist*, 13 August 2016.

39. According to a senior official closely involved in these plans, teams had previously been dispatched to India, Vietnam and China to explore options for banking liberalisation.

40. When they announced plans in late 2023, the financial services authorities said there would be a ceiling on the maximum number of shares foreign investors could own in local banks to avoid the latter being swallowed by foreign rivals.

41. 'Ethiopia's prime minister plans telecoms privatisation', *Financial Times*, 4 February 2010.

42. 'Land privatisation once again on the table,' *The Reporter*, 19 November 2022.

8. BRIDGE OF LOVE

1. On 18 May 2018, Suraphel told his congregants that "the people who miss each other will be without restrictions, in the name of Jesus! In the name of Jesus, the people will move back and forth without checkpoints! They will be one": https://www.youtube.com/watch?v=mdVy0hiEKdY

2. 'An unexpected embrace', *The Economist*, 7 October 2018.

3. 'Prison break', *The Economist*, 11 October 2018.

4. On a visit to Mogadishu in 2018 Abiy said that he and Somalia's president had "discussed undergoing full economic integration shortly. And to integrate the people in the process and fully unite and become one country in the long run."

5. Paul Kenyan, *Dictatorland: The Men Who Stole Africa* (2008), p. 436.

6. 'Bio Notes on Eritrean President Isaias Afewerki', *WikiLeaks*, 12 November 2008.

7. A notorious early example was Isaias's execution of his old friend, Mussie Tesfamikael, during the EPLF's "*menqa*" (bat) purges of the 1970s. In September

2001, as president, Isaias rounded up and jailed eleven of his closest colleagues. Twenty-three years later none have been freed and many are known to have died.

8. Gaim Kibreab, *From Ally to Enemy* (2021), pp. 125–8.

9. According to former Eritrean defence minister Mesfin Hagos, Isaias floated the idea of joining the EPRDF coalition in an EPLF central committee meeting in 1991: Mesfin Hagos and Awet Tewelde Weldemichael, *An African Revolution Reclaimed* (2023), pp. 293–4.

10. In a press conference in Addis Ababa in 1993, Isaias said that "full integration of Ethiopia and Eritrea, beginning with an economic integration programme, and ending possibly in the form of some political integration, is the possibility."

11. 'Eritrea pushes to get U.S. base', *Washington Post*, 21 November 2002.

12. Robert Kaplan, *Surrender or Starve* (1988), p. 206.

13. Richard Reid, *Shallow Graves* (2020), p. 113.

14. Report of the Commission of Inquiry on Human Rights in Eritrea (June 2015): https://www.ohchr.org/en/hr-bodies/hrc/co-i-eritrea/report-co-i-eritrea-0

15. The moniker was unpopular even with Eritrean critics of the government. Though inexact, the parallels between the two regimes were nonetheless quite striking: 'Why Eritrea is called Africa's North Korea', *The Economist*, 14 August 2018.

16. 'The surprising triumph of Africa's Kim Jong Un', *1843*, 29 September 2023.

17. Awet T. Weldemichael, 'Neither Old nor New', in *Ethiopia in the Wake of Political Reforms* (2020), p. 528.

18. There is some disagreement about what exactly the EPRDF executive committee had agreed by this point. In *War on Tigray: Genocidal Axis in the Horn* (2023), the Tigrayan journalist Daniel Berhane claims that a team to prepare a proposal for the implementation of the Algiers Agreement was all that had been established.

19. Ibid., p. 529.

20. Abiy had also told Parliament in his inaugural speech: "We want from the bottom of our hearts that the disagreement that has reigned for years to come to an end."

21. Technically, however, even this offer fell short of Eritrea's long-standing demand for unconditional withdrawal of Ethiopian troops prior to any dialogue.

22. See, for example, Martin Plaut and Sarah Vaughan, *Understanding Ethiopia's Tigray War* (2023).

23. 'President Isaias's Speech on Martyrs' Day', *Eritrea Profile*, 23 June 2018.

24. Awet T. Weldemichael, 'Neither Old nor New', in *Ethiopia in the Wake of Political Reforms* (2020), p. 531.

25. 'The Great Land Rush', *Financial Times*, 1 March 2016.

26. 'The Rehabilitation of Africa's Most Isolated Dictatorship,' *Foreign Policy*, 21 June 2017.

27. For example, Abiy spoke warmly of the UAE's federal system in a speech on 17 January 2022: https://youtu.be/NF_eM7gpCFs

28. 'This is Dubai now', *The Guardian*, 16 October 2019.

29. 'Muddled meddling by the UAE', *Africa Confidential*, 10 June 2021.

30. 'The Most Powerful Arab Ruler Isn't M.B.S. It's M.B.Z.' *New York Times*, 2 June 2019; 'A Saudi Prince's Quest to Remake the Middle East', *New Yorker*, 2 April 2018.

31. The finances of the Gulf states, particularly its vast sovereign wealth funds, are notoriously opaque, making it difficult to track where and how exactly they were spent in Ethiopia in these years.
32. 'Abiy dials down Pax Ethiopia', *Africa Confidential*, 10 August 2018.
33. The prominent Ethiopianist activist, Abebe Gellaw, claimed in an interview in 2023 that Abiy had told him five years earlier how he and Isaias had mulled plans to bind Ethiopia and Eritrea in a form of economic or even political union.
34. Farmaajo may, however, have briefly persuaded Abiy not to follow through with a controversial 2018 deal with Somaliland, in which Ethiopia was to acquire a 19% stake in the recently expanded Emirati-funded port of Berbera. The deal was in any case revived—and expanded—to much fanfare in January 2024.
35. Muktar Robow, a former leader of Al-Shabaab, told me in 2022 that Ethiopian soldiers in the AMISOM peacekeeping force had arrested him in order to prevent his running for president of Somalia's South-West region.
36. https://twitter.com/PMEthiopia/status/1069640490260123648/photo/3
37. Willow Berridge et al., *Sudan's Unfinished Democracy* (2022), p. 99.
38. Abiy did, however, help to persuade the leaders of Somaliland and Somalia to meet in Djibouti in 2020 (though nothing came out of it): 'Somalia-Somaliland: A Halting Embrace of Dialogue', International Crisis Group, 6 August 2020.
39. 'Abiy spells out expansionist plans', *Africa Confidential*, 16 November 2023.

9. "IT WAS CHAOS"

1. https://reliefweb.int/report/ethiopia/ethiopia-gedeo-and-west-guji-displacement-snapshot-march-2019
2. 'The young Ethiopians working for peace', *New Humanitarian*, 11 November 2019.
3. Kibru Mamo, *Ye Gedeo Hizb ye zemenet Tiyake* (2022). p. 91.
4. The estimates were quite wide-ranging: between 1.4m and 2.9m new IDPs in 2018. But even the lower estimates put Ethiopia in the top spot globally that year.
5. Politicisation of IDP numbers was a problem on both sides of the conflict; the highest tallies had almost certainly been inflated by the respective zonal administrations. But there is little reason to doubt that those displaced numbered in the hundreds of thousands.
6. 'Abiy Ahmed and the struggle to keep Ethiopia together', *The Africa Report*, 11 October 2019.
7. https://www.acleddata.com/2018/10/13/change-and-continuity-in-protests-and-political-violence-pm-abiys-ethiopia
8. '"Leba! Leba!" Abiy inspires farmers' revolt in North Shoa village', *Ethiopia Insight*, 21 November 2018.
9. Jawar later retracted the statement in an interview in 2013.
10. 'Anguish for Harari as Oromo claim rights', *Ethiopia Insight*, 2 January 2019.
11. According to the Ethiopian Investment Commission, the country lost out on $300m of investment in the first quarter of 2019, as committed investment was pulled out due to political instability, above all in Oromia.

12. 'Ethnic federalism and its discontents', International Crisis Group, 4 September 2009.

13. Dagne Shibru, 'Conflict and conflict resolution mechanisms in Ethiopia: the case of Gedeo and Guji ethnic groups,' PhD dissertation (2013).

14. 'Ethnic federalism and its discontents', International Crisis Group, 4 September 2009.

15. See, for example, Jon Abbink, 'Ethnicity and conflict generation in Ethiopia: some problems and prospects of ethno-regional federalism', *Journal of Contemporary African Studies*, vol. 24, no. 3 (2006).

16. 'Drivers of ethnic conflict in contemporary Ethiopia', *Institute for Security Studies*, 9 December 2019.

17. Ibid.

18. According to UN sources, there were as many as 841 people per square kilometre on average in the most densely populated parts of Gedeo and Guji.

19. https://www.acleddata.com/2018/10/13/change-and-continuity-in-protests-and-political-violence-pm-abiys-ethiopia

20. Abiy to Parliament, 15 June 2018.

21. 'Drivers of ethnic conflict in contemporary Ethiopia,' *Institute for Security Studies*, 9 December 2019.

22. Abiy's first press conference, 25 August 2018.

23. One such discussion forum, organised by the Prime Minister's Office as "Addis Weg", soon became little more than a platform for government propaganda.

24. 'Ethiopia's democratic predicaments: state–society dynamics and the balance of power', *Institute for Security Studies*, 7 December 2022.

25. In Oromia, there were reports of local police even creating clandestine "Qeerroo" groups in order to loot.

26. 'Ethiopia must end culture of impunity to heal from decades of human rights violations', *Addis Standard*, 2 June 2020.

27. See, for example, Abiy's speech to Parliament on 6 July 2023: "It is more important to seek forgiveness for past wrongs rather than pursue retribution."

28. See, for example, Abiy's first press conference, 25 August 2018.

29. 'Shadow falls over Ethiopia reforms as warnings of crisis go unheeded', *The Guardian*, 14 March 2018; one crowd-funding campaign, led by an Ethiopian-American activist, ESAT's Tamagn Beyene, raised more than $1.3 million for the Gedeo cause.

30. Addressing the displaced Gedeos on 17 March 2019, Abiy said: "the federal government received a report on March 10 and it responded on March 11, the next day": https://www.youtube.com/watch?v=i-r7ACaC8Wk&ab_channel=EBC

31. https://reliefweb.int/report/ethiopia/ethiopia-forced-displacement-guji-and-gedeo-zones-dg-echo-humanitarian-partners-echo

32. According to the AU's Kampala Convention—which Ethiopia had signed but not ratified—displaced persons are entitled to freedom of movement and to adequate humanitarian assistance wherever they need it.

33. Abiy to Parliament, 6 July 2023.

34. See, for example, '"Rot is so much deeper"—decades of Ethiopia aid manipulation', *Devex*, 28 August 2023.

10. "OUR SON-OF-A-BITCH"

1.   https://web.archive.org/web/20080227131228/http://130.238.24.99/library/resources/dossiers/local_history_of_ethiopia/d/ORTDEB2.pdf
2.   Ibid.
3.   Martin Plaut and Sarah Vaughan, *Understanding Ethiopia's Tigray War* (2023), p. 89.
4.   'Collective Punishment', Human Rights Watch, June 2008.
5.   Ibid.
6.   'Ethiopians Said to Push Civilians Into Rebel War', *New York Times*, 15 December 2007.
7.   'Nobody will kneel!' Reuters, 16 December 2018.
8.   Abiy to Parliament, 30 November 2020.
9.   https://twitter.com/addisstandard/status/1010433172667060224?s=20
10. 'Political Violence Could Derail Ethiopia's Democratic Transition', *Foreign Policy*, 20 September 2020.
11. 'Death on the Nile haunts Ethiopia's rebirth', *Bloomberg*, 2 August 2019.
12. See, for example,, the large-scale land deals in Gambella in the late 2000s, which had almost exclusively gone to well-connected Tigrayans: Fana Gebresenbet, 'Land Acquisitions, the Politics of Dispossession, and State-Remaking in Gambella, Western Ethiopia', *Africa Spectrum*, vol. 51, no. 1, 2016. Likewise, for example, see the ownership of Afar region's salt mines: 'Afar's Salty Politics', Rift Valley Institute, September 2023.
13. 'We are like the dead', Human Rights Watch, 4 July 2018.
14. 'It wasn't me!' *OPride*, 12 July 2018.
15. https://www.lse.ac.uk/ideas/Assets/Documents/Conflict-Research-Programme/crp-memos/Inter-ethnic-conflicts-SRS-Final-April-2020.pdf
16. 'Upheaval in Somali Region Tests Ethiopian PM's Ability to Unify', *VOA*, 10 August 2018;   https://www.lse.ac.uk/ideas/Assets/Documents/Conflict-Research-Programme/crp-memos/Inter-ethnic-conflicts-SRS-Final-April-2020.pdf
17. Abiy to Parliament, 30 November 2020.
18. In the same 2020 speech Abiy insisted he had waited until the very last possible moment before intervening.
19. http://aigaforum.com/amharic-article-2020/when-facing-history.htm
20. 'Lessons from an open-air prison', *The Economist*, 3 October 2019.
21. 'Afar's Salty Politics', Rift Valley Institute, September 2023, p. 22.
22. 'All is not quiet on Ethiopia's western front', *Foreign Policy*, 6 January 2021.
23. In a televised ceremony inaugurating the new Republican Guard in December 2018, some of the soldiers were wearing T-shirts bearing Abiy's face: https://www.youtube.com/watch?v=2uct1VsInDA&ab_channel=TigraiOnline
24. "I came to realise […] it is a force within which is going to kill me": Abiy to Parliament, 30 November 2020.

25. However, not all were Tigrayan: the deputy CEO of METEC, for instance, was Oromo.

26. Regional state broadcasters such as the Oromia Broadcasting Network were given the relevant material by federal officials and ordered to broadcast it: "*Yefitih Sekoka*" (The Wailing of Justice), 11 December 2018 (Amhara Media Corporation): Part one: https://www.youtube.com/watch?v=3JKZs7Kk3CY Part two: https://www.youtube.com/watch?v=c48h55XR3ns

27. In a speech given on 19 November 2018, Debretsion said the regional administration would not assent to what he deemed "politicised arrests".

28. 'Rounding up the suspects', *Africa Confidential*, 23 November 2018.

29. 'Debretsion's Final Nail in the EPRDF Coffin', *Awate*, 28 December 2019.

30. 'The Special Police in Ethiopia', *European Institute of Peace*, October 2021. According to sources in the TPLF, the Tigrayan special police increased in size from roughly 2,000 to 25,000 troops between 2018 and the start of the Tigray War.

31. Kjetil Tronvoll, 'Falling from Grace: The Collapse of Ethiopia's Ruling Coalition', *Northeast African Studies*, vol. 21, no. 2, 2021, pp. 11–56. *Project MUSE.*

11. "THEIR PROTECTOR"

1. In this respect, it was telling that the most celebrated figure in Ethiopian history among many Amharas was Emperor Tewodros II, who killed himself rather than be taken captive by the British at the Battle of Magdala in 1868.

2. 'Abiy Ahmed's Reforms Have Unleashed Forces He Can No Longer Control', *Foreign Policy*, 4 July 2019.

3. In a speech in the UAE in February 2020, Abiy said Asaminew's appointment was his decision.

4. See, for instance, his 2018 speech at the graduation ceremony of new special forces, in which Asaminew warned: "If we look back at our history, we've not faced a challenge as great as this for 500 years… The challenge we face now is even stronger than that one." https://www.youtube.com/watch?v=TyM2OcJtqiU

5. https://www.youtube.com/watch?v=Ei9LLm5C3u0&ab_channel=AyalewD

6. https://youtu.be/I-muBJ5rLcw?si=TYD6plFsPXxzT9TL

7. See, for example, Tezera Tazebew, 'Amhara nationalism: The empire strikes back', *African Affairs*, vol. 120, issue 479, April 2021, pp. 297–313.

8. S Pausewang, 'The two-faced Amhara identity', *Scrinium*, 1(1), 2005, pp. 273–86.

9. Tegegne Teka, 'Amhara Ethnicity in the Making', in Markakis and Salih (eds), *Ethnicity and the State in Eastern Africa* (1998).

10. Donald Levine, *Wax and Gold* (1974), p. 78.

11. Christopher Clapham, 'Centralization and local response in Southern Ethiopia', *African Affairs*, 74, 294, 1975.

12. See, for example, Abinet Hunegaw, *The Case for Amhara Nationalism* (2017).

13. The All-Amhara People's Organisation (AAPO), founded by the renowned medical doctor Asrat Woldeyes in the 1990s, was a notable—though unsuccessful—

exception. Dr Asrat was arrested in 1994 and imprisoned for four years on charges of attempting to violently overthrow the government.

14. Terje Ostebo, *Islam, Ethnicity and Conflict* (2020).

15. John Young, 'Along Ethiopia's Western Frontier: Gambella and Benishangul in Transition', *The Journal of Modern African Studies*, 37, no. 2, 1999: 321–46. http://www.jstor.org/stable/161849

16. United States Bureau of Citizenship and Immigration Services, Ethiopia. Status of Amharas, March 1993: https://www.refworld.org/docid/3ae6a6077.html

17. 'Driven away by conflict, thousands of Ethiopians stranded without a home,' Thomson Reuters Foundation, 21 June 2021.

18. 'The Authoritarian Liberation of the Western Lands,' *Justice Spatiale*, July 2015.

19. Muluken Asfaw, *Amhara Holocaust* (2017).

20. 'Why Ethiopia has postponed its census', *The Economist*, 29 March 2019.

21. Birtukan Sebsibie wept in the House of Federation two days after a massacre of Amhara civilians in Wollega on 1 November 2020: https://www.youtube.com/watch?v=gHZQLm2ys3w

22. Tadesse Tamrat, *Church and State in Ethiopia 1270–1527* (1972), p. 301.

23. Martin Plaut and Sarah Vaughan, *Understanding Ethiopia's Tigray War* (2023), p. 19.

24. Mehdi Labzae, 'The Wolkayt Question in Amhara Nationalism' (2023).

25. One such movement was *Mahibere Kidusan*, formed several years earlier to meet the challenge posed by the rise of Pentecostalism. Some of its most prominent members, notably Daniel Kibret, joined Abiy's government, which caused major internal frictions in the movement.

26. 'The war in Ethiopia is not over', *Mail and Guardian*, 9 February 2023.

27. 'Beyond Law Enforcement', Amnesty International, 29 May 2020.

28. For a more detailed discussion of the parallels between Ethiopia and the former Yugoslavia, see, for example, 'Abiy Ahmed and the struggle to keep Ethiopia together', *The Africa Report*, 11 October 2019.

29. The article in question was: Carol Skalnik Leff, 'Democratization and Disintegration in Multinational States: The Breakup of the Communist Federations', *World Politics*, vol. 51, no. 2, 1999.

30. The presence of Muslims in NaMA was limited but not non-existent: one of its founders and a deputy chairman, Yusuf Ibrahim, for instance, was a Muslim from Wollo. However, Islamophobia was common among rank-and-file Amhara nationalists. The popular 'Patriot' and *Fano* leader Mesafint Teka, for instance, was recorded saying that it was "okay to eat and dine with Muslims… But a Muslim becoming a political leader is unacceptable." https://twitter.com/isaacEthio/status/1520769318010724352

31. 'Bridging the divide in Ethiopia's troubled north,' Crisis Group, 12 June 2020.

32. https://youtu.be/I-muBJ5rLcw?si=TYD6plFsPXxzT9TL

33. 'Bridging the divide in Ethiopia's troubled north,' Crisis Group, 12 June 2020.

34. Slobodan Milošević rose to power in the late 1980s by highlighting the alleged oppression of minority Serbs by the Albanian majority in Kosovo and, from 1992 to 1999, launched successive campaigns of ethnic cleansing. Unlike Asaminew,

though, observers have tended to stress Milošević's cynical adoption of Serbian nationalism for political advantage. Few doubted, by contrast, the sincerity of Asaminew's convictions.

35. 'Drivers of ethnic conflict in contemporary Ethiopia,' *Institute for Security Studies*, 9 December 2019.

36. In the recording, Asaminew is heard telling Muluken Setiye of Amhara Media Corporation over the phone that "we have taken action on ADP leaders": https://www.youtube.com/watch?v=qE2pZyh_Lcc

37. Tefera Mamo, Asaminew's close colleague and head of the Amhara special forces at the time, later wrote that his late friend had carried out the attacks on the basis of a "grudge" stemming from the critical evaluation three days earlier. He described it as a "suicide mission": 'June 22nd: From What I Have Seen and Heard', *Feteh Magazine*, June 2020.

38. Milkessa Midega, a former OPDO colleague, argued that Abiy's use of crisis was deliberate and strategic: 'Manufacturing crises for the birth of a "new" dictatorship', *Addis Standard*, 4 July 2023.

39. Source: Full Gospel church leader present at the meeting (my interview).

40. Abiy also claimed that this was the reason he had sent his family abroad to America for their safety, and erroneously claimed that he—rather than Hailemariam—had been the one to release Asaminew from prison in 2018.

12.   *THE HIJACKED REVOLUTION*

1. Terrefe Woldetsadik, 'The Unification of Ethiopia (1880–1935) Wälläga', *Journal of Ethiopian Studies*, vol. 6, no. 1, 1968, pp. 73–86.

2. Allesandro Truilzi, 'Nekemte and Addis Ababa: the dilemmas of provincial rule' in Donham & James (eds), *The Southern Marches of Imperial Ethiopia* (1986).

3. See, for example, ibid., p. 11.

4. J Hultin, 'Rebounding Nationalism: State and Ethnicity in Wollega 1968–1976', *Africa,* 73(3), 2003, pp. 402–26.

5. The number of Amhara officials in the local administration increased slightly after the Second World War; as part of an increasingly rigid language policy, Afan Oromo was, for instance, banned in Protestant mission schools in 1942: ibid., p. 141.

6. The most prominent was Emanuel Abraham, who held several ministerial posts between the 1950s and 1970s and came from Gimbi in western Wollega.

7. John Binns, *The Orthodox Church of Ethiopia: A History* (2016), pp. 201–6.

8. Ezekiel Gebissa, 'The Italian Invasion, the Ethiopian Empire, and Oromo Nationalism: The Significance of the Western Oromo Confederation of 1936,' *Northeast African Studies*, vol. 9, no. 3, 2002, pp. 75–96.

9. For example, Negasso Gidada—an OLF member who later became the first President of the FDRE in 1991—was the son of one of the first local Protestant ministers in Dembi Dollo. Lencho Lata, one of the OLF's founders, was the son of a Protestant evangelist.

10. 'The fracturing of the Oromo elite and return of Ethiopia's law and order State', *Addis Standard*, 13 August 2020.

11. *Feteh*, November 2018.

12. Although Abiy's mother was likely Amhara by birth, the fact that Abiy had been raised an Oromo would, in earlier times, have qualified him as ethnically Oromo. Oromo nationalism in the twenty-first century, however, tended to place rather more value on bloodline 'purity'.

13. 'Toll from Ethiopia bloodshed at least 58: rights group, source,' *AFP*, 19 September 2018.

14. Many Oromos would later claim that the killings had been orchestrated by the government. Former OPDO official Milkessa Midega, for instance, claimed in an address given to the March 2022 Oromo Studies Association conference that the lethal violence had been deliberately sparked by government agents provocateurs so as to tarnish the reputation of *Qeerroos*. Jawar himself claimed the violence was part of a conspiracy "to dismantle the federal system": https://twitter.com/Jawar_Mohammed/status/1043850961519869958

15. 'Oromo political victory masks volatile region,' *Ethiopia Insight*, 14 August 2018.

16. Ibid.

17. 'OLF integration underway yet tensions remain,' *Ethiopia Insight*, 1 March 2019.

18. 'A hidden war threatens Ethiopia's transition to democracy,' *The Economist*, 19 March 2023.

19. Some OLF leaders in Addis Ababa suggested splinter groups once part of the front could have been responsible: 'Drivers of ethnic conflict in contemporary Ethiopia', *Institute for Security*, 9 December 2019.

20. Most informed sources, however, believed that the OLA maintained cover lines of communication with the OLF leadership in Addis Ababa even after the official split.

21. 'Failed politics and deception,' *Addis Standard*, 20 March 2020.

22. https://reliefweb.int/report/ethiopia/ethiopia-humanitarian-access-snapshot-january-december-2020

23. 'Rebel or bandit? His life illuminates Ethiopia's hidden insurgency', *Washington Post*, 21 May 2023.

24. Taped conversation between Jaal Marroo and Jaal Segni leaked in April 2022. OLA representatives didn't deny that the recording was authentic: https://youtu.be/uGyS5bIOONO

25. Several senior Oromo officials had relatives who were kidnapped in this period, including the former minister of mines, Takele Uma.

26. 'Rebel or bandit? His life illuminates Ethiopia's hidden insurgency', *Washington Post*, 21 May 2023.

27. Ibid.

28. According to one estimate, Amharas represent up to 10 percent of the Oromia region's approximately 40 million people.

29. Parents of the students who visited the Amhara regional government in March 2020 seeking answers were rebuffed and sent home, as recorded in the documentary, *The Battle for Ethiopia* (Al Jazeera, October 2020).

30. 'Over 50 ethnic Amhara killed in attack on village by armed group', Amnesty International, 2 November 2020.

31. 'Conflicting narratives as violence hits East Wollega again,' *Addis Standard*, 26 August 2021.

32. 'Over 200 Feared Dead in Ethiopia Massacre', *New York Times*, 19 June 2022.

33. 'More Than 150 Reported Killed in 'New Massacre' in West Oromia', *Addis Standard*, 5 July 2022.

34. Hangassa Ibrahim, 5 July 2022: https://www.facebook.com/Hangaasaahmedibraahim/ videos/347033280935313

35. 'A hidden war threatens Ethiopia's transition to democracy,' *The Economist*, 19 March 2023.

36. 'Failed politics and deception,' *Addis Standard*, 20 March 2020.

37. Ibid.

38. Ibid.

39. 'Beyond Law Enforcement', Amnesty International, 29 May 2020.

40. 'Security forces in Oromia execute a young man in public view', *Addis Standard*, 12 May 2021.

41. Getachew Balcha said that a "directive has been put in place to take a similar measure against a person who kills people".

42. As Jawar admitted, "there is really no ideological difference between Oromo political parties… just tactical difference": 'Preaching unity but flying solo,' *Ethiopia Insight*, 25 February 2020.

43. See, for example, Abiy interview with the Oromia Broadcasting Network on 16 July 2020: https://www.youtube.com/watch?v=xCcKBVq13NE

44. Abiy's speech in Haraghe, Oromia, 31 October 2019: https://www.youtube.com/watch?v=CfYVGMAYE6w

45. An Oromo security officer told members of the Ethiopian Human Rights Commission in 2021 that they could be doing "much worse" and that they were "only doing a fraction of what [they] were told to do."

46. 'In Ethiopia, a secret committee ordered killings, arrests', Reuters, 23 February 2024.

47. 'How Abiy Ahmed Betrayed Oromia and Endangered Ethiopia', *Foreign Policy*, 25 January 2022.

48. See, for example, "It has been a long-held view that leaders need to assert themselves by episodically inflicting violence on recalcitrant subjects, lest the latter think the ruler dead or incapacitated": Richard Reid, *Shallow Graves* (2020), p. 103.

49. Abiy Ahmed, *The Stirrup and the Throne* (2016), p. 38.

13. "MEDEMER"

1. 'Africa's New Talisman', *Financial Times*, 21 February 2019.

2. Ibid.

3. Official figures cited in: 'This is Dubai now', *The Guardian*, 16 October 2019.

4. 'Did a Nobel Peace Laureate Stoke a Civil War?' *New Yorker*, 26 September 2022.

5. In a promotional video released in September 2019, Abiy gave a tour of his office, explaining how potential donors and investors were more open to invest large sums after admiring the renovations. When the World Bank offered additional financial support, Abiy claimed, "there [were] many reasons but the influence of the office was a major one": https://www.youtube.com/watch?v=K6KrJDfHTDk&ab_channel=AlMariam

6. See also Biruk Terrefe, 'Urban layers of political rupture: the "new" politics of Addis Ababa's megaprojects', *Journal of Eastern African Studies*, 2020.

7. The convention was organised by his friend and advisor Dr Mehret Debebe, a motivational speaker and pop-psychologist on 19 May 2018: https://www.youtube.com/watch?v=WwF8NsWxlLU&feature=youtu.be

8. 'Africa's new talisman', *Financial Times*, 21 February 2019.

9. 'What are the tasks of the transition period?' *DW*, 21 December 2018.

10. Abiy speech to PP officials, 8 October 2020: https://www.youtube.com/watch?v=4DClE6-GRQs&feature=youtu.be

11. Abiy interview on EBS on 12 January 2020: https://www.youtube.com/watch?v=mmxoOJqMj6s

12. 'Abiy Ahmed—a Philosopher King or a Sophist?', *Ethiopia Insight*, 5 April 2020.

13. Abiy's address to the Pente congregation of Prophet Yonatan Aklilu on 7 September 2019: https://www.youtube.com/watch?v=1ZYqg292p_k

14. 'The politics and problems of Prosperity Party gospel', *Ethiopia Insight*, 4 April 2020.

15. Abiy's televised lecture to Ethiopian army officers on 14 April 2022: https://www.youtube.com/watch?v=P1z8uK5OcqU&t=416s

16. Abiy to Parliament on 19 October 2020: https://youtu.be/QT_W2Up2jyU

17. A well-known example was OVID Construction, a major local contractor.

18. Berhanu Nega was, however, ethnic Gurage, and distinctly unpopular with many Amhara nationalists.

19. Andargachew publicly claimed to have written the "road map", though in an interview with me in 2023 he downplayed its significance, describing it as an "innocuous paper we gave to all opposition parties and the government".

20. See, for example, Abiy's depiction of Addis Ababa as microcosm of the nation in a speech at the inauguration of the renovated Meskel Square on 14 June 2021: https://www.youtube.com/watch?v=q47Waju3h2o&embeds_referring_euri=https%3A%2F%2Falmariam.com%2F&source_ve_path=MjM4NTE&feature=emb_title; see also Abiy's documentary about the city, broadcast on 10 June 2021, in which the capital is presented as a national symbol: https://www.youtube.com/watch?v=-evyxfd-KNw

21. Historical references to "*Medemer*" in archives from the Haile Selassie era were uncovered by the Ethiopian academic Serawit Debele.

22. Jawar Mohammed's interview on LTV 20 October 2019: https://www.youtube.com/watch?v=JyKIJGZREdY

23. Martin Plaut and Sarah Vaughan, *Understanding Ethiopia's Tigray War* (2023), p. 158.

24. In a speech to Parliament on 1 February 2019, Abiy also said that: "What every

citizen should understand is that regions are only administrative borders; they are not sovereign states. There is only a sovereign country, not a sovereign state. As a result, it is immoral and unconstitutional to displace people."

25. 'Abiy Ahmed—a Philosopher King or a Sophist?', *Ethiopia Insight*, 5 April 2020.

26. 'Ethiopia urgently needs inclusive national dialogue', Al Jazeera, 30 March 2021.

27. https://www.facebook.com/awol.allo/posts/10156622629126918

28. Plaut and Vaughan, *Understanding Ethiopia's Tigray War*, p. 158.

29. 'Fineline', *Addis Fortune*, 14 December 2019.

30. Kjetil Tronvoll, 'Falling from Grace: The Collapse of Ethiopia's Ruling Coalition.' *Northeast African Studies*, vol. 21, no. 2, 2021, pp. 11–56.

31. 'Keeping Ethiopia's transition on the rails', Crisis Group, December 2019.

32. Abiy at the launch of *Medemer* in October 2019: https://www.youtube.com/watch?v=8BmG8uKNPiQ&t=98s&ab_channel=EBC

14. "MENGISTU DRIFT"

1. For more on the expressive power of Hachalu's lyrics, see, for example, 'Haacaaluu Hundeessaa: A towering musician and an Oromo icon', Al Jazeera, 5 July 2020.

2. Abiy's address to the nation on 30 June 2020: https://youtu.be/a9i_7H9Jeu0

3. 'My son died the worst kind of death', *Mail & Guardian*, 14 July 2020.

4. Report from the Ethiopian Human Rights Commission, January 2021.

5. https://twitter.com/PMEthiopia/status/1288459077736161282

6. Interview with Jawar on LTV, 22 October 2019: https://youtu.be/AS6rmXlWNVY?si=milvBBPWnsrF8nk5

7. 'Justice Needed for Deadly October Violence', Human Rights Watch, 1 April 2020.

8. Charts showing rise in social media use of "*Neftegna*" and "*Galla*" between October 2019 and July 2020: https://twitter.com/CARDEthiopia/status/1291029092477947915/photo/2

9. '"Better to kill us": Ethiopian residents fear evictions from satellite towns', Thomson Reuters Foundation, 19 April 2019.

10. Lemma's address to the Oromia regional parliament on 26 February 2019: https://www.youtube.com/watch?v=OWu7q3FZE4I

11. Abiy's address to the nation on 7 May 2020: https://www.youtube.com/watch?v=acvALtjNU1o&t=3s&ab_channel=AbiyAhmedAli

12. Abiy to Parliament, 30 April 2020: https://www.facebook.com/watch/live/?ref=watch_permalink&v=522823591729232

13. 'Two-track talks on the dam', *Africa Confidential*, 7 November 2019.

14. Harry Verhoeven & Michael Woldemariam, 'Who lost Ethiopia? The unmaking of an African anchor state and U.S. foreign policy', Contemporary Security Policy, 43:4, 2022.

15. Guyo Wariyo, however, vehemently denied to me that any sensitive comments had been edited.

16. Hachalu's interview on OMN, 20 June 2020: https://www.youtube.com/watch?v=ERAHOGwogCg&ab_channel=OMN

17. Two incriminating videos appeared on OMN's Facebook the night after Hachalu's murder. These were later removed by Facebook (Meta).

18. Shimeles Abdissa, for instance, heavily insinuated in a speech on 30 June that the TPLF had organised the assassination in order to "regain the power which they had lost": https://www.youtube.com/watch?v=y8HBJbJNQpg

19. Kassaye Chemeda's comments were broadcast on Walta TV on 8 July 2020; he called again for war on 23 July 2020, arguing that "the [federal] government should plan well, and they [Tigray] should be attacked": https://youtu.be/KYRA5uHe0S8

20. On 7 October 2020, ESAT's "Eletawi" programme aired calls to close Tigrayan businesses and Tigrayan bank accounts—specifically, it said, because "the most important point is that the federal government must take actions that disrupt the livelihood of the Tigrayan people": https://www.youtube.com/watch?v=-MTHYJ869do

21. Zadig Abraha, then Abiy's minister in charge of democratisation, told me at the time that more than twenty-five mayors in Oromia had been fired following Hachalu's assassination, and that ten to twelve of them had been charged on the grounds that "they were working to support Jawar".

15. "GAME OVER"

1. 'Tigray Blocks General's Appointment In Swipe At Abiy,' *AFP*, 30 October 2020.

2. The new North-Western and Central Commands had officially been announced late 2018 but it took until 2020 to get them operational. Originally, they were intended to be stationed in Bahir Dar and Addis Ababa.

3. After Abiy came to power there followed multiple changes to the territorial configuration of the regional commands and their composition. After the dissolution of the Central Command based in Shire in 2018, the Northern Command with its headquarters at Wukro was redesigned to cover the whole of Tigray as well as adjoining parts of Amhara; of the sixteen divisions stationed in Tigray, eight were redeployed to other commands. The move was already heavily criticised by the Tigray government and, in some cases, there were attempts to block the movements of divisions.

4. https://twitter.com/daniel_berhane/status/1320395747993571329?s=20

5. See, for example, 'Bracing for change under new leadership,' *Aiga Forum*, 29 March 2018.

6. Elleni Centime Zeleke, *Ethiopia in Theory: Revolution and Knowledge Production* (2019), pp. 61–2. By contrast, in *Greater Tigray and the Mysterious Magnetism of Ethiopia* (2023), the historian Haggai Erlich argues that such a distinct Tigrayan identity can indeed be traced back as far as ancient Axum.

7. See, for example, Mulugeta Gebrehiwot Berhe, *Laying the Past to Rest* (2020).

8. 'Unrest in Ethiopia: the ultimate warning shot?' *Open Democracy*, 2 February 2016.

9. See, for example, Terrence Lyons, *The Puzzle of Ethiopian Politics* (2020), p. 26.

10. For example, Nebiyu Sehil Mikael, the first leader of Tigray branch of the Prosperity Party.

11. Abiy's apparent slur against the late TPLF fighter, Hayelom Araya, during his 2018 US tour was, by many accounts, one of the key early contributors to Tigrayan suspicion of him: https://www.youtube.com/watch?v=9ehVfkoIf6M

12. 'Daytime hyenas' meant, in effect, 'thieves in broad daylight', someone shameless and brazen in their corruption, while also 'dirty': a 'scavenger' who would rather eat carrion than make a kill themselves. Abiy first used it publicly to describe those allegedly sabotaging his administration on 15 June 2018: https://www.youtube.com/watch?v=byuH_kjQSzE

13. Abiy to Parliament, 1 February 2019: https://www.youtube.com/watch?time_continue=88&v=ur_wToXbzLY&feature=emb_logo

14. Speaking to Parliament after war began on 30 November 2020, Abiy likened the TPLF's bid for regional autonomy to the secession of Taiwan from mainland China in the 1940s.

15. By October 2020, the Northern Command possessed considerable heavy weaponry but no fully mechanised divisions; of the ENDF's eight mechanised divisions, two of them were in the Northern Command but stationed outside of Tigray.

16. Interview with Isaias on Eri-TV, 7 February 2020: https://www.youtube.com/watch?v=NFElBdDLY5Y

17. Most meetings took place without aides or note-takers present: 'The Nobel prize that paved the way for war,' *New York Times*, 15 December 2021.

18. Ibid.

19. In an updated edition of *Against All Odds: A Chronicle of the Eritrean Revolution*, released in 2021, Dan Connell claimed that Isaias, likely concerned about the continued loss of manpower for his army, had made action against Eritrean refugees a condition for continuing normalisation talks following a meeting with Abiy in Asmara.

20. The same *New York Times* article included a quote from a senior Ethiopian official, confirming that "Ethiopian military cargo planes began to make clandestine flights at night to bases in Eritrea."

21. According to Mesfin Hagos, the former Eritrean minister of defence with sources inside the Eritrean military, these locations were around Om Hajer and Humera; around Shilalo and Shambko; between Adiquala and the Mereb river; and between Senate and Zalambessa.

22. See, for example, Daniel Berhane, *War on Tigray: Genocidal Axis in the Horn of Africa* (2023).

23. See, in particular, the TPLF's statement on the day of its 45th anniversary in February 2020: http://aigaforum.com/current-issue/tplf-statement-lekatit11-2020-english.htm

24. In his 30 November speech to Parliament after the outbreak of war, Abiy pointed to what he saw as the hypocrisy of TPLF officials trying to forge alliances with opposition members who'd been outlawed under the EPRDF, while at the same time complaining when the Prosperity Party did the same: "Now they have formed a 'federalist forum' with those who they labelled a terrorist before. They don't feel any shame."

25. An ETV report on 16 September 2020, for example, blamed attacks on Amharas

in Benishangul-Gumuz on a guerrilla group supported by "OLF-Shane and anti-reform groups and Tigrinya speakers." The attack, the report claimed, was intended to disrupt the construction of the Grand Ethiopian Renaissance Dam.

26. In my September 2020 interview, the minister put it slightly more delicately: "We have our blueprint for a post-TPLF Tigray—but we are not interested in regime change … social movements are enough… our non-interference policy is working very well… so let it handle itself."

27. 'Who and what is behind the Oromia crisis—a view from Abiy's camp', *Africa Report*, 3 August 2020.

28. In the same interview, broadcast on 27 July 2020, Abiy also made striking criticisms of the TPLF's ideology and, implicitly, the outdated thinking of the student movement, arguing that "neither Tigray nor Ethiopia can be led by ideas which are more than fifty years old": https://youtu.be/ixEAJVHwnuU

29. There is a considerable range of estimates for the numbers of Tigrayan troops. On the eve of war, the International Crisis Group estimated the total number of Tigrayan forces to be around 250,000. Getachew Reda, by contrast, would later claim they'd begun the war with only 9,800 special police, between 40–50,000 militiamen, and 800 commandos (https://youtu.be/mn1PGo8_MNk). To my knowledge, the most reliable estimate is of 60,000 troops at the outbreak of the war, of which some 25,000 were Tigrayan special police. The rest comprised former soldiers of the Ethiopian army, regular police and local militia.

30. General Tsadkan Gebretensae, who met with Abiy on several occasions before the war began, later said that the prime minister had remarked to him that "there isn't anything that can't be solved through money and force; the people of Tigray are no different and will be subdued through money and force; I will solve this; don't lose your sleep over this issue": https://www.youtube.com/watch?v=0znM0zm7nj8

31. A video statement given by Abiy to his opponents on 7 May 2020: https://www.facebook.com/watch/?v=656991138477284

32. Nonetheless, in the days before the Tigray election in September the House of Federation stopped short of ceding to demands, reportedly from the Prosperity Party's Amhara wing, to license "action" against the TPLF—suggesting that internal party divisions concerning the wisdom of war were still salient at that point, and that alternative outcomes were still conceivable even at this late stage.

33. For many months the Tigrayan authorities had complained that construction projects as well as federal development programmes in the region had been cut or delayed; COVID-19 testing reagents were not delivered to the region; and foreign investors were prevented from flying to Mekelle.

34. Abiy spoke at length about what he called "Project X" in September 2020: https://www.youtube.com/watch?v=fQRuOrSUWQE&ab_channel=OfficeofthePrimeMinister-Ethiopia

35. When I met with General Ibrahim Jaber, a senior officer in Sudan's Sovereign Council, in Khartoum in July 2021 he provided a similar account of the meeting between the two leaders: "Our president told Abiy: 'please don't go to war.' Abiy replied that it would only take 'seventy-two hours' to arrest and apprehend the

leaders." General Jaber then added: "One to two days after the war began the Ethiopians asked us to turn off telecoms at the border. We said, 'No, we cannot do it like that.' They asked us to close the border—we said 'okay'."

36. The Sudanese ambassador also noted that on the matter of the Grand Ethiopian Renaissance Dam, Abiy had offered to give Sudan an office at the site of the project.

37. The federal government at first denied that its troops had encircled Tigray prior to fighting; several of its generals, however, later confirmed the military's general state of readiness for war in public interviews.

38. 'Ethiopian Airlines and the Tigray Conflict,' *Substack; Actual Control*, 17 August 2021.

39. Around the time of the incident, according to some local sources, an OLA commander wrote a Facebook post—later deleted—noting that there was an ongoing operation against "PP informants" in the area. According to these sources, the incident was a revenge attack after local Amhara residents informed the Ethiopian military of the OLA's location, leading to OLA losses.

40. Four of the eight divisions of the Northern Command, each comprising a maximum 6,000 soldiers, were by then stationed outside Tigray.

41. Leon Trotsky, *The Revolution Betrayed* (1936).

42. Local sources estimated that about half of the Northern Command's personnel went over to the Tigrayan side; about 25 percent remained neutral in their positions, and a further 25 percent withdrew to Eritrea.

43. Abiy's own account of the alleged massacre was also inconsistent. In a speech to Parliament in June 2022, for instance, he claimed that the soldiers were not killed but were rather abducted in their sleep: https://www.youtube.com/watch?v=DSu-ARGyRag&ab_channel=AmharaMediaCorporation

44. The federal government didn't deny that these supposedly civilian cargo planes flew to Mekelle that evening, though its claim that they were simply delivering bank notes was questionable. It is also notable that an early report by the United Nations Office for the Coordination of Humanitarian Affairs (UN OCHA) described the first fighting that evening as taking place near the airport rather than the Northern Command in Mekelle: Martin Plaut and Sarah Vaughan, *Understanding Ethiopia's Tigray War* (2023), p. 210.

45. https://twitter.com/ETFactCheck/status/1327568678326575104?s=20

46. A senior Tigrayan general later claimed that an unnamed federal official had leaked information to TPLF about the federal government's military planning shortly before the war began: "A person who was present at the time when Abiy and Isaias made an agreement to attack us, called me and told me about it. We received information that they were preparing to attack us on November 7. We gathered and discussed as soon as we received the information." https://m.facebook.com/story.php?storyfbid=pfbid0aP6EQheDNiAwvPLfUvpUGxZEHk9d8ThAnQHSoZYoVyuRt6EXysRPMk2scgMKHB4fl&id=100003210969223&mibextid=Nif5oz

47. As one Tigrayan commentator close to the TPLF put it to me days before the war: "To tell you the truth, they are actually itching for a fight. The sense of betrayal is so hard they can't let it go."

48. For example, General Tsadkan Gebretensae told the French scholar René Lefort before the war: "There is not one army in the Horn of Africa which can defeat us."

49. Daniel Berhane on Tigray Media House, 21 October 2020: https://www.youtube.com/watch?v=GhDQwEjv3ds&ab_channel=TigraiMediaHouse. Similarly, a veteran Tigrayan diplomat wrote in October 2020: "When confronted face to face with history, the only option is to hit with the fist. We have reached here." http://aigaforum.com/amharic-article-2020/when-facing-history.htm

50. https://www.nytimes.com/2021/12/15/world/africa/ethiopia-abiy-ahmed-nobel-war.html. See, for example, 'The Nobel prize which paved the path to war,' *New York Times*, 15 December 2021. Abiy's book *Medemer's Path*, published in 2021, also provided some insight into the prime minister's fears in the run-up to the war.

51. For example, Mike Pompeo, then America's secretary of state, condemned the TPLF's missile attack on Eritrea in the early days of the war, while staying silent about Eritrea's own military engagements: https://twitter.com/SecPompeo/status/1328721926643195907. Tibor Nagy later warned the TPLF not to "internationalise" the conflict by launching "unjustifiable" strikes on Eritrea: https://twitter.com/asstsecstateaf/status/1328015362999414786

52. Abiy himself told Parliament on 30 November 2020 that what his government had faced was similar to what Unionists faced in the American Civil War.

16. "JUST WAITING TO DIE"

1.   The term 'ethnic cleansing' was coined when Yugoslavia broke apart in the early 1990s, and, unlike 'genocide', is not codified in law and does not obligate a diplomatic or military response. Nonetheless, acts such as targeted killings and rapes and forced displacement that make up ethnic cleansing are the same as those that could constitute genocide.

2.   Local Wolkait identity was fluid and complex: a foreign academic noted, for instance, the example of a Tigrinya-speaking woman who was able to claim Amhara identity after the territory changed hands despite not speaking Amharic. Such "code-switching" was also vividly expressed by a Tigrayan refugee from the Western Tigray town of Adebay who told me in eastern Sudan in December 2022 that "before [Wolkaites] were with us; now they are with the Amharas."

3.   'We Will Erase You From This Land,' Human Rights Watch, Amnesty International, 6 April 2022.

4.   'Preaching unity but flying solo,' *Ethiopia Insight*, 25 February 2020.

5.   Ibid.

6.   Arming and training the special police was not entirely unprecedented: the ENDF's Eastern Command had trained and armed the Somali special police after its establishment in 2008.

7.   In Raya, southern Tigray, a similar committee was established in 2018 with the aim of achieving recognition of the bilingual Raya identity to establish an autonomous administrative zone. The Amharic-speaking part expressed a wish to return the area under Amhara administration.

8. 'Amhara region police chief reveals how region's police force guided federal steel-clad mechanized forces to join "war" in Tigray', *Addis Standard*, 4 January 2021.

9. According to the researcher who was present at the time, these "*kebele*" militia were the first to rush into the lowlands of Western Tigray on 4 November, shooting into the air to call others to follow them.

10. 'How ethnic killings exploded from an Ethiopian town,' Reuters, 7 June 2021.

11. Colonel Demeke Zewdu, the leader of the Wolkait Committee, for instance, had a sister who was a member of the TPLF. Getachew Reda, the future Tigray president who came from Raya, had a sister who was a member of the Amhara regional police. Similarly, the *Financial Times* reported early on in the war of an Amhara-identifying father going to fight against his own Tigrayan-identifying son: "'A political mess that makes fathers fight sons'", *Financial Times*, 18 November 2020.

12. 'Duelling information campaigns', *The Media Manipulation Case Book*, Harvard University, August 2021.

13. Harry Verhoeven & Michael Woldemariam, 'Who lost Ethiopia? The unmaking of an African anchor state and U.S. foreign policy', *Contemporary Security Policy*, 43:4, 2022, pp. 622–50.

14. Amnesty International's early report stopped short of attributing responsibility for the massacre. A joint report with Human Rights Watch published in 2022 found that the first wave of killings were mostly carried out by Tigrayan youth in Mai Kadra, and that this was swiftly followed by widespread retaliatory killings of Tigrayan civilians: https://www.hrw.org/news/2022/04/06/crimes-against-humanity-and-ethnic-cleansing-ethiopias-western-tigray-zone

15. An employee of the EHRC who took part in the investigation later admitted to a Western diplomat that the investigative team had been given a list of more than 600 people by the local Amhara authorities, which the employee said was almost certainly inaccurate.

16. Abiy to Parliament, 30 November 2020.

17. The so-called "Samre" group in Mai Kadra was not a formal organisation with ties to the TPLF but rather a colloquial name for young, often underemployed men from a specific neighbourhood of the town.

18. 'We Will Erase You From This Land,' Human Rights Watch, Amnesty International, 6 April 2022.

19. This was a reference to a concept developed in the 1930s in response to European fascism which broadly meant the use of legal restrictions on political expression and participation to curb extremist actors in democratic regimes.

20. Abiy to Parliament, 30 November 2020.

21. The documentary, broadcast on 8 November 2020, was produced by the federal authorities, and sent to all government media for publication.

22. Abiy to Parliament, 30 November 2020.

23. What was undeniable was that during these years that the TPLF—especially via its media outlets—had provided rhetorical and moral support to Abiy's opponents, including, in particular, Oromo and Qemant activists. Communication between the TPLF and elements of the OLA also predated the Tigray War, though solid

evidence of—for instance—any money and arms transfers in this period was hard to come by.

24. Abiy to Parliament, 30 November 2020.

25. "*Tut nekash*" literally means "biting the breast that feeds you". In this context it suggested a parasitic traitor sucking the country dry: 'Ethiopia's war of words as divisive as fighting on the ground', *Financial Times*, 2 December 2020.

26. Some of those held in a detention camp in Amhara in 2022, for instance, reported that federal police and soldiers guarded them from *Fanos* in the surrounding area who had threatened to enter the facilities and kill the Tigrayan detainees. It is also worth noting that the vast majority of Tigrayan civilians held in detention during the war were eventually released.

27. The "Cancer of Ethiopia" statement was shared by the official account of the Prime Minister's Office on 18 July 2021.

28. 'Briton released from death row accused of inciting genocide in Ethiopia', *The Telegraph*, 28 November 2021.

29. Pekka Haavisto, the EU's special representative at the time, told a European Parliament committee in a televised briefing that such words had been expressed to him by the "Ethiopian leadership". Some of those with first-hand knowledge later confirmed to me that the senior leader in question was Abiy.

30. The other two recalled generals were Lt General Bacha Debele, an Oromo, and Lt General Yohannes Gebremeskel, a rare Tigrayan said to be particularly loyal to Abiy.

31. Abiy to Parliament, 30 November 2020.

32. https://www.youtube.com/live/h962lZgFjss?si=mRM3nCggdiMkZ5Xs

33. 'We Will Erase You From This Land,' Human Rights Watch, Amnesty International, 6 April 2022.

34. Also worth noting is the role of prominent Amhara businessmen in the Afar region's salt industry after 2018, and the alleged use of profits from there to fund the *Fano* in Western Tigray.

35. Dansha, Western Tigray, 17 March 2021. A militiaman told the same academic: "We don't need a single one of them anymore. They cannot be trusted."

36. The Amhara special policeman who shared the video, a former member of Ginbot 7, was killed in December 2022 on the Dedebit front in northwest Tigray. The destruction shown in the video, he said, took place around Adi Goshu in Western Tigray. The Amharic verb "*matsedat / tseda*", meaning "to clean", was widely used in Western Tigray in this period and was generally used with reference to the "junta", a term which by this point could be taken to mean Tigrayans in general.

37. 'Men are marched out of prison camps. Then corpses float down the river', *CNN*, 10 September 2021.

38. Sometimes Abiy did appear to endorse Amhara resettlement of the territories. For instance, in a speech to Parliament on 15 November 2022 he appeared to advise the new administrators—cryptically—to "do their job" of changing population patterns on the ground before a future referendum: "Each zone, each woreda has to do their job. They shouldn't cling on to the federal [government]. They must do

their jobs. If they do that, the rest is easy. It won't be that difficult": https://www.youtube.com/watch?v=t55jyzpeikQ

39. At times Abiy seemed to share the Amhara nationalist interpretation of history. In a speech in July 2021, for instance, he noted that the territories of Wolkait and Tsegede had once belonged to the historical province of Begemeder governed from Gondar: https://www.youtube.com/watch?v=xBiu32v3wLc. Speaking about the Border Commission in March 2021, moreover, he argued that "the reason the 'junta' refused to accept [recognise] the commission is because it knows what it did": https://www.youtube.com/watch?v=b-2cN-3KK0A

17. "DIRTY WAR"

1. https://2017-2021-translations.state.gov/2020/11/17/the-united-states-condemns-the-attack-on-eritrea-by-the-tigray-peoples-liberation-front/index.html

2. Abiy to Parliament, 30 November 2020.

3. Fetsum Berhane, a Tigrayan commentator close to the TPLF, similarly told me in October 2020: "Abiy doesn't have an army".

4. The AU's Peace and Security Council did not discuss Tigray until almost a year into the conflict.

5. 'UN Security Council: End Inaction on Ethiopia', Human Rights Watch, 2 July 2021. The UNSC issued only two press statements in the course of the entire conflict.

6. The EU Commission suspended budget support for Ethiopia worth $107 million until humanitarian agencies were granted full humanitarian access; the EU commission also proceeded to withhold regular programme disbursements to Ethiopia.

7. Speaking to Parliament on 30 November 2020, Abiy claimed that he had been developing the drone programme for years in full view of the TPLF; rather than conceal it, he claimed, he had "pleaded with them not to think of war, telling them we have equipped ourselves with such weapons."

8. "We give them gold, they give us drones," a former senior Ethiopian official told me. Ethiopia's official gold exports increased from $71.9m to $880m between 2020 and 2021.

9. Sources in Ethiopia's black market for foreign exchange said that the rising parallel rate in 2021 was due (among other factors) to the fact that Eritrean soldiers were paid in birr—and which they then had to change into dollars. A report by the diaspora satellite channel Ethio360 in March 2021, which a senior government official later corroborated to me, claimed that Eritrean soldiers were being paid a monthly salary by the Ethiopian government: https://youtu.be/wwiPd2mCTAo

10. 'Eritrea's Role in Ethiopia's Conflict and the Fate of Eritrean Refugees in Ethiopia', *African Arguments*, 4 December 2020.

11. In the video, an Eritrean officer appears to be in charge, and in several instances the Ethiopian officers appear to be taking orders from him: https://youtu.be/KIcXkali8RU

12. Researchers at the University of Ghent identified 4,453 victims by name: https://ethiopiatigraywar.com/incidents.php

13. The University of Ghent's revised figures in 2023 estimated civilian deaths from hunger and disease ranging from 162,000 to 378,000.

14. Senior Tigrayan military sources told the British academic Alex de Waal in 2023 that the Ethiopian army had lost, by its own calculation, between 260,000 and 520,000 soldiers killed or missing in action, plus 374,000 wounded. The top Ethiopian general, Bacha Debele, later said to a French journalist that probably 1.2 million lives—combatants and civilians combined—were lost overall.

15. The camps were first entered and attacked by Eritrean troops, who also abducted Eritrean refugees and took them back to Eritrea. Soon after Tigrayan forces entered the camps and also killed, threatened and sexually assaulted refugees who they accused of collaborating with the Eritreans: 'Eritrean refugees targeted in Tigray', Human Rights Watch, 16 September 2021.

16. 'Eritrean troops' massacre of hundreds of Axum civilians may amount to crime against humanity', Amnesty International, 26 February 2021. By July 2021 the University of Ghent's *Tigray: Atlas of the humanitarian situation* had counted 245 individual massacres, defined as incidents in which at least five people died on the same day at the same location. The September 2023 report of the International Human Rights Experts on Ethiopia also counted dozens of mass killings.

17. https://www.ohchr.org/sites/default/files/documents/hrbodies/hrcouncil/chreetiopia/A_HRC_54_55_AUV.pdf

18. In September 2023, the UN's International Commission of Human Rights Experts on Ethiopia estimated at least 10,000 women and girls in Tigray were raped between November 2020 and July 2023. Tigray's regional authorities put the figure at closer to 100,000, a figure later supported by a comprehensive study conducted by the Columbia University biostatistician Kiros Berhane.

19. See, for example, Birhan Gebrekirstos and Mulu Mesfin, *Genocidal War: Women and Girls' Stories from Tigray War* (2023).

20. 'Practically this has been a genocide', *CNN*, 19 March 2021.

21. 'I don't know if they realized I was a person', Amnesty International, 11 August 2022.

22. See, for example, Dara Kay Cohen, 'The Ties That Bind: How Armed Groups Use Violence to Socialize Fighters', *Journal of Peace Research*, vol. 54, no. 5, 2017, pp. 701–14.

23. 'Sexual violence and the war in Tigray,' *Lawfare*, 16 June 2021.

24. The UN convention on genocide defines the term broadly: it is not only killing that counts, but also "measures intended to prevent births", if their aim is "to destroy, in whole or in part, a national, ethnical, racial or religious group".

25. M. Bassiouni and Marcia McCormick, 'Sexual violence: an invisible weapon of war in the former Yugoslavia' (1996).

26. '"Practically This Has Been a Genocide"', *CNN*, 22 March 2021; '"A Tigrayan womb should never give birth"', Al Jazeera, 21 April 2021.

27. 'US blasts "dangerous" rhetoric by ally of Ethiopia PM', Ahram Online, 20 September 2021.

28. Richard Reid, 'Atrocity in Ethiopian History', *Journal of Genocide Research*, 24:1, 2022, pp. 97–108.

29. In his prescient memoir, *Shallow Graves* (2020), Reid noted that after the 1998–2000 war ended, "the fact of living with sexual violence [remained] the biggest obstacle to peace", p. 71.

30. Mohammed Hassen, 'Genocidal Conquest, Plunder of Resources and Dehumanization of the Oromo in Ethiopia', *Journal of Genocide Research*, 24:1, 2022.

31. Isaias's first public discussion of Eritrea's role in the Tigray War was in an interview with state media on 8 January 2022: https://www.youtube.com/watch?v=0qaGpf0HsoQ

32. The claim was amplified by, among others, Ann Fitz-Gerald, a Canadian academic whose work was facilitated by the Ethiopian government and subsequently used to lobby foreign governments on their behalf: see, for example, 'Peace prospects in Ethiopia,' Royal United Services Institute, 15 December 2022.

33. Abiy to Parliament, 21 March 2021.

34. https://twitter.com/AbiyAhmedAli/status/1375308233754173440

35. 'Ethiopia's Hard Road to Peace,' *Foreign Affairs*, 26 December 2022.

36. 'Addis and Asmara exchange vows,' *Africa Confidential*, 15 April 2021.

37. Abiy's address to Parliament on 23 March 2021: https://t.co/Sa7nWUUWpl?amp=1

38. The video of Redwan Hussein briefing Ethiopian diplomats was leaked in March 2021: https://www.facebook.com/watch/?v=121053947543474

39. The Mahbere Dego massacre was among the best documented of the entire war. See, among other investigations: 'Evidence suggests Ethiopian military carried out massacre in Tigray,' *BBC*, 1 April 2021.

40. 'The Secret Plot Against the Head of World Health Organization', *Bloomberg*, 2 October 2023.

41. https://twitter.com/EthioHRC/status/1365054381729714179

42. Daniel Bekele's political views were well known and broadly aligned with those of the federal government. In a 2021 statement to the UN Human Rights Council in Geneva, for instance, he stressed Ethiopian sovereignty, and criticised what he described as a "disinformation campaign" and "social media frenzy". For a full summary of the commissioner's highly partisan comments and interventions, see: https://hrp.law.harvard.edu/the-ethiopian-human-rights-commission-a-champion-of-transitional-justice/

43. https://www.ohchr.org/Documents/Countries/ET/OHCHR-EHRC-Tigray-Report.pdf

44. https://www.ungeneva.org/en/news-media/meeting-summary/2021/12/le-conseil-decide-de-nommer-une-commission-dexperts-chargee

45. The statement was published by the EHRC, but the investigation had in fact been undertaken by the taskforce led by Filsan Abdi.

46. See the September 2022 update from the inter-ministerial task force set up to bring war criminals to account: https://drive.google.com/file/d/1KsuoIDUBPib FMRPFRxfWCVZjHceSuATk/view

18. "OUR ADWA MOMENT"

1. International Commission of Human Rights Experts on Ethiopia (September 2022): https://www.ohchr.org/en/hr-bodies/hrc/ichre-ethiopa/index

2. According to TDF sources, between early November 2020 and early June 2021, they received between 25,000–45,000 new volunteers.

3. 'Salvaging a failing state', *Responsible Statecraft*, 10 November 2021.

4. Abiy's address to an applauding crowd on 30 June 2023: https://www.facebook. com/157746334716558/posts/1133404873817361/

5. Abiy to Parliament, 30 November 2020.

6. https://twitter.com/reda_getachew/status/1411621680280113156/photo/2

7. An economic advisor close to Abiy told a well-connected local researcher at the time that the federal government's plan was to lay siege to Tigray, with a view to splitting the Tigrayan leadership and then negotiating with a faction.

8. Cases of aid being diverted from its intended recipients were not unheard of in Ethiopia. Though it wasn't the reason it defeated the Derg, subsequent investigations have suggested the TPLF used some food aid to feed its fighters in the 1980s. In an interview with Fana TV on 23 June 2021 Abiy promised this would never happen again: https://youtu.be/rmOMyRa72t8

9. https://www.ohchr.org/sites/default/files/documents/hrbodies/hrcouncil/ chreetiopia/A_HRC_54_55_AUV.pdf

10. Nor was it unique to the rebel side: in 2023, ENDF generals openly complained to USAID that the suspension of food aid meant their own soldiers were going hungry.

11. Getachew Reda told the BBC on 11 August 2021: "If Abiy is removed from office […] that would be the icing on the cake. Ethiopia would be better off without Abiy."

12. See, for example, Susan Rice, Director of the United States Domestic Policy Council from 2021 to 2023, who had played a key role in mediating a ceasefire during the 1998–2000 Ethio-Eritrea War.

13. 'Did a Nobel Peace Laureate Stoke a Civil War?' *New Yorker*, 26 September 2022.

14. See, for example, Abiy Ahmed, *Generation Medemer* (2023), pp. 131–43.

15. Rather than attend the 31st Ordinary Session of the Assembly of Heads of State and Government of the African Union held in July 2018 in Nouakchott, Mauritania, Abiy sent a state minister. No previous Ethiopian prime minister had missed one of these, with the one exception of Meles when terminally ill in hospital in Brussels in 2012.

16. Abiy's speech in the Afar region on May 2021: https://youtu.be/ilQhcYYyUfc

17. https://www.facebook.com/854166034606545/posts/4231749680181480/

18. Abiy's speech at the inauguration of a sugar factory on 6 June 2021: https://www. facebook.com/541629952535552/posts/4483804101651431/?d=n

19. The government launched a national "Hands Off Ethiopia" campaign against interference in Ethiopia's internal affairs on 19 May 2021.

20. The billboards were the handiwork of a fire-and-brimstone preacher advertising his YouTube channel. Tellingly, the government let them stay up for several months.

21. Quoted in Gebru Tareke, *The Ethiopian Revolution* (2009).

22. 'Duelling information campaigns', *The Media Manipulation Case Book*, Harvard University, August 2021.

23. The controversial Ethiopianist activist, Yonatan Tesfaye, was appointed as deputy director of the media authority in April 2021.

24. The WhatsApp group was called "Leadership Convergence", and included scores of government officials.

25. See, for example, https://www.geopolitics.press/from-basma-to-ethiopia-how-c2fc-is-using-lethal-journalism-to-conduct-information-warfare-and-lawfare-against-ethiopia/; https://newafricainstitute.medium.com/disinformation-in-tigray-manufacturing-consent-for-a-secessionist-war-275544445c53

26. Ann Fitz-Gerald, Director of the Balsillie School of International Affairs in Canada, for instance, collaborated with GLEAN and Actum, a lobbying firm hired to defend the Ethiopian government.

27. See, for example, 'Somali troops committed atrocities in Tigray as new alliance emerged, survivors say,' *Mail and Guardian*, 20 January 2022.

28. *Min Litazez?* had been previously taken off air for several weeks in 2019 for mocking the prime minister too directly.

29. See, for example, his dig at the TPLF's "whiskey-drinkers" in a speech on 19 October 2019: https://www.youtube.com/watch?v=8BmG8uKNPiQ&t=98s

30. On p. 144 Abiy argued that Ethiopia's low level of literacy and education made "modern journalism" inappropriate. This was an argument consistent with the EPRDF's idea of "developmental journalism".

31. In Ethiopia, homosexual acts are punishable by up to fifteen years in prison.

32. See, for example, Gideon Rachman, *The Age of the Strongman* (2022).

33. According to René Lefort, Abiy told business leaders: "I am the leader for the next five years; if I don't get enough votes in the ballot boxes, I will rig the elections": 'Preaching unity but flying solo', *Ethiopia Insight*, 25 February 2020.

34. Birtukan said the board's preference would have been to hold the elections in September 2021.

35. 'Ethiopia's democratic predicaments', *Institute for Security Studies*, 7 December 2022.

36. By 2022, the Prosperity Party claimed twelve million members.

37. Local *woreda* (district) elections were not held in 2021; they were supposed to be held in 2018 but had been postponed due to instability. By 2023, there had been no local elections for a decade, and there were some 3.6 million local councillors without a formal mandate.

38. "'Finish Them Off'", *New York Times*, 17 March 2022.

39. https://twitter.com/reda_getachew/status/1418563919241793539?lang=en

40. General Wedi Gebregziabher Beyene in a speech to TDF fighters on 20 June 2021: https://www.youtube.com/watch?v=lfdh1QEcdn8&t=14s

41. Few, if any, of the Somali special forces ever made it to the battlefield, apparently preferring to run away than fight.

42. See, for example, the infamous photo of Amhara youth in Debark wielding machetes posted on Facebook in August 2021: https://www.facebook.com/654684251716987/posts/1209001489618591/?sfnsn=mo

43. This was the common, and of course erroneous, allegation made about foreign journalists during the Tigray War, and was fanned by the federal government and state media. It stemmed in large part from the widespread misapprehension that reporting the atrocities committed in Tigray amounted to support for the TPLF. See, for example, "I was a war reporter in Ethiopia. Then I became the enemy", *1843*, 24 June 2022.

44. "'Then the killing started'", Associated Press, 25 September 2021.

45. 'Summary killings, rape and looting by Tigrayan forces in Amhara,' Amnesty International, 16 February 2022.

46. This was shown most notably in a leaked internal report by Ahunna Eziakonwa, UNDP's Assistant Administrator and Regional Director for Africa, whose positions on the war were almost indistinguishable from those of Abiy's government. Maureen Achieng, the IOM's chief of mission to Ethiopia was fired in late November 2021 for leaked remarks about the war in which she called the TPLF "dirty" and "vicious", and vowed never to return to Tigray. Similarly, in his book, *At the Centre of the World in Ethiopia*, published in early 2023, the former WFP Ethiopia Director, Steven Were Omamo, defended the government's conduct in the war—including its restriction of aid to Tigray—as unexceptional and broadly legitimate, while downplaying reports of famine.

47. There is scant evidence of any foreign troops, besides a single Italian man, fighting alongside the TDF, though Sudan and most probably Egypt did supply it with arms.

48. Abiy to government officials, 1 November 2022: https://www.facebook.com/863485070524876/posts/1925488354324537/

49. 'Ethiopia and 3 Rebel Groups Look Toward U.S.-Led Peace Talks,' *New York Times*, 14 May 1991.

50. https://www.youtube.com/watch?v=0znM0zm7nj8

51. Abiy's lecture to journalists on 11 November 2021: https://www.youtube.com/watch?fbclid=IwAR3GgBqGC_kEM_jKNQbNbW4ztI_qcg9faQM2GrkTBsLKaMqXDoQSD5nWccQ&v=Osk0y6SG6ks&feature=youtu.be

52. In a speech given on 3 November 2021 to commemorate the attack on the Northern Command, Abiy explicitly compared himself remaining in Ethiopia to Christ choosing to stay on a boat among his disciplines during a storm: https://www.youtube.com/watch?v=vx5-8tpUpH0&feature=youtu.be

53. Richard Reid, 'Atrocity in Ethiopian History', *Journal of Genocide Research*, 24:1, 2022, pp. 97–108.

54. By July 2022, Andrew DeCort, an American academic and close observer of

Christianity in Ethiopia, had catalogued only ten public statements from Christian leaders in Ethiopia and Eritrea which condemned the war.

55. Abiy was blessed in his office by a group of Orthodox bishops including the now late Patriarch Abune Merkorios on 7 October 2021: https://www.youtube.com/watch?v=3brTDd0hnvM

56. Abiy's speech at a diaspora fundraising dinner in Addis Ababa on 17 January 2022: https://youtu.be/NF_eM7gpCFs

19. "DO YOU LOVE ME?"

1. In his speech to Parliament on 30 November 2020, Abiy had likened negotiating with the TPLF to cutting a deal with "Satan".

2. The "United Front of Ethiopian Federalist and Confederalist Forces" was formed by nine anti-government factions including the TPLF and OLA on 4 November 2021.

3. 'Foreign Drones Tip the Balance in Ethiopia's Civil War', *New York Times*, 20 December 2021.

4. 'Abiy juggles truce with force', *Africa Confidential*, 26 May 2022.

5. In a speech to the Ethiopian diaspora at a fundraising dinner on 17 January 2022, Abiy said that the decision to release prisoners was given to him by God: https://youtu.be/NF_eM7gpCFs

6. Abiy's official Christmas statement, 6 January 2022: https://www.facebook.com/112704996810839/posts/694927258588607/

7. In the same interview, Isaias also denounced ethnic federalism: (Eri TV, 8 January 2022): https://www.youtube.com/watch?v=0qaGpf0HsoQ

8. The first photo of the two in public since 2020 appeared in July 2020, when the two attended a regional conference in Cairo.

9. In 2023, Abiy repeatedly told colleagues as well as businessmen that Ethiopia needed to get a port, whether by peaceful means or through force. In a widely watched documentary on the issue broadcast on state media in October 2023, Abiy stated that access to the Red Sea "is not a luxury but a matter of existence for Ethiopia. What option do we have?": https://www.youtube.com/watch?v=HdQM85O5tk4

10. As early as December 2020, trucks loaded with cereals were witnessed crossing into Eritrea from Western Tigray.

11. See, for example, Seeye Abraha's argument in *Foreign Policy* on 4 May 2021: "Why Eritrea won't leave Ethiopia".

12. According to relatives of top Eritrean military officers, the commanders in charge of training Amhara forces were Brigadier-General Simon Uqbe Kelete, Colonel Tsehaye Mekonnen and Brigadier-General Tekle Kiflay. The training centre was at the town of Baeker. Eritrea was also training several thousand Afar Special Forces at this time.

13. The document, which was leaked in mid-2022, described the strengthening of bilateral relations between Eritrea and Amhara as a "strategic conundrum" for Tigray.

14. Of particular concern was the proposed creation of "Sheger City" surrounding

Addis Ababa, an integrated metropolitan area made up of satellite towns under Oromia's jurisdiction. Many Amharas saw it as a scheme for ethnically cleansing Amhara residents from the outskirts of the capital through demolition works.

15. The US government finally announced on 20 March 2023 that it had formally determined that war crimes and crimes against humanity had taken place in Ethiopia.

16. The central bank recorded FDI of $9.1bn in Q2 2021.

17. 'Ethiopia Macroeconomic Handbook', *Cepheus* (January 2023).

18. 'Unlikely to replicate exceptional growth again', *Capital Economics*, 10 August 2022.

19. 'Ethiopia Macroeconomic Handbook', *Cepheus* (January 2023).

20. By September 2022, central bank advances made up a quarter of the government's outstanding domestic debt stock. Ethiopia's inflation rate averaged 34% during 2022. On the parallel market the value of the Birr dropped by 50 percent to the dollar in just a year (*Cepheus*, January 2023).

21. 'Ethiopia seeking $2 billion under IMF program, sources say,' Reuters, 13 April 2023.

22. Ethiopia's announcement in January 2021 that it planned to restructure its debt triggered a selloff of its $1 billion of Eurobonds.

23. 'Abiy Ahmed's loyal allies tasked with keeping the money coming', *Africa Intelligence*, 11 April 2023.

24. A major change came in the first half of 2022 with the formation of the Ethiopian Investment Holdings (EIH) answerable to the Prime Minister's Office and with Abiy as the Chairperson of its Board of Directors. Twenty-seven state-owned enterprises were placed under it in 2022.

25. 'New breed regional conglomerates replicating EFFORT', *The Reporter*, 12 March 2022; 'Gold glitters, grievances grow', Rift Valley Institute, June 2023.

26. 'PM unveils vision to see construction giant born from GERD', *The Reporter*, 16 September 2023.

27. Donor funds had also been used to effectively subsidise the war effort, for instance, when, in 2021, donor-supported government ministries donated money to the military.

28. A 2023 report by the Federal Anti-Corruption Commission indicated that 98 percent of PP officials had registered inaccurate financial information: *Ethio Forum*, 26 January 2024.

29. 'An imperial palace in the Yeka Hills,' *Africa Confidential*, 30 June 2023.

30. Ibid.

31. 'U.S. Suspends Food Aid for Ethiopia, Citing Widespread Theft', *New York Times*, 8 June 2023.

32. 'Tigray, land of hunger', *ARTE TV* (30 June 2022).

33. Debretsion's speech to a party conference in Mekelle on 11 May: https://www.facebook.com/282348198530030/posts/pfbid02LBMhtyYsvcVcfnpfb3kjPCfHoJjaSjmkafWkZxMP6ZK4Buy7cPZCEu75RRpWUL1Tl/?app=fbl

34. 'New Military Adventure of the TPLF', *Shabait*, 17 May 2022.

35. Yilikal Kefale, 11 May 2022: https://www.youtube.com/watch?v=Bm8OuH HsG_A&list=WL&index=3&t=313s

36. The TPLF also noted that Obasanjo had blessed Abiy's election victory that previous year in his capacity as the head of the AU's election observation mission.

37. 'The African Union cannot deliver peace to Tigray,' *The Africa Report*, 22 August 2022.

38. 'After Secret U.S. Talks Fail, a Hidden War in Africa Rapidly Escalates', *New York Times*, 8 October 2022.

39. 'Facing famine, Tigray concedes to Ethiopian government, and Abiy', *Responsible Statecraft*, 16 November 2022.

40. Abiy to Parliament, 7 July 2022: https://www.youtube.com/watch?v=XoXpCqyT6Lc

41. The diaspora-based news outlet, Ethio Forum, was by 2023 perhaps the most common beneficiary of top-level leaks, with government officials, MPs and security officers routinely sharing sensitive information with its journalists.

42. 'Decoding the Cabinet Reshuffles in Ethiopia', *Reqiq Insights*, 11 April 2023; Demeke Mekonnen was finally given permission to leave office in January 2024.

43. Abiy to his Cabinet on 4 June 2023: https://www.youtube.com/watch?v=Eisss58KAHE

44. Diplomats, particularly Tigrayan ones, were the key exception: large numbers resigned or refused to return to Ethiopia in 2022 (some applied for asylum in the West instead).

45. https://ethiopiatigraywar.com/incidents.php

46. Ethio Forum, 25 October 2023: www.youtube.com/watch?v=E5xO511tdYs

47. 'Tigray faces a new onslaught,' *Responsible Statecraft*, 14 October 2022.

48. Abiy addressing a rally in Gamo, southern Ethiopia on 3 November 2022: https://www.youtube.com/watch?v=agfiWuS_Zyc

49. https://twitter.com/danielkibret/status/1587869907714285569?s=20&t=w-AR0LMVqDFeCc0xmkzOCw

50. 'Today or tomorrow, they should be brought before justice', Amnesty International, 4 September 2023.

51. 'War crimes in Tigray may be covered up or forgotten,' *The Economist*, 9 July 2023; 'Ethnic Cleansing Persists Under Tigray Truce,' Human Rights Watch, 1 June 2023.

52. 'Ethiopia's plan to rebuild in the wake of a "brutal" war', *Financial Times*, 4 October 2023; in February 2024, Getachew Reda put the number at as high as 270,000 in a public press conference.

53. https://www.ohchr.org/sites/default/files/documents/hrbodies/hrcouncil/chreetiopia/A-HRC-54-CRP-2.pdf

54. By one estimate in 2022, the total of all regional forces plus *Fanos* and equivalents was by then double the size of the federal army, even without counting the local "kebele" militias: 'Abiy's botched centralization fuels Ethiopia's feuding centrifugal forces', *Ethiopia Insight*, 30 April 2022.

EPILOGUE

1. Originally coined by French theorist Edgar Morin, the term has more recently been popularised by the historian Adam Tooze to describe the interaction of multiple crises at once.

2. Abiy to Parliament, 6 February 2024: https://www.youtube.com/watch?v=iEANF_hdfG8

3. Ibid.

4. 'Can Justice Bring Peace to Ethiopia?' *Foreign Affairs*, 15 November 2023.

5. Besides Eritrea, one can count South Sudan plus still-unrecognised Somaliland.

INDEX

INDEX

INDEX

INDEX

INDEX

INDEX

INDEX

INDEX

INDEX

Rohingyas, 146
Rondos, Alex, 52, 138, 258, 280
Russian Federation, 348
    Chechnya, 160
    Eritrea, relations with, 129, 248
    Sochi Summit (2019), 226, 233
    Tigray War (2020–22), 279, 280,
        281, 303
    Ukraine War (2022–), 265, 280,
        281, 299
Rwanda, 39, 57, 178

Safaricom, 326
Sahle-Work Zewde, 116
samna-warq, 91
Samora Yunis, 43, 53, 77, 106, 158
Samre, 266
San Francisco, California, 65
Sapiens (Harari), 65–6
satire, 112
Saudi Arabia, 135–6, 138, 300
science museum, 3
Scoop (Waugh), 267
Scramble for Africa (c. 1870–1914), 12
Seare Mekonnen, 158, 183, 184
Sebhat Nega, 106, 168, 243, 278, 319
Seeye Abraha, 56, 318
Selale, 226
self-help, 3, 47, 206, 208
self-sufficiency, 139, 207, 325, 328,
    330
Selsay Woyane, 245
Semera, Afar Region, 310
Semitic languages, 16
September 11th attacks (2001), 51,
    126
Serbia, 180, 181, 264, 284
Serit-Humera, 264
sesame crops, 97, 179, 261, 274, 321
seven mountain theology, 47
Sewyew (Facebook page), 106
Sewyew (Hassen), 32
sexual violence, 145, 160, 191, 263,
    283–5, 287, 290, 293, 309, 311

Seychelles, 315–17, 331, 332
Seyoum Mesfin, 249, 254
al-Shabaab, 127
Shabelle River, 160
Shane, 199, 270
Shashemene, Oromia, 146, 222, 228
Sheger Park, Addis Ababa, 203
Sheraton Hotel, Addis Ababa, 79, 121,
    204
Shewa region, 13, 19, 69, 175, 226
Shiferaw Shigute, 104–5
*shifta*s, 31
Shimelis Abdissa, 90, 91, 131, 183,
    214, 226
Shinfa River, 179
Shire, Tigray, 244, 286, 316, 339
shopping malls, 69
Siad Barre, 139
Sidama, 214
Simegnew Bekele, 159
Sisay Tola, 64
al-Sisi, Abdel-Fattah, 232–3
slavery, 5, 12, 31, 32
smart cities, 3
smuggling, 101, 329
Sochi Summit (2019), 226, 233
socialist revolution (1974), 11, 12, 14,
    17, 22, 29, 48, 148, 352
Solomon Girmay, 176
Solomon, King of Israel, 13, 205, 313
Somali People's Democratic Party, 212
Somalia, 12, 22–3, 53, 346
    Eritrea, relations with, 138–40
    Ethiopian occupation (2006–9), 52
    Kenya, relations with, 141
    Ogaden War (1977–8), 22–3, 34,
        155, 166
    Somaliland, relations with, 141,
        351
    Tigray War (2020–22), 140, 304
    tripartite alliance, 138–40
Somaliland, 141, 350–51
Somalis; Somali Region, 18, 99–101,
    146, 154, 155–66, 178

INDEX

INDEX